Transborder Los Angeles

WESTERN HISTORIES
William Deverell, series editor

Published for the Huntingon–USC Institute on California and the West by University of California Press.

1. *The Father of All: The de la Guerra Family, Power, and Patriarchy in Mexican California,* by Louise Pubols

2. *Alta California: Peoples in Motion, Identities in Formation,* edited by Steven W. Hackel

3. *American Heathens: Religion, Race, and Reconstruction in California,* by Joshua Paddison

4. *Blue Sky Metropolis: The Aerospace Century in Southern California,* edited by Peter J. Westwick

5. *Post-Ghetto: Reimagining South Los Angeles,* edited by Josh Sides

6. *Where Minds and Matters Meet: Technology in California and the West,* edited by Volker Janssen

7. *A Squatter's Republic: Land and the Politics of Monopoly in California, 1850–1900,* by Tamara Venit Shelton

8. *Heavy Ground: William Mulholland and the St. Francis Dam Disaster,* by Norris Hundley Jr. and Donald C. Jackson

9. *The Other California: Land, Identity, and Politics on the Mexican Borderlands,* by Verónica Castillo-Muñoz

10. *The Worlds of Junípero Serra: Historical Contexts and Cultural Representations,* edited by Steven W. Hackel

11. *Braided Waters: Environment and Society in Molokai, Hawai'i,* by Wade Graham

12. *Transborder Los Angeles: An Unknown Transpacific History of Japanese-Mexican Relations,* by Yu Tokunaga

Transborder Los Angeles

*An Unknown Transpacific History
of Japanese-Mexican Relations*

―

Yu Tokunaga

UNIVERSITY OF CALIFORNIA PRESS

University of California Press
Oakland, California

© 2022 by Yu Tokunaga

Library of Congress Cataloging-in-Publication Data

Names: Tokunaga, Yū, 1982– author.
Title: Transborder Los Angeles : an unknown transpacific history of
   Japanese-Mexican relations / Yu Tokunaga.
Other titles: Western histories ; 12.
Description: Oakland, California : University of California Press, [2022]
   | Series: Western histories ; 12 | Includes bibliographical references
   and index.
Identifiers: LCCN 2022006826 (print) | LCCN 2022006827 (ebook) |
   ISBN 9780520379787 (cloth) | ISBN 9780520379794 (paperback) |
   ISBN 9780520976931 (epub)
Subjects: LCSH: Immigrants—California—Los Angeles—20th century. |
   Japanese—United States—20th century. | Mexicans—United States—
   20th century. | Agriculture—Social aspects—California—Los Angeles—
   20th century.
Classification: LCC JV6926.L67 T65 2022 (print) | LCC JV6926.L67 (ebook) |
   DDC 304.8/79494—dc23/eng/20220411
LC record available at https://lccn.loc.gov/2022006826
LC ebook record available at https://lccn.loc.gov/2022006827

31 30 29 28 27 26 25 24 23 22
10 9 8 7 6 5 4 3 2 1

*To my wife, Sakiko Tokunaga,
and our kids, Sotaro, Keijiro, and Rinzaburo*

The publisher and the University of California Press Foundation
gratefully acknowledge the generous support of the Lisa See
Endowment Fund in Southern California History and Culture.

CONTENTS

List of Illustrations and Tables ix
Acknowledgments xi

Introduction: Exploring Japanese-Mexican Relations
in Los Angeles and the US-Mexico Borderlands   1

1. The 1924 Immigration Act and Its Unintended Consequence
   in the US-Mexico Borderlands   12

2. The Deepening of Japanese-Mexican Relations in Triracial
   Los Angeles   52

3. Transpacific Borderlands: Japanese Farmers and Mexican Workers
   in the 1933 El Monte Berry Strike   76

4. Ethnic Solidarity or Interethnic Accommodation:
   The 1936 Venice Celery Strike   105

5. Japanese Internment as an Agricultural Labor Crisis:
   Wartime Debates over Food Security versus Military Necessity   137

6. Enduring Interethnic Trust in Rancho San Pedro   160

   Conclusion   177

Notes   181
Bibliography 235
Index   249

ILLUSTRATIONS AND TABLES

MAPS

1. Japanese farms in Los Angeles County, 1942   *10*
2. Rancho San Pedro, 1937   *161*
3. Horita and Haijima's farms in Rancho San Pedro   *165*
4. Buildings owned by former Japanese tenant Henry Chiyozō Takeuchi in Rancho San Pedro   *175*

FIGURES

1. An aerial view of Los Angeles farmland, ca. 1924   *22*
2. An aerial view looking south toward Seventh Street and the Los Angeles produce market, ca. 1928   *23*
3. Advertisement of the Hara Company in *La Opinión*, 1926   *70*
4. Advertisement of Dr. Ichioka's clinic in *La Opinión*, 1928   *70*
5. Japanese farmers and workers in the Palos Verdes area, July 1933   *82*
6. Statement of Japanese immigrants in Mexicali, June 1933   *94*
7. Statement of Japanese immigrants in Ensenada, July 1933   *101*
8. Japanese *giyūdan* workers helping harvest celery in Venice, 1936   *111*
9. Japanese and Mexican representatives signing a provisional agreement, 1936   *126*

TABLES

1. List of Japanese tenants in Rancho San Pedro along the rural routes from the post office in Compton, February 10, 1942   *170*
2. List of Mexican tenants in Rancho San Pedro along the rural routes from the post office in Compton, 1943   *171*

ACKNOWLEDGMENTS

The seed of this book was first sown in Costa Rica in 2000, when I flew there as a high school exchange student from Japan. Surrounded by mango trees, I spent a year and learned Spanish. This experience gave me a completely new geographical and cultural perspective on the United States. Having lived in Costa Rica, I came to see the United States as not only to the east of Asia but also to the north of Latin America. On my way back to Japan, I stayed at a hotel near the Los Angeles International Airport for one night before taking a connecting flight. At the hotel, I clearly recognized the United States as a Spanish-speaking country because I was able to communicate with the hotel employees only in Spanish. Around this time, I became increasingly interested in the historical context of immigrants in both Japan and the United States today. I wanted to learn about how immigrants faced and overcame difficulties and how peoples of different ethnoracial backgrounds could live together in the era of globalization. My interests in immigration history remained strong during my undergraduate years in Kyoto University and my subsequent four-year experience as a newspaper reporter. Thus, I decided to return to university to gain expertise in US immigration history. I first entered a master's program at Kyoto University in 2010 and, two years later, the doctoral program in history at the University of Southern California. As a doctoral student, I conducted research on the history of Japanese-Mexican interethnic relations in the United States. My experience of living in Costa Rica gave me the language skills to readily access Spanish-language documents preserved in the United States and Mexico. I analyzed such documents along with Japanese and English-language sources to shed a methodologically and conceptually new light on the history of multiethnic Los Angeles. This book is the fruit of these years living on either side of the Pacific Ocean.

The book, furthermore, was only made possible with the support of many people. I would like to express my sincerest gratitude to Lon Kurashige, my adviser, for his guidance and encouragement since my doctoral years at the USC History Department. Lon sensei has been a great mentor in my professional and private lives. I learned the importance of the emerging field of transpacific history by studying and spending time with him on and off campus in both the United States and Japan. I am deeply grateful to William (Bill) Deverell for supporting me first as the History Department chair and more recently as the Western Histories series editor. Bill introduced me to the fascinating world of multiethnic California history and, with words of encouragement, helped me feel confident about my own work. I feel truly blessed that I could study Mexican American history with George J. Sánchez. In George's classes, I was always impressed by his insightful comments and wealth of knowledge. It was also memorable for me to study with Jody Agius Vallejo. Jody's sociology class reminded me of the importance of connecting academia with activism for social justice. I am truly thankful to these four professors for supporting me as my dissertation committee members. My special thanks are extended to Kyung Moon Hwang, who helped me broaden my perspective through intensive readings for the qualifying exam, and Steve Ross, who carefully instructed me how to write a good journal article in his research seminar. I also learned a great deal as a student or teaching assistant in the undergraduate classes of other professors in the History Department, including Philip Ethington, Clinton Godart, Richard Fox, Nathan Perl-Rosenthal, Joshua Goldstein, and Diana Williams.

During my doctoral years, I benefited from the friendship of my colleagues Angelica Stoddard, Christina Copland, David Neumann, Darci Ohigashi, Young Sun Park, David-James Gonzales, Nadia Kanagawa, Dylan Ellefson, Michael Block, Rosanne Sia, Jillian Barndt, William Cowan, and Carlos Parra. In particular, I am grateful to Carlos for helping me edit my dissertation draft and make it more readable and meaningful. It was also fun to share our graduate school experiences abroad with Yuko Konno, Go Oyagi, Yasuhito Abe, Kohki Watabe, and Rio Katayama, all from Japan. I wish to acknowledge the help provided by Lori Rogers and Melissa Calderon of the History Department office and by Grace Ryu and Alexandria Eloriaga of the USC East Asian Studies Center. The History Program at USC proved to be the best place for me to study the history of California and beyond.

It was fun and important to meet and talk with people in my life in Los Angeles and during archival research in Japan, Mexico, and the United States. I would like to express my gratitude to Yoshiko Hayashi, Chiyoko Nishimori, her son Steve Nishimori, Fuyu Kiyota, and Iwao Ichikawa for sharing their family histories with me. Their stories helped me contextualize my findings and better understand Japanese American and Japanese Mexican histories. I am grateful to

Thomas Philo and Gregory Williams, respectively archivist and director in California State University, Dominguez Hills' University Library, for their support and generosity, and Eileen Yoshimura for showing me her undergraduate paper on Japanese immigrants in Rancho San Pedro submitted to the CSUDH in the 1980s. I am deeply thankful to Alex and Emma for letting me stay at their house during my archival research in Mexicali, and to Yolanda Sánchez Ogás, local historian of Baja California, for kindly giving me a tour on Japanese immigration history there. The Gardena Valley Japanese Cultural Institute showed me that the Japanese American experience helped people continue to revitalize their community and pass down their history to following generations. The KIWA (Koreatown Immigrant Workers Alliance) gave me a precious opportunity to work as a volunteer during the summer of 2013 and taught me the importance of grassroots activism to support immigrant workers. My graduate school experience could not have been this fruitful without the financial support I received from the USC, the Japan-US Educational Commission (Fulbright Japan), and the Association for Japan-US Community Exchange-Nikaido Fellowship.

I am also indebted to Brian Hayashi, Reiko Maekawa, and Yasuko Takezawa, with whom I studied as a master's student at Kyoto University for encouraging me to study abroad in the United States. As my adviser at Kyoto University, Hayashi sensei taught me how a historian should conduct research and make an evidence-based argument. I also want to thank Paul Kramer and Takakazu Yamagishi who further motivated me to study in the United States at an international graduate seminar hosted by Nanzan University in 2011. It was also a pleasure to meet and study with other graduate students in Japan, especially Hironori Watari, Mishio Yamanaka, Aki Son-Katada, Yumi Saito, Crystal Uchino, and Daniel Milne. I am very thankful to Daniel, now my colleague, for his friendship and his assistance in revising my book manuscript. After I returned from Los Angeles to Japan to work at the Institute for Research in Humanities at Kyoto University in 2016, I received vital support from my colleagues and friends. Takezawa sensei gave me a precious opportunity to join her research project that explored racialization processes in the Pacific Rim region. I am grateful to Toru Onozawa for giving me a teaching opportunity and helping me reconnect with Japanese scholars of US history. While working there, I received generous research funding from the Kyoto University Research Coordination Alliance to visit the United States and conduct additional archival research for my book project. In 2020, my affiliation at Kyoto University changed to the Graduate School of Global Environmental Studies with a joint appointment at the Graduate School of Human and Environmental Studies. I want to convey my thanks to colleagues and office staff of both graduate schools, particularly Mari Oka and Aki Yamamura for their guidance and advice regarding my new assignments. Inside and outside my institution, it has been enjoyable to work with scholars particularly in the fields related to Japanese and

US history. I am appreciative of Tomoe Moriya, Mitsuhiro Sakaguchi, Akihiro Yamakura, Kazuhiro Oharazeki, Norifumi Kawahara, Rika Lee, Mari Yoshihara, Yujin Yaguchi, Sanae Nakatani, Masumi Izumi, Akiko Ochiai, Fuminori Minamikawa, Valerie Matsumoto, Shelley Sang-Hee Lee, Mariko Iijima, Andrew Elliott, William Gow, Kotaro Nakano, and many others for sharing their knowledge and giving me opportunities to present papers and publish articles.

It took longer than I expected to revise my book manuscript and get this book out due to the coronavirus pandemic, a significant historical event of our time. I would like to thank again William Deverell, and Niels Hooper, executive editor of the University of California Press, for their support and understanding. Naja Pulliam Collins, editorial assistant of UC Press, was very helpful, too. I was able to make many improvements on my manuscript thanks to insightful comments and suggestions given by Greg Robinson and Devra Weber. I am also appreciative of David Yoo and Phuong Tran Nguyen for giving me helpful advice and encouragement regarding my book project. In addition, I would like to express gratitude to Merry Ovnick, editor of the *Southern California Quarterly*, and Marc Rodriguez and Brenda Frink, respectively editor and associate editor of the *Pacific Historical Review*, for publishing articles that became part of this book. An early version of chapter 3 was published as "Japanese Farmers, Mexican Workers, and the Making of Transpacific Borderlands" in the *Pacific Historical Review* 89, no. 2 (Spring 2020), which won both the W. Turrentine Jackson (Article) Prize and the Louis Knott Koontz Memorial Award. An early version of chapter 5 was published as "Japanese Internment as an Agricultural Labor Crisis: Wartime Debates over Food Security versus Military Necessity" in the *Southern California Quarterly* 101, no. 1 (Spring 2019). Part of chapter 1 appeared in Japanese as "Hainichi imin hō to zai Mekishiko nihonjin: Beiboku kokkyō chiiki ni okeru nihonjin imin shakaiken no hatten" (The Japanese Exclusion Act and Japanese immigrants in Mexico: The development of the transborder ethnic Japanese community in the US-Mexico borderlands), *Imin kenkyū nempō* 24 (June 2018). I am obliged to UC Press, Huntington Library Press, and the Huntington-USC Institute on California and the West for publishing this book.

I want to use this opportunity to thank my former colleagues at the Asahi Shimbun company as well. Taro Tamaki and Kenji Kimoto always make me feel still connected with my former workplace and help me retain a journalistic viewpoint on international migration. I have been a member of a volunteer organization that supports immigrant children in Shiga Prefecture, Japan, for more than ten years. By interacting with immigrant children, their parents, and fellow volunteer members, I could see more clearly the value of learning from immigration history for building a more equal and inclusive society in an age of globalization. My deep gratitude also goes to my host parents Guillermo and Eida, other family members, and many friends in Costa Rica. I want to thank Joe and Ian, my roommates at UC

Riverside, where I studied as an undergraduate exchange student in the academic year 2004–2005, for letting me simply enjoy an American campus life. It has also been important for me to share time to laugh and relax with my old friends in Kyoto.

Without the love and support from my mother Kayo and my late father Muneo, I would not be where I am today. Finally, my wife Sakiko and our kids Sotaro, Keijiro, and Rinzaburo are always the source of my energy and happiness. This book is dedicated to them.

Introduction

*Exploring Japanese-Mexican Relations
in Los Angeles and the US-Mexico Borderlands*

This book explores the social history of interethnic relations between Japanese and Mexican immigrants in Los Angeles County from 1924 to 1942 by paying careful attention to international relations between Japan, Mexico, and the United States. In this period, Japanese, Mexicans, and white Americans in Los Angeles developed mutual relations, which were not always rigid and dominated by domestic racial and economic factors but were rather fluid and situational due to the immigrants' agency to negotiate interethnic relations and international factors around the Pacific Ocean and across the US-Mexico border. This study focuses on farmland in Los Angeles County as a site of particularly close Japanese-Mexican interactions and of overlapping experiences as immigrants. Japanese and Mexicans played a significant role in developing local agriculture, one of the major industries of Los Angeles County before World War II. By looking at the Japanese-Mexican interactions within the correlations of their experiences as racialized minorities in this turbulent period, we can see the Japanese immigrant experience, such as the ban on Japanese immigration and the wartime Japanese relocation and internment, and the Mexican immigrant experience, such as agricultural strikes in the 1930s and the Bracero Program, not in isolation but in a single narrative of transpacific history.[1]

In this eighteen-year period, Japanese-Mexican relations in Los Angeles farmland became fully incorporated as an integral part of local agriculture along with two socioeconomic and geopolitical relationships developing particularly after the implementation of the Immigration Act of 1924. The first relationship is the development of a unique triracial hierarchy in which Japanese tenant farmers leased lands from white landowners and hired Mexican farmworkers, which was the consequence of the upward mobility of Japanese immigrants into land tenancy and the increase of Mexican immigrants in Los Angeles County, particularly after the 1920s. Although this triracial hierarchy functioned to strengthen racial and class divisions and conflicts among Japanese, Mexicans, and white Americans, their regular interactions resulted in efforts toward mutual understanding and interethnic accommodation in unexpected ways even during the periods of Japanese-Mexican labor conflict during the 1930s and strong anti-Japanese sentiment during the Pacific War. The other relationship is the development of a transborder ethnic Japanese community in the US-Mexico borderlands in which the experience of Japanese immigrants in Mexico affected that of their co-ethnics and their relations with Mexican immigrants in Los Angeles County. By taking these two important factors into consideration, this book describes the development and sudden demise of Japanese-Mexican relations in Los Angeles farmland from 1924 to 1942, providing a better understanding of why and how interethnic and international relations played into not only racial and economic inequalities but also interethnic accommodation in a multiethnic Los Angeles, a global meeting place located at the historical intersection of Asia, Latin America, and the United States.

In the first three decades of the twentieth century, the ethnic Japanese and Mexican populations in Los Angeles County increased dramatically.[2] In Los Angeles County, the number of ethnic Japanese residents rose from 209 in 1900 to 35,390 in 1930 and the Mexican counterpart from 1,618 (as a foreign-born population) in 1900 to 167,024 (as a racial group) in 1930, together constituting 9 percent of the total population and 78 percent of the whole nonwhite population in Los Angeles County in 1930. Japanese and Mexican minorities made up the majority of nonwhite Los Angeles before World War II.[3]

In early twentieth-century Los Angeles, Japanese and Mexicans were major racialized minorities. With the development of scientific racism such as eugenics, American racial nationalism reinforced the idea of Anglo-Saxon superiority and materialized in the Immigration Act of 1924.[4] This new immigration policy prohibited Japanese immigration altogether. The law banned the entry of immigrants who were ineligible for naturalization. The ineligibility of Japanese immigrants to become US citizens was the legal basis for the California Alien Land Laws of 1913 and 1920 that prohibited Japanese from purchasing and leasing land. The *Ozawa v. United States* case in 1922 firmly established the nonwhite racial status of Japanese as ineligible for naturalization by rejecting an appeal filed by a Japanese immigrant Takao Ozawa who applied for naturalization. The 1924 Immigration Act reaffirmed the racial status of Japanese as undesirable and ineligible to become part of the American nation. On the other hand, Mexicans were legally regarded as white based on the Treaty of Guadalupe-Hidalgo of 1848 and exempted from the numerical restriction institutionalized by the 1924 Act largely due to growing demands for Mexican labor in the Southwest. However, new entry requirements imposed by the 1924 Act and the establishment of the US Border Patrol in the same year functioned to racialize Mexicans increasingly as nonwhite and illegal immigrants.[5]

Although the US state power and its racial nationalism considerably affected the lives of Japanese and Mexican immigrants, these immigrants were also under the influence of the new international regime of the post–World War I period and the development of racial ideology in their respective home countries, Japan and Mexico. Looking at the international context of the 1920s, Japan emerged as a new leading power and competed with the United States in the world following the devastation of Europe.[6] During this decade, Japanese nationalism took a Pan-Asianist framework in justifying its imperial expansion in East Asia, positioning the Japanese as a leading *minzoku* (race or ethnicity) in Asia in competition with the West.[7] On the other side of the Pacific Ocean in Los Angeles, Japanese nationalism provided emotional support to Japanese immigrants who needed to survive the anti-Japanese environment.[8] The 1920s was also an important period for Mexico to modernize as a nation. After the Mexican Revolution, the Mexican government sought to modernize and unify the diverse Mexican population. In the 1920s Mexican cultural nationalist movement, post-revolutionary Mexican nationalism envisioned *mestizaje* (racial mixing) as the basis of the greatness of the Mexican nation.[9] Again in Los Angeles, located on the other side of the US-Mexico border, Mexican nationalism and government intervention occasionally empowered Mexican immigrants who identified themselves as *mexicanos* or *raza* (race or people) and transformed local labor conflicts in Los Angeles into international issues that affected both sides of the Pacific Ocean.[10]

Japanese and Mexican immigrants were not simply passive victims of American racialization but, as this book clarifies, were also positive agents who could utilize their racial and national identities to survive a Los Angeles society dominated by white Americans. Furthermore, in order to understand the political and emotional connections between Japanese and Mexicans with their respective home governments, this study pays special attention to the role played by the Japanese and Mexican consulates in Los Angeles, established in 1915 and 1885, respectively. Particularly in times of Japanese-Mexican interethnic conflicts, the Japanese and Mexican consulates played a significant role as the proxy of the respective immigrant communities as well as of their governments. The consulates, however, did not always work for the sake of immigrants per se and immigrants did not always follow the instruction they gave. By doing archival research in Japan, Mexico, and the United States and analyzing primary sources written in three languages, this book illustrates the transpacific dimension of local Japanese-Mexican relations in Los Angeles agriculture.

LITERATURE ON INTERETHNIC RELATIONS

An increasing number of scholars have explored interethnic relations in California, particularly in Los Angeles, to understand the history of immigration and racial dynamics. Yet, no one has detailed the relations between ethnic Japanese and Mexicans. I regard this as a major hole in the literature, given that in 1930 these two groups combined constituted the majority of nonwhite population in Los Angeles County. I also agree with Natalia Molina, who argues that "there are limits to examining racialized groups in isolation" because the experience of one nonwhite group affected the other.[11] As far as the history of Japanese immigration is concerned, much scholarly attention has been paid to growing US-Japan conflict generated through early twentieth-century crises over Japanese immigration to the West Coast. But the Mexican dimension to this conflict remains largely unknown. What role did Mexico and Mexican immigrants play in the Japanese immigrant experience including various acts of anti-Japanese discrimination, immigration exclusion, and the removal and internment of the ethnic Japanese population during World War II? How did the influx of Mexican immigrants shape the development of the ethnic Japanese community? *Transborder Los Angeles* explores these questions through a largely unknown transpacific history of Japanese and Mexican agricultural and labor relations that highlights the emergence of Southern California as a transpacific meeting place among peoples from the East, West, and South.[12]

This book takes a *relational* approach to examine Japanese-Mexican relations, paying special attention to their labor and political interactions in Los Angeles farmland. Broadly speaking, there are two kinds of studies on interethnic relations in existing scholarship: comparative studies and relational studies. Comparative studies look at several ethnoracial groups separately, compare them with each other, and obtain a relational understanding on these groups. In this way, they reveal a larger picture of immigration and racial dynamics in a city like Los Angeles or in a larger area such as the US-Mexico borderlands. Such studies are important and effective in revealing the dominant institutional power structures that situate ethnoracial minorities in disadvantaged positions in the United States.[13] Nevertheless, comparative studies are not much concerned with actual interactions between ethnoracial groups in the area. On the other hand, relational studies shed light on actual interactions between ethnoracial groups, rather than comparing their experiences independently.[14] Interethnic interactions can be observed within different spaces such as the family, neighborhood, and workplace. For example, Karen Isaksen Leonard's work on Punjabi-Mexican families in the Imperial Valley provides a great example of intimate interethnic relations, while George J. Sánchez's study on Boyle Heights, Los Angeles, teaches us about the importance of the multicultural neighborhood relations in creating interracial harmony.[15] The current book highlights interethnic relations in the workplace and provides a clear picture of Japanese-Mexican interactions in Los Angeles farmland in contrast to previous works that have focused on one ethnic group, either Japanese or Mexican, or examined these groups comparatively.[16]

Furthermore, it situates Japanese-Mexican relations in the intersection of the Pacific Ocean and the US-Mexico borderlands and weaves the local history of Japanese-Mexican relations with the history of international relations involving Japan, Mexico, and the United States. Immigration history is almost inevitably transnational history.[17] This book examines the transnational processes in which the triangular relationship between peoples and governments of three Pacific Rim countries generated not only racial and economic inequalities but also efforts toward mutual understanding and interethnic accommodation. In this regard, Grace Peña Delgado's study of ethnic Chinese residents in the Arizona-Sonora borderlands provides an important insight into the question of the historical intersection between the US-Mexico borderlands and the Pacific Ocean. Her work has contributed to the making of a transnational turn in the historiography of interethnic relations. Peña Delgado illuminates the US-Mexico borderlands as "trans-Pacific-borderlands," as a space in which Chinese residents built socioeconomic and legal relationships with Mexican neighbors and officers while local and transnational factors of China, Mexico, and the United States operated simultaneously and helped create US and Mexican immigration policies in the region at around the turn of the twentieth century.[18]

This book adopts Peña Delgado's conceptualization but focuses more specifically on Los Angeles farmland as a central site of the transpacific borderlands. Los Angeles is of great significance to historians interested in exploring multiethnic relations in the American West, in which Asians and Latin Americans began to interact with each other as minority groups from the late nineteenth century. In other words, the historiography of this region tells us how scholars have understood multiethnic relations over time. This book shows that Los Angeles witnessed significant and extensive triracial negotiations between Japanese, Mexicans, and white Americans for the first time in US history, providing a new understanding of multiethnic relations in Los Angeles and the American West. The history of the American West and US-Mexico borderlands cannot be fully understood by looking only at biracial relations between one nonwhite minority and the white majority because many communities in this region were multiethnic. We have yet to fully explore these ethnoracially diverse communities in the international context around the Pacific Ocean.

Similar to Peña Delgado's, Eiichiro Azuma's work is important in terms of the transnational turn in the multiracial historiography of the American West. Azuma has examined triracial interactions between Japanese, Filipinos, and white Americans in 1930s Stockton in Northern California and provided a historical perspective indispensable for us to understand the Japanese immigrant experience. Azuma adeptly describes the dual status and transnationalism of Japanese immigrants as simultaneously citizen-subjects of imperial Japan and resident members of white America. With this understanding, Azuma examines the world view of Japanese tenant farmers and merchants who "envisioned a simple, three-tiered, overlapping race and class hierarchy, where white elites, Japanese entrepreneurs, and Filipino union laborers formed the pyramid in descending order." He argues that Japanese immigrants "appropriated the ruling ideology of white supremacy as their own and endeavored to turn perceived social relations into real ones." Therefore, being a proper Japanese national was compatible with becoming a good American resident who would understand the dominant white racial ideology.[19] Azuma applies a similar perspective to the Japanese immigrant experience in the US-Mexico borderlands. In understanding the Japanese immigrant world view in relation to Mexicans, Azuma emphasizes California Japanese as settler colonialists who thought it "easy to dominate" Mexicans and become a "master" race in Mexico when they faced the anti-Japanese movement in 1890s California.[20]

Azuma's work has made a significant contribution to our understanding of multiracial relations in California, particularly showing the compatibility of Japanese imperial nationalism with white supremacy in multiracial California. However, his work describes the triracial hierarchy of Japanese, Filipinos, and white Americans as a stable and rigid social structure divided along existing racial and class boundaries under the influence of white supremacy. It downplays, however, the social dimension that was not totally dominated by white supremacy and overlooks the agency of minority residents and white people who did not always fit in the dominant triracial hierarchy. In contrast, by looking at the triangular relations between Japanese, Mexicans, and white Americans on Los Angeles farmland, this book demonstrates their triracial hierarchy as an unstable and fluid relationship, not simply dominated by existing racial and class factors. I would argue that the social factor of working together in Los Angeles farmland over a long time despite their racial and class differences played an important role in changing the dominant racial and class structure. This change was substantiated by the efforts and compromises of some Japanese, Mexicans, and white Americans who cooperated with each other even in periods of serious Japanese-Mexican labor conflicts in the 1930s and very strong anti-Japanese sentiment following the Pearl Harbor attack in the 1940s. To understand the nature of triracial interactions, we need to look conceptually beyond white supremacy and geographically beyond the Pacific Ocean and the US-Mexico border and take a different methodological approach by drawing on primary sources in three languages. By doing so, we can get a fuller picture of triangular interactions between Japanese, Mexicans, and white Americans in prewar Los Angeles agriculture.

I regard Los Angeles farmland as a *transpacific workplace* that functioned as a contested site in which their local relations operated within the context of increasingly precarious international relations around the Pacific Ocean from 1924 to 1942. The *transpacific workplace* concept helps us to identify specific sites where Asian and Latin American immigrants interact with one another as racialized minorities in white-dominant US society and where their interactions were partly a product of international relations between their home countries and the United States. As shown in this book, in the 1920s, Los Angeles farmland transformed into a *transpacific workplace* on a full scale along with the rapid economic development of Los Angeles as a major American city.[21]

THE ORGANIZATION OF THE BOOK: TRANSBORDER LOS ANGELES

Today we can find many *transpacific workplaces* where Asian and Latin American immigrants interact with each other largely due to the implementation of the Immigration Act of 1965 that abolished the exclusionist quota system. We can better observe their lives not simply in a domestic context but also in a larger global context in which local and international factors around the Pacific Ocean influence each other to shape their immigrant experiences. This social history of Japanese-Mexican relations speaks of the contemporary importance of understanding increasingly complicated multiracial relations in the international context around the Pacific Ocean and of grasping their workplace not simply as a site of conflict and exploitation but also as a site of mutual understanding. In Los Angeles farmland, Japanese, Mexicans, and white Americans together formed interethnic relations beyond racial and class boundaries in both local and transnational contexts. In other words, this study is about transborder Los Angeles. By paying close attention to this situational and fluid nature of race and class relations, we can see Los Angeles farmland as a formative site of transborder Los Angeles.

Chapter 1 briefly explains the local history of Los Angeles. To provide background for what would happen in Japanese-Mexican relations in Los Angeles farmland, it starts by looking at the pre-1924 period from a global perspective. It then explores the impact of the Immigration Act of 1924 on Japanese immigrants in Los Angeles County and the subsequent development of a transborder ethnic Japanese community in the US-Mexico borderlands. Japanese exclusion made Los Angeles Japanese seriously concerned about their future in an anti-Japanese US society and increasingly interested in migrating southward to Mexico where no anti-Japanese laws existed. At about the same time, people in Japan felt the same way and began to talk about Mexico as a hopeful destination for future Japanese emigrants. While most California Japanese remained in the United States, newly arriving immigrants from Japan substantially increased in Mexico and developed an ethnic Japanese community in Baja California, which became firmly incorporated into a southern part of a transborder ethnic Japanese community in the US-Mexico borderlands with Los Angeles as its nucleus. Chapter 1 details the development of the transborder ethnic Japanese community, an unintended consequence of the 1924 Act, which provided an important historical setting that led to local Japanese-Mexican interactions in Los Angeles farmland having international repercussions in the 1930s.

Chapter 2 demonstrates the increase of Mexican immigrants in Los Angeles County after Japanese exclusion as an indispensable factor in the development of a triracial hierarchy in the Los Angeles agriculture of the 1920s. After Japanese exclusion, white nativists quickly replaced the "Japanese Problem" with the "Mexican Problem" (and the "Filipino Problem") as their major target, while white agribusiness leaders opposed any immigration restriction by racializing Mexicans as inferior but also as a very "safe" source of labor. Meanwhile, Japanese tenant farmers continued to lease lands from white landowners and increasingly relied on Mexican workers, stabilizing the triracial hierarchy of Los Angeles agriculture. Under this localized immigration regime, Japanese and Mexicans were fully incorporated in growing capitalist agriculture despite the fact that they were deemed undesirable and deportable. In an increasingly multiethnic Los Angeles, Japanese immigrants often portrayed Mexicans as criminals and inferior to the Japanese. On the other hand, they deepened their relations in urban and nonurban areas to the extent that they invested in emerging ethnic Mexican businesses including the Spanish-language newspaper *La Opinión*, which would later play an important role in supporting Mexican strikers and criticizing Japanese farmers in the 1930s.

Chapters 3 and 4 examine interethnic conflicts between Japanese and Mexican immigrants in Los Angeles farmland during the Great Depression years by focusing on two large-scale agricultural strikes launched by Mexican workers against Japanese tenant farmers. Chapter 3 examines the El Monte Berry Strike of 1933 and its international repercussions across the Pacific Ocean as well as the US-Mexico border. The El Monte strike became one of California's largest labor conflicts in 1933. The strike evolved from a local interethnic conflict into an international problem in which anti-Japanese sentiment traveled across the US-Mexico border, merged with Mexican nationalism, and forced Japanese residents in Mexicali, Baja California to issue an unexpected pro-labor and pro-Mexican statement against their co-ethnics in Los Angeles. By focusing on the transpacific character of the Japanese-Mexican interethnic relations in Los Angeles agriculture, this chapter details the process in which Mexican nationalism trumped ethnic solidarity among Japanese immigrants in their transborder community and that the exacerbating situation in Mexico, rather than in California, played a decisive role in the settlement of the strike. The pro-Mexican action taken by the Mexicali Japanese destabilized the existing racial and class boundaries in Los Angeles farmland, forcing the Los Angeles Japanese to make a compromise with Mexican strikers.

Chapter 4 continues to examine the Japanese-Mexican conflict by looking at another large-scale agricultural strike, namely the Venice Celery Strike of 1936, and explores the growth of interethnic alliances in Los Angeles farmland. Unable to see improvements to their working and living conditions after the El Monte strike, Mexican farmworkers went on the Venice strike against Japanese farmers in 1936. Largely influenced by the enactment of the National Labor Relations Act of 1935, Mexican strikers began to demand union recognition and some Japanese began to express sympathy toward Mexicans and their demand. While most Japanese farmers vehemently opposed union recognition that they thought would devastate their ethnic agriculture and sought to maintain the rigid racial and class boundaries, more than fifty Japanese farmers signed a contract with Mexican strikers challenging the existing norm of the triracial hierarchy. By exploring the Venice strike in the context of the New Deal pro-labor political climate, chapter 4 illustrates how the Japanese-Mexican interethnic conflict pushed Japanese immigrants to reconsider their position as a nonwhite minority in a highly multiethnic Los Angeles society and how Japanese immigrant nationalism responded to the growing need for interethnic accommodation in mid-1930s Los Angeles. Although those efforts to achieve mutual understanding and interethnic accommodation appeared more clearly in the actions taken by people in the Japanese side as documented in this book, it is crucial to understand that such actions, often followed by compromises, were generated through interactions with the Mexican side. In other words, without Mexican farmworkers going on strike and urging farmers to better understand their poor working conditions, Japanese farmers could not have had a chance to rethink their relationship with Mexican workers. In Los Angeles farmland, agricultural strikes played a significant role in prompting efforts for interethnic understanding from the Japanese side, while there were also moments where Mexican workers made compromises through interethnic negotiations.

Chapters 5 and 6 focus on the sudden demise of Japanese-Mexican relations as well as of the transborder ethnic Japanese community by analyzing Japanese relocation and internment as an agricultural labor crisis in California, particularly in Los Angeles farmland. Chapter 5 examines the economic impact of the Japanese Internment on California agriculture and political debates over food security versus military necessity. While Japanese Internment inflicted a grave injustice on Japanese immigrants and Japanese American citizens, it also resulted in the sudden loss of ethnic Japanese farmers in California. Just like the ethnic Japanese in Hawai'i, their co-ethnics in California were also economically vital as an integral part of local agriculture and an important element of wartime food security. Thus, the Japanese removal prompted voices sympathetic to the ethnic Japanese among federal agricultural officials and California Governor Culbert Olson, which questioned the necessity of the full-scale implementation of mass evacuation and also led to a growing demand for Mexican farmworkers who would come through the

10   INTRODUCTION

MAP 1. Japanese farms in Los Angeles County, 1942. "Map Reveals Jap Menace," blazoned a March 4, 1942, headline in the *Los Angeles Times*. It was accompanied by a map indicating that Japanese farms were located suspiciously near strategic oil fields, defense industries, and the harbor. SOURCE: *Los Angeles Times*, March 4, 1942.

Bracero Program. Consideration of these processes helps us to better understand the Japanese Internment as not solely about race but also about economics in wartime, multiethnic California.

Chapter 6 continues to explore the agricultural labor crisis caused by Japanese removal by focusing on issues regarding tenant farmers in former Japanese farms. In Los Angeles, some white landowners were upset and concerned about how to find new tenant farmers to keep their Japanese farms operational without the Japanese. The Bracero Program was not designed to bring tenant farmers from Mexico. In fact, it was very difficult for some white landowners to find replacement tenants when many people were finding their jobs in booming war industries in Los Angeles County. The last chapter details the process in which Japanese farms were taken over by non-Japanese farmers in Rancho San Pedro, the site of an old Spanish rancho in Los Angeles County. It details how the sudden loss of Japanese tenant farmers turned into an economic opportunity for Mexican "workers to take over the former Japanese lands and become tenant farmers themselves. In this last chapter, we see that the mutual understanding between Japanese tenant farmers and white landowners and even between some Japanese and Mexicans unsettled the hardening racial and political boundaries in wartime Los Angeles.

In March 1942, the *Los Angeles Times* ran an article with the headline "Network of Japanese Farms Covers Vital Southland Defense Areas" and a map made by Los Angeles County authorities (see Map 1). The map showed in black the locations of Japanese agricultural settlements in order to sound the alarm on the alleged internal Japanese military threat following the Pearl Harbor attack. As the map's caption states, "Depicting how Japanese landholdings are spaced throughout the Los Angeles County area in a manner to permit disastrous assaults on every military objective," it reflected the alarm and suspicion among local authorities toward Japanese farmers, many of whom lived near the militarily important areas of Los Angeles County such as "dams, oil refineries and tank farms, bridges, aircraft plants and other defense factories," unlike their fellow co-ethnics living in the downtown Little Tokyo. Over the coming chapters, *Transborder Los Angeles* explores the forgotten history of Japanese-Mexican relations that disappeared from this map in the summer of 1942.[22]

1

The 1924 Immigration Act and Its Unintended Consequence in the US-Mexico Borderlands

During World War I, Japanese writer and future Lower House member Kōji Higashi traveled across the United States to observe anti-Japanese racism. Higashi believed that US-Japan relations would be the most crucial factor for Japanese diplomacy after World War I. Next in importance was Europe, where he planned to visit after leaving the United States. His plans changed, however, when he came to see that Mexico was more important than Europe to understand US-Japan relations. In *Beiboku jūō* (Traveling down and across the United States and Mexico), a book published in Japan in 1920, Higashi explained that the United States had been aspiring to rule Mexico since its independence in 1821, as seen in the subsequent US annexation of Texas and its acquisition of California and other Southwestern regions. He viewed the Mexican-American War (1846–1848) as "the explicit revelation of the US invasionism." He believed that the United States was currently targeting Baja California when he learned that US Senator Henry Ashurst of Arizona had proposed the annexation of this region. Located next to California, Ashurst considered Baja California as an important region for US national security.[1]

Although Japan also was expanding its influence over China, Higashi found the US attitude toward Mexico "much more daring and astute" than Japan's own attitude toward China. At the same time, he saw parallels in both powers' imperial relationship to its weaker neighbors. "It is true," he wrote, "that US-Mexico relations significantly resemble Japan-China relations in terms of political, diplomatic, social, economic concerns, and so forth. I strongly believe that there are many things that we must take into consideration regarding US-Mexico, US-China, Japan-Mexico, and Japan-China relations if we want to solve Japan-US problems in the future." The key to resolving US-Japan tension, Higashi suggested, was Japan's relationship to Mexico because Americans were irrationally fearful that Japan would purchase lands and establish a military base in Baja California. Learning about the historical importance of Mexico in US expansionism, Higashi emphasized that Japan should develop its diplomatic strategies related to the United States and Mexico based on the fact that Americans were very sensitive to Japan-Mexico relations.[2]

Higashi's conception of US-Japan relations as triangulated by Mexico is important for understanding immigration as well as diplomatic history. Mexico and its immigrants north of the border played a salient, though often unacknowledged, role in the experience of Japanese immigrants and Japanese Americans in Southern California, the largest settlement of its kind in the continental United States. Shortly after the US government prohibited Japanese immigration in 1924, Japanese people on both sides of the Pacific Ocean began to express sentiments such as "[Japanese] migration to Mexico is hopeful" and "Send emigrants to Mexico!"[3] In addition to small-scale secondary migrations to Mexico, Japanese farmers in Los Angeles would later confront labor and racial conflicts with Mexican immigrants that blew up into international crises that concerned government representatives from Japan, Mexico, and the United States.

LOS ANGELES FARMLAND: A GLOBAL MEETING PLACE ON THE PACIFIC RIM

Los Angeles is a long-standing global meeting place. Peoples of diverse backgrounds coming across land and sea have interacted, conflicted, and understood each other for centuries. The region was first inhabited by Native Americans before it came to be ruled by Spain and named Los Angeles in the late eighteenth century. The nineteenth century saw two regime changes from Spain to Mexico and then to the United States. Before the Spanish Empire claimed its rule over the region, five to ten thousand Native Americans, today known as the Gabrieliño-Tongva, lived there. They interacted with other Native Americans including those living near the Colorado River and Arizona and had a valuable source of knowledge of trade routes beyond the region. Meanwhile, California came to be seen increasingly as an important area for the Spanish Empire to maintain its trade with Asia across the Pacific Ocean. The Spanish Empire considered it necessary to prevent any other European power, particularly Russia, from entering California, dreaming that California could guide them to the mythical sea passage from Europe to Asia called the "Strait of Anián."[4]

The future US state of California was established as a colonial crossroads in the Pacific Rim beginning in 1769, when the Spanish Empire sent missionaries, soldiers, and settlers to the region. Two years later, the San Gabriel Mission was founded about eight miles east of downtown Los Angeles and became one of the richest and most important of the missions established in the region. Yet, as a way to limit the power of the Catholic Church over the Gabrielino-Tongva and other Native Americans, California's governor, Felipe de Neve, founded a civilian agricultural settlement called Nuestra Señora de Los Angeles with forty-two settlers in 1781. In this civilian settlement, Native Americans grew crops such as corn, beans, and melons for Spanish-Mexican settlers. In return, the settlers did not demand that the former should convert to Christianity and gave them one-third to one-half of the harvest or manufactured goods such as cotton cloth, glass beads, and knives. Although the Spaniards imposed their cultural norms, including the Spanish language, on Native Americans, they socialized with one another on an everyday basis. Some settlers formally married with Indian women and others spoke the Indian languages fluently. By the turn of the nineteenth century, the Los Angeles region had already been an important place for its transpacific connection to Asia, agricultural activities, and interethnic interactions.[5]

The Independence of the Republic of Mexico from the Spanish Empire in 1821 had a significant impact on the migration flows in and out of the Los Angeles region. With the new republic's secularization policy, most Native Americans left their missions for the interior valleys. The Native American population of the larger Los Angeles region marked 28,643 in 1820 but plummeted down to 2,553 after secularization. In the Los Angeles civilian settlement, however, their population increased from 200 in 1820 to 553 in 1836, and 650 in 1844, since former neophytes (mission residents) chose to settle in the town where they could work as servants for wealthy ranchero families.[6]

At the same time, the Los Angeles settlement attracted new migrants from Mexico, particularly from Sonora and Sinaloa, as well as other European American immigrants from New Mexico and the Mississippi Valley. Although the Los Angeles population increased only slightly from 1,088 in 1836 to 1,250 in 1844, the Mexican period saw the expansion of ranchos for the growing hide and tallow trade, thanks to the liberalized land policy. By the 1830s, the trade lines had been firmly established between California rancheros and New England traders. These maritime traders brought to California manufactured goods from New England such as shoes, while they took sea otter pelts to China. On their return voyages the New Englanders brought Chinese goods to California before taking hides and tallow from the region back to New England. In what is now Southern California, Manuel Domínguez, a prominent ranchero who inherited one of the original Spanish land grants and owned more than 25,000 acres of land, worked closely with American traders. Since he was politically active and spoke English fluently, Manuel Domínguez became mayor of Los Angeles in 1832.[7]

Mexican California also saw the reification of the expansionist ideology, often explained by the doctrine of Manifest Destiny, that justified the American rule of the northern Mexican territory.⁸ In 1848, the United State acquired California, New Mexico, and other northern Mexican territories through the stipulations of the Treaty of Guadalupe-Hidalgo after defeating its southern neighbor in the Mexican-American War. Nevertheless, Los Angeles remained culturally as a Mexican town, as half of its population still consisted of Mexicans in 1860, while the region was increasingly connected to the transcontinental and transpacific markets.⁹ As detailed in chapter 6, Manuel Domínguez's descendants would play an important role in supporting ethnic Japanese farmers during World War II, merging the Spanish colonial history with the Mexican, American, and Japanese histories into a global history.

Not long afterward, the United States went through the devastating Civil War. The triumph of the North, supported by abolitionists, Whigs, and free-soilers, prevented the westward expansion of slavery but accelerated the westward development of the railroad network. During the Civil War, northern Republican Party legislators enacted a variety of laws for the United States to develop economically through government promotion and large-scale enterprise. One such law was the transcontinental railroad bill that authorized public land grants for the westward railroad construction. As a result, in 1869, the first transcontinental railroad was completed between the Missouri River and Sacramento, California. Chinese immigrants, who had arrived in California during the Gold Rush, constructed the western half of the transcontinental railroad, while Irish immigrants did the eastern half. By 1890, the entire mainland United States had been connected by 167,000 miles of railroad tracks, serving as the extensive bloodstream of the growing US economy.¹⁰ In this period, Los Angeles came to be firmly incorporated into the transcontinental railroad network as the Southern Pacific Railroad reached the city via San Francisco in 1876 and the Atchison, Topeka and Santa Fe Railroad did in 1887, which resulted in the transformation of the city's demography and local economy with the influx of migration from other areas of the United States.¹¹

The influx of these American newcomers had a considerable impact on the racial and cultural representation of Los Angeles, since they consisted mainly of middle-class white Protestant migrants dissatisfied with their lives in the Midwest. Their arrival resulted in the significant expansion of the city's population from about 11,000 in 1880 to 102,000 in 1900, making Los Angeles increasingly a white Protestant city. In 1900, nearly 78 percent of the city's population was American-born white, while the percentage of foreign-born white population in the city was 18 percent and that of the nonwhite population 4.3 percent. The city's boosters knew that the population growth was crucial for the development of the Los Angeles region. They declared, "No happier paradise for the farmer can be found than Los Angeles County," in order to attract white American migrants from the interior. Yet the boosters were also aware that these prospective newcomers did not intend to engage in large-scale farming. Therefore, they did not emphasize their economic prosperity in agriculture but rather portrayed the city as a comfortable place where "nature seems to work with man, and not against him" liberating them from "the restless rush and haste of our usual life." The development of the highway network made it much easier for the newcomers to live in the neighboring areas around the city such as the San Fernando Valley, San Gabriel Valley, Long Beach, and Santa Monica. As a result, Los Angeles County's population increased from 504,131 in 1910 to 936,455 in 1920, 92 percent of which were the native and foreign-born white population except Mexican-born residents. With the presence of the overwhelming white majority, white reformers and municipal officials drew the dividing line between white suburbs and nonwhite "slums" not only in their imagination but also in the actual city landscape through measures such as zoning ordinances and public health policy among other policies.[12]

In the early twentieth century, European immigrants such as Italians, Russians, and Poles supplemented the white population of Los Angeles County, thanks to the improved transportation facilities such as the new transportation route connecting the Southern Pacific Railroad with the steamship service between New Orleans and Naples, Italy. In 1920, the foreign-born white population in Los Angeles County numbered 166,579, about an 88 percent increase from 1910. African Americans also arrived at Los Angeles escaping the discriminatory socioeconomic situation in the South and their number doubled from 9,424 to 18,738 in Los Angeles County in the same period.[13] Los Angeles history, however, cannot be understood within the Black-white racial paradigm because the region's demography was becoming increasingly multiracial and multicultural due to the influx of farmers and laborers, particularly from two Pacific Rim countries: Mexico and Japan. These countries experienced rapid modernization and development around the turn of the twentieth century as Los Angeles did. The downside of rapid modernization in Mexico and Japan was the impoverishment of many of their respective citizens, who suffered from drastic reforms and became potential emigrants to Los Angeles located in the intersection of Latin America and Asia. Mexican and Japanese immigrants would play an indispensable role in developing agriculture in the remaining rural area of rapidly growing Los Angeles County.

The development of Los Angeles farmland as a global meeting place needs to be understood as part of the larger history of California agriculture. From the 1870s, bonanza wheat farms developed thanks to the strong commercial connection between San Francisco and Liverpool, England. In the 1880s, due to the arrival of the Southern Pacific Railroad and the Atchison, Topeka and Santa Fe Railroad in Southern California and the development of refrigerated train cars, citrus and vegetable production dramatically increased, contributing to the population growth of Los Angeles County. Although the traditional American agrarian philosophy weighs the importance of small-scale self-sufficient farmers as the basis of a democratic society, California agriculture developed with large-scale farming based on the system of monopolistic landownership inherited from the Spanish colonial period. California farmers sought larger profits with the belief that large-scale production, the disciplined use of irrigated water, specialized marketing cooperatives that would avoid middlemen and encourage consumption, and, most importantly, cheap farm labor were fundamental for their economic success. In Wheatland in 1913, farmworkers challenged their employers and went on strike with the support of the Industrial Workers of the World, which resulted in the arrest of union leaders and gave agribusiness confidence in their aggressive measures against workers. By the mid-1910s, California agriculture had become firmly industrialized and profit-driven, drawing a sharper line between agribusiness and farm labor and deeming the latter rather as a commodity. In Southern California, the Los Angeles Chamber of Commerce functioned as the promoter and defender of agribusiness along with other growers' organizations.[14]

Industrialized agriculture in California forced farmworkers into a position characterized by harsh working and living conditions including low wages, irregular work, constant migration, social isolation, and individual powerlessness, even though or rather because farmworkers were indispensable for large-scale, labor-intensive agriculture. In booming wheat farming in the late nineteenth century, leaders of large-scale agriculture hired a large number of Chinese workers, now dismissed from railroad construction sites, and regarded them almost equivalent to slaves, as a leading farm employer William Blackwood wrote in 1884, "The laborers of China are born to servitude—it has become ingrained in their natures." In 1888, the *Kern County Californian* also described, "With the Chinese, field hands could be treated like the beasts of the field." On the other hand, the presence of Chinese immigrants reinforced anti-Chinese sentiment among whites who perceived the importation of Chinese workers as a threat to the status of free white labor just like the African slave trade. As the number of Chinese farmworkers decreased after the enactment of the so-called Chinese Exclusion Act (initially known as the Chinese Restriction Act) in 1882, unemployed urban whites engaged temporarily in farm work during the depression of the 1890s, and soon after, Japanese farmworkers began to increase. In the beginning of the new century, many Japanese immigrants still shared with Mexicans the same class status as laborers. In 1903, Japanese and Mexican farmworkers successfully organized a bi-national labor union in Oxnard, Ventura County, although their coalition eventually dissolved as the American Federation of Labor rejected the membership of Asian workers. Not long afterward, many Japanese became small-scale tenant farmers in regions such as Los Angeles County, while Filipinos and Mexicans became the major source of farm labor in California.[15] In the Depression years of the 1930s, the decade that would see further diversification of farm labor with the influx of white Dust Bowl migrants from the Great

Plains, farmworkers of different ethnoracial backgrounds stood up against the exploitative structure of California agribusiness, as will be examined in terms of Japanese-Mexican relations in chapters 3 and 4.

Class and race functioned simultaneously and consolidated the racial capitalism that defined the relations between agribusiness and farmworkers in California agriculture.[16] While the urban history of Los Angeles is well known, this book highlights the multiethnic nonurban history of Los Angeles farmland from the 1920s to the 1940s by focusing on Japanese and Mexicans as its protagonists. Their history demonstrates unique social relations in California agriculture that were not always determined by their race and class differences.

MODERNIZATION OF MEXICO AND JAPAN AND EMIGRANTS TO THE UNITED STATES

As the Los Angeles region was once ruled by Mexico, old Mexican barrios still existed in late nineteenth-century California. But their presence would be overwhelmed by the large-scale migration of newly arriving Mexicans in the first three decades of the twentieth century. The increase of Mexican immigrants in Los Angeles had a lot to do with the modernization of Mexico that started with the presidency of Porfirio Díaz in 1876. The land reform and railroad construction were the two major reforms implemented by Díaz that largely influenced the Mexican migration north to the United States. Believing that large-scale agriculture was indispensable for the economic development of Mexico, the Díaz administration rapidly built up the land system ruled by powerful landowners and companies by depriving small farmers of their traditional communal lands whose ownership was not clear from the government's perspective. As a result, in 1910, only 1 percent of the Mexican population owned 90 percent of the entire national territory, leaving 95 percent of the ten million farmers landless. Many of these landless people had no choice but to become migratory workers. At the same time, the Díaz administration eagerly received foreign investment particularly for the development of mines and the expansion of railroad tracks. In Mexico, the track mileage increased from 663 kilometers in 1875 to 19,748 kilometers in 1910, which shrunk the temporal distance between the city and the countryside and developed the country's market economy. Thus, many landless Mexicans took a ride on the train heading north to the United States particularly in times of political and economic disturbances during and after the Mexican Revolution (1910–1920). On the other side of the border, the expansion of agriculture and the enforcement of restrictions on Asian labor in California enlarged the demand for agricultural labor provided by these Mexican immigrants. By 1920, in California, ethnic Mexicans comprised about 75 percent of the state's agricultural labor force (and nearly 17 percent of its unskilled construction labor force).[17]

Although the number of Mexican-born residents in California was merely 8,086 in 1900, it jumped more than tenfold to 85,610 in 1920. Los Angeles County counted by far the largest concentration in California where 33,644 Mexican-born residents lived (3.6 percent of the total county population). Most Mexican immigrants first settled in the downtown Plaza area before World War I. With the urban development and the increase of native-born white Americans who settled in the western parts of the city, many Mexican immigrants concentrated in the eastern side of the Los Angeles River such as Boyle Heights as well.[18]

When we analyze the immigrant experience in an international context, we need to look at the activities of the consulate of their home country in the United States since the consulate served as the official agency that protected its overseas nationals and negotiated with the local and federal governments of the United States regarding immigration issues. The Mexican consulate had been established in Los Angeles much before the increase of the Mexican population in the early twentieth century. For decades after the Mexican-American War, the Mexican government did not pay much attention to its nationals in Los Angeles. But in 1885 when Los Angeles was about to be fully connected to the transnational railroad network, the Mexican government established its consulate in Los Angeles, understanding the necessity to protect Mexican residents and foreseeing the economic potential of the city. With the rapid increase of the Mexican population in the Los Angeles region, the Mexican consulate would play a more proactive role in the protection and control of their nationals, particularly in the 1930s as detailed in chapters 3 and 4.[19]

Japanese immigrants were another major nonwhite minority in Los Angeles, although the Chinese preceded them as an Asian immigrant group.[20] The Japanese became visible and incorporated into the multiethnic economy in Los Angeles especially in the early twentieth century. As was the case of Mexican immigrants, the political reform of Japan affected the overseas Japanese migration across the Pacific Ocean. In 1868, fifteen years after Commodore Matthew Perry's first visit to Japan, which brought an end to Japan's seclusion policy, and only eight years before the beginning of the Díaz administration in Mexico, the Meiji Restoration took place and drastically modernized the Japanese society and economy. The equivalent of the Porfirian land reform was the tax reform called *chisokaisei* implemented in 1873. The new Meiji government began to impose tax on the land instead of crops, mainly rice, to assure the stable tax revenue that would not be influenced by crop failures or successes. Furthermore, in the 1880s, the Japanese government took a drastic deflation policy in order to solve the serious inflation caused by the military expenses on suppressing the uprisings of former *samurais* deprived of their privileges by the regime change. The rapid decline of the rice price hurt the livelihood of rural farming families. As a consequence of the combination of the tax reform and deflation policy, both of which were necessary for the new government to continue the path of modernization with a stable fiscal base, many Japanese farmers became landless and then migratory workers. Meanwhile, Japanese steamship lines connected Japan with Seattle and San Francisco in the late 1890s making their transpacific transportation more feasible. In the hope of having a better life, many Japanese laborers particularly from the southwestern prefectures of Japan such as Hiroshima, Yamaguchi, Kumamoto, and Fukuoka took on the transpacific journey first to Hawai'i and then to the mainland United States particularly from the 1890s.[21]

While the enactment of the Chinese Exclusion Act of 1882 certainly increased demands for substitute immigrant labor, the financial inflation after the Sino-Japanese War of 1894 and 1895 directed impoverished Japanese workers and jobless war veterans to the United States. In addition, in 1894, the Japanese government set up regulations on the protection of emigrants that put private Japanese emigrant companies in charge of sending Japanese laborers abroad, while those companies actively recruited would-be emigrants making profits from their brokerage business. As the result, the Japanese population in the United States increased from about 4,500 in 1892 to 35,000 in 1897 and many of them used the Hawaiian Islands as a stepping-stone to the mainland United States.[22]

Natural disasters also affected the destiny of Japanese immigrants in the United States. Although San Francisco was the first Japanese settlement in California starting from the 1870s, the Great Earthquake of 1906 destroyed the city and turned Los Angeles into the main destination for Japanese immigrants. While the Japanese had existed in Los Angeles County since as early as the 1880s, their population in the county dramatically increased from 209 in 1900 to 19,911 in 1920 (2.1 percent of the total county population, which was equivalent to the African American population).[23] Japanese immigrants worked in a variety of industries such as construction, canneries, fishing, and domestic service, but one of the most important industries was agriculture. First-generation Japanese, known as Issei, most of whom had farming experiences in Japan, had skills to grow fruits and vegetables effectively. Landowners were willing to employ the Japanese, not only because of their skills suitable to intensive agriculture, but also because of the rapid growth of agricultural industry in California and the lack of other low-wage foreign workers, such as the Chinese, whose entry was banned in 1882.[24]

The defining characteristic of Japanese agriculture in Southern California was its large percentage of tenant farmers. In Los Angeles County in 1940, about 90 percent of Japanese farmers were tenant farmers, while about less than half were tenant farmers in other places such as Fresno, Merced, Placer, and Sacramento Counties. There were two main reasons for the high percentage of Japanese tenancy in Southern California even before the enactment of the California Alien Land Laws that prohibited Japanese nationals from purchasing and leasing lands. Firstly, most lands in Southern California were being held for speculative purposes, not for sale. Secondly, Japanese immigrant farmers considered that leasing would be more profitable for them than purchasing lands.[25]

After the enactment of the Alien Land Laws in 1913 and 1920, Japanese farmers began to lease lands under the names of their children who were US citizens eligible for leasing and purchasing lands. Although the Alien Land Laws were certainly a serious obstacle faced by Japanese farmers, the productivity of Japanese farmers did not change in Southern California, as they came to dominate the production of a variety of crops. In 1941, Japanese farmers grew more than 90 percent of the production of at least seventeen fruits and vegetables including strawberries and celery, two major crops whose fields became the very sites of Japanese-Mexican conflicts in 1930s Los Angeles County. Although they operated only 4.8 percent of all 596,552 acres of Los Angeles County farmland in 1940, the importance of Japanese farmers in perishable crop agriculture was undeniable in Los Angeles by the time of the Pearl Harbor attack.[26] Yet it also meant the importance of Mexican farmworkers who provided indispensable labor for Japanese tenant farmers in Los Angeles County. The Gentlemen's Agreement made by both Japan and the United States in 1907 and 1908 restricted the entry of Japanese laborers to the United States, so that by the early 1910s it had already been impossible for Los Angeles Japanese farmers to grow crops without the help of non-Japanese laborers such as Mexicans, Filipinos, and even white workers.[27] In Los Angeles County, the Japanese farmers' dependency on Mexican workers became even larger after the implementation of the Immigration Act of 1924 that stopped the entry of Japanese immigrants.

The expansion of Japanese farmland meant the expansion of Japanese-Mexican interactions in Los Angeles County. The first Japanese agricultural settlement in Los Angeles County was established by two Japanese immigrants who began to farm in Tropico, about six miles north of downtown Los Angeles in 1901. Then Japanese farmers began to work in areas such as the Gardena and San Gabriel Valleys. Japanese farms in the Gardena Valley first succeeded in the strawberry industry in the Gardena and Moneta area, about ten miles south of downtown. In 1910, 531 Japanese farms existed in Los Angeles County and the Gardena and Moneta area was the largest concentration of Japanese immigrants at the time. From the mid-1910s, they began to grow vegetables and expanded to its northwestern and southeastern areas such as Torrance, Hawthorne, Inglewood, and Compton. The southward expansion of Japanese agriculture reached the former Spanish land grant of Rancho San Pedro, which overlaps mainly with the South Bay cities, such as Torrance and Carson and the Wilmington area of Los Angeles. In the San Gabriel Valley, Japanese farmers appeared in the early 1900s and expanded widely in the valley. They had been a major producer of celery until around 1920 and then cauliflower and berries particularly in the El Monte area, about thirteen miles east of downtown. Meanwhile, in the mid-1910s, Japanese immigrants also established

FIGURE 1. An aerial view of Los Angeles farmland, ca.1924. SOURCE: USC Digital Library. California Historical Society Collection.

agricultural settlements in the Venice area, about ten miles west of downtown, where they became major celery producers on a national level.[28]

This book highlights these agricultural areas before World War II. Throughout the period from 1920 to 1940, about 40 percent of the total ethnic Japanese population in Los Angeles County lived mostly in nonurban agricultural areas outside downtown (Figure 1), while downtown Los Angeles served as their economic, cultural, and political center.[29] The expansion of Japanese agriculture helped develop Little Tokyo as a visible and vibrant Japan town in multiethnic Los Angeles from the early 1900s. It also resulted in the openings of two major agricultural wholesale markets, the Ninth Street and Seventh Street Markets (Figure 2), established, respectively, in 1909 and 1918 downtown, which played crucial roles in shipping and selling Japanese crops within and beyond Los Angeles County. In 1915, the Japanese government established its consulate in downtown Los Angeles, responding to the decade-long request from Japanese residents. Like the Mexican counterpart, the Japanese consulate became seriously concerned and involved in the Japanese-Mexican conflicts in 1930s Los Angeles farmland.[30]

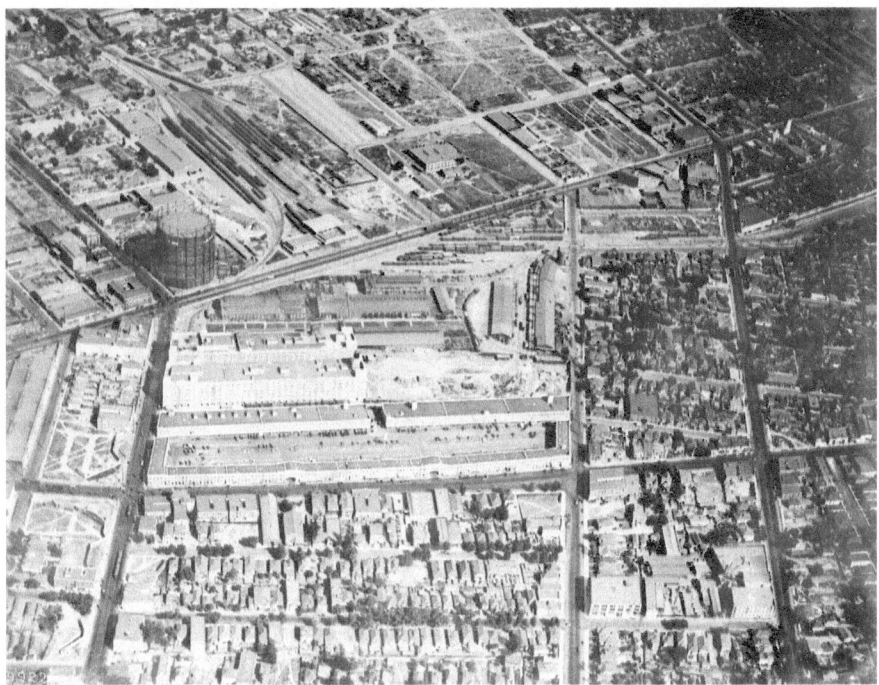

FIGURE 2. An aerial view looking south toward Seventh Street and the Los Angeles produce market, ca.1928. SOURCE: USC Digital Library. California Historical Society Collection.

"MEXICO IS WAITING FOR YOU" IN THE TIME OF JAPANESE EXCLUSION

In the first three decades of the twentieth century, Los Angeles developed dramatically, outpacing every other American metropolis. Los Angeles County's population doubled from 936,455 in 1920 to 2,208,492 in 1930, which counted for nearly 40 percent of the total population of California. One of the major driving forces of the region's rapid development was its oil industry, which fueled trains, ships, and other industrial machines. During the 1920s, the Los Angeles harbor came to handle a large number of various cargoes, including oil, and overtook the trade volume of any other port except that of New York. Regarding the transpacific trade between the United States and Japan, at the end of the decade, the Los Angeles harbor dealt with the largest amount of export to Japan among US ports on the Pacific Coast. On the other hand, agriculture remained one of the major industries of Los Angeles County, utilizing water coming from the Los Angeles River and the Owens Valley. As far as the agricultural labor in Los Angeles was concerned, Japanese and Mexican immigrants continued to play an important role as farmers and workers, while their respective ethnic communities developed along with the rapid growth of the metropolitan region.[31] However, relations between these two groups faced new challenges.

The Immigration Act of 1924 affected Japanese and Mexicans differently, since the law prohibited Japanese immigration and thus increased demands for Mexican agricultural labor. The impact of this demographic change is clear in census records. In Los Angeles County, the number of ethnic Japanese residents increased from 19,911 in 1920 to 35,300 in 1930, thanks to a growing second generation. Meanwhile, the number of ethnic Mexican residents jumped from 33,644 (as a foreign born white population) in 1920 to 167,024 in 1930, due to both the influx of newcomers and its own growing second generation.[32] In other words, although the number of ethnic Mexicans was less than twice as large as that of Japanese in 1920, the former grew almost five times larger than the latter in 1930.

But it was not only the demographic character of Los Angeles ethnoracial minorities that the 1924 Act changed. While Japanese exclusion promoted the migration of Mexicans to the United States, in part to replace Japanese labor, it pushed a small number of disgruntled Los Angeles Japanese to resettle in Mexico. More importantly, it also resulted in the substantial migration of people from Japan to Mexico, particularly to Baja California. The increasing size of the ethnic Mexican community in Southern California and the development of the ethnic Japanese community south of the border in Baja California in the 1920s laid the foundation for serious interethnic and international conflicts between Japanese and Mexicans in both the United States and Mexico in the following decade.[33]

The goal of the Immigration Act of 1924 was to maintain the United States as a country dominated by white Anglo-Saxon Americans. For that goal, the 1924 Act introduced the national origins quota system that largely restricted Eastern and Southern European immigrants and prohibited Japanese immigrants from entering the United States altogether except certain groups of people such as government officials, merchants, students, and tourists. The 1924 Act symbolized the triumph of Anglo-Saxon racial nationalism over civic virtues such as liberty and equality and thus brought an end to the era when immigrants envisioned the United States as a promised land. In this year, Los Angeles Chamber of Commerce official Clarence Matson wrote in their business periodical, "Anglo Saxon civilization must climax in the generations to come.... The Los Angeles of Tomorrow will be the center of this climax."[34]

Regarding Japanese immigrants, restrictionists and nativists succeeded in excluding them by inciting demographic, economic, racial, moral, and ideological fears among the white majority regarding the Japanese. Lon Kurashige argues that these five fears related to Asian immigration, such as human flood, labor competition, mongrelization, racial disruption of social order, and ideologically driven actions, together produced the "perfect storm of exclusion" as materialized in the 1924 Immigration Act. In this process, despite the presence of pro-Japanese white Americans who were often in close interactions with ethnic Japanese residents, California's "Progressive Era" politicians succeeded in incorporating the Japanese exclusion clause in the 1924 Act.[35]

In contrast, Mexicans did not face the numerical restriction of the quota system because of the low-wage labor demands for expanding US industry and agriculture. This policy was also justified as an expression of Pan-Americanism and Good Neighbor policies of the US State Department that wanted to keep amicable relations with its neighboring countries in the Western Hemisphere. The 1924 Act institutionalized an immigration control policy that aimed to maintain the Anglo-Saxon Americans as the "original [Nordic] stock" of the country, while allowing Mexican workers to enter the United States in the way in which it responded to the expectations of capitalists. No matter whether Mexicans came legally or illegally, they came to be seen increasingly as "illegal" due to other legal provisions and enforcement newly implemented by the 1924 Act. This act had a serious cultural consequence racializing Asian and Mexican Americans as "alien citizens" who were illegal, criminal, foreign, and unassimilable regardless of their actual citizenship.[36]

Being targeted for exclusion, an immediate response of the Los Angeles Japanese community was anger, as they denounced the law as the Japanese Exclusion Act or *hainichi imin hō* in Japanese.[37] An editorial of the *Rafu Shimpo*, a major Japanese immigrant newspaper in Los Angeles founded in 1903, showed their concern that the 1924 Act would result in a future "race war" between whites and nonwhites but also called on the Japanese to their nation's discriminatory attitude towards the Chinese in Japan, saying, "Is there any difference between anti-Japanese discrimination in the United States and anti-Chinese discrimination in Japan?" In the early 1920s, the Japanese government was strengthening its control over Chinese workers in Japan and issued deportation orders on the prejudiced assumption that most Chinese were engaged in industries such as construction and transportation in which the Chinese were not allowed to engage. In 1922, a Chinese student in Japan, named Zhaocheng Wang, wrote up to the *Tokyo Asahi Shimbun*, a major newspaper, and criticized the Japanese government's deportation order against Chinese workers as inappropriate. Wang stressed, "Such an action of the Japanese government is starkly inconsistent with its own proposal for the anti-racial discrimination clause at the Paris Peace conference," and "Look at the anti-Japanese movement in the United States. You should know what the problem is."[38] Nevertheless, these voices did not influence the Japanese public in general.

The Japanese on both sides of the Pacific Ocean called and remembered the day of its enactment May 26, 1924 as *kokujokubi* (The day of national disgrace). In

Tokyo, one Japanese man felt infuriated and protested the United States by disembowelment, or *hara-kiri*, which many Los Angeles Japanese thought was a respectable patriotic act.[39] On the other hand, Japanese immigrants had to think about the future of their ethnic community in the United States, since US immigration policy officially deemed them undesirable. They were concerned particularly about the future of their US-born children or Nisei. In order to prevent anti-Japanese sentiment from growing further, Japanese immigrant parents began to regard and educate their children as a bridge (*kakehashi*) of understanding between the United States and Japan.[40] Their US-born children had the dual citizenship due to the *jus sanguinis* principle of Japan and the *jus soli* principle of the United States. Issei regarded the dual citizenship as an obstacle for the future of Nisei because anti-Japanese nativists criticized their dual citizenship and doubted their loyalty to the United States. Responding to their concern, in 1916 and in 1924, the Japanese government amended the Nationality Act to make it possible for Nisei to renounce their Japanese citizenship. From December 1924 to November 1925, out of 5,993 children of Japanese ancestry born in San Francisco, Los Angeles, Seattle, Portland, and New York, 4,245 or 70.8 percent renounced the Japanese citizenship, while 1,748 retained dual citizenship. The amendment of the Nationality Act was also for the sake of the Issei, who believed that Nisei's US citizenship was "a faint glimmer [of hope]" for their survival in the United States.[41] Although renouncing citizenship might have sounded unpatriotic to Japanese nationalists, the Japanese government recognized the need to provide a better legal environment for the ethnic Japanese community during the peak of anti-Japanese sentiment in the 1920s United States.

The 1924 Act redirected Japanese immigrants to settle in South American countries such as Brazil and Peru, expanding the range of the Japanese diaspora. The peak of Japanese immigration to Brazil was between 1928 and 1934, when about 108,000 Japanese entered Brazil.[42] While emigration from Japan was reorienting itself toward these South American countries, some Japanese immigrants already living in the United States at the time of the passage of the 1924 Act also developed interest in migrating to other less-hostile destinations.[43] Although many Japanese families had established a settled way of life in Southern California by the early 1920s, the 1924 Act ignited the desire of Japanese immigrants for migrating to neighboring Mexico, a desire that had existed since the enactments of previous anti-Japanese legislations such as the Gentlemen's Agreement and California Alien Land Law controversies.[44] Before World War II, the most influential ethnic Japanese organization in Southern California was the Central Japanese Association of Southern California (Nanka Chūō Nihonjin Kai). Tsuneji Chino, who was the association's chairman in 1920 and 1921, recalled later in the 1950s, "Feeling the necessity to find new places for the Japanese to prosper after the enactment of the malignant land law, we [Shirō Fujioka and I] advocated and organized a study group to learn about Mexico with other like-minded members."[45] Regarding the legal status granted to the Japanese, Mexico appeared much more attractive than California, since the Mexican government allowed the Japanese to immigrate, purchase lands, and get naturalized, although the Mexican government did not recruit or receive many Japanese immigrants until 1924 because of the Gentlemen's Agreement, as will be explained later in this chapter.

Migration to Mexico quickly became a major agenda in the ethnic Japanese community in Los Angeles. Japanese ethnic organizations and newspapers led the discussion and portrayed Mexico as a new promised land with vast lands free from anti-Japanese sentiment and with plenty of chances for Japanese farmers and investors. In February 1924, three months before the enactment of the 1924 Act, the Central Japanese Association held a regular meeting, which was attended by about forty immigrant leaders from Los Angeles and from other places in Southern California such as Santa Barbara and San Diego. At the meeting, they discussed the necessity of helping those who wanted to find new lands outside California or in Mexico.[46] In April, the association held a board meeting in which ten board members decided to set up a team to conduct research in Mexico. They put importance on exploring Mexico as a measure to save Japanese farmers who faced growing anti-Japanese hostility in Southern California. At the same time, the members brought up the idea of petitioning the Japanese government to set up a branch consular office in Mexico under the control of the Japanese consulate in Los Angeles, not the Japanese Legation in Mexico City.[47]

In May, responding to "the voices calling for the development of the Japanese outside California and migration to Mexico," Japanese immigrant leaders quickly made a start in field research in Mexico in order to determine whether Mexican lands were suitable for Japanese immigrants. The secretary general of the association Masuo Hiratsuka emphasized Mexico as the right destination for the Japanese, arguing, "even outside of the state [of California], if we remain in the United States, we will face anti-Japanese legislations."[48] By 1924, other states such as Washington, Oregon, and Arizona had passed their alien land laws against the Japanese. Texas also passed its alien land law which prohibited newly arriving immigrants from owning land in the Lone Star State after its enactment, although the law conceded that Japanese immigrants were still able to lease land.[49] Given the increase of anti-Japanese legislation in various states across the United States, Mexico appeared as an intriguing option in the anxious hearts of Los Angeles Japanese. In July, the *Rafu Shimpo* cited a local English newspaper and reported that a Japanese government official visited Los Angeles after conducting research on the availability of Mexican lands and encouraged Japanese farmers to go south to Mexico. He also emphasized the absence of anti-Japanese legislation against Japanese farmers, saying, "The vast untouched land in Mexico is waiting for Japanese people under especially favorable conditions. In Mexico, the Japanese can purchase lands.... Those already engaged in agriculture in California can use their experiences as a capital and work hard without restraint in their new lands in Mexico."[50]

Right after the enactment of the 1924 Act, the Japanese Association of Los Angeles (Rafu Nihonjin Kai), another important ethnic organization, began to gather information about Mexico in hope of finding a place for Japanese settlements. The association asked a Japanese resident in Mexico, Fusao Kasai, who worked as a doctor in the state of Chihuahua, about whether Los Angeles Japanese could migrate to Mexico. In mid-May 1924, Kasai sent the association a reply and recommended Mexico as a great place for the future prosperity of fellow Japanese immigrants. Kasai stressed that Mexican newspapers reported that there was no reason for Japanese immigrants to stay in anti-Japanese California. His white friend, probably American, who owned large ranches and mines in the state of Jalisco, was asking him to find Japanese people interested in purchasing properties in Mexico. He even contrasted Mexico with Canada, which "is already infected by American anti-Japanese sentiment." His reply appeared in the *Rafu Shimpo* with the title "Mexico is waiting for you."[51] As seen in Kasai's comments, Japanese immigrants in Mexico perceived anti-Japanese sentiment as a disease spreading from the United States. As Kasai feared, the Canadian government decided to limit the number of Japanese immigrants to under 150, responding to anti-Japanese pressure in the 1920s. Anti-Japanese sentiment was strong especially in Vancouver, where Japanese workers were denied membership in the mainstream unions. However, in Canada, the Japanese were still able to purchase lands and even gain Canadian citizenship (without the right to vote).[52] While overlooking these facts, Kasai understood that Canada was "infected" because it was a country dominated by anti-Japanese whites just like the United States. What is interesting is that his rhetoric that linked race with disease was similar to the American yellow peril discourse in the early decades of the twentieth century which used the metaphor of disease to criticize the increase of the Japanese population in the United States.[53] Probably the disease that Kasai considered "infected" Canada was a disease of white hysteria over the yellow peril.

At the very moment in which the US government declared the Japanese undesirable and restricted their immigration, the presumed absence of anti-Japanese legislations and anti-Japanese sentiment in Mexico appealed to the Los Angeles Japanese. Yet, they needed more information regarding both merits and demerits of migrating to Mexico. To give them a more accurate picture of Mexico, the *Rafu Shimpo* published serial articles about Mexico written by a Japanese resident in Mexico, Torimatsu Ozono, who immigrated to Mexico from the United States before 1924 and was farming bananas in the state of Sinaloa. Based on his experiences in both the United States and Mexico, he could provide a comparative view about the two countries and discuss the possibility of Japanese migration to Mexico.⁵⁴ In contrast to growing expectation of Japanese immigrants in Los Angeles, however, Ozono did not encourage them to migrate south of the border. He contended that Japanese Issei in California were too old to begin agriculture from scratch in Mexico because it would take at least five years to harvest enough crops. Instead, he argued that a new Japanese immigrant community in Mexico should be built by Japanese investors living in Japan and by newly arriving immigrant workers from Japan who were supposedly younger and stronger than Japanese immigrants in Los Angeles. So what role could Los Angeles Japanese play in Mexico? Ozono argued that the Japanese in the United States should take part in building a new Japanese community in Mexico by providing the newly coming Japanese with knowledge to cultivate their lands and information to sell their produce in the US market.⁵⁵

In addition to his concern over difficulty in initiating land cultivation from scratch, Ozono also pointed out the lack of adequate education for Japanese children in Mexico as another reason why Los Angeles Japanese should not migrate to Mexico. He argued, "I am not impressed by Mexican ways of education. It seems that ordinary Mexicans are satisfied with their hand-to-mouth life and unaspiring, as they lack an ambition for savings. And liquors, philandering with women, dancing, and gambling were common." Ozono warned that "[Japanese children] would become Mexicanized" unless "a large number of Japanese immigrants live together in the same place to build an orderly Japanese colony modeled after the US or Japanese society in every aspect." Instead, Ozono encouraged Japanese American youth to use the "knowledge and skills that they earned from the best education and civilization [in the United States]" to help Japanese immigrants in Mexico.⁵⁶ He envisioned a transpacific Japanese network which would link labor in Mexico, capital in Japan, and knowledge in the United States. But his suggestion was based on the idea that Mexico was culturally and economically inferior to both Japan and the United States.

Despite the appeal of Mexican prospects, Japanese immigrants were not free from anti-Japanese sentiment in Mexico, either. In 1924, Itarō Ishii, a Japanese diplomat stationed in Mexico City, conducted field research in the Mexican border city of Mexicali. In his report on the *Rafu Shimpo* published in early May, he warned that anti-Japanese sentiment in California could influence how ordinary Mexicans would treat Japanese immigrants in Mexico. In Mexicali, he had discussions with local Mexicans on Japanese immigration to Mexico. It was their unanimous opinion that "they would welcome the Japanese simply because they were sorry to learn about Japanese exclusion in California." On the other hand, he was "concerned that anti-Japanese sentiment in the United States could sway Mexicans in the border region and make them treat Japanese migrants in a condescending manner," although "the wind of pro-Japanese sentiment might blow" in the inland region of Mexico.⁵⁷ Ishii recognized that the regional difference regarding Mexicans' sentiment toward the Japanese also lay in the fact that the border region had larger Asian populations and a record of anti-Asian violence, particularly against the Chinese.

During the Mexican Revolution, in the Mexican northern region, Mexican nationalism merged with anti-Chinese sentiment and caused physical and economic harm to Chinese residents. In 1911, a Mexican revolutionary mob killed 303 Chinese in Torreón in the state of Coahuila. In this city, Chinese immigrants had strong economic power. They owned a large Chinese bank and dominated local agriculture, which drew strong resentment from local Mexicans. The Japanese government immediately investigated the Torreón massacre since they heard the rumor that the mob killed some Japanese, too. Eventually, the Japanese government found that there was no Japanese killed in the massacre but warned that Japanese immigrants could face the same tragedy if they amassed significant wealth and incurred resentment from local Mexican residents.[58] In 1917, the anti-Chinese campaign in the northwestern state of Sonora became intensified. Mexican nationalists regarded Chinese immigrants as supporters of the deposed President Porfirio Díaz as well as contaminators of the Mexican race. In response, Governor Plutarco Elías Calles implemented several anti-Chinese regulations including a special taxation of Chinese farmers and merchants and the denial of reentry of Chinese residents who had left Mexico.[59] The anti-Chinese campaign was still active in 1924. In early June, the *Rafu Shimpo* reported rumors of an anti-Chinese campaign in the northern border region of Mexico, which led the Mexican government to immediately repudiate the story.[60] In September, however, the anti-Chinese campaign developed strength in several Mexican states, especially in Sonora. Anti-Chinese Mexican nativists sent petitions asking the Mexican government to solve the "Chinese Problem" and criticizing the Chinese for lowering wages, posing a threat to public health, and creating disorder in society. In reporting this, the *Rafu Shimpo* mentioned that the Mexican government was doing research on various anti-Chinese regulations that would make the Chinese ineligible for immigration, intermarriage, land lease, and naturalization.[61] It was important for the Los Angeles Japanese to be aware of the situation of Chinese immigrants in Mexico because they could face a similar situation if they migrated to Mexico.[62]

In Mexico, the Japanese had occasionally been the victims of xenophobic violence, although their small population did not pose a significant economic threat to ordinary Mexicans. According to a Japanese government investigation, at least fifty-one Japanese suffered physical and economic harm during the Mexican Revolution. Most cases were robbery, but some Japanese lost their lives. For example, in October of 1913 in Nayarit, revolutionary soldiers robbed the grocery store of Kenjirō Sakaguchi and set his store on fire destroying his entire fortune valued at five thousand pesos. In March of 1918 in the same area, soldiers robbed a grocery store and killed a Japanese shopkeeper, Ryūsaku Kikuchi.[63] If the Japanese population increased in Mexico, sporadic attacks against the Japanese could turn into a concerted anti-Japanese campaign. While some Japanese in Los Angeles had an optimistic view that they could live in Mexico because of the absence of anti-Japanese sentiment, their migration and concentration could be a source of anti-Japanese attitudes in Mexico. In 1924, Los Angeles Japanese were gathering information and considering very carefully whether they should or could go to Mexico.

The Central Japanese Association of Southern California appointed Wataru Dobashi, vice president of the association, and Ryōsaku Matsuoka, agricultural engineer, to lead the expedition. Dobashi and Matsuoka spent two months in Mexico and came back to Los Angeles in early September of 1924. On September 6, they gave a talk on their expedition at a meeting of the Central Japanese Association and invited leaders of local Japanese farming communities and other Japanese interested in migrating to Mexico.[64] Soon after the *Rafu Shimpo* reported the details of their talk in serial articles to share the information with the larger Japanese community in Los Angeles and beyond.

In their talk, Dobashi and Matsuoka encouraged their audience to migrate and build new Japanese colonies in Mexico, because of relatively favorable public feeling toward the Japanese, the low price of lands in Mexico, and the successes of other non-Japanese immigrants such as Italians and Canadians in building their colonies. They also emphasized that "Mexico cannot help but depend on foreign agricultural immigrants" to develop unattended lands. They explained that two hundred thousand square-miles of farmlands were farmed by three million workers and six hundred thousand landlords in Mexico but still three hundred thousand square-miles were waiting to be cultivated. But the availability of lands would not guarantee the success of Japanese immigrants in agriculture in Mexico. There were already about twenty-five hundred Japanese residents in Mexico and most of them were not engaged in agriculture. In fact, many Japanese had tried and failed in agriculture in Mexico because they neither selected the right types of crops and sales outlets nor had enough capital and transportation network. Thus, Dobashi and Matsuoka recommended that the Japanese should migrate in a large group, not as individuals, and work together to overcome difficulties, particularly the lack of capital. As a possible destination, they suggested the western states of Nayarit and Colima, located along the Pacific Ocean, where immigrants could use enough water from rivers for farmlands.[65]

What is interesting about Dobashi and Matsuoka's explanation is that it gives us an idea of how Japanese immigrants in Los Angeles mapped the world and found locations for future Japanese settlements in the 1920s. Dobashi and Matsuoka described Mexico as a safe place for the Japanese by comparing Mexico with the northeastern Chinese region of Manchuria. They contended, "Mexico is not quite dangerous compared to places like Manchuria. In Manchuria, bandits might kill you and rob you of your money, but in Mexico, they tell you 'hold up' and take money from you if you have any." They also mentioned the geographical advantage of Mexico, which "is significantly important from the global perspective" because Mexico faced the United States, Europe, and Asia.[66] Since the Russo-Japanese War in 1904 and 1905, the Japanese government regarded Manchuria as an important frontier and as a "life line" of the Japanese Empire in terms of economic interests and national security. Before the Manchuria Incident in 1931, the Japanese government infiltrated into Manchuria in the name of protecting Korean immigrants, who were treated as Japanese subjects after the Japanese annexation of Korea in 1910. But the Japanese army leadership held the idea that the increase of Japanese immigrants was indispensable to gain full control of Manchuria.[67] In fact, the number of Japanese immigrants in Manchuria increased in the 1920s, although it was not until Japan founded its puppet state Manchukuo in 1932 that the Japanese population expanded in Manchuria in full scale. In 1923, Sakio Tsurumi, the director of the commerce department of the Ministry of Agriculture and Commerce of Japan, gave a talk at the conference on Japanese overseas migration in Tokyo and reported that "an increasing number of Japanese went to the Manchuria region recently," leading to more sales of Japanese products such as *sake*, *miso*, soy sauce, clothes, and even *geta* (traditional Japanese wooden clogs) not only among the Japanese but also among the Chinese in the region.[68]

Although Dobashi and Matsuoka described Manchuria as an awful place for immigration, their explanation tells us that Manchuria was, if not desirable, one of the possible destinations for Japanese immigrants in the 1920s. Compared to Manchuria, Mexico was located right next to California so that Los Angeles Japanese could migrate with less expense and still benefit from the growing market of the United States. In addition, Mexico was still connected to the larger Japanese diaspora via the Pacific Ocean. Thus, Mexico appeared a better option for Los Angeles Japanese not simply from a borderlands perspective but from a transpacific perspective as well. Their expedition report also had a self-complacent view toward Mexican women and men, which made Mexico look even more attractive than Manchuria. According to a *Rafu Shimpo* article about their expedition titled "Mr. Wataru Dobashi and a Mexican princess," "Dobashi looks better than Mexican men, so that the Mexican lady fell in love with Dobashi at first sight." Although Dobashi did not interact with the woman, this episode implies that Los Angeles Japanese found themselves both attracted to Mexico and superior to Mexicans.[69]

Nevertheless, as mentioned earlier, Mexico's proximity to the United States raised concern about anti-Japanese sentiment in the US-Mexico borderlands. Dobashi and Matsuoka echoed the same concerns voiced by the diplomat Itarō Ishii who recently warned that anti-Japanese sentiment in the United States could affect how Mexicans would treat the Japanese. They said, "It is true that Mexicans welcome the Japanese and treat the Chinese like beasts. But we witnessed Americans promoting the idea that the Japanese and the Chinese are the same group of people. American newspapers belonging to the [anti-Japanese] Hearst Press were widely read in major Mexican cities." They were also "appalled to learn that Americans built an American school in the middle of Mexico and boldly promote [American] nationalism in Mexico." At the same time, they alerted the audience to the influence of American money in Mexico, explaining that many American capitalists were trying to purchase Mexican lands at low prices and would not sell their lands to the Japanese at reasonable prices.[70] Although Los Angeles Japanese wanted to find a place free from anti-Japanese sentiment in the United States, their expedition made them realize that Japanese immigrants could hardly escape from the American sphere of influence even if they migrated south to Mexico.

Dobashi and Matsuoka were not the only Japanese who studied the prospects for Japanese immigrants in Mexico. Based on reporting in the *Rafu Shimpo*, at least three more groups of Japanese immigrants in Los Angeles County took a research trip to Mexico within four months after the enactment of the 1924 Immigration Act. One of them, Genpei Nakamura, lost his life during his trip to Mexico. Nakamura owned farmlands in Lancaster in the northern part of Los Angeles County, where Japanese immigrants farmed from as early as 1910, but decided to sell his lands and move to Mexico. In September, Nakamura left Los Angeles on his expedition by car with four other Japanese men to explore Ensenada, a Mexican coastal city in the Baja California Peninsula, 180 miles from Los Angeles. On their way, their car ran off the road near Oceanside in San Diego County and rolled down when they attempted to overtake the car in front of them, killing Nakamura and severely injuring the other passengers.[71] The death of Nakamura was an unexpected consequence of the Immigration Act of 1924, but it did little to stop other Japanese in Los Angeles from thinking about the possibility of migrating to Mexico. The *Rafu Shimpo* reported both the death of Nakamura and the talk of Dobashi and Matsuoka on September 16, which happened to be the Independence Day of Mexico. Mexican immigrants in Los Angeles held an event to celebrate the day in Lincoln Park and invited the Japanese consul in Los Angeles Kaname Wakasugi.[72] We do not know what Wakasugi said to the Mexican audience at the event, but he was increasingly interested in Japanese migration to Mexico. When the 1924 Act was enacted, Wakasugi questioned the attitude of Americans and candidly said, "How could the Japanese assimilate when they are socially excluded?"[73]

The desire of Japanese immigrants to leave the United States was inextricably linked with their nationalism and national pride. Shirō Fujioka, editor-in-chief of the *Rafu Shimpo*, favored the idea of migrating to Mexico over waiting for a softening in US public opinion or going back to Japan.[74] Fujioka was born in 1879 in Aomori, the northernmost prefecture of the Honshū island of Japan. After studying at Waseda University in Tokyo, he arrived at the United States in 1897. He then began to work as a journalist for ethnic Japanese papers in New York and Seattle. When the state of California implemented its first Alien Land Law in 1913, he moved to California to investigate the case on behalf of Japanese farmers. In 1914, he settled in Los Angeles as the secretary general of the Japanese Association of Southern California. Since then, he had worked for several Japanese organizations and contributed many articles for the *Rafu Shimpo* as the editor-in-chief. By the 1920s, he had become a well-known intellectual and political leader of the Japanese community in Southern California.[75] When the US government implemented Japanese exclusion in 1924, Fujioka denounced the law as the revelation of white Americans' racial prejudice and wrote, "The white race has the strongest sense of superiority by birth. . . . We must break down white Americans' sense of superiority by making full efforts to build up our strength."[76]

Although *Rafu Shimpo*'s editorials were anonymous, Fujioka was most likely the person responsible for many articles advocating for Japanese migration to Mexico in 1924, as independent scholar Kaori Hayashi argues based on her extensive research about the history of the ethnic paper.[77] When a Japanese man committed suicide in Japan as his protest against the United States in June of 1924, the editorial wrote, "I cannot help but respect his sincere efforts to care and love the nation. . . . If it is impossible [to repeal the law], we will need to search for places outside the United States such as South America or Mexico for the development [of the Japanese nation]." When Dobashi and Matsuoka reported back to Los Angeles in September, another editorial emphasized Mexico as "the most ideal place to prosper not only for the Japanese in the United States but also for the Japanese as a nation in the future."[78] The 1924 Act made Fujioka determined to advocate for the development of Japanese overseas communities in order to eventually stand equally with white Americans. While many Japanese immigrants hoped that their US-born children could build better relations between Japanese and whites, many others found a chance in Mexico to make a contribution to the development of the Japanese imperial state and its people that was strong enough to confront white American racism in the future. In the 1950s, Fujioka looked back on the 1920s and wrote, "Those with guts searched for a new life in another state or another country in the hope of escaping the bond of humiliation and infringement on freedom [in the United States], which I see was the natural course of events. Thus, it is understandable that the Japanese in the United States advocated for migrating to Mexico."[79]

Around the time when the Japanese Exclusion Act was enacted, Japanese government officials and intellectuals began to discuss more seriously possible new destinations for the development of overseas Japanese populations. For example, in 1925, geography teacher Satarō Yamada published a book on the overseas Japanese migration titled *Gojin no kaitaku subeki kaigai yūbō no fugen* (My thoughts regarding promising overseas sources of wealth for our development). In the preface, he wrote, "the problem of our overseas migration became a major discussion topic among the general public after the enactment of the Japanese Exclusion Act effective from July 1, 1924, in the United States" and "nothing would be more pleasing than doing research to find a solution and establish a solid emigration policy." He believed that sending Japanese people from agricultural areas to other countries would solve two major problems in Japan: the battered economy in rural areas and overpopulation. Yamada picked up eight overseas regions as possible destinations for future Japanese emigrants: Manchuria, Siberia, Southeast Asia, South Africa, Mexico, Cuba, Brazil, and other South American countries (Peru, Chile, and Argentina). Regarding Mexico, Yamada explained that Mexicans "are not comfortable with the autocratic United States because their country has always been hampered by the United States and they have a strong will to develop businesses with the Japanese. Thus, it is imperative that we establish the basis for the development of our fellow countrymen [in Mexico] by acquiring interests in the fertile land, forests, mines, and so forth."[80]

Meanwhile, the Japanese consulate in Los Angeles was busy checking the passports of Japanese immigrants planning to travel to Mexico. While understanding enthusiasm among those Japanese, the Japanese consulate was concerned that they might bring back inaccurate information on Mexico, which could be beneficial only for themselves and misleading for many others. The consulate also wanted Japanese immigrants to share their findings about Mexico with the Japanese government, since the government was also planning on conducting research on Latin America. In late September, Tetsuo Umimoto, the Japanese vice-consul in Los Angeles, proposed the creation of a study group on Mexico. He claimed, "In Southern California, there is no other place like Los Angeles convenient to learn about Mexico directly and indirectly. . . . I hope that our study group, as a support organization, finds out where [the Japanese government] should send Japanese emigrants in the future from a national perspective."[81] Aligned with the argument of Umimoto, an editorial of the *Rafu Shimpo*, most likely written by Fujioka, agreed with the vice-consul's idea of creating a study group in Los Angeles and sharing their information on Mexico with fellow Japanese in the United States and Japan. The editorial asserted, "We must understand that this is our responsibility to our home country."[82] On October 8, 1924, Umimoto and twenty-eight Japanese immigrant leaders in Los Angeles gathered and celebrated the foundation of a study group on Mexico, called the Mexico Study Society (Bokukoku Kenkyū Kai). They adopted a resolution that their organization should work closely with the Japanese government and contribute to the prosperity of Japanese people in Mexico.[83] The Japanese consulate, the *Rafu Shimpo*, and immigrant leaders in Los Angeles emphasized that the Japanese in Los Angeles were privileged and even responsible for studying on Mexico and opening up new possibilities of Japanese migration in cooperation with the Japanese in their home country.

In 1925, the Mexico Study Society published a guidebook for settling in Mexico and recommended that Japanese in the United States migrate to the Mexican state of Colima, located in the Pacific coast region, which was comfortable with a mild and dry climate and convenient for transportation to Japan across the Pacific Ocean. The guidebook, written by two Japanese who had done considerable research in Mexico, explained that "the ideal site for our place of future burial" should have "mountains with green trees, rivers with pure water, and flat and fertile lands in between, and hopefully be located near the ocean with abundance of seafood that can be served fresh and raw at the table just like our homeland." The farmland in Colima was "indeed an ideal place to set up our settlement" that "meets all the conditions." The guidebook also emphasized, "What we need to do most for our settlement in Mexico is to develop agriculture in Mexico, which is closely related to our settlement project, and live and prosper together with Mexican farmers by instructing and supporting them" and "to help Mexico develop its industries and increase its wealth so that Mexico can stave off other strong countries' intervention and maintain its independence forever." There, Japanese immigrants should raise their children as proud descendants of the *yamato* (Japanese) nation and, at the same time, make them study in the Mexican education system so that they would become "Mexicans who will make a heroic leap in Mexico with the *yamato* spirit in the future."[84] Although their settlement project positioned Japanese immigrants as those who would lead Mexican farmers with better farming skills, it does not seem to have implied settler colonialism but rather suggested an attempt to merge Japanese immigrant nationalism with Mexican patriotism from a bottom-up perspective by demonstrating Japanese migration as beneficial for Mexico's development and independence.

At the same time, some Japanese in Los Angeles did not follow such a concerted effort and attempted to explore Mexico in their own way. Regardless of whether Japanese immigrants and the consulate worked together, many Japanese were so enthusiastic about Mexico that some wanted to learn more about the country, including its language. In July of 1924, the *Rafu Shimpo* advertised the *Mexican Almanac*, published by the *Los Angeles Times* and distributed to the Japanese through the *Rafu Shimpo*. One copy of the almanac cost $7.50 (approximately $114 in 2020), which was neither too cheap nor too expensive (The hourly wage in Japanese berry farms was thirty-five cents in 1924). The paper emphasized, "Since this book has sufficient and detailed information about Mexico, it will be the only guide and repository for those who want to move to Mexico."[85] In the following month, a Spanish-language school placed an advertisement in the *Rafu Shimpo*. A man named A. E. De Moran, who claimed to be a former university professor in Mexico, wrote, "I will teach you Spanish with kindness."[86]

Around the same time, Japanese enthusiasm for Mexico grew on the other side of the Pacific Ocean. In Tokyo, Japanese business, political, and military elites, who had personal connections with Mexico, felt the same necessity to learn more about Mexico. On October 17, 1924, they established an organization named the Japan-Mexico Society (Nichi-Boku Kyōkai) to promote amity between the peoples of Japan and Mexico. Since 1913, a group of people who had some relationship with Mexico had held meetings to discuss Japan-Mexico relations, but Japanese exclusion in 1924 seems to have persuaded them to make a more formal and well-organized group. At their first meeting on that day, thirty-seven Japanese elites celebrated the foundation of the organization and appointed Lieutenant General Keizaburō Moriyama of the Japanese Navy as the first president. Other founding members included Masaji Inoue, who was a businessman and a Lower House member; Ichijirō Itani, who was a prominent fisheries scientist; and Jūtoku Saigō, who was an army general and a nephew of well-known Meiji revolutionary Takamori Saigō. The list of members proves that the Japan-Mexico Society was not a civilian amity society, but a quasi-governmental organization with serious political weight behind it designed to pursue national interests in response to the adversarial immigration law of the United States.[87]

At their first meeting, Moriyama appreciated the welcoming and sympathetic attitude of Mexicans toward the Japanese, drawing on the historical facts that a Japanese *samurai* named Tsunenaga Hasekura visited Nueva España (Mexico) in the early seventeenth century and that Mexico made an equal treaty with Japan in the late nineteenth century. In his speech, Mexico appeared as the complete opposite of the United States, which had forced Japan to sign an unequal treaty in the nineteenth century and recently prohibited Japanese immigration because of white supremacist racism. Moriyama proceeded to explain that the main goal of the Japan-Mexico Society was to "contribute to mutual prosperity and cooperation between the peoples of Japan and Mexico by deepening understanding of the situation and real intent of both nations." For that purpose, the Japan-Mexico Society aimed to conduct investigations in Mexico and provide the Japanese people with their findings, so that it could help people who would migrate between Japan and Mexico.[88] As the news about the foundation of the Japan-Mexico Society in Tokyo arrived at Los Angeles, the *Rafu Shimpo* cheerfully reported it as a timely event that would brighten up the hearts of Japanese immigrants who had created their own study group about Mexico, the Mexico Study Society.[89]

In contrast to the Los Angeles study group, the Tokyo group consisted of elites, and had better and quick access to Mexican government officials stationed in Tokyo. Right after the closing of their first meeting on October 17, they held a welcoming party for the minister of the Mexican Legation in Japan, Eduardo F. Hay, who was active during the Mexican Revolution and would later become the Mexican secretary of foreign affairs in the mid-1930s. In his speech, Hay appreciated the foundation of the Japan-Mexico Society and provided his idea that commerce was the most effective way to deepen the relationship between the peoples of

Japan and Mexico. He did not touch upon Japanese immigration to Mexico.[90] But the Mexican Legation in Japan had been paying attention to domestic discussions on Japanese migration to Mexico. In 1922, for example, the Legation informed the Mexican Ministry of Foreign Affairs that it became easier for Japanese to enter Mexico via the United States due to new regulations implemented by the United States.[91] Two years later, Hay was well aware of growing expectations among the Japanese for the Mexican government to accept Japanese immigrants. On June 2, 1924, Hay sent correspondence from Tokyo to the Ministry of Foreign Affairs of Mexico in Mexico City and reported possible consequences of the Immigration Act of 1924 on Mexico. He explained, "[As a] consequence of the new American law prohibiting Japanese immigration, Japan will need to direct immigration to other countries [from the United States]. I urgently need you to let me know the attitude of the Mexican government regarding the acceptance of immigrants and indicate conditions [such as] an approximate number of immigrants admissible annually. The Japanese [are] indignant with the United States."[92]

Although Japanese immigrants increased after 1924, as detailed later, the Mexican federal and local governments did not openly advocate for the acceptance of Japanese immigrants on a large scale. In April 1924, the *Tokyo Asahi Shimbun*, a major newspaper in Japan, reported excitedly, with a strapline "Mexico, a new destination for Japanese immigrants," that Mexican president Álvaro Obregón had told the press that Mexico would welcome a large number of Japanese immigrants. Not long afterward, Obregón denied what the media had reported, although he said that he was open to discussing the possibility of accepting the Japanese after researching its impact on the Mexican society.[93] In the same month, a group of Japanese in California visited the state of Sinaloa and asked local Mexican officials about whether the Japanese could move and find a place to live in Mexico. According to the report of the *Yomiuri Shimbun*, another major newspaper in Japan, the Mexican officials responded negatively, saying, "We would not encourage the immigration of Asians and other nationals because it could cause conflicts with the United States."[94] They probably needed to consider how the US government would react to Japanese immigration to Mexico, because Japanese immigrants in Mexico could be a source of illegal Japanese immigrants into the United States.

Likewise, the Japanese government worried that sending a large number of immigrants to Mexico could worsen the already deteriorated US-Japan relations. In the 1950s, Shirō Fujioka revealed an episode about how the Japanese government considered the impact of Japanese immigration to Mexico on US-Japan relations. According to Fujioka, the minister of the Japanese Legation in Mexico, Shigetsuna Furuya, told the Japanese minister of foreign affairs, Kijūrō Shidehara, that the Mexican government was interested in accepting Japanese immigrants and providing them with necessary farming implements and housing after the US government prohibited Japanese immigration. Shidehara, known for his policy of international cooperation, reproached Furuya and said that such a move between Japan and Mexico could hurt US-Japan relations, which were more important for Japan's position in the international society.[95] The 1920s was indeed the period of international cooperation between the United States and Japan, who came to the forefront as great powers after Europe's devastation from World War I. But Japan aroused mistrust from the United States by pressuring China with the notorious Twenty-One Demands in 1915. Shidehara considered it necessary to regain trust from the United States, and he achieved historic international agreements such as the Washington Naval Treaty.[96]

On May 25, 1925, the Japan-Mexico Society held a meeting and invited as a guest speaker Eiichi Kimura, a Japanese diplomat who had come back from his field research in Mexico. Above all else, Kimura emphasized the abundance of petroleum in Mexico and the influence of American capital in the Mexican oil industry. Then, regarding how Japan should build good relations with Mexico, he argued that Japanese immigrant farmers could develop Japan-Mexico economic relations and turn the Pacific Ocean into an international site of trade and investment between the two countries. "If Japanese immigrants prosper in the Pacific Coast of Mexico, a region with various types of terrains such as plains, highlands, and tropical and temperate zones, we can easily gain resources our country needs in this region. . . . The United States has already dominated the oil, gold, and silver industries, and retained control over railroads. Thus, it is only agriculture that our people can find room to invest in." In addition, Kimura explained that native Mexicans believed that their ancestors were Asians and had a good feeling especially toward the Japanese, saying, "It is very interesting to see some similarities between them and us in terms of manners, customs, looks, and other things."[97]

In December of the same year, the Japan-Mexico Society held another meeting and Minister Hay attended to share his idea about organizing an exposition of Japanese products in Mexico. This time he touched upon the possibility of Japanese migration to Mexico. While emphasizing the importance of economic relations between Japan and Mexico, he discouraged the audience about Japanese immigration to Mexico. Hay said that "right after anti-Japanese voices rose in the United States, many Japanese shifted their focus to Mexico, which urged both Japan and Mexico to cooperate closely." Yet, large-scale immigration was not the solution from the perspective of the Mexican government. He explained that if the Japanese government wanted to send a large number of immigrants to Mexico, there needed to be three conditions: (1) the socioeconomic situation of Mexico should be better than that of Japan, (2) Japanese immigrants should contribute to national interests of Mexico, and (3) the immigrants should not take jobs from Mexican workers. "However, if we look at the current situation of Mexico, it is one level lower than that of Japan. Mexican workers are crying over difficulties in their lives" because of the downturn of the world economy and consequences of the Mexican Revolution. He continued, "You may say that Mexico will benefit from Japanese immigrants if they arrive at Mexico and exert their skills to develop lands and resources, but at present Mexico does not have enough capital to respond to such expectations. And even if we had it, Japanese immigration would decrease job opportunities for Mexicans. It is my sincere thought that this is not the right time to send Japanese immigrants to Mexico."[98]

Despite the reluctant response of Hay, Japanese enthusiasm about going to Mexico, developing in both Los Angeles and Tokyo, did not fade away, regarding Mexico as a strong candidate for Japanese emigration in the 1920s. While the *Rafu Shimpo* in Los Angeles advocated for the development of Japanese settlements in Mexico, the *Yomiuri Shimbun* in Japan ran an editorial that called for sending the Japanese to Mexico as "the policy that Japan should take after being extremely insulted [by the United States]."[99] These voices resonated with each other to make a transpacific campaign for Japanese migration to Mexico and resulted in the creation of groups such as the Mexico Study Society in Los Angeles and the Japan-Mexico Society in Tokyo. Soon after, the number of Japanese immigrants increased in Mexico, which would contribute to the formation of a transborder ethnic Japanese community that would connect the Japanese in Southern California with their co-ethnics in Baja California.

THE DEVELOPMENT OF THE TRANSBORDER ETHNIC JAPANESE COMMUNITY

The Immigration Act of 1924 embodied Anglo-American ethnocentrism and anti-Japanese sentiment in the 1920s United States and infuriated many Japanese in the United States and Japan. However, it had an unintended consequence of forming a relatively large Japanese population in Baja California, Mexico. The key point was the Gentlemen's Agreement made by the US and Japanese governments. The history of Japanese immigration to Mexico began in 1897 with a group of thirty-five Japanese settlers sent by former Japanese minister of foreign affairs Takeaki Enomoto, who advocated for sending Japanese people abroad as a "great and urgent need [for the development of Japan] for domestic and international reasons." Although Enomoto's settlement project failed because the settlers lacked funding and farming skills necessary in Mexican coffee farms, Japanese immigrants continued to land in Mexico through Japanese emigration companies, particularly from 1901, and worked at mines in the northern region, coffee and sugar cane fields in the southern region, and railroad construction sites in the central region. By 1907, Japanese immigrants in Mexico numbered 8,697, arriving through emigration companies.[100] However, most Japanese in Mexico clandestinely entered the United States, prompting the US government to restrict the influx of Japanese from Mexico by negotiating with the Japanese government. In this context, the

Gentlemen's Agreement led the Japanese government to refrain from sending its subjects to neighboring countries of the United States such as Mexico in order to prevent illegal immigration into the United States, while Theodore Roosevelt had issued an executive order to stop further immigration of Japanese from Hawaiʻi, Mexico, and Canada. As a result, the number of Japanese immigrants to Mexico dropped from about 9,000 in 1906 and 1907 down to zero in 1908.[101]

The 1924 Immigration Act nullified this Gentlemen's Agreement. Consequently, the nullification of the agreement made it easier for the Japanese government to issue passports to those who desired to go to Mexico. Speaking before the Japanese Diet in 1926, the Ministry of Foreign Affairs of Japan explained, "After the demise of the so-called Gentlemen's Agreement, the government had nothing to worry about regarding Japanese immigrants in Mexico, but it is still difficult for ordinary workers to build a stable life [in Mexico]." Thus, the Japanese government allowed the emigration of only "*yobiyose* [relatives of Japanese residents in Mexico], immigrants who aim to reenter, and those who have enough capital to be self-reliant in agriculture or commerce."[102] As a result, most Japanese who arrived in Mexico after 1924 were *yobiyose*. Historian María Elena Ota Mishima demonstrates that 2,950 Japanese immigrated to Mexico from 1921 to 1941 and 74 percent of them did so from 1925 to 1932, mostly as *yobiyose*.[103] In 1933, the total Japanese population in Mexico was 5,297 according to a Japanese government report.[104] In fact, Los Angeles Japanese, who paid close attention to US immigration policy, were aware that the 1924 Act would nullify the restriction on Japanese immigration to Mexico and the Japanese government would not deny passport applications of those planning to go to Mexico.[105] The increase of *yobiyose* Japanese in Mexico was an unintended, if predictable, consequence of the 1924 Act, which largely affected Japanese migration in the US-Mexico borderlands. As will be seen, however, most *yobiyose* Japanese in Mexico were not from Los Angeles.

It was the Mexican border city of Mexicali that received the largest number of Japanese *yobiyose* immigrants after 1924. Mexicali is located about three hundred miles southeast of Los Angeles and just across the border from California's Imperial County. In the beginning of the twentieth century, Mexicali was a small town with a scarce population of less than one thousand people because of its poor communications and transportation conditions as well as its harsh desert climate. However, by 1930, Mexicali evolved into a center of cotton cultivation in Mexico with about thirty thousand people.[106] The process of this transformation involved the water from the Colorado River, a huge amount of money coming from Los Angeles, and immigrant workers, first the Chinese and later the Japanese. In 1908, the Colorado River Land Company, an American company owned by powerful and wealthy Americans such as *Los Angeles Times* owner Harrison G. Otis, invested twelve million dollars to construct canals, dikes, roads, and other improvements in order to utilize lands of Mexicali. The company monopolized the land for agricultural use and hired a large number of Chinese immigrants as tenant farmers and farmworkers, who entered Mexicali legally or illegally and played an indispensable role in the early development of Mexicali cotton agriculture.[107]

When World War I boosted the Mexicali economy, the Japanese came on the scene, as they found an economic opportunity in the speculative cotton industry. There were two groups of Japanese immigrants, one coming from the United States and the other wanting to enter the United States. The first group came from California with capital enough to become cotton farmers in the lands free from anti-Japanese sentiment and regulations in the United States such as the California Alien Land Laws. The second group arrived there from other parts of Mexico or Peru in the hope of entering the United States clandestinely.[108] A Japanese man, Sankichi Tsutsumi, recalled that when he arrived at Mexicali in 1919, there were six or seven hundred Japanese waiting for their chance to slip into the United States.[109] But many decided to settle in Mexicali and work for the Japanese cotton farmers, not only because the local cotton economy was booming but also because it was not difficult to enter the United States as temporary visitors if they lived in Mexicali. The Japanese workers stepped up to become foremen and later tenant farmers as they got used to their new life in Mexicali. They leased lands from the Colorado River Land Company like the Chinese, hired Japanese workers, and paid the company about 10 percent of their harvest income. Japanese farmers also hired local Mexican workers to reclaim land, plant seeds, eradicate weeds, and harvest crops. By 1924, Mexicali had developed as an ethnic Japanese community in a unique way, in which the southward migration of Japanese from California met with the northward migration of Japanese from other parts of Mexico.[110] According to the Mexican census of 1930, the number of Japanese immigrants in the northern region of Baja California increased from 393 in 1921 to 958 in 1930. As the Japanese Association of Mexicali claimed that the ethnic Japanese population was nearly 1,000 in 1931, Mexicali became one of the largest concentrations of ethnic Japanese residents in Mexico.[111]

One of the Japanese people who gave up his plan to enter the United States but built a stable life in Mexicali was Gensaku Nakaoka. In April 1919, he landed at the port of Salina Cruz in southern Mexico after staying temporarily in Peru and Chile and joined more than two hundred Japanese with the same intention to enter the United States. After arriving in the port of Guaymas in the state of Sonora, he began to walk in the blazing heat with about twenty Japanese toward Mexicali, some of whom died during their journey in a foreign land. In Mexicali, after finding a high-paying job cutting down trees and leveling the land, he decided to settle in Mexicali to become a cotton farmer.[112] An immigrant story like Nakaoka's has been narrated in the context of Japanese Mexican history. But if he had successfully entered the United States and stayed there, his life would have been part of Japanese American history. In the mind of immigrants like Nakaoka, the distinction between Japanese American history and Japanese Mexican history did not matter. The experiences of immigrants who passed or stayed in Mexicali were part of a larger Japanese immigration history of the US-Mexico borderlands.

However, with the implementation of the 1924 Immigration Act, which automatically nullified the Gentlemen's Agreement, Japanese immigrants who had already lived in Mexicali began to call their relatives over from Japan at full scale, and they developed the border city as one of the most important sites of Japanese Mexican history. After 1924, the ethnic Japanese population increased and played a larger role in the local cotton agriculture in Mexicali. There were probably around five hundred Japanese in Mexicali in 1925. By that time, cotton cultivation in Mexicali expanded to about twenty thousand hectares, of which the Japanese cultivated 70 percent, while the Chinese and Americans cultivated the rest.[113] A contemporary report issued by the Japanese consul in Los Angeles, Chūichi Ōhashi, tells us a slightly different number. In 1926, Ōhashi reported the situation of Mexicali Japanese in the Overseas Business Bulletin, a daily report published by the Ministry of Foreign Affairs of Japan. His report was based on an investigation conducted by Mokichi Fukushima, a Japanese diplomat stationed at an outpost of the Ministry of Foreign Affairs in Baja California, and later included as a chapter in the Japan-Mexico Society bulletin. This report said that in 1926 the ethnic Japanese population numbered about four hundred, out of which one hundred were engaged in cotton agriculture and the other three hundred were running restaurants, barber shops, bars, hotels, pool halls, and so forth. Ōhashi added that the ethnic Chinese population was thirty-five hundred and that "one half of them are day laborers at cotton farms, but the other half have a hold on the city's commerce."[114] Anti-Chinese xenophobia growing from the early 1920s forced many Chinese to leave cotton farms and move to the downtown area, leaving more chances for the Japanese to engage in cotton farming in the countryside of the Mexicali region.[115]

The personal stories of newly arriving Japanese immigrants in the border town of Mexicali reveal much about their *yobiyose* background. Kieya Hayasaka was one of the *yobiyose* Japanese in Mexicali. In 1924, he began to live in Mexicali at the age of twenty-two, when his brother, who had already lived in that arid border town, called him over from Japan. In 1929, he became a naturalized Mexican citizen, because he did not think of "returning to his country by virtue of having the majority of his family members in Mexico and his interests," as written in his naturalization application. In his application, he wrote the names of two Mexican friends and his savings of $727 (approximately $11,000 in 2020), which demonstrated his stable social and economic basis.[116] The United States did not allow the Japanese to become naturalized as American citizens based on the Naturalization Act of 1790 and the *Ozawa v. The United States* case of 1922, which deemed the Japanese ineligible for naturalization because they were neither African nor white, who were people "of what is popularly known as the Caucasian race."[117] In contrast, the Mexican government allowed the Japanese to become Mexican citizens. In fact, the Mexican Census of 1930 recorded that forty-one people of Japanese origin had become Mexican citizens by 1930 in Baja California where about one thousand Japanese nationals lived at that time.[118] One of the economic reasons for naturalization was that foreigners were not allowed to purchase land or water rights in the range of one hundred kilometers from the national borders or fifty kilometers from the coasts.[119] The number of Japanese immigrants who got the Mexican citizenship was relatively small, most likely because they could lease and purchase lands without Mexican citizenship and did not need to purchase properties in these regions near the borders and coasts.

Kiyoshi Nakazawa was another *yobiyose* who arrived at Mexicali in 1924. In the beginning, his plan was to enter the United States from Mexicali. He stayed there for a couple of years, but thought twice and decided to settle in Mexicali because of the reinforcement of the US border control. After working at grocery stores, he began to engage in agriculture with his fellow Japanese in Mexicali in 1931.[120] Naoki Hata was a good example of transpacific Japanese migration. In 1918, he crossed the Pacific Ocean and arrived at the Peruvian capital city of Lima where he lived as a barber for five years. In Lima, it was very common for Japanese to work at barber shops, since they could start out the business with relatively little capital and skills. By the mid-1910s, 80 out of 110 barber shops in Lima were operated by Japanese immigrants. Then in 1923, Hata traveled to Mexico in search for a better life and began working at a cotton farm in Mexicali. In 1925, he entered the United States, most likely without documents, but only six months later, he returned to Mexicali to open his barber shop based on his experience in Peru. In 1930, he called over his wife Sueko from Japan and later raised four girls in Mexicali. There were many women like Sueko who arrived in Mexicali as *yobiyose* wives, too. As these examples illustrate, Japanese immigrants who arrived at Mexicali in the early 1920s started their lives as Japanese of the US-Mexico borderlands, not knowing whether they were going to stay in Mexico or in the United States.[121]

And in Mexico, it was common for Japanese men to marry Mexican women, since intermarriage was legal, unlike in the United States. But due to the development of cotton agriculture and the *yobiyose* immigration, many Japanese men in Mexicali married Japanese wives and had Mexican-born children, forming an ethnic community similar to that of their co-ethnics in Los Angeles.[122] The growth of the Japanese community in Mexicali after 1924 resulted in creations of several important ethnic organizations. Mexicali Japanese founded the Japanese School of Mexicali in 1925, the Japanese Agricultural Association of Mexicali in 1928, and the Women's Association of Mexicali in 1929.[123]

Another Mexican city in Baja California that attracted Japanese was Ensenada, a city facing the Pacific Ocean and located fifty miles south of the US-Mexico border. Many Japanese fishermen settled in Ensenada and worked for Japanese fishery companies based in Southern California. The Japanese on both sides of the US-Mexico border developed their ethnic fishery business together. From the 1910s, Japanese fishery companies based in Southern California were recruiting Japanese fishermen in Mexico, since Japanese could not enter the United States after the implementation of the Gentlemen's Agreement. After the nullification of the agreement by the 1924 Act, it became easier for Japanese fishermen to bring their relatives to Mexico as *yobiyose*.[124] For example, a Japanese fishery company MK Fisheries based in San Diego had been hiring Japanese immigrants in Mexico since 1913. For hiring fishermen, the company's president Masaharu Kondō used an immigration recruitment company and also relied on the support of his friend, the scientist Ichijirō Itani, who later became a founding member of the Japan-Mexico Society. Kondō then brought over thirteen Japanese from several prefectures in Japan. By 1926, the company had brought about one hundred *yobiyose* to Baja California.[125] The *Periódico Oficial*, the official organ of the government of the northern district of Baja California, recorded the activity of MK Fisheries in 1924. Kondō applied for a permit to operate his fishing ships at nineteen places along the coast of Baja California that covered San José del Cabo, the southern edge of the peninsula, with the purpose of catching and exporting lobsters, abalones, and seaweeds.[126] According to a report submitted by the Japanese consul in Los Angeles Ōhashi, in 1926, about two hundred Japanese were registered as residents in the Ensenada area but only sixty were actual residents, because the rest were out of town working on the voyage for California-based Japanese fishery companies.[127] Hajime Tomita, a former Japanese fisherman, recalled that Japanese fishermen had a strong sense that they had immigrated to the United States although they were in Mexico on paper, since they worked on the ocean and got on shore mostly at San Diego.[128] These Japanese fishermen were also the Japanese of the US-Mexico borderlands just like Mexicali Japanese residents.

Japanese fishing activities in Baja California developed partly thanks to the renewal of the Japan-Mexico Treaty of Amity, Commerce, and Navigation in October of 1924. The original treaty between Japan and Mexico was first signed in 1888, which was the first equal international treaty for Japan after the Meiji Restoration. Although the treaty did not strengthen economic ties much between Japan and Mexico, it certainly opened the door for Japanese to immigrate to Mexico.[129] However, the 1888 treaty was unable to correspond to changing international relations in the early twentieth century, when Mexico underwent its years-long revolution and Japan evolved into an empire. While Japan became a country that received immigrants from its colonies such as Korea and Taiwan, the country was still searching for places abroad to send emigrants and decrease the unemployed within the Japanese archipelago. The new Japan-Mexico Treaty of 1924 continued to allow Japanese nationals to enter and travel in Mexico. It also permitted them to engage in economic activities in Mexico by giving them the same status as Mexicans, or a most-favored-nation status. Yet the treaty exempted fishery activities from its application. Although it did not mean that the treaty prohibited Japanese fishery activities, it indicates that the Mexican government wanted to develop the Mexican fishery industry by Mexicans themselves by limiting the influence of Japanese fishermen and fishery companies to a certain extent. In addition, the renewal of the Japan-Mexico Treaty in 1924 was not exactly the Japanese government's countermeasure against the US exclusionist law, since the negotiation between the two countries had begun in 1916 but became suspended due to the political instability caused by the Mexican Revolution.[130] It was, however, significant and symbolic for the Japanese government to be able to manifest its amicable relations with Mexico, an important neighbor country of the United States. Although Eiichiro Azuma emphasizes that American diplomats were deeply concerned about the Japanese presence in Mexico and argues that Baja California held "a symbolic site of a hemispheric race war and inter-imperial contestation," I argue that Baja California was also a symbolic site for Japan-Mexico transpacific amity in the 1920s as seen in the increase of Japanese population in the region as already explained.[131] At a time when the US government declared that the Japanese were undesirable aliens, the Mexican government made clear that the Japanese were still desirable or at least acceptable immigrants.

The Japanese community in Baja California developed their relations with the co-ethnics in Southern California. Japanese diplomats knew that the Japanese Mexican community would grow after 1924 with *yobiyose* from Japan as well as the Japanese coming from the United States. In May 1924, Minister of the Japanese Legation in Mexico Shigetsuna Furuya sent an encrypted telegram to Minister of Foreign Affairs Keishirō Matsui, writing that Japan should build a new consulate in Mazatlán, a harbor town at the Pacific Coast in the state of Sinaloa, to protect Japanese immigrants in the region and take a preventive measure against anti-Japanese propaganda of the United States. But it was not just about Japanese immigrants but also about the power relationship with European countries sending immigrants to Baja California. Nine countries including England, the United States, Germany, Italy, and Spain had their respective consulates in Mazatlán. In contrast, Japan had no consulate in the entire Mexican territory. Furuya called for the creation of a consulate because otherwise Japan "would regret greatly sometime later in terms of competition with other countries."[132]

The Japanese consulate in Los Angeles, not the Japanese Legation in Mexico City, was in charge of protecting and monitoring the Japanese in Baja California, because Baja California was a part of the larger Southern California metropolitan economy. Additionally, the Japanese consul in Los Angeles Kaname Wakasugi also felt the necessity to create a new consulate in Mazatlán. In June 1924, he sent the Ministry of Foreign Affairs in Tokyo an encrypted telegram and gave four reasons why Japan needed to set up a new consulate in Mazatlán. First, "Japanese farmers in the Los Angeles area were increasingly interested in migrating to Mexico as a countermeasure against the oppression of anti-Japanese land laws and immigration laws." And Japanese fishermen based in California but working along the Pacific Coast of Mexico could move their base to Mexico if American laws became more exclusionist against them. Second, the Japanese government should send emigrants to Mexico directly from Japan just like emigrants to South America, given the "unilateral action taken by the United States" that nullified the Gentlemen's Agreement. With the increase of the Japanese population, the new consulate in Mazatlán could develop the commercial market of Japanese in Mexico. Third, the Japanese government should create a consulate in advance to give guidance to newly arriving Japanese immigrants so that they could prevent the development of anti-Japanese sentiment in this region. Finally, Wakasugi added that the Ministry of Foreign Affairs should enhance the capability of overseas agencies by setting up a consulate in Mazatlán.[133] Soon after in the summer of 1924, the Ministry of Foreign Affairs of Japan took the diplomats' suggestions seriously and started consular activities in Mazatlán (The Japanese consulate of Mazatlán formally opened in 1927 after securing a sufficient budget).[134]

In October 1924, the Mexico Study Society held a welcome party at a Japanese restaurant in Los Angeles for Masaki Yodogawa, a Japanese diplomat assigned to work at the new consular office in Mazatlán, when he visited Los Angeles on his way to Mexico. Twenty-four members of the study group attended the party and showed him their enthusiasm and explained why Los Angeles Japanese created a group to do research on Mexico.[135] The new consulate in Mazatlán at the Pacific Coast near Baja California was another consequence of the Immigration Act of 1924 that reflected worries and expectations among the Japanese immigrants and government officials regarding Japanese migration in the US-Mexico borderlands and international competition between Japan and Western countries.

There remains one question: how many Japanese migrated from Los Angeles to Mexico after 1924? Despite several expeditions and the high expectations Los Angeles Japanese had, only a small number of Japanese actually moved from Los Angeles to Mexico after 1924. In Mexico, there were still many places politically too unstable for the Japanese to build a new ethnic community. The risks of ongoing instability likely convinced many to remain in Los Angeles. In fact, by December of this year, the *Rafu Shimpo* had begun to show negative prospects of leaving California. An editorial, although not written regarding the 1924 Act, stated, "You need to be well knowledgeable and well prepared [to engage in agriculture in other places outside California or the United States], so I think you cannot expect much."[136]

Even in the border city of Mexicali, most Japanese immigrants were not from the United States. According to Ōhashi's report, the majority of Japanese immigrants there came from other places in Mexico or Peru and decided to stay and work in Mexicali since they became short of money at the time they arrived at Mexicali. "Recently some Japanese in Los Angeles," explained the report, "came to this region to purchase several thousand acres of land from American landowners in order to sell the land in lots, but ... it is quite hard to make ends meet in agriculture in this region," since they were not able to find lands with good irrigation. From his report, it is clear that only a few Los Angeles Japanese moved to Mexicali.[137] In the same year, another Japanese diplomat Fukuoka traveled in the southern half of Baja California. He found few Japanese residents and reported that "agriculture is almost impossible due to very bad irrigation," adding, "There is little hope from the viewpoint of Japanese in the United States."[138]

Historian María Elena Ota Mishima has analyzed the alien registration cards (tarjetas del Registro Nacional de Extranjeros) of 3,626 individuals recorded as Japanese immigrants by the Mexican government between 1890 and 1949. She has found that 3,471 individuals were born in Japan and immigrated to Mexico between 1890 and 1949 (155 were born in Mexico) and that only fifteen Japanese immigrants came from the United States, arguing that "Japanese immigrants sporadically came to Mexico from other countries" but mostly from Japan.[139]

Despite the initial enthusiasm in most of 1924, Los Angeles Japanese did not carry out a large-scale migration to Mexico.[140] Dobashi and Matsuoka, representing the Central Japanese Association of Southern California, did not mention Mexicali as a possible destination for Japanese migration but recommended Mexican northwestern states such as Nayarit and Colima, since these places had lands with enough water for farming. Their suggestion, however, did not result in any organized project that could successfully transfer Japanese people from Los Angeles to those coastal destinations in Mexico. In 1927, Teizō Egashira, a navy lieutenant colonel stationed at the Japanese Legation in Mexico, contributed a report to the Japan-Mexico Society's bulletin on the Mexican coastal states of Nayarit, Sonora, and Sinaloa facing the Pacific Ocean and the Gulf of California. His report mentioned that about 350 Japanese lived in these three states and those who had come from the United States tended to be successful in agriculture. But the number of Japanese immigrants in Mexico was still small because it required serious efforts for newcomers to reclaim uncultivated lands in Mexico with fewer resources than they had in California. To quell optimism, Egashira touched upon a Japanese who came from the United States in the hope of succeeding in agriculture in this region but decided to give up his plan immediately after looking at underdeveloped lands in Mexico. Egashira added, "Those who assume that they could use things like a car and a telephone from the beginning have no right to talk about starting a business in this country" and "[If you want to succeed] you need to have the same willingness of fellow Japanese immigrants who could reclaim wilderness of the United States in the past."[141]

High expectations for Mexico expressed by Los Angeles Japanese in 1924 were the reflection of their anger against the American exclusionist law and strong desire to find somewhere better than the United States. Such expectations, however, did not materialize because it was still economically and culturally better for Japanese immigrants to live in Los Angeles than in Mexico despite anti-Japanese regulations in the United States. Nevertheless, it does not mean that the Japanese communities in Los Angeles and in Mexico existed separately. Despite its location within the northern fringes of the Mexican polity, Baja California vividly belonged to the larger economic sphere of Southern California with Los Angeles as its nucleus. At the time, Mexican border cities like Mexicali were not able to survive without goods and information emanating from Southern California. In the early 1930s, Mokichi Fukushima, a Japanese diplomat stationed in Baja California, reported, "almost all materials including consumer staples, building materials, and so forth, are imported from the United States" in Mexicali, Ensenada, and Tijuana. The US dollar was widely circulated there. In addition, Baja Japanese immigrants were reading the Los Angeles-based ethnic press such as the *Rafu Shimpo*, while serving as local correspondents for those papers.[142] In addition, the Japanese consulate in Los Angeles, not the Japanese Legation in Mexico City, was in charge of protecting and monitoring Japanese subjects in Baja California until 1931 when the Japanese consulate in Mazatlán took over that role.[143] Japanese residents of Baja California survived in the periphery of both the United States and Mexico by keeping economic, cultural, and political ties with the Los Angeles Japanese. The Immigration Act of 1924 did not dramatically increase the number of Japanese moving from the United States to Mexico but certainly brought more *yobiyose* from Japan to Mexico, especially Mexicali, developing a transborder ethnic Japanese community in the US-Mexico borderlands.

In the 1920s, Japanese immigrants were not the only nonwhite group in California who idealized Mexico as a haven free from racial discrimination. African Americans in California also attempted to build a colony in Baja California seeking self-sufficiency. Hugh Macbeth, an African American in Los Angeles who was born in South Carolina in 1884 and earned a law degree from Harvard University in 1908, found an economic opportunity in Baja California focused on land speculation. As World War I increased demand for agricultural products in the United States and beyond, in 1918, Macbeth founded the Lower California Mexican Land and Development Company and began to offer land tracts at twenty dollars per acre in order to form an all-Black farming colony, which the *Los Angeles Times* called "Little Liberia." His company advertised the colonization project to African American investors and prospective settlers who sought to be "sovereigns of [their] own labor, who want to be really free!" One African American stockholder in Little Liberia envisaged that Mexico was "the land of freedom and opportunity—where a man breathes the atmosphere of tolerance, where his ambitions and dreams be within himself for realization and not within his COLOR." The colony, however, did not last long. In 1923, the Mexican government restricted the entry of African Americans into Mexico to prevent "the ethnic problem," treating African Americans like the indigenous population in Mexico. Macbeth's company then went bankrupt in 1927.[144] Although Little Liberia was short-lived, its history provides another example of the economic connection between Los Angeles and Baja California developed by a nonwhite group of people in the 1920s.

Returning to Japanese immigrants in the borderlands, deepening relations between Los Angeles and Mexicali Japanese were not always good for Mexicali Japanese. After 1924, the Japanese Association of Mexicali came to play an increasingly important role in strengthening ethnic solidarity and economy in the Mexican dominant society. The association was first founded in 1917 as an outpost agency for the Japanese consulate in Los Angeles and took care of immigration paperwork. In December 1926, this association unexpectedly turned into a crime scene, when the association secretary Saburō Mashiko was found dead and buried under the patio of the incinerated association building. Mashiko immigrated to Mexico in 1907 to work at a coal mine in the northern state of Coahuila and served as a supervisor of immigrants. He could speak Spanish, since he had studied the language at a school specializing in foreign studies in Tokyo. He was a well-respected immigrant leader in the Japanese community in Mexico, who worked hard to support other Japanese workers facing difficult working conditions. When eight Japanese miners died from an explosion at a mine in the state of Veracruz in 1908, Mashiko brought their bodies back from the mine and held a funeral for them. Then in 1925, he moved to Mexicali to work as the secretary of the Japanese Association, which unfortunately resulted in his death a year later.[145]

After his body was found, the Mexican local authority arrested two Japanese men, Shin'ichi Morishita and Kiyoji Shōda, for the murder of Mashiko. Why was Mashiko killed by fellow Japanese? *History of Japan-Mexico Interactions*, a comprehensive history of Japanese immigrants in Mexico edited by first-generation Japanese, explains the cause of this homicide. At the time, there were Japanese women who migrated to Mexicali as *yobiyose* immigrants but worked as prostitutes in Mexicali or in the north of the border. A Japanese mafia organization called the Tokyo Club, based in Los Angeles, was behind the entry of such women in Mexico. When Mashiko was killed, the Tokyo Club might have used its influence to remove Mashiko, who attempted to repatriate five Japanese women who he thought would become prostitutes. According to *History of Japan-Mexico Interactions*, Shōda was a member of the Tokyo Club, while Morishita was an owner of a pool hall and bar in Mexicali. Mitsu Ichikawa, a Japanese female resident who began to live in Mexicali in 1924, remembered the incident, saying, "My eldest son was born on December 7 [of 1926]. Back then, the Japanese Association was like a city hall [for the Japanese]. So, I was going to visit the association building to report the birth of my son within three or four days later. But Mr. Mashiko was not there when I visited the building. It was the night of that day [December 9] when the association building was burned down."[146]

The *Rafu Shimpo* reported the murder of Mashiko as a tragedy for both Mexicali and Los Angeles Japanese. Although the paper did not mention the involvement of the Tokyo Club, it recorded that Shōda was arrested in Calexico, an American border city directly across from Mexicali, and that Japanese consular officials and immigrants in Los Angeles visited Mexicali to investigate the situation and encourage their co-ethnics amid that horrible experience.[147] In 2016, I visited Mexicali and met with Ichikawa's son, Iwao Ichikawa. When I asked him what he knew about the influence of Los Angeles Japanese in Mexicali, he immediately told me about the death of Mashiko. His death is still remembered by descendants of Mexicali Japanese.[148] Mashiko's death proved how deeply the Japanese communities in Los Angeles and Mexicali were connected with each other and how they formed a transborder ethnic Japanese community before World War II. As will be explained in detail later in this book, this transborder community would serve as a significant background that complicated interethnic relations between Japanese farmers and Mexican workers in Los Angeles farmland in the 1930s.

2

The Deepening of Japanese-Mexican Relations in Triracial Los Angeles

While the 1924 Immigration Act forced many Los Angeles Japanese to think about their future in Mexico as detailed in the previous chapter, the law also made white business leaders and nativists focus more on Mexicans in the United States. The number of both legal and undocumented Mexicans increased in Southern California, as the growing agribusiness needed more Mexican workers. Mexicans became the major source of farmworkers for Japanese tenant farmers gradually from the 1910s and particularly after the exclusion of Japanese immigrants in 1924. In fact, by this time, there were almost no Japanese farms that operated only with Japanese labor. In Los Angeles County in 1929, the number of Japanese residents engaged in agriculture increased to 8,882 and their children to 12,355. As Japanese farmers increasingly employed Mexican farmworkers, they came to develop interethnic relations that were mutually dependent though charged with labor and racial tension.[1]

As a result, a triracial hierarchy developed in Los Angeles agriculture as Japanese tenants leased lands from white landowners and hired Mexican farmworkers.[2] Major ideological and economic forces that created this hierarchy were white supremacy and agricultural industrialization, as it placed white landowners and business leaders on the top and marginalized Japanese tenants in the middle and Mexican workers on the bottom. This divide-and-rule structure certainly helped strengthen the character of what Carey McWilliams called *factories in the field* in Los Angeles agriculture, although this characterization itself was a historical product of the 1930s as David Vaught contends.[3] In this situation, the Japanese played the role of a middleman minority who built ethnic solidarity and economy to endure an anti-Japanese society, while buffering direct criticism from Mexican labor against white American capital.⁴ While white landowners and Japanese tenant farmers in Los Angeles became increasingly dependent on Mexican farmworkers, Mexican immigrants were not inclined to own or lease farmland in the United States except certain areas of Texas, as reported by the Chamber of Commerce of the United States in 1930.⁵ Many Mexicans did not become tenants most likely because farm prices were falling in the early 1920s and because the relationships between white landowners and Asian tenants had already been established, not leaving much room for Mexican newcomers, which was the case for Filipinos and Japanese late comers in the same period.⁶ A 1925 study in the Claremont area of a local Americanization organization observed that most Mexican residents leased land for their temporary houses and had plans to go back to Mexico.⁷

In order to better understand the triracial hierarchy of Los Angeles agriculture, this chapter examines the increase of Mexican immigrants in Los Angeles after Japanese exclusion. First, it details how white agribusiness leaders explained the importance of Mexican agricultural workers in response to anti-Mexican exclusionists as a background of the triracial hierarchy. Agribusiness leaders racialized those who would come to the United States specifically as the "Mexican peon" and thus a group of Indians who would do no harm to US society. Second, this chapter explains how Japanese immigrants perceived the growing presence of Mexican residents and interacted with them in Los Angeles County by highlighting their differentiated use of racial terms such as *meki* and *dojin*. Finally, it explores how Mexicans themselves developed their ethnic community by focusing on the foundation of the ethnic Mexican press *La Opinión* and a pioneer Mexican labor union, la Confederación de Uniones Obreras Mexicanas, in the 1920s. *La Opinión* and the Mexican labor union members would significantly influence Japanese-Mexican conflicts in Los Angeles County in the 1930s as the former strongly supported the labor movement through its coverage of the conflicts and the latter organized Mexican farmworkers who demanded better wages from Japanese tenant farmers.

THE RACISM OF WHITE AGRIBUSINESS ON MEXICANS

The exclusion of Japanese immigrants and the increase of Mexican immigrants simultaneously propelled the transition from the "Japanese Problem" to the "Mexican Problem" as the major target of nativism in California, which decreased nativist pressure on Japanese farmers who survived in Los Angeles. In fact, despite the immigration ban and land-use restrictions imposed by the California Alien Land Laws, Japanese farmers of Los Angeles County would enter the period of the "rise and prosperity" within the stable framework of the triracial agricultural system even during the Great Depression years. Although the Great Depression damaged the ethnic Japanese economy as in the case of Little Tokyo merchants,

Japanese agriculture endured the recession and even developed in the 1930s. Historian Masakazu Iwata contends, based on his own experience, that Japanese immigrants overcame economic difficulties of the Depression "because of the general steadfastness and tenacity of the Issei inured to hardships coupled with their cohesiveness as a group." Edna Bonacich and John Modell also argue that as a middleman minority, Japanese immigrants in the United States "were not only able to survive but could actually thrive within capitalist society."[8]

Although Mexicans did not face restrictions based on the quota system, they had to go through a variety of entry requirements institutionalized by the 1924 Act, compelling many to avoid formal admission and inspection. In fact, after the implementation of new entry requirements including a ten-dollar fee to secure a visa, legal immigration dropped from 90,000 to 32,378 in 1924. At the same time, among legal Mexican immigrants, many entered the United States as "temporary visitors" who would work as farmworkers but did not have to submit passport or visa. Such instability of immigration control met the labor demand of local agribusiness, but immigration officials perceived it as opportunities for illegal immigration. Historian Mae Ngai observes that "it was ironic that Mexicans became so associated with illegal immigration because, unlike Europeans, they were not subject to numerical quotas and, unlike Asiatics, they were not excluded as racially ineligible to citizenship."[9]

The new entry requirements on Mexicans coincided with the reinforcement of border control enforcement, namely the establishment of the US Border Patrol in 1924. As the Border Patrol intensified the significance of the political border among Mexicans in the Southwest, the term "alien" began to be used toward Mexicans in the Southwest. As George J. Sánchez argues, they came to be perceived as "interlopers on familiar land, even as their labor became increasingly crucial to its economic development."[10] Until the 1920s, the Chinese and Japanese had long been considered as major "illegal aliens." In fact, the predecessors of the Border Patrol officers were the Mounted Chinese Inspectors of the Chinese Division of the Immigration Service, who were assigned to enforce the Chinese Exclusion Act in 1904. As Kelly L. Hernández has demonstrated, 24 percent of the original 104 Border Patrol officers hired by July 1, 1924, were former Mounted Chinese Inspectors.[11] Even after Japanese exclusion, the US government continued to worry about continued undocumented immigration from Japan and other Asian countries by way of Mexico. The establishment of the Border Patrol, however, symbolized the geographical divide between the United States and Mexico, racializing Mexicans as "illegal aliens" whose presence became increasingly visible particularly in the farmlands of the Southwest.[12]

Anti-Mexican restrictionists raised several concerns about the increase of Mexicans in California. In the mid-1920s, many Americans came to reaffirm their belief that Mexicans were unassimilable and thus a racial and economic threat to white America. One of the prominent restrictionists was Texas representative John C. Box. In 1928, Box attempted to pass a so-called Box Bill to restrict immigration from Mexico by applying the quota system to Mexicans. He thought it necessary in order to protect "American racial stock from further degradation" because he believed that the "Mexican peon" was "a mixture of Mediterranean-blooded Spanish peasants with low-grade Indians who did not fight to extinction but submitted and multiplied as serfs." The restrictionist discourse resembled that against Asians in the past decades and resonated with the development of eugenics in the 1920s. The American Eugenics Society claimed, "The Mexican birth rate is high, and every Mexican child born on American soil is an American citizen, who, on attaining his or her majority, will have a vote. This is not a question of pocketbook or the 'need of labor' or of economic [necessity]. It is a question of the character of future races. It is eugenics, not economics." Yet, the "Mexican Problem" was both a racial and an economic problem for many other anti-Mexican restrictionists, who insisted that Mexican workers were displacing American workers. For example, the *Saturday Evening Post* concluded that Mexican exclusion would be the "only salvation" for American workers.[13]

However, for agribusiness leaders in Southern California, Mexican exclusion meant the devastation of agriculture, and thus Mexican inclusion was the only salvation for agriculture. Likewise, Filipino labor was the salvation for agriculture in Northern and Central California. A report of the California State government on Mexican farm workers published in 1930 demonstrated that Mexicans consisted of 84 percent of nonwhite farm labor in Southern California (not including Imperial and Coachella Valleys), while they were 56 percent and 32 percent, respectively, in the San Joaquin and Sacramento Valleys. The use of Filipino farm labor covered 17 percent, 18 percent, and 6 percent, respectively, in the San Joaquin Valley, the Sacramento Valley, and Southern California. The percentage of Japanese farmworkers remained relatively large in San Joaquin Valley and Sacramento Valley, as it was 17 percent and 29 percent, respectively, because many Japanese farmers used the labor provided by their family members. Yet, the percentage of Japanese farm labor was only 5 percent in Southern California, showing the heavier dependency on Mexican labor among farmers, including both white and Japanese operators in Southern California.[14]

During the first half of the twentieth century, California agriculture was rapidly growing and transforming into highly industrialized agriculture, which promoted the concentration of farms for large scale production and labor exploitation for large profits. The number of farms in California rose from 88,197 in 1910, to 117,670 in 1920, and then 150,360 in 1935. The number of large-scale farms of a thousand acres or more increased from 4,906 in 1920 to 5,939 in 1945.[15] In 1926, the agricultural production of California reached $453,267,000.[16] Mexican labor was an indispensable element for California industrialized agriculture, particularly for the cultivation of perishable crops such as fruits and vegetables. In Los Angeles, agriculture attracted many Mexican workers, who came to their work sites using the highly developed railroad network.[17] In order to maintain this agricultural labor, agribusiness leaders of Southern California readily countered anti-Mexican restrictionist arguments by employing unique discourses that reflected the racism of white agribusiness.

In 1928, the California Development Association, an organization devoted to the economic growth of California and supported by prominent business leaders of Los Angeles and other areas in Southern California, prepared a survey report titled the *Survey of the Mexican Labor Problem in California*. The purpose of this report was to counter anti-Mexican arguments by portraying Mexicans as indispensable and harmless labor in California agriculture. The survey explained that California agriculture needed more farm labor since "each successive bar was dropped against existing adequate labor—first Chinese and, more recently, Japanese" and "fluid casual labor is this farmer's only salvation. It is the prime necessity of his success. Restrictive immigration has shut out Europe and Asia from the California farmer. He has only the Mexican to turn to," which clearly linked their pro-Mexican labor argument with the recent enactment of the Immigration Act of 1924. Comparing with East Coast agriculture "accustomed to intensive harvest labor only in the autumn months," the report emphasized that "the land works 365 days" in California because of a series of peaks of crops in different places throughout a year. Mexican workers accommodated themselves "by nature much more readily than the white farm laborer" to the circulatory working style drifting from one crop peak to another, since "the Mexican is inherently a nomad, little prone to rooting himself and with an instinct for accommodating himself to his surroundings." Since farmers depended on Mexicans for works that could not be done by machines, the report repeated that Mexican labor was necessary "until Thomas Edison or Henry Ford develop machinery which will take the drudgery out of the harvest, or until the idealist becomes amenable to developing callouses on his hands."[18]

While arguing against restrictionists who used racist explanations, the *Survey of Mexican Labor Problem in California* provided equally racist views on Mexicans. To portray Mexicans as docile and better labor compared to other foreign labor, the report wrote, "[The Mexican] is not acquisitive and, therefore, is not concerned in laying up for a rainy day. He has no sense of time, nor idea of values. He still adheres to many of the principles and precepts of tribal life. He is generous, sympathetic, kind, artistic and has his own ideas in regard to perfection. He possesses great capacity for happiness." This racist and ambiguous characterization of Mexicans was followed by the explanation of George P. Clements, who worked as the manager of the Agricultural Department of the Los Angeles Chamber of Commerce from 1918 to 1939 and would play an important role in the Japanese-Mexican conflicts in the 1930s.[19] Clements was in the forefront of defending Southern California agribusiness.[20] In order to refute the anti-Mexican exclusionist argument that Mexican immigrants were nonwhite Indians who would pose a racial and economic threat to US society, Clements employed a unique and racist discourse in support of California agribusiness. According to Clements, there were three types of Mexicans: the ruling class, the "greaser" class, and the "Mexican peon." First, he emphasized that the "greaser" class of Mexicans were "the riff-raff of the Mexican race, found along the railroads and in the larger centers of population [in Mexico]. They are the criminal Mexicans; worthless in labor and always a social problem; chronic beggars and sizzling with disease." For these reasons, "this class should never pass the immigration officer on the Border, even though he did happen to be a healthy specimen." Following this, Clements provided a much more positive picture of the "Mexican peon." According to Clements, Mexicans who came to the United States were the peon-class Mexicans, "made up of hundreds of distinct Indian tribes as primitive as our own Indians were when the first colonists arrived in America" and "they are clean and healthy and are still strongly tribal in their recognition of responsibility—a characteristic which may appear soviet or communistic to those not understanding it."[21] In short, Clements racialized Mexican immigrant workers as safe Indians, simultaneously attempting to avoid anti-communist criticism, and thus easy to handle, while highlighting Mexican city dwellers as dangerous "greasers" who assumed all characteristics deemed as problematic by exclusionists.

Clements's argument that Mexicans could be categorized into three types was not true in either reality or theory, simply because it was too difficult to racially categorize the Mexican population. The majority of the Mexican population consisted of indigenous people and mestizos, a racially mixed people resulting from the Spanish colonization of Mexico from the sixteenth century. The term *mestizo* referred to the Mexican middle class, which included indigenous groups of people acculturated to Western ways and accounted for half of the entire Mexican population. In addition, during the 1920s, Mexican intellectuals such as Manuel Gamio and José Vasconcelos were still in the middle of developing their theories to explain the modern Mexican nation.[22] On the other hand, Mexican immigrants in the United States, as Neil Foley summarizes, identified themselves "simply as *mexicanos*, a national identity that embraced the concept of *mestizaje*, or racial mixture." Devra Weber also writes that ethnic Mexicans felt interethnic tensions not only with Anglo Americans but also with other groups of people in the highly multiethnic environment of Los Angeles and that segregation, racism, and working conditions of Mexican immigrants in the city tended to reinforce their identity as "mexicanos" even though they came from various regions and social classes in Mexico.[23] However, Clements, known as a man who "made himself thoroughly acquainted with Mexican character," ignored the demographic reality of Mexico and Mexican immigrants' perspective. In addition, the report said that Mexicans "may be deported" unlike other nonwhite alternative workers such as African Americans from the South, Filipinos, and Puerto Ricans.[24] White agribusiness leaders described Mexican immigrants as primitive, deportable, and thereby nonthreatening to US society. In other words, the pro-Mexican argument of white agribusiness was based on what can be called *redirecting racism* that attempted to turn away the attention of exclusionists from Mexican immigrants to a more "dangerous" type of Mexicans who inhabited Mexican urban centers.[25]

Clements's racial categorization deemed Mexican immigrants premodern Indian and urban Mexican "greasers" unable to live a modern life. Either way, Mexicans were not modern and thus inferior to white Americans. His categorization was different from the racial assumption that Chamber leaders had in the fall of 1924, when plague was found in Los Angeles and the California Board of Health implemented the quarantine and demolition of Mexican neighborhoods. At that time, Chamber leaders cooperated with the Board of Health and regarded "typical Mexicans" as a vector of the disease, as William Deverell has detailed.[26] Four years later, when they needed to keep Mexican labor for California agriculture, they deemed only those Mexicans who lived in Mexican urban centers susceptible to disease, while explaining that Mexican immigrants in California were "clean and healthy." Their changing racial discourse shows us the arbitrary and opportunistic nature of capitalist racism.

Nevertheless, the acknowledgment that Mexicans could be deported would not be persuasive to exclusionists who wanted both Mexicans and Filipinos deported from the United States. A year before the *Survey of Mexican Labor Problem in California* was published, the California State Federation of Labor adopted a resolution demanding the exclusion of Filipinos who "threaten American standards of wages and living conditions" and "the communities in which they have congregated because of their immoral conduct." After Japanese Exclusion, Filipinos were facing a similar restrictionist pressure. Such a pressure materialized during the Depression years as the Tydings-McDuffie Act of 1934, which would change the legal status of Filipinos from "national" to "alien," subject to a restrictive immigration quota, and as the Filipino Repatriation Act of 1935, which would encourage Filipinos to return to the Philippines (yet, once they returned, it would be almost impossible for them to return to the United States because they would be regarded as "alien" under the provisions of the Tydings-McDuffie Act).[27] Furthermore, the California Development Association's report ludicrously asserted that "there is no distinctly Mexican town or land-owning Mexican colony in the State" because Mexicans would return to Mexico after the heavy peaks of harvest. The report downplayed or intentionally did not talk about the development of Mexican barrios and the increasing visibility of Mexican immigrants in 1920s Southern California. By 1930, Los Angeles housed the largest concentration of Mexican immigrants in the United States and many Mexican immigrants began to see themselves more rooted in US society.[28]

Despite the development of culturally rich and economically active ethnic Mexican communities in 1920s Los Angeles, the *Survey of the Mexican Labor Problem in California* attempted to forge the image of Mexican immigrants as "primitive" and deportable Indians. Their ultimate purpose was to prove Mexicans nonthreatening to the white-dominant society, as it concluded that "the Mexican farm laborer does not in any sense constitute a menace to the so-called Anglo-Saxon blood strain."[29] In fact, their argument partly reflected the contemporary common sense among whites regarding the number of Mexicans, as Ricardo Romo argues that "because Mexicans, at least the vast majority, had arrived in the 1900–1930 migration wave at a time when the West was still economically and politically marginal to the eastern seaboard region, census takers, government officials, and scholars assumed that they were relatively few in number and therefore insignificant."[30] Although it is not clear to what extent the California Development Association's "pro-Mexican" argument was persuasive to restrictionists, it is clear that both white American opponents and advocates for Mexican labor used racist rhetoric to explain that Mexicans were inherently threatening or nonthreatening. Equally important is that such an ostensibly "pro-Mexican" argument reflected the racism of white agribusiness that underpinned the triracial hierarchy in Los Angeles farmland.

SUSPICIOUS "MEKI" AND UNCIVILIZED "DOJIN": THE JAPANESE RACIAL VIEW ON MEXICANS

When it comes to the multiethnic Los Angeles society, racial prejudice against Mexicans was developed not exclusively by white Americans but also by the Japanese who increasingly interacted with Mexicans in 1920s Los Angeles. The *Survey of the Mexican Labor Problem in California* mentioned the end of Japanese immigration as a major reason why agribusiness needed Mexican labor. Yet it did not mention the role of Japanese tenant farmers in Southern California, probably because the very existence of such Japanese farmers proved to be a loophole in anti-Japanese legislation and the economic alliance between white landowners and business leaders and Japanese farmers who leased lands under the name of their US-born children. Most Japanese involved in Los Angeles agriculture were small tenant farmers who cultivated relatively small plots of land. For example, as of 1924, eleven Japanese farmers in Santa Monica leased about 350 acres, meaning that their average acreage per farmer was about 32 acres.[31] In the 1920s when California agriculture became highly industrialized and large-scale farms over 1,000 acres increased, small-scale farms under 50 acres also increased, including those plots operated by both Japanese and non-Japanese farmers. Between 1920 and

1945, the number of farmers under 50 acres increased by 25,169, while the number of farmers between 50 and 999 acres decreased by 12,201. As Lawrence J. Jelinek has pointed out, "California's industrialized agriculture meant not only increasing land concentration, or horizontal integration, but increasing polarization between very small and very large farms."[32] As small-farm operators, Japanese farmers maintained their niche in California agriculture dominated by large-scale business farms.

The California Development Association's *Survey of the Mexican Labor Problem in California* implicitly explained why Mexican casual labor mattered to Japanese tenant farmers, who usually relied on the unpaid labor of family members but needed Mexican labor for the harvest seasons. The report wrote, "For the small farmer particularly, success depends solely upon his handling his crop so as to keep production costs at the lowest possible figure.... At harvest time, particularly if he has a perishable crop, the small farmer needs casual labor—ten, twenty or fifty—and he needs that labor quickly to get his crop off and into market."[33] This was the case for most Japanese tenant farmers in Los Angeles. As early as the 1910s, it was "virtually impossible" for the Japanese to operate their farms without non-Japanese workers such as Mexicans and Filipinos. Their dependency on Mexican labor became larger as they worked more farmlands. The total acreage of land cultivated by ethnic Japanese farmers in California increased from 134,058 acres in 1908 to 328,350 acres in 1929, although it reached a peak in 1920 and soon after decreased by 30 percent in the 1920s because of the California Alien Land Law of 1920. In 1929, Japanese farmers in Los Angeles County cultivated 33,730 acres, 98 percent of which were lands leased by tenant farmers.[34]

A conversation between a Japanese farmer and a white landowner in 1924 shows us a clear picture of the triracial hierarchy in which Japanese farmers leased lands from white landowners and hired Mexican farmworkers. The Del Amo Estate Company that inherited part of Rancho San Pedro, one of the original Spanish land grants in the South Bay region of Los Angeles County, sent a letter to a Japanese American tenant named Ken'ichi Kodama, asking about Japanese immigrant workers the company found in Kodama's farmland. Those Japanese used to be the company's tenants but needed to leave the land after the enactment of the California Alien Land Law of 1920 unless they were employed by Kodama, an American citizen entitled to lease farmland and hire laborers. The company wrote to Kodama, "If they are not your employees they have no legal right to be upon the land and you are hereby directed to order them to vacate immediately." Kodama responded in his imperfect English: "I have seven formans working for me stardy and some extra work men when ever they are nesecely, I am paying monthly wages for my formans and by the hours for the extra men. My employees are mostly Japanese and a few Mexicans but, I have right to hiaring any nationality as I desir, as you know, so you need no worry about this lease as long as

I am operating your Domingzue Hill Ranch."³⁵ To answer the same inquiry from the landowner, another Japanese American farmer wrote that he hired "Japanese and Mexicans at times . . . when their services are required. I cannot give you their names right now because they are there temporarily."³⁶ Mexicans provided indispensable labor for Japanese farms as proved in these conversations. In the 1920s, the restrictionist shift in US immigration policy and the development of Southern California agribusiness strengthened the triracial hierarchy.

The 1924 Immigration Act helped generate more interactions between Japanese and Mexicans in both agricultural and nonagricultural areas in Los Angeles. Their interactions were not always amicable and sometimes reinforced the racial prejudice that the Japanese had toward Mexicans in Los Angeles. We can observe such prejudice in *Rafu Shimpo* articles that used derogatory terms toward Mexicans. When the Japanese ethnic paper reported about crimes committed by Mexicans against the Japanese, writers used the Japanese term *meki* to refer to Mexican criminals. Like *Jap* used by white Americans against the Japanese, *meki* was used against Mexicans as a derogatory abbreviation of the formal term used to refer to a Mexican person in the Japanese language, *mekishikojin*.³⁷ For example, in June 1924, the *Rafu Shimpo* run an article titled "Mekidoro ga shin'nyū" (A Mexican robber broke in). The term *doro* is also an abbreviation of *dorobō* (robber), such that *mekidoro* functioned as a derogatory way of referring to a Mexican robber. A young Mexican man broke in a Japanese jewelry shop, the Yamamoto Jewelry, in downtown Los Angeles early afternoon and stole golden clocks and a precious jar. In this incident, the robber was arrested soon after he stole the goods, and the jewelry shop ultimately suffered no loss. But the article added, "It is said that this *mekidoro* was the same man who broke in the Tomio Store [another Japanese store] the other day."³⁸ The next day, in another article titled "Chihō nōka wo arasu sagikan to mekidoro" (Bandits and Mexican robbers looting rural farmers), the *Rafu Shimpo* reported that a sheriff officer visited the Japanese Association of Los Angeles and warned about crimes committed by bandits and Mexicans in the rural farm area of Los Angeles. The sheriff told the Japanese Association members that three Mexicans had visited a Japanese farmer and one of them began to talk with the farmer while the other two robbed his house.³⁹ The *Rafu Shimpo* reinforced a negative image of Mexicans as dangerous and suspicious by using the derogatory term *meki*.⁴⁰

Although these *mekidoro* stories were only about Mexican robbers, Mexican residents were aware of Japanese immigrants' contemptuous attitude towards them, which added another layer of discomfort and difficulty in their lives in the United States. In 1927, Miguel Alonso, a Mexican tenant farmer planning to return to Mexico, looked back at his experiences in Los Angeles in an interview conducted by Luis Felipe Recinos, a research assistant hired by anthropologist Manuel Gamio. Alonso explained, "I don't believe that I will ever return to this country for I have here spent the hardest days of my life; it is here where I have worked the hardest and earned the least. Besides the people here don't like us, for even the 'chapanises [Japanese]' treat the Mexicans without considerations of any kind. They think that we aren't as good as they and as we are submissive they do whatever they want to with our labor which they often steal with impunity." On the other hand, other Mexicans had different feelings about the Japanese. Zeferino Velázquez, who lived in Los Angeles and worked with Japanese farmers in the Imperial Valley, said, "I don't have anything to say against the 'chapos [Japanese]' for they have been very good people to me. They showed me how to use a plow, the cultivator, the disc and the planting machines and they have been my best bosses."[41] Although Los Angeles Japanese frequently interacted with Mexican residents and their relationships varied, probably many of them did not know well how fellow Mexican residents perceived their everyday attitude toward Mexicans.

The Japanese racial prejudice toward Mexicans seems to have affected how the Japanese regarded mixed-race children of Japanese-Mexican couples in Los Angeles as well. In 1924, a Japanese-Mexican child named Tony Kishi, thirteen years old, whose father was a Japanese rental car shop owner and whose mother was a Mexican, was arrested for several robbery cases in Los Angeles and sent to a reformatory called the Whittier State School. Although Kishi was a son of a Japanese immigrant, the *Rafu Shimpo* described him rather as a non-Japanese foreigner. The article stated, "*Konketsuji* [mixed-blood child] Tony has been known as a delinquent kid who could be handled neither by his father nor by the general public."[42] The Japanese term *konketsu* literally means "mixed-blood," but it implies that mixed-blood children are not "pure-blood" Japanese. Scholar Hyoue Okamura explains that the term *konketsu* inherited the racist ideology of nineteenth-century Europe as it first appeared in written form in Japanese in 1903 when Ōgai Mori, one of the greatest Japanese novelists, introduced the term *konketsu* from Comte de Gobineau's *An Essay on the Inequality of the Human Races*.[43] The article emphasized Kishi as not "pure Japanese" and contrasted him with his father and the general Japanese community. In other words, it implicitly portrayed Kishi as a foreign person outside the "pure Japanese" community. Kishi was a minority within the Japanese community in Los Angeles because it was not common for Japanese immigrant men to intermarry non-Japanese women in California and have mixed-race children.

California law, with its prohibition on intermarriage between "Mongolian" and white women, discouraged mixed marriages between Japanese and other ethnoracial groups at the time, while the long-established picture bride system (fostering unions between Japanese men and women) continued until 1920. Aside from the picture bride system and California's anti-miscegenation laws, the social pressure within the ethnic Japanese community discouraged intermarriage, as suggested by historian Paul Spickard.[44] From 1924 to 1933 in Los Angeles County, the total number of Japanese who married was 1,163. Only 27 or 2.3 percent of them married non-Japanese such as Chinese, African Americans, Filipinos, and "white Americans" who could be ethnic Mexicans. Constantine Panunzio, who examined the marriage licenses in this period, suggested that the county clerk might not have been informed of the anti-miscegenation law or regarded such "white Americans" as outside the prohibition if they came from foreign countries. On the other hand, only 46 or 0.4 percent of 11,016 ethnic Mexicans who married in the same period had Asian, Black, or Native American spouses. In 1942, among Japanese Americans removed to "relocation centers," there were only 192 Japanese Americans of mixed white and Japanese ancestry and 183 whose ancestry was Japanese and another nonwhite minority including Mexicans.[45] For these reasons, mixed-race children of Japanese-Mexican couples suffered social pressure and racial prejudice not only within the larger white-dominant society but also within the ethnic Japanese community.

The Japanese racial prejudice toward ordinary Mexicans did not come only from their encounters with Mexican robbers but also from their understanding that Mexicans were indigenous people rooted in the Western Hemisphere. The Japanese rarely called Mexicans in the United States "immigrants" (*imin*), but did sometimes use that term for Europeans.[46] A similar view appeared in both the *Rafu Shimpo* and in Japanese government documents when they used the Japanese term *dojin* to refer to ordinary Mexicans living in Mexico. The term *dojin* literally meant "a person of land" or "a native person," so the term was used to describe not only Mexicans in Mexico but other native populations, such as Filipinos in the Philippines.[47] But it implied "uncivilized person." As early as 1869, a year after the Meiji Restoration, Yukichi Fukuzawa, one of the most influential intellectuals in the modernization of Japan, whose portrait appears on the ten-thousand-yen bill (in use until 2024), used the term *dojin* in his work on world geography to explain "the lowest people" in the uncivilized region in the world as opposed to the people in the civilized region, mentioning indigenous peoples in Africa and Australia.[48]

The term *dojin* appeared clearly in the Japanese colonization policy of the northern island of Hokkaidō and the following marginalization of the island's native Ainu people. In 1869, the new Japanese government established the Kaitakushi (Development Commission) and further promoted the political inclusion of its native people as imperial subjects of Japan, while denying their history and traditional ways of life as a distinct ethnic group in Hokkaidō. Although the Japanese government claimed that the Ainu people were equal to the ethnic Japanese, the government registered the Ainu as *kyū-dojin* (former natives), which meant that they were originally uncivilized people.[49] Japanese newspapers occasionally used the term *dojin* even without *kyu* (former) to refer to the Ainu people.[50] A Japanese-language dictionary *Daigenkai* published in 1934 continued to explain that *dojin* meant a native person born in that territory or "a native race who lived a primitive life."[51]

While Mexican land seemed very promising to the Japanese of Los Angeles, who were worried about rising discrimination in the United States, Japanese occasionally described Mexican people in Mexico with the *dojin* term. Torimatsu Ozono, a Japanese resident who lived in Mexico and sent his reports to the *Rafu Shimpo* in 1924, explained that Japanese immigrants could save half of their salary in Mexico if they spent money on food like *dojin* did and that *dojin* boys earned fifty cents or $1 a day while Japanese workers could earn $1.22 to $1.75 a day.[52] In 1926, the Ministry of Foreign Affairs of Japan also used the *dojin* term when it issued a report on Mexican agriculture, probably responding to growing interests among the Japanese in migrating to Mexico. Saichirō Koshida, a Japanese diplomat in Mexico and the author of the report, wrote, "The production of minerals, petroleum, and a considerable amount of agricultural products for trade depend on foreigners from the United States, Spain, and Germany" but "the village industry depends on *dojin*."[53]

These documents tell us about a transpacific prejudice that the Japanese on both sides of the Pacific Ocean had toward ordinary Mexicans regarding them as uncivilized or less civilized compared to the Japanese. Keiichi Itō, former acting deputy minister of the Japanese Legation in Mexico, observed in 1925, "There is a tendency among the Japanese in the United States to look down on Mexico and Mexicans and even scorn the fellow Japanese in Mexico," arguing, "I doubt that there is a superior or inferior country if we compare the people of each nation with one another, although our country honors the unbroken imperial line that makes our national polity significantly different from young republics in Latin America."[54] The notion of Japanese superiority over other nonwhite racial groups developed along with the growth of imperial Japan, especially after the victory over Russia in 1905. Los Angeles Japanese, living within the imagined Japanese community around the Pacific Ocean and getting the latest news about Japan and the world in the Japanese language media, shared such notions. For example, editor-in-chief of the *Rafu Shimpo* Shirō Fujioka, although he was very critical about those Japanese who discriminated against other racial groups, still asserted in 1924, "It is clear that our country Japan became a first-rate country in the world and thus should not be considered equal to countries of other colored races."[55] Some Mexicans noticed a strong sense of nationalism among Japanese residents. Fortino V. Tenorio, interviewed in Los Angeles by the Manuel Gamio's research team, told how he had learned what patriotism was by interacting with Japanese workers who worked with him in the same field. Japanese workers distinguished themselves by their industriousness and came together to discuss things about Japan. The experience of working with patriotic Japanese workers made Tenorio decide to join a Mexican patriotic society named the Zaragoza.[56]

Los Angeles Japanese used derogatory terms toward ordinary Mexicans such as *meki* and *dojin*, but this did not mean that they never appreciated their interactions with Mexicans. For example, in October 1918, the Japanese Chamber of Commerce of Southern California organized a carnival at an empty lot in front of the Japanese-operated Pacific Hotel (Taiheiyō Hotel) on San Pedro Street in downtown Los Angeles. The main event in their carnival was a Mexican dance show. The Japanese Chamber spent $600 (approximately $10,300 in 2020) on the carnival. Within this budget, they leased the lot, set up a stage for dancers and a music band, and distributed fifty Spanish fliers in the ethnic Mexican neighborhood. This was a unique multiracial event organized by Japanese immigrants, as they distributed fliers to nearby white residents and set up another stage for Mexican residents to dance. Before the carnival, they were planning to take one hundred Japanese on a two-week excursion in Mexico, which was later canceled due to the lack of funds. After the carnival, the Japanese Chamber invited the Mexican consul Leandro Garza Leal to a party with the purpose of developing friendship. Ujirō Ōyama, Japanese consul in Los Angeles, also attended the party and made welcoming remarks. Although their meeting minutes do not explain in detail, it is most likely that both the Japanese Chamber and the Japanese government wanted to strengthen economic relations with the Mexican government officials and business leaders by organizing events such as the carnival and the party.[57] It seems that Los Angeles Japanese regarded Los Angeles Mexicans as "modernized" because they lived in the United States, while calling ordinary Mexicans in Mexico uncivilized (*dojin*) despite the fact that they were the same Mexicans. The country where Mexicans lived or their physical proximity to Los Angeles, therefore, affected Japanese people's racial view of Mexicans. In other words, *meki* and *dojin* were localized racial terms employed by Japanese immigrants in Southern California toward ethnic Mexicans in Los Angeles and in Mexico, respectively.

The Japanese-Mexican trusting relationship also developed through the interactions between the two groups in schools and multiethnic neighborhoods such as Boyle Heights.[58] Above all, the Japanese had to interact with Mexicans because they needed to work with them on their farms, which would require a certain level of trust and decency for fellow Mexican immigrants. Nevertheless, the racial prejudice as well as understanding that the Japanese had toward Mexicans added an underlying factor that would complicate Japanese-Mexican interethnic relations in the 1930s, as will be discussed in the next chapter.

THE BIRTH OF THE ETHNIC MEXICAN PRESS WITH JAPANESE BUSINESS: AN INTERETHNIC HISTORY OF LA OPINIÓN

While Japanese immigrants advocated for migrating to Mexico and white business leaders discussed the importance of Mexican agricultural labor, Los Angeles became the largest ethnic Mexican community in the United States in the 1920s due to the city's rapid industrialization and urbanization.[59] Although Mexicans were legally considered as white and thus eligible for naturalization unlike Asians, the dominant white society looked down on them as nonwhite and set up a variety of racist legal barriers such as discriminatory housing covenants, school segregation, and city zoning laws, which forced Mexicans to live in Mexican barrios particularly in East Los Angeles. However, thanks to the proximity to their home country and the increase of their population, Mexicans also developed a culturally rich and economically vibrant ethnic community. They operated Mexican restaurants, patronized ethnic businesses, organized community organizations, attended Catholic churches, and enjoyed Spanish-language radio programs.[60] As historian Albert Camarillo summarizes, "barrioization in the early part of the century reflected positive elements (cultural, ethnic, and linguistic reinforcement) as well as negative forces (impoverishment, physical deterioration of neighborhoods, and lack of adequate municipal services)."[61]

Discriminated against as cheap labor in the white-dominant society, many Mexican immigrants maintained strong attachment to Mexico. Regarding the naturalization rates among Mexicans, only 5.5 percent of Mexican residents in Los Angeles were naturalized in 1930.[62] Before World War II, a longtime Mexican resident in Hicks Camp, a Mexican barrio in El Monte, Los Angeles, responded to a California government researcher and said, "I'm not interested in being a citizen because first of all it would mean nothing to anyone—I would be a citizen in name only—with no privileges or considerations. I would still be a 'dirty Mexican.'"[63] Mexican immigrants' low rates of naturalization also reflected the fact that they needed to keep their Mexican citizenship in order to rely on the Mexican consulate in Los Angeles for protection and assistance. In the 1920s, the Mexican consulate became increasingly involved in the public life of its expatriates, while many Mexicans began to see themselves increasingly rooted in Los Angeles.[64] In the 1920s, Luis Felipe Recinos, a research assistant hired by Manuel Gamio, visited Los Angeles to interview Mexican immigrants. He noticed Mexican flags and pictures of Mexican heroes in many houses of Mexican immigrants and observed that such items gave "patriotism . . . an almost religious character."[65] In 1930, sociologist Emory S. Bogardus wrote, "By remaining a citizen of Mexico and by calling on the Mexican consul for assistance the Mexican immigrant often can secure justice, whereas if he becomes an American citizen, he feels helpless. He does not understand our courts and is not able to secure as adequate a hearing as if he remains a Mexican citizen."[66]

Likewise, the Japanese consulate in Los Angeles also had a close connection with ethnic Japanese residents. During the period when the Gentlemen's Agreement was effective, the Japanese government had the direct organizational authority over local immigrant organizations. The Japanese government delegated to the local Japanese associations, through its consulates, part of its bureaucratic functions of creating the immigrant registry needed for the implementation of the Gentlemen's Agreement. This registry was considered the only valid document for Japanese laborers who had already settled in the United States to continue to reside in the United States. After the enactment of the Immigration Act of 1924, this type of registry became no longer necessary, bringing an end to the direct organizational relationship between the Japanese consulates and immigrant associations in 1926.[67] Nevertheless, Japanese immigrants, ineligible for naturalization, continued to depend on the Japanese consulates for their protection. When Toshito Satō became the Japanese consul in Los Angeles in 1929 after working at the Japanese Embassy in Washington, D.C., for three years and a few months, he explained that his position was like the *sonchō* (village mayor) of the Los Angeles Japanese community, and the *Rafu Shimpo* reported his remark with the headline highlighting the term *sonchō*.[68]

Mexican immigrants were not silent about the socioeconomic difficulties and discriminations that they faced in Los Angeles. In the 1920s, the increase of Mexican immigrants expanded the possibility and generated the need to strengthen their ethnic solidarity. Some of the most important developments in the Mexican community in 1920s Los Angeles were the publication of an ethnic Mexican newspaper *La Opinión* in 1926 and the creation of a large-scale labor union, la Confederación de Uniones Obreras Mexicanas (Confederation of Mexican Labor Unions, CUOM) in 1928. Both *La Opinión* and the CUOM would shape Japanese-Mexican relations in 1930s Los Angeles.

Ignacio Lozano, the founder of *La Opinión*, was one of many Mexican immigrants who moved and found a chance to start a business in Los Angeles, an emerging metropolis on the Pacific Coast. The development of the Mexican community meant an expansion of markets for goods that Mexican consumers wanted to purchase. In 1913, after leaving his hometown in northern Mexico during the outbreak of the Mexican Revolution, Lozano founded a Mexican newspaper titled *La Prensa* in San Antonio, Texas, which at the time had the largest concentration of Mexican immigrants in the United States. Lozano succeeded in making *La Prensa* the largest Mexican paper in San Antonio. By distributing papers via the railroads, he expanded the sales network to other big cities, such as Chicago, New York, and Los Angeles. Impressed by the growth of the Mexican population and the market in Los Angeles, in 1926, Lozano founded *La Opinión* in Los Angeles. In the same period, several other Spanish-language newspapers, including his own *La Prensa*, were published in Los Angeles, showing an increasing demand for the Spanish-language media that would provide Mexican residents with useful information. Lozano regarded *La Opinión* as "a Mexican newspaper whose purpose was to pay close attention to what was happening in Mexico, to call to task the politicians for what they were doing, and to continue to watch and ensure that there was progress in Mexico," as his granddaughter Monica Lozano later recalled in an interview. The Mexican government of the 1920s and 1930s did not allow him to go back to Mexico, viewing as problematic his political writings, which tried to be journalistically objective and were not allied with any particular political party. Thus, Ignacio Lozano needed to stay in the United States and write what should be discussed about his country without censorship and suppression by the Mexican government.[69] In 1928, the paper reached a circulation of about twelve thousand copies.[70] From the beginning, his intention had been to send his paper to readers in Mexico, as the newspaper announced that a subscription cost ninety cents per month in Los Angeles, two dollars in the rest of the United States, and three dollars outside of the United States. The price was almost same as the *Rafu Shimpo*, which cost one dollar per month in the same year.[71]

The editorial page of the first issue, published on September 16, 1926, Mexico's Independence Day, proclaimed Los Angeles as an "importantísima región" (very important region) and demonstrated that *La Opinión* would be a serious and useful newspaper for readers based on the publishers' experience of publishing *La Prensa* in San Antonio for the last fourteen years. Mexican intellectuals such as Teodoro Torres Jr, a well-known journalist, and José Vasconcelos, a former secretary of public education, contributed columns to the editorial page. Writing from Mexico, Torres discussed the responsibility of journalists in relation to Mexican politics. Sending a message from France, Vasconcelos wrote passionately about the importance of spiritual activities for the development of the Spanish-speaking people.[72] According to Raul D. Tovares, who has analyzed *La Opinión*'s editorials during its early years, Lozano considered that "the Mexican nation was seen and evaluated through the image Mexicans in the United States were projecting in public." With Lozano's goal to succeed in his business and with the loyalty of the Mexican community, *La Opinión* made efforts to provide Mexican immigrant readers with enough information about Mexico, which would not be available in Los Angeles without *La Opinión*.[73]

Although its editorials reflected an assumption that Mexicans would return to Mexico once Mexican politics stabilized, *La Opinión* provided practical advice for Mexicans to adapt to a new environment in Los Angeles. One such tip was an encouragement to learn English. An editorial on October 11, 1926, wrote, "If those Mexicans, instead of feeling faint, would preoccupy themselves with learning a little bit of English every day and something about the method of working the American way, they would soon see that they are not as inept for the struggle to succeed as they think they are."[74] Even before this editorial, advertisements on *La Opinión* had already encouraged readers to learn English. An advertisement printed on the very first issue, which was likely placed by a textbook company, said "English in a few weeks," "We guarantee success to each disciple for sure," and "Give us your name and address to send you interesting information." Another advertisement also promoted an English textbook, saying, "the edition we offer now, which has been considerably revised, contains a DICTIONARY OF FIVE THOUSAND WORDS." Lozano himself might have been the person selling this textbook, since the name of the company that placed this advertisement was Librería Lozano (Lozano bookstore).[75] While Los Angeles Japanese felt the need to learn English and Spanish as they might have to go to Mexico, Los Angeles Mexicans were encouraged to learn more English.[76]

There were also Japanese immigrants who studied Spanish or hired somebody fluent in Spanish to interact with Mexicans in Los Angeles. Just like Lozano found an economic chance in the growing Mexican community, Japanese merchants and doctors wanted Mexican residents to patronize their businesses. On October 3, 1926, only seventeen days after Lozano launched *La Opinión*, a Japanese company named the Hara Company placed an advertisement in the paper. This company sold clothes and shoes on North Main Street near the Plaza in downtown Los Angeles, where many Japanese had businesses. One of the company's advertisements pictured two young girls. One girl appeared to be white and the other appeared to be a Japanese girl with short, straight black hair, a hairstyle common among Japanese girls (Figure 3).[77] The Hara Company became one of the major advertisers for *La Opinión* in the early years after the paper's founding. Mexican customers patronized the Hara Company with affection, as they called the owner "Japonesito," a mixture of *Japonés* (Japanese) and *-ito* (an affectionate Spanish diminutive suffix). In January 1927, the Hara Company placed an advertisement in the paper saying, "El Japonesito's store, as our friends call us, wishes a Happy New Year to its friends, its fellow merchants, and the Mexican, American, and Japanese communities."[78]

Japanese merchants built an amicable customer-business relationship with Mexican residents in multiethnic Los Angeles, which seemed to improve Mexican workers' impression toward Japanese employers. In the late 1920s, the Commission on International and Interracial Factors in the Problems of Mexicans in the United States, organized by religious leaders, conducted a comprehensive study on Mexicans in California, gathering information from more than one hundred people such as local Chamber of Commerce secretaries, professors, ranchers, business people, local officials, pastors, and missionaries. Their report indicated that "Mexicans are frequently employed in large numbers by Japanese" and that "they prefer Japanese employers as they receive better treatment from them. Japanese have been accused of exploiting the Mexicans, but evidently this is not a common feeling. Japanese stores and pool halls are frequent in Mexican communities. The relations between proprietor and customers are on a purely business basis, but apparently the Mexicans receive fair treatment. Japanese and Chinese are much more likely than Americans to learn Spanish for business purposes."[79]

Japanese doctors provided medical care to Mexican residents in Los Angeles, too. In December 1928, two Japanese clinics, treating patients along First Street between Main and Los Angeles Streets in downtown Los Angeles, placed

FIGURE 3. Advertisement of the Hara Company in *La Opinión*, 1926. SOURCE: *La Opinión*, October 17, 1926.

FIGURE 4. Advertisement of Dr. Ichioka's clinic in *La Opinión*, 1928. SOURCE: *La Opinión*, December 1, 1928.

their respective advertisements on *La Opinión*. Both surgeon Dr. T. Ichioka and ophthalmologist Dr. M. Shinohara emphasized, "Se Habla Español" (We speak Spanish), in order to make their clinics look accessible to Mexican immigrants (Figure 4). Japanese doctors including Ichioka and Shinohara continued to place their advertisements in *La Opinión* into the 1930s, which proves the long-lasting relationship between Mexican patients and Japanese doctors in downtown Los Angeles.[80] In 1920s Los Angeles, Japanese businesses were part of the income source for *La Opinión* from the very beginning and formed a multiracial cityscape of Los Angeles for newly arriving Mexican immigrants. While Mexicans interacted increasingly with the Japanese in the urban downtown area, they also faced the Japanese in the nonurban agricultural areas around Los Angeles. In the next decade when Japanese-Mexican relations deteriorated due to the labor conflict between Japanese farmers and Mexican farmworkers, *La Opinión* would play an important role in the fight for Mexicans and in promoting Mexican nationalism mixed with anti-Japanese sentiment.

As Mexicans increased and became an indispensable labor force in Los Angeles, they also came to be aware of the need to make a larger effort to organize and fight against exploitation. On November 10, 1927, a committee of la Confederación de Sociedades Mexicanas (Federation of Mexican Societies), an umbrella organization of ethnic Mexican mutual and beneficent societies in Los Angeles, adopted a resolution that recited the "deplorable condition of abandonment and isolation" in which Mexicans lived in the United States, "deprived of food, cooperation and mutual help."[81] Alfonso Pesqueira, Mexican consul in Los Angeles, told them that he considered their efforts "extremely favorable for all the Mexican community of workers who live in the West [of the United States]."[82] Soon after this resolution, local Mexican unions merged into la Confederación de Uniones Obreras Mexicanas (CUOM). On March 23, 1928, the Committee on Laws of the CUOM formulated a constitution, modeled after la Confederación Regional Obrera Mexicana (CROM), the largest Mexican union in Mexico, founded in 1918. The CUOM adopted the constitution declaring:

1. That the exploited class, the greater part of which is made up of manual labor, is right in establishing a class struggle in order to effect an economic and moral betterment of its conditions, and at last its complete freedom from capitalistic tyranny.
2. That in order to be able to oppose the organization, each day more complete and intelligent, of the exploiters, the exploited class must organize as such, the base of its organization being the union of resistance, in accord with the rights which the laws of this country concede to native and foreign workers.
3. That the corporations, possessors of the natural and social wealth, being integral parts of the international association of industry, commerce and banking, the disinherited class must also integrate by means of its federations and confederation into a single union of all the labor of the world.[83]

Their constitution shows both the national and transnational characteristics of the CUOM, since they modeled themselves after the largest union in their home country but put emphasis on the rights guaranteed by their host country.

The CUOM also issued their manifesto to make clear that Mexican workers needed to be united for the "prosperity of the laboring classes, promoting their defense, stimulating remunerative salaries and the constant betterment of the proletarian" and that "this movement['s] aim is not to agitate, nor to spread or instigate dis[s]olvent ideas. All that is desired is to equalize Mexican labor to American labor and to obtain for them what the Law justly allows them." What is more important is that in order to improve the working conditions of Mexicans in the United States, the CUOM advocated for "solid relations with the organized Labor of Mexico (Confederación Regional Obrera Mexicana) and to try to stop the immigration of unorganized Labor into the U.S. which is harmful to the working men of both Countries."[84] Prior to the 1930s, the American Federation of Labor did not make efforts to organize unskilled workers of any nationality, especially migratory farm workers, regarding them unorganizable.[85] The CUOM showed their restrictive stance toward newly arriving immigrant workers in order to lessen the tension between them and American workers.

The CUOM also intended to improve the living conditions of Mexican families as a Mexican mutual-aid organization, as they demonstrated that while "animat[ing] by all possible way[s] the conservation of our racial and patriotic principles," they would "promote a strong cultural campa[i]gn giving preference to the education of our children, for which we shall build schools and libraries as is possible," "raise a beneficence fund towards helping our indigent countrymen and to build up or help other Mexican Societies for the establishment of exclusive Mexican hospitals, orphan asylums, alm[s] houses," and "constitute Committees of defense which will have competent lawyers paid by the Mexican colonies themselves so that these with the help of the [Mexican] consulate can effectively defend Mexican[s] who are put in jail, in many cases by mere ignorance of the law."[86] These efforts seemed to be what they meant by "moral betterment" in their constitution. While working closely with the Mexican consulate, the CUOM assumed the role of *mutualistas*, Mexican mutual-aid societies that had existed since the late nineteenth century and increased in the early twentieth century in ethnic Mexican neighborhoods in the Southwest.[87]

In contrast to *La Opinión*'s early assumption that Mexicans would return to Mexico, the CUOM positioned Mexican immigrants in Los Angeles as exploited laborers who would *stay* in the United States and thus fight against exploitation and discrimination, working with both Mexicans and non-Mexicans. On the other hand, a major Japanese mutual-aid association in 1920s Los Angeles was the Central Japanese Association of Southern California (Nanka Chūō Nihonjin Kai), which was established in 1915 and originally founded as the Federation of Japanese Associations in Southern California (Minamikashū Rengō Nihonjin Kai) in 1910. From the beginning, one of the major goals of the Central Japanese Association was to develop Japanese agriculture in Southern California. In the 1920s, when anti-Japanese sentiment became strong, the association adopted a resolution to encourage Americanization of the ethnic Japanese population, which indicates that many Japanese immigrants were determined to settle in the United States despite Japanese exclusion, similar to Mexican immigrants of the CUOM who showed their willingness to stay in the United States.[88]

The CUOM was born just at the moment in which American restrictionists were engaged in heated discussions on the so-called "Mexican Problem." Only five days after the CUOM formulated its constitution, California Governor C. C. Young appointed the Mexican Fact-Finding Committee and ordered the committee to prepare a report that "would contain only *facts* relating to the industrial, social and agricultural aspects of the problem of Mexican immigration into California." The core members of the committee were Will J. French, director of the Department of Industrial Relations, Anna L. Saylor, director of the Department of Social Welfare, and George H. Hecke, director of the Department of Agriculture. Their report, published in 1930, touched upon the CUOM as part of their analysis on Mexican labor unions. In contrast to the image of Mexicans forged by business leaders such as Clements, the report pointed out that "the fact that the Mexican laborers are beginning to organize into unions is significant from the standpoint of those employers who look upon Mexican laborers as tractable and docile persons." But it provided a rather optimistic view about the CUOM because "Mexicans themselves consider that there is already an oversupply of Mexican workers in California, as evidenced by the fact that they have incorporated in their constitution articles pertaining to the limiting of further Mexican immigration into the United States."[89]

The restrictionist stance of organized Mexican workers in the United States was not influential enough to limit the actual influx of immigrants, given the huge demand for Mexican labor in the ever-growing Southern California agricultural industry.[90] However, once the economic growth halted and unemployment rose due to the Great Depression in the 1930s, Mexicans came to be seen as a burden on US taxpayers, compelling the Los Angeles County government to repatriate a large number of Mexicans and their US born children. From Los Angeles County, about thirteen thousand ethnic Mexicans returned to Mexico from March 1931 to April 1934.[91] The Great Depression also helped *La Opinión* evolve from a Mexican newspaper to a Mexican American one, if subtly. Witnessing that Mexicans were scapegoated despite their economic contribution, *La Opinión* raised voices of protest against the forced repatriation of Mexicans.[92] In the 1930s, about one-third of the ethnic Mexican population in Los Angeles, particularly single men and young families, returned to Mexico, which made the immigrant generation numerically smaller than the second generation. George J. Sánchez argues that "the major outcome of repatriation was to silence the Mexican immigrant generation in Los Angeles and make them less visible." Increased residential segregation, decreasing interethnic contact, the efforts of local officials to remove the Mexican population, for example, as seen in the construction of the Union Train Terminal, forced ethnic Mexicans further into specific areas such as the downtown area or into East Los Angeles.[93]

Los Angeles business leaders were concerned that repatriating too many Mexicans would negatively affect local industries that had been using cheap Mexican labor and that the repatriation campaign would worsen the image of Los Angeles.[94] In May 1931, J. A. H. Kerr, the president of the Los Angeles Chamber of Commerce, posted a letter titled "To Our Mexican Friends" on the Chamber's bulletin, saying, "This community [of Los Angeles] has been privileged to be designated as the largest city in Mexican population outside of the Republic" and "they should in no wise be influenced in leaving this section because of idle rumors that the people of Los Angeles do not entertain for them the most cordial friendship or that the government of the United States is embarked upon any wholesale deportation plan aimed principally at our Mexican people." The Chamber had *La Opinión* print Kerr's message and agree to read it over the radio broadcast by the paper's editor in Spanish.[95] On the other hand, the Mexican consul in Los Angeles Rafael de la Colina, who worked closely with Mexican nationals in Los Angeles, did not take such a statement of Kerr as sincere enough and thought that local business leaders viewed the "Mexican laborer as a docile beast of burden, hard-working, economical, and cheap."[96]

Colina's view grasped accurately the racial understanding of business leaders. As discussed earlier in this chapter, George P. Clements, the manager of the Chamber's Agricultural Department, countered the exclusionist argument in 1928 by confidently explaining that Mexican immigrants should be allowed to stay and work in Los Angeles because they consisted of a type of Mexicans who were "clean and healthy" and had their sense of "responsibility" unlike the dangerous "greaser" type of Mexicans. After the Great Depression began, Clements still maintained his racist view of Mexican immigrants as safe and docile. In June 1931, Clements wrote a letter to his superior A. G. Arnoll, the Chamber's secretary and general manager, about the feasibility of keeping nonwhite agricultural labor in California even during the Depression. He contended, "Unemployment has nothing whatever to do with certain types of agricultural labor" because "a Mexican, Chinaman or Jap at the present wages could make a good living and give service for wage to his employer." In the same letter, Clements also said, "I think that I thoroughly understand the Mexican people, and particularly the type of Mexican whom for years we have solicited from Mexico. We have been very careful to demand a sandalled Mexican. These men are drawn from tribes all over Mexico, and the majority of them have no real knowledge of their own government or their governmental workings. In fact, it might be correct to say that the majority of them do not know that such a thing as a Mexican consul exists."[97]

As the Depression worsened the living and working conditions of the remaining Mexican workers and their families, they felt an even larger need to organize and fight against labor exploitation. Japanese tenant farmers in Los Angeles were part of the economically exploitative structure in Southern California agriculture, holding a middleman-minority position between white landowners and Mexican workers. In 1933, Armando Flores, one of the founding members of the CUOM, became a leader who worked closely with the Mexican consulate and *La Opinión* and mobilized Mexican farmworkers against Japanese tenant farmers in El Monte, at the time one of Los Angeles's neighboring agricultural communities.[98] The El Monte strike became one of the largest strikes in 1933. It started as a local interethnic conflict in Los Angeles but evolved into an international conflict between Japan, Mexico, and the United States, which unexpectedly affected the lives of Japanese immigrants across the border in Mexicali. The 1920s saw the development of the transborder ethnic Japanese community and the triracial hierarchy in Los Angeles farmland, which laid a foundation of transpacific Japanese-Mexican conflicts in the 1930s.

3

Transpacific Borderlands

Japanese Farmers and Mexican Workers in the 1933 El Monte Berry Strike

The Immigration Act of 1924 resulted in the increase of Japanese immigrants in Baja California, Mexico, and Mexican immigrants in Southern California. Japanese tenant farmers of Los Angeles County increasingly depended on Mexican workers, further institutionalizing the labor-management relationship between these two immigrant groups within the triracial hierarchy of the local agriculture. The post-1924 development of the triracial hierarchy increased the possibility of Japanese-Mexican interethnic conflicts and resulted in a large-scale agricultural strike by Mexican workers against the Japanese in the early 1930s.

The Great Depression triggered a significant development in the labor movement of the 1930s. Losing their jobs and seeing their wages fall, many farmworkers attempted to improve their working conditions by joining strikes. There were 156 strikes between 1933 and 1939. In the early 1930s, unorganized farmworkers came to constitute the backbone of the Communist-led labor movement in California to organize semiskilled and unskilled workers who had been ignored by the established craft unions. The Imperial Valley Lettuce Strike marked the beginning of the serious involvement of Communist organizers in agricultural strikes in California. It was also a multiethnic project since two white and one Japanese organizer, who formed a branch of the Agricultural Workers Industrial League (AWIL), were assigned to support Mexican and Filipino strikers. The AWIL changed its name twice and became the Cannery and Agricultural Workers' Industrial Union (CAWIU) in 1931. After taking the passive approach of waiting for spontaneous strikes, in 1933 Communist organizers of the CAWIU seized opportunities to mobilize farmworkers who needed an organizational force against labor exploitation. Yet, Mexican workers, or *raza*, who had been ignored by the American

Federation of Labor but had brought a tradition of labor protest from Mexico and established ethnic organizations in the United States, played a proactive and indispensable role in the development of the labor movement in California along with Communist organizers.[1]

In June 1933, Mexican farmworkers went on strike against Japanese tenant farmers in the small community of El Monte in Los Angeles County. Quickly spreading to other areas of Southern California, involving more than five thousand strikers, and lasting more than a month, the El Monte Berry Strike became one of the state's largest labor conflicts in a Great Depression year that was witness to at least thirty-seven agricultural strikes.[2] More than just a labor and interethnic issue, the El Monte strike was an international problem involving the peoples and governments of Japan, Mexico, and the United States. This process strengthened the racial and class boundaries in the local context of Los Angeles agriculture but unsettled the racial and class boundaries in the transnational context of the US-Mexico borderlands. The strike's transnational dimension was evident in a letter to the editor of *La Opinión*. What is intriguing about the letter is not that it supported the Mexican strikers and opposed the Japanese farmers, but that it was written by Japanese immigrants living across the border in Mexicali, Baja California, who condemned the labor exploitation by the Japanese in Los Angeles as "inhumane and contrary to friendly and cooperative relations that must exist between the employer and the worker."[3] This unexpected action taken by Mexicali Japanese eventually affected the way in which Los Angeles Japanese made a compromise in their negotiation with Mexican strikers, turning the racial and class boundaries temporarily fluid and leading to the settlement of the strike.

Historians have studied the El Monte strike not simply as a local conflict but also in terms of US-Mexico relations. Abraham Hoffman argues that the El Monte strike "claimed the distinction of direct involvement by the government of Mexico, in the form of diplomatic pressure, monetary assistance, and consular intervention" through his analysis of diplomatic correspondence between Mexican and US officials and politicians. Francisco E. Balderrama has discussed the El Monte strike in his book that examined an international dimension of the Mexican American community by assessing consular-colonia relations in Los Angeles. Gilbert G. González has analyzed the close communication exchanged between the Mexican consulate in Los Angeles and the Mexican government during the El Monte strike. He interprets the nature of the Mexican government's involvement in the strike as conservative Mexican nationalism that would neither help Mexican farmworkers in a radical way nor harm US capitalism.[4]

In the 1970s, several scholars including Hoffman studied the Japanese-Mexican conflicts in the 1930s, presumably inspired by the labor conflicts that occurred between the United Farm Workers and the Nisei Farmers League in the 1970s to explore the earlier cases of Japanese-Mexican relations. Ronald W.

López provided a detailed overview of the El Monte Strike, revealing the Mexican government's involvement in the strike. Devra Weber explored the ideological relationship between the El Monte strike and the Mexican Revolution. Charles Wollenberg paid careful attention to the interethnic aspect of the strike, describing the historical process in which Japanese and Mexicans came into conflicts in the agricultural industry in 1930s Los Angeles.[5]

Yet no one has examined the strike from the perspective of the Japanese government and Japanese immigrants in both the United States and Mexico.[6] This book does so by focusing largely on Japanese diplomatic documents and Japanese immigrant newspapers *Rafu Shimpo* and *Kashu Mainichi*, while drawing on Mexican diplomatic documents as well as Spanish-language newspapers. These sources reveal that the El Monte strike generated anti-Japanese sentiment in Southern California, which spread across the border to Mexico and eventually pressured Japanese immigrants in Los Angeles to soften their uncompromising stance on the strike and to accept a settlement. In this way, conflict between Japanese farmers and Mexican workers in Southern California contributed to the further reification of transpacific borderlands framed by intersecting local and diplomatic concerns of Japan, Mexico, and the United States.[7] A key, but often overlooked, dimension of the history of US-Mexico borderlands was the interactions between the Japanese in Southern California and their co-ethnics in Baja California, Mexico, which developed the transborder ethnic Japanese community after 1924 as detailed earlier in this book. Although Japanese immigrants on both sides developed cultural and economic ties with each other across the border, the El Monte strike exposed the limits of this transborder ethnic solidarity as the Japanese in Mexico supported the strikers in Los Angeles and thus fell in line with Mexican nationalism. In the end, such nationalism trumped ethnic solidarity among Japanese immigrants in the transpacific borderlands.

AN INTERNATIONAL PROBLEM GENERATED IN LOS ANGELES BERRY FARMS

In 1930, Japanese and Mexicans constituted about 78 percent of the nonwhite population in Los Angeles County.[8] By the 1930s, a triracial hierarchy had developed in Los Angeles agriculture where Japanese tenant farmers took on the role of the middleman minority while leasing lands from white landowners and hiring Mexican workers. El Monte was one of many *transpacific workplaces* in Southern California where Mexicans worked for Japanese farmers. A small community in the San Gabriel Valley, El Monte was about thirteen miles east of downtown Los Angeles, with a population of sixteen thousand. Ethnic Mexicans made up approximately 20 percent of the community's population, while ethnic Japanese accounted for about 5 percent, with the rest being white Americans. Throughout the broader San

Gabriel Valley, Japanese farmers leased land from white landowners and hired Mexican farmworkers to cultivate approximately 80 percent of six to seven hundred acres of berries. Jesusita Torres, a Mexican American woman, remembered, "[Japanese farmers] would work in the field, but you knew they were the boss." In El Monte, both ethnic Japanese and Mexican residents faced racial segregation that excluded nonwhites from more affluent white areas. For example, Japanese and Mexican children went to the same segregated school, where no white children attended.[9] Yet a cultural divide existed between Japanese and Mexican children, as Mexican American resident Patty Holguin recalled, "I thought it was so weird to see the food [the Japanese] ate, just as they probably thought we were weird with our tacos."[10]

The Great Depression hit this triracial community of El Monte, particularly afflicting Mexican residents. Since May of 1933, Mexican farmworkers in El Monte had been demanding a pay increase from fifteen cents (approximately $3 in 2020) to thirty-five cents an hour, due to that season's abundant harvest. Japanese farmers, however, rejected the farmworkers' demand, arguing that they could not afford to increase wages because the price of their crop had declined due to the Depression.[11] Carey McWilliams demonstrated how difficult it was for Japanese farmers to raise wages for Mexican workers in the 1930s based on a Los Angeles County survey conducted in 1935. According to the survey, the average annual gross return for 157 farms, 94.3 percent of whom were Japanese, was $6,415. The average annual expense for paid workers was 33.3 percent of the gross return, while overhead expenses such as rent, water charges, and fertilization reached 50.1 percent. It is most likely that an average annual income of a Japanese farm was less than $1,065 (approximately $20,100 in 2020) in the mid 1930s.[12]

On June 1, Communist organizers of the CAWIU, whose strike committee included several Mexican, Japanese, and Filipino members, successfully mobilized about eight hundred Mexican farmworkers at a barrio called Hicks Camp in El Monte. The CAWIU became the major force in organizing agricultural workers in 1933, leading twenty-four strikes out of thirty-seven in the year.[13] Following its initial outbreak, the El Monte strike rapidly spread to other parts of the San Gabriel Valley and then into farther areas within Los Angeles County such as Venice because Communist organizers of the CAWIU held local meetings and distributed leaflets to farmworkers right after the strike was set in motion. Women and children actively took part in picketing and distributing leaflets printed in Spanish, Japanese, and English. Learning from their failure in mobilizing farmworkers during a pea strike in Alameda and Santa Clara Counties in April, the organizers placed importance on the publication of leaflets for "ideological control" over farmworkers to lead a militant and successful strike.[14]

On June 6, *La Opinión* ran the first detailed account of the El Monte strike and reported that Japanese farmers had refused to improve labor conditions for the "numerous Mexicans [who] had three and four children to support."[15] Although CAWIU organizers first launched the strike, another Mexican workers' organization played an active role from the early stages of the strike. Calling itself la Unión de Campesinos y Obreros Mexicanos (UCOM) by the end of the strike in early July, this union originated from la Confederación de Uniones Obreras Mexicanas (CUOM), which was founded in 1928 as a mutual aid society for Mexican workers in California as explained in the previous chapter. It emphasized patriotic principles rather than the international solidarity of workers. Armando Flores, a print shop owner and an original signer of the CUOM and the general secretary of the UCOM in 1933, was especially active in leading those on strike. By June 6, with the support of Flores, the leaders of the ethnic Mexican community formed a pro-strike committee. They held a meeting at Flores's print shop and decided that the committee should not only support picketing by strikers but should also provide the government and workers in their home country with information of the strike. They also agreed to express their gratitude to *La Opinión* for "their dedicated and spontaneous support for the movement," which was not surprising since the newspaper catered to Mexican immigrant readers in Los Angeles.[16] The strike was also endorsed by the Partido Liberal Mexicano (PLM), an ethnic Mexican organization originally formed in Mexico by the Mexican revolutionary Ricardo Flores Magón and later recreated by him in Los Angeles after he fled to the United States in 1904. Reflecting the long-lasting impact of the Mexican Revolution in the 1930s labor movement in Los Angeles, an immigrant leader, Jesús Solórzano, confirmed the PLM's support and stated, "The strike is just and the comrades deserve all the support of labor organizations of Mexicans in Los Angeles."[17] While most strike leaders were men like Flores, Mexican women were also actively supporting the strikers behind the scenes, cooking food and taking it to the strikers.[18]

Following a request from Japanese farmers, more than ten local sheriffs began to protect their farms from the activities of labor organizers. The Central Japanese Association of Southern California (Nanka Chūō Nihonjin Kai), the ethnic organization that sent an expedition team to Mexico in 1924 as explained in chapter 1, quickly responded to the strike under the leadership of the association's president Katsuma Mukaeda. Mukaeda was a respected community leader in the ethnic Japanese community because of his educational background and bilingual abilities. He was born in Kumamoto Prefecture in 1890 and immigrated to California in 1908. After working on his uncle's strawberry farms in Arcadia near El Monte, he attended the University of Southern California and the Southwestern University School of Law, which enabled him to serve as a court interpreter for the ethnic Japanese community.[19] Takashi Fukami, the general secretary of the association, was assigned to negotiate with the Mexican side. Given the absence of the Mexican farmworkers, Japanese farmers tried to find more permanent replacement workers, while using their children to harvest the crop in the meantime.

By June 10, Japanese farmers had advertised in local newspapers and distributed fliers to recruit new farmworkers. The *Rafu Shimpo* reported that many white Americans, responding to the call for work, "flooded to the Japanese association in El Monte and some brought their wives, students, and children" and that they were not skilled workers, but "the most powerful weapon against the strike." The ethnic newspaper covered the strike in a nationalistic tone with aggressive words such as "weapon," "risk his life [to save fellow Japanese]," and "flames [of the strike]." In an interview article, an anonymous Japanese farmer explained his experience, saying, "It was like a war" when both strikers and sheriffs came to his farm. Resentment against Mexican strikers was evident in the Japanese side.[20]

Meanwhile, two young Japanese American representatives of the recently established San Gabriel Valley Japanese American Citizens League, Shizuko Shirane and David Shiratake, got the principal of El Monte Union High School to grant a special permission to sixty-five Japanese students to work on the farms, additionally postponing the students' exams until after the harvest. A *Rafu Shimpo* headline declared, "Good job! Miss Shizuko Shirane," and noted "all the fellow farmers were moved by the beautiful action of the Nisei [second generation]." By emphasizing the "beautiful" role of young Japanese Americans, the article romanticized their action, at the expense of the Mexican farmworkers.[21] In the English section of the *Rafu Shimpo* for Nisei readers, a bilingual Nisei editor George Hideo Nakamoto wrote, "In cooperating with their parent organization in Los Angeles, [Nisei members of the newly formed JACL of San Gabriel Valley] have really shown to the Japanese community what organized effort can do in the way of coming to the rescue of their harassed parents."[22] It was not until the late 1930s that the second generation began to take a larger role in the Japanese farming community. Yet, in the El Monte strike, the US-born children of Japanese farmers played an important role. For Japanese farmers, their US-born children enabled them to lease land and provided them with useful temporary labor during an emergency.[23]

El Monte's white landowners association, headed by Tom Lambert, backed the Japanese farmers, who were their tenants, too. Lambert was concerned that the strike "would unquestionably be reflected directly back on the land owner" who knowingly let the Japanese lease lands under their children's names, which was a legal loophole of the Alien Land Laws. He was "very much concerned about the suit brought by the Mexican strikers against Japanese vegetable growers by Flores," which would question the legality of Japanese tenant agriculture. Although the strike caused serious concerns among white landowners, posing the possibility of breaking down the triracial hierarchy in local agriculture, they continued to support Japanese farmers to protect their economic interests over the welfare of Mexican farmworkers.[24]

The strike spread quickly to other areas such as Venice and Gardena, since Mexican farmworkers were working throughout the county.[25] In 1933, the Mexican

FIGURE 5. Japanese farmers and workers in the Palos Verdes area, July 1933. Courtesy of Ishibashi Collection, Gerth Archives and Special Collections, CSU Dominguez Hills.

consulate in Los Angeles estimated that there were 21,500 ethnic Mexican families in Los Angeles County and reported to the Ministry of Foreign Affairs of Mexico, "Even when there is a shortage of jobs in all branches, Mexicans always find jobs two or three days a week in harvesting fruits or vegetables."[26] In Venice, about 125 Mexican farmworkers went on strike on the same day when the strike was voted for in El Monte. About sixty Japanese tenant farmers, most of whom grew celery, held a convention on the first evening of the strike. Mexican strikers demanded thirty-five cents an hour instead of the fifteen or twenty cents they had been receiving, but Japanese tenant farmers dismissed their demand as "futō yōkyū" (inadequate claim). In the Gardena Valley, most Mexican farmworkers quickly joined the strike, while eight or nine Mexicans remained in the field since they had been working with Japanese tenant farmers for years. According to the *Rafu Shimpo*, a "threat group" organized mainly by Communists came to the field by three cars and "threatened" those remaining Mexican workers to leave the field, so that no Mexican remained by mid-June. In Dominguez Hills, a group of ten Mexicans came to stop other Mexicans from working at Japanese farms, so that Japanese farmers immediately asked local sheriffs to protect them. The strike also affected the nearby Palos Verdes area (Figure 5), although it did not prevent Japanese farmers from harvesting tomatoes because they could hire temporary workers such as unemployed Japanese workers. Consequently, the El Monte strike became serious enough to involve both the Japanese and Mexican consulates in Los Angeles as well as the state government and the business community of Southern California.[27]

In El Monte and other areas of Los Angeles County, strikers asked the Mexican consulate for support. Quickly responding to their request, on June 6, the vice consul Ricardo Hill visited Venice to take necessary steps to settle the problem under the auspices of the Department of Protection of the Mexican Consulate.[28] Hill, one of three vice consuls working at the Mexican consulate in Los Angeles, was the chief of its Department of Protection. This department dealt with issues related to the protection of Mexican residents and to Comisiones Honoríficas Mexicanas (Mexican Honorary Commissions), locally established organizations of Mexican residents that functioned to facilitate the communication between Mexican immigrants and the Mexican consulate in downtown Los Angeles.[29] The relationship between Comisiones Honoríficas and the Mexican consulate was not the same but similar to that between local Japanese associations (Nihonjin Kai) and the Japanese consulate in the sense that immigrant organizations mediated the communication between immigrants and their home government.

The Mexican consulate also supervised the flow of relief supplies for Mexican strikers. After launching the strike, the Mexican pro-strike committee assigned a member named Vicente Pinto to collect provisions, funds, and any other assistance from people who wanted to help Mexican strikers in El Monte. Accordingly, an owner of a Mexican grocery store M. Pacheco was asked to provide strikers with "30 sacks of wheat, 8 sacks of beans, 200 pounds of salt, 500 pounds of sugar, 10 boxes of condensed milk, and 10 cans of butter that were worth 171.95 dollars." The pro-strike committee estimated that these supplies could prolong the strike until almost the end of June and decided that these should be handed to strikers only through the order issued by the Mexican consulate. The Mexican consulate provided assistance to the strikers from the beginning because the El Monte strike appeared to be a chance to unite Mexican nationals in Los Angeles, some of whom were "forgetting the sentiment of solidarity, brotherhood, and patriotism that every Mexican should cherish for their fellow [Mexican] citizens," as recorded in the consular monthly report.[30] *La Opinión* also reported that "the Mexican Consulate and the Pro-Strike General Committee, the two forces leading the strikers, work together to achieve the triumph of the movement" and that strike leaders sent telegrams to the Labor Department of Mexico to ask for financial and moral assistance.[31]

On June 7, an official of the California Department of Industrial Relations met with Japanese consul Toshito Satō and told him that the wage of farmworkers was too low. Later that day, Hill visited Satō to ask him to "interpose their valuable influence before the group of Japanese farmers." Hill had worked at the Mexican Legation in Tokyo from October 1923 to June 1924, which he might have told Satō at some point or another.[32] But Satō answered that there was little either consulate could do to settle the problem, since Japanese farmers had already determined not to compromise. According to the *Kashu Mainichi*, another major Japanese immigrant newspaper, Satō told Hill that if Japanese farmers increased wages, Mexicans would lose their jobs because Japanese workers would take their position instead and that Japanese farmers are hiring Mexicans just because their wages are low.[33] The Japanese consulate assumed a hands-off approach to the conflict in its early stage, standing by the side of farmers. In Japanese diplomatic correspondence, Satō later explained to Tokyo that he had refrained from intervening in the strike "because of the character of the conflict." Although Satō did not specify the meaning of its "character," he considered that the consulate "should not deal with it directly but support them [Japanese farmers] indirectly," probably because he thought that the consulate's intervention in the early stage could promote the internationalization of this local interethnic conflict.[34]

Satō became the consul in 1929 after working in the Japanese Embassy in Washington for more than three years. Japanese immigrants later remembered him as one of the consuls who worked most closely with their ethnic community in Los Angeles prior to World War II. Satō had to handle the US-Japan relations carefully, due to the international tension heightened by Japan's invasion of Manchuria in 1931 and due to Japanese dependence on US exports such as oil and cotton, many of them produced in or near the Los Angeles area.[35] Japanese immigrants in Los Angeles fervently supported Japan's foreign policy in Manchuria, while attempting to build amicable relationships between Japanese and Americans.[36] Even though the peak of prewar anti-Japanese sentiment came with US exclusion of Japanese immigration in 1924, Japanese communities continued to face nativist harassment and local conflicts always had the potential of hurting US-Japan relations. When Satō was assigned to the Japanese consulate in Los Angeles, he gave a speech at a welcome party for himself. In his speech, he acknowledged Los Angeles as a growing industrial center and emphasized the importance of the US-Japan relationship. To maintain stable diplomatic and trade relations between Japan and the United States, Satō directed Japanese immigrants to abide by US laws and settle in US society without causing any problems, knowing "a considerable number [of Japanese residents] faced legal punishment for offences against laws such as the traffic and prohibition laws."[37]

In contrast, the Mexican consulate played an active role in the El Monte strike from its beginning. Despite the initial success of CAWIU organizers in mobilizing strikers, their presence ironically gave a good reason for the Mexican consulate to take over the leadership in the strike by using anti-Communist rhetoric and emphasizing Mexican nationalism. When mass picket lines set up by the CAWIU organizers resulted in a confrontation with sheriffs in El Monte, the Mexican consul Alejandro Martínez came to El Monte and denounced the CAWIU organizers as "reds" who did not represent the rights of farmworkers. Actually, it was the strike leader, Flores, who requested Martínez's visit. On June 10, when local authorities finally arrested and jailed eight of the CAWIU organizers involved in the El Monte strike, Martínez appeared in public and denounced the CAWIU leadership again. After this incident, strikers began to fight against Japanese farmers along nationalistic lines.[38] It was not difficult for them to switch their leadership from Communists to the Mexican consulate, since few strikers were actual members of the CAWIU and non-Communist leaders like Flores gained confidence in directing the course of the strike, as historian Cletus E. Daniel argues.[39]

Predictably, the Japanese farmers welcomed the arrest of Communist organizers due to the threat they posed to their business. When local authorities arrested a Japanese Communist named Hiroshi Tōi and a group of Mexican workers on June 7, the ethnic Japanese newspaper *Nichibei Shimbun* praised the action.[40] Although prominent Japanese American Communists such as Karl Yoneda played an important role in building a multiracial and multiethnic coalition, Japanese immigrant farmers and the *Rafu Shimpo* regarded Communism as a threat to their ethnic solidarity and farmers' profits.[41] One Japanese farmer maintained that "the strike spread widely because of the agitation of leftists and lazy unemployed people" and that farmers could solve the conflict "by separating professional agitators from workers and negotiating directly with workers."[42] The Japanese consul Satō also emphasized, "If individuals such as Communists are disturbing Japanese farmers, it is my thought that we should take an appropriate action in cooperation with authorities."[43] In the El Monte strike, both Japanese and Mexican leaders regarded Communist organizers as harmful to their respective economic and political solidarity.

Meanwhile, Flores was active in making the Japanese-Mexican conflict an international problem. He asked for support from US and Mexican politicians such as President Franklin D. Roosevelt and the former president of Mexico Plutarco Elías Calles. Calles, known as the "Jefe Máximo" (supreme leader), maintained strong political power in Mexico. By June 23, Calles had donated at least $750 (approximately $15,000 in 2020) through the Mexican consulate in Los Angeles, while Mexican president Abelardo Rodríguez, loyal to Calles, donated $1,000 for strikers. A strike leader praised Calles's assistance as "very timely" and said, "I was sure that the strike would have failed if he had not intervened so kindly."[44] Given the reality of the transborder migration of Mexican farmworkers in the early twentieth century, Calles found in the El Monte strike an opportunity to forge a positive image of himself among the Mexican working class beyond the US-Mexico border. Historian Ronald W. López contends that "this would be an opportunity for Calles to get good publicity and simultaneously Flores would be getting support for the strike" since "labor groups in Mexico were disenchanted with Calles and his puppet president, Abelardo Rodríguez." As the Mexican secretary of foreign affairs, José M. Puig Casaraunc, later mentioned, Calles's interest was due chiefly to "his geographical propinquity." Gilbert G. González argues that "Calles had no deep interest in the strike other than his own driving political ambition."[45]

The strike received stronger support from labor organizations in Mexico as well. On June 20, the pro-strike committee received a memorandum from an organization named the Executive Committee of the United Front of Workers of Los Angeles stating that they had begun to lobby the Mexican government and labor organizations to support Mexican strikers in Los Angeles. The Executive Committee explained that their representative in Mexico, Luis F. Bustamante, had visited the Mexican Ministry of Foreign Affairs together with the secretary general of la Confederación Regional Obrera Mexicana (CROM) to request financial support for the strike and that the CROM was ready to call a nationwide boycott against Japanese products while sending circulars to all the related organizations begging for an immediate dispatch of funds for strikers.[46] Two days later, Mexican labor unions in Ciudad Juárez in the state of Chihuahua, just across the border south of El Paso, agreed to launch an anti-Japanese boycott as a way to express their solidarity with strikers in Los Angeles.[47] Although the CROM's political influence dwindled from 1928 due to the internal division, the El Monte strike operated in cooperation with the organized labor in Mexico.[48] At the same time, problems were beginning to mount not only for Japanese immigrants but also for their country's diplomats in Japan, Mexico, and the United States.

The expansion of the strike along with the active intervention of the Mexican consulate and political leaders persuaded Satō to change his hands-off approach and intervene in the conflict in order to prevent the souring of relations between Japan, the United States, and Mexico. On June 23, Satō sent a telegram to the minister of foreign affairs, Yasuya Uchida, in Tokyo, writing that the strike was "considerably organized" and that he had been working hard to solve the conflict with Japanese farmers and local business leaders of the Los Angeles Chamber of Commerce. Satō explained that the US economy depended on Mexican farmworkers because of the "historical relationship between the United States and Mexico" after the US government banned Japanese immigration in 1924. Satō reported to Tokyo that the number of Mexican strikers in the San Gabriel Valley had increased to two thousand, and strike leaders were working with the Mexican government and planning for a boycott against Japanese merchants.[49]

Since both Japanese farmers and Mexican farmworkers were an integral part of the unique triracial hierarchy of Los Angeles agriculture, their interethnic conflict became a serious problem for white landowners and agribusiness leaders. While the strike involved Mexican farmworkers, Japanese farmers, and their respective consulates, white business leaders in the Los Angeles Chamber of Commerce, who attempted to keep Mexican labor in Los Angeles during the period of the Mexican repatriation as mentioned in chapter 2, also got involved and sought to convince Japanese farmers and Mexican farmworkers to resolve the strike through a compromise. They too were concerned that the strike by farmworkers would reinforce anti-immigration sentiment and rekindle the argument for Mexican immigration restriction that could lead to a labor shortage. When the Los Angeles County government repatriated a large number of Mexicans in 1931 due to the Great Depression, some chamber members expressed their concerns that the repatriation program could severely damage local industries. In May of that year, Chamber President J. A. H. Kerr stated, "We regret that a considerable number of our Mexican people are returning to their home land" and "all those who have come into this country legally not only are permitted to stay here but are welcome." To prevent a labor shortage, on June 26, 1933, the Chamber of Commerce leaders proposed a compromise and called on the US Labor Department to mediate a settlement of the El Monte strike. The proposal demanded that the Japanese farmers pay eighteen cents an hour to berry pickers. Japanese tenant farmers agreed to the deal, but Mexican farmworkers declined it, demanding an arrangement that covered all vegetables and fruits as well as berries.[50] Ross H. Gast, the Chamber's official who arranged the first round of negotiations, had increasing concerns about the precarious situation of the strike. One day after the first negotiation ended in failure, Gast sent a letter to his superior George Pigeon Clements, the manager of the Chamber's Agricultural Department, writing, "My opinion is that unless something is done, this local situation is dangerous in that it will spread throughout the state as a whole. In my opinion this is the most serious break of the Mexican workers here."[51] Reflecting his concern, by this time, the total number of strikers had reached over five thousand in Los Angeles and Orange Counties.[52]

Gast correctly grasped the potential of the strike to spread far beyond the Los Angeles area, drawing the larger involvement of the California State government. Furthermore, the failure to reach an agreement exacerbated the situation not only in Los Angeles but also in Mexicali, home to the largest concentration of ethnic Japanese residents in Baja California, Mexico. Anti-Japanese sentiment in Los Angeles traveled across the US-Mexico border and began to disturb ethnic Japanese residents in Mexicali, who played an important role in the local cotton agriculture as explained in chapter 1. Consequently, Japanese diplomats in Mexico became increasingly concerned about the impact of the El Monte strike on Japan-Mexico relations.

GROWING ANTI-JAPANESE SENTIMENT IN THE US-MEXICO BORDERLANDS

After the failure to reach a compromise on June 26, the Japanese consul Satō became increasingly concerned over the strike's negative impact on international relations involving Japan, Mexico, and the United States and discarded his early uncritical stance toward Japanese farmers. By monitoring *La Opinión*, he was already aware of the exacerbating situation in Mexico as the most influential Mexican leaders such as Calles and Rodríguez were supporting the strikers. In addition, two days before the failed negotiation, the minister of the Japanese Legation in Mexico, Yoshiatsu Hori, warned Satō of the possibility that the strike would bother the Mexican government by driving a large number of unemployed immigrants in Los Angeles back to Mexico. Hori added, "I hope that you take our region's situation into consideration, although I understand that you are working hard to solve the problem in an amicable way."[53]

On June 27, Satō summoned thirty-five leaders of Japanese farm communities in Los Angeles and Orange County to his consulate building and recommended that they reach a compromise with Mexican farmworkers. By this time, he came to consider that without his intervention, the strike "could complicate the relations of Japan, the United States, and Mexico." At the meeting, Satō stated to Japanese farmers, "It would be wise for the Japanese side to make a concession at necessary costs," and attempted to persuade them to pay twenty cents an hour since the strike had become "increasingly important locally and internationally." The El Monte strike could stir up anti-Japanese sentiment, which had troubled US-Japan relations since the early twentieth century, as seen in the Gentlemen's Agreement of 1907 and 1908, the first California Alien Land Law of 1913, the second California Alien Land Law of 1920, and the Immigration Act of 1924. Satō was concerned that mounting anti-Japanese sentiment caused by the strike would lead to further legal restrictions against Japanese land use, which would go beyond the restrictions laid out in the Alien Land Laws.[54]

Nevertheless, Japanese farmers rejected the consul's recommendation, explaining that it was hardly possible for them to raise wages due to the continuing economic recession and that some farmers had difficulty paying their land rent and water bills. They concluded, "Even with the current wages, fifteen cents per hour, Japanese farmers get into the red. So it is impossible for us to raise wages until the economy gets well."[55] Nakamoto, the Nisei editor of the *Rafu Shimpo*'s English section, echoed Japanese farmers' concerns and described Mexicans' demands as "impossible for the Japanese growers to accept without seriously jeopardizing the position of the Japanese farmers in general throughout the Southland."[56] Although Japanese agriculture in Los Angeles County had continued to develop by overcoming legal restrictions on land use, their average income was much below that of all residents in California and many Japanese women and children were supporting family farming through unpaid labor.[57] In addition, Japanese farmers were reluctant to make a concession because 60 to 70 percent of the struggling Mexican strikers had already returned to work by the beginning of July. The strike did not seem to be working.[58] Despite the ongoing internationalization of the strike, the fact that Japanese tenant farmers had sufficient political autonomy to reject the consul's recommendation further complicated the situation. What was evident was that the Japanese consulate began to work closely with farmers as the Mexican counterpart had been doing with strikers, making clear the national boundary between the Japanese and Mexican sides which intersected with their racial and class boundaries.

In attempting to resolve the strike, two *Rafu Shimpo* reporters visited the Mexican consulate in Los Angeles and interviewed the consul Martínez, vice consul Hill, the strike leader Flores, and their lawyer David Marcus about the ongoing Japanese-Mexican conflict. On June 29, their conversation appeared in the *Rafu Shimpo*. Martínez simply reaffirmed their basic stance in the strike saying, "It is my viewpoint that the Mexicans are entitled to better wages. It is also my hope that the Japanese producers may find a way to cooperate in our efforts to help the Mexican families of California as I consider that both factors have [been] a great force for the development of the State of California." In this meeting, the Japanese reporters were particularly eager to interview Flores, regarding him as "the most influential person among Mexicans." Flores told the reporters, "What we want the Japanese farmers to understand is that we are not making an inadequate claim." He added, "It is my sincere hope that we concede to each other to reach a peaceful solution. Otherwise, we need to take a different measure." When the reporters asked what he meant by a "different measure," Flores answered, "I can't tell you clearly since it depends on the situation."[59] Flores did not seem to have a definite idea of a different measure, and so this interview proved that the situation was quite uncertain.

The situation soon worsened for those on both sides of the conflict. *La Opinión* sensationally reported that two Mexican children died allegedly from hunger caused by the strike, although infant mortality rates were high among Mexican farmworkers in Los Angeles County even before the strike.[60] In Mexico, la Cámara Nacional del Trabajo (National Chamber of Labor), a newly established and short-lived labor organization whose director was a former CROM leader and politically close to the leading Mexican political party, el Partido Nacional Revolucionario (National Revolutionary Party, hereafter as PNR), and Calles, issued a decree to boycott Japanese products, urging, "No Mexican worker will buy Japanese merchandise nor sponsor Japanese establishments."[61] Three days after the failed negotiation, Japanese berry farmers in El Monte and nearby Arcadia opened their fields and let the public pick berries at one cent per box, five to six cents below the retail price. The move was a huge financial loss for the farmers, but they decided to do so in a desperate attempt to salvage part of the money invested in their crop. After newspapers and local radio stations announced this emergent pick-your-own day, "Hundreds of men, women, and children, carrying baskets, buckets and various other containers, invaded the berry fields."[62] This event hurt the strikers' efforts. Later the same day, at least two thousand strikers began to gather around the Hicks Camp and about half of them entered the berry fields to urge those harvesting the berries to quit. Nearly a hundred local police officers quickly responded to the intrusion. The *Los Angeles Times* reported that on the next morning, some strikers beat a Japanese farmer and his wife near Arcadia. The *Rafu Shimpo* took up the alleged incident seriously and investigated only to find that the stories of the violence on the Japanese were fabricated by English-language newspapers and radio stations. This kind of exaggeration about strikers' violence in the *Los Angeles Times* explains the newspaper's long reputation of being anti-labor.[63] Satō knew that the *Los Angeles Times* reported as little as possible about the strike, so that many residents in Los Angeles did not know that several thousands of Mexican farmworkers were fighting against Japanese farmers.[64] Regardless of injuries, local interethnic relations between Japanese and Mexicans were getting worse.

The Mexican consulate responded to this worsening situation. On June 30, Mexican consul Martínez exchanged telegrams with governor of California James Rolph Jr., asking him to intervene in the dispute. In their communication, Martínez forwarded a telegram sent by former president Calles describing Mexicans' working conditions as "intolerable" and their wages as "inhumanly low." Rolph ordered the Director of the Department of Industrial Relations and the chief of the Division of Labor Statistics and Law Enforcement to "amicably adjust the dispute." The next day, Rolph's decision headlined *La Opinión*'s front page, which generally buried local news in other sections.[65] According to the monthly consular report of June 1933 to the Ministry of Foreign Affairs of Mexico, the Mexican consulate also called Rolph's attention to "the illegal intervention of the police authorities of Arcadia and San Gabriel and other parts affected by the strike" because "it is known based on a reliable source that Japanese farmers have paid police officers in the already mentioned areas."[66] The strike leader Flores played an important behind-the-scenes role. Following the failed negotiation, Flores left Los Angeles for Baja California to meet Calles, who had been supporting the strikers. On his way to El Sauzal in Baja California where he would meet Calles, Flores told *La Opinión*, "Our principal objective is to personally show gratitude to Mr. General Calles for his moral and material support" and to relay the details of the fight against the Japanese. On June 29, just a day after Flores met Calles, Calles sent a message to Governor Rolph, explaining, "The Japanese employers . . . lack all humanitarian sentiment and deny workers the rights they have in the modern world." This message appeared in *La Opinión* the next day.[67] Both Martínez and Flores needed the political power of the former Mexican president to support the strikers.

On the other hand, Japanese consul Satō was paying careful attention to the actions of the Mexican consulate. Satō reported to Tokyo, "The Mexican consul openly supports the strikers as he kept the funds for the strike and distributed fliers to encourage the strike while asking the US Labor Department and the Governor of California to intervene." Actually, Satō speculated that Flores was Calles's right-hand man and that Flores was manipulating the Mexican consulate as his *tesaki* (puppet) by using the power of Calles. Satō developed a sense of distrust toward Mexican strikers and their consulate, leaving no room to problematize the dominant structure of Los Angeles agriculture that marginalized both the Japanese and Mexicans. Instead, the Japanese consul functioned to affirm the status quo by cooperating with the Los Angeles Chamber of Commerce that represented the interests of white landowners.[68]

The Los Angeles Chamber of Commerce proved far more sympathetic to the Japanese. Ross H. Gast believed the strike leaders were exploiting the workers by preventing them from working. He regarded Flores as "a pretty smart operator" who "was able to point out that if the Mexican government and particularly Calles and Rodríguez would show sympathy" to Mexican farmworkers in Southern California, they would gain the labor support in Mexico. In addition, Gast thought that it was necessary to take a "humanitarian standpoint" to solve the strike because "workers want to go back to the fields" liberated from strike leaders who "are exploiting workers." He clearly lacked a humanitarian viewpoint to understand the farmworkers' plight, although he was partly right in the sense that the Mexican government had a political stake in the strike. First, it was understandable why the strike leaders rejected the compromise offered by Japanese farmers. The proposal covered only the berry industry despite the fact that Mexican farmworkers worked a variety of fruit and vegetable crops on a number of farms throughout Los Angeles, just like those harvesting celery in Venice. Second, and more importantly, the wages of farmworkers were extremely low, compared to the state's minimum wages for industrial workers, thirty-three cents an hour, which did not apply to farmworkers. According to a survey conducted by the Los Angeles County government and the Works Progress Administration in the 1930s, a farmworker's household income was approximately $491 and their average expenditure for food was about $412. There was little money left for farmworkers to use for housing, medical care, clothing, and other necessities. About 98 percent of those interviewed lived in "frame houses," which could best be described as "wooden shacks."[69]

By this time, the El Monte strike had taken a transnational twist when anti-Japanese sentiment spread beyond the small town of El Monte and unexpectedly developed in Mexico. In mid-June, anti-Japanese activities in Mexico prompted a call for a boycott against Japanese merchants to protest the actions of Japanese farmers in Los Angeles. Anti-Japanese sentiment grew stronger in Mexico after Calles took an unfavorable attitude toward Japanese farmers and provided financial support for Mexican strikers in Los Angeles.[70] Calles helped transform the strike into an international problem by providing support from Mexico and mobilizing the Mexican public. He also sent messages to California's Governor

Rolph, President Franklin D. Roosevelt, and the PNR's chairman to urge their support. The minister of the Japanese Legation in Mexico, Hori, sent a telegram to the minister of foreign affairs, Uchida, in Tokyo on June 29, warning that since local newspapers widely reported the action taken by Calles, the situation of the Japanese side was "seriously deteriorating" in Mexico, so much so that it might have a negative effect on Japan-Mexico relations.[71] By the end of June, the PNR had declared that they would donate $1,000 to Mexican strikers in Los Angeles. According to the monthly consular report of July 1933 to the Ministry of Foreign Affairs of Mexico, the Mexican consul Martínez, who was in close contact with Calles, "received also a thousand dollars that el Partido Nacional Revolucionario sent the undersigned for the support of the strike." The *Kashu Mainichi* observed that the PNR donated the money on Calles's advice and did so in order to "make Mexicans fully feel a sense of awe and gratitude to the party when they face the worst of living conditions." By July 1, the Mexican consul had received $4,490.75 as donations from Calles and his friends.[72]

Even before the strike began, Hori was aware of growing anti-Japanese sentiment in Mexico, especially in its northern region including Baja California, due to the territorial expansion of the Japanese empire in Manchuria. In May 1933, Mexican newspaper *El Excélsior* ran an anti-Japanese article warning of a possible Japanese invasion of Mexico with the large headline "A grave danger to Baja California," which Hori countered. Frustrated with the prolonged strike in Los Angeles and the worsening situation in Mexico, Hori sent another telegram to Uchida in Tokyo the next day. He insisted, "I had been dealing with this problem as a local problem of California that had nothing to do with us, but I would need to explain the position of Japanese tenant farmers [of Los Angeles] depending on the future situation. Thus, I beg you to send us a telegram *immediately* about the points of contention over wages claimed by both sides of the conflict, the number of Mexican workers who are returning to work, and the latest situation of the conflict" (italics added).[73]

Japanese diplomats in Mexico also needed to prevent anti-Japanese sentiment from spreading and turning into some organized campaign against Japanese immigrants. Although their small population did not pose a significant economic threat to ordinary Mexicans, the Japanese had occasionally been the victims of xenophobic violence in Mexico as mentioned in chapter 1. In the 1930s, the Great Depression made the Japanese in Mexico increasingly concerned about anti-Japanese sentiment, as it created a large number of frustrated, unemployed Mexicans. In September of 1932 in Veracruz, for instance, a group of unemployed Mexicans demanded that seventeen Japanese shop owners hire Mexicans. After the Japanese rejected their request, they forced the closure of two Japanese shops, denouncing the Japanese as foreigners exploiting Mexicans.[74]

The El Monte strike took place in this historical context of anti-Japanese violence and became another source that fueled anti-Japanese sentiment in Mexico. The strike's impact was serious among Japanese residents in Mexico, especially in the Mexican border city of Mexicali, Baja California. By the 1930s Mexicali became the largest concentration of ethnic Japanese residents in Mexico with nearly one thousand people and was incorporated into the southern region of the transborder ethnic Japanese community.[75] Despite their economic, cultural, and political ties with Japanese immigrants in Los Angeles, the Japanese in Mexicali initially did not take sides in the El Monte strike. Nevertheless, they were facing anti-Japanese sentiment that developed in El Monte and spread beyond the US-Mexico border.[76]

Mokichi Fukushima, a Japanese diplomat stationed at a consular outpost in Tijuana, reported the situation of Mexicali Japanese to Tokyo. The consular outpost in Tijuana began to operate in 1931 by the decision of the Ministry of Foreign Affairs of Japan given the growing population of ethnic Japanese residents and the development of Japanese fishermen's activities along the coast of Baja California.[77] Fukushima wrote, "Mexicans here [in Mexicali] who had been relatively cool began to launch the activity to collect donations and the boycott against Japanese merchants as an act of revenge," because Calles intervened in the conflict. The Mexicali Japanese became increasingly concerned about Calles and the impact of anti-Japanese sentiment on their cotton farming. Japanese cotton farmers employed Mexican farmworkers on favorable terms granted by the local government of Baja California. They, however, became fearful that mounting anti-Japanese sentiment in Mexicali could motivate the Governor of Baja California Agustín Olachea to end that accommodation for Japanese cotton farmers.[78] On the day after the failed negotiation in Los Angeles, the Mexicali Japanese finally decided to publicly express their support for Mexican strikers, rather than for fellow Japanese immigrants in Los Angeles, as an attempt to deflect any anti-Japanese sentiment. This decision was especially difficult because the Mexicali Japanese had received financial support from the Los Angeles Japanese when they suffered a poor cotton harvest in the previous year. In their public statement, they noted the bonds between Japanese on both sides of the border, but clearly sided with the Mexican strikers: "The members of this Japanese Association of [Mexicali], Mexico, putting aside the spiritual and racial bonds that unite us with such Japanese residents in California, U.S.A, for humanitarian reasons, for moral reasons, and for the directions of conscience and of rights, we unite for very righteous protests of Mexicans against the unfair conduct of those subjects of the Japanese Empire" (Figure 6).[79] Transborder anti-Japanese sentiment seemed to have resulted in the cooperation of Mexicali Japanese, if only temporarily, for the Mexican nationalist pro-strike campaign.

The Mexicali Japanese sent their pro-strike statement to Calles, Olachea, and the media on June 27. Three days later, *La Opinión* published it in Los Angeles.

> **MENSAJES DE LOS JAPONESES DE BAJA CALIFORNIA, APOYANDO LA HUELGA DE LOS PIZCADORES**
>
> Son dirigidos al Presidente Rodríguez, al Gral. Calles y a Olachea.—Los agricultores nipones abren al público sus campos para no perder la cosecha
>
> (Sigue de la 1a. Pág.)
>
> mejor entendimiento en sus relaciones con los trabajadores mexicanos, de quienes ha recibido una cooperación ilimitada tanto en las épocas de auge como en las críticas, estando por ello agradecido.
>
> Y no siendo justa la actitud del elemento japonés residente en el Estado de California, Estados Unidos de Norteamérica, los miembros de esta Asociación Japonesa de la Baja California, México, haciendo a un lado los lazos espirituales y de raza que nos ligan con dichos japoneses residentes en California, E. U. A., POR HUMANIDAD, POR MORAL Y POR LOS DICTADOS DE LA CONCIENCIA Y DEL DERECHO, NOS AUNAMOS A LAS MUY JUSTAS PROTESTAS DE LOS MEXICANOS EN CONTRA DEL INICUO PROCEDER DE AQUELLOS SUBDITOS DEL IMPERIO JAPONES, QUE SIN RECORDAR LAS CORDIALES RELACIONES QUE NUESTRA PATRIA HA TENIDO Y TIENE CON LA REPUBLICA MEXICANA, TRATAN DE EXTORSIONAR A CIUDADANOS MEXICANOS.
>
> Mexicali, Baja California, a 27 de junio de 1933".
>
> gar a un acuerdo en la fijación de salarios, habiendo el último lunes rechazado el Comité General Pro-Huelga de los mexicanos las proposiciones presentadas por la Asociación Japonesa, considerándose desventajosas para los huelguistas.
>
> Entre 1,000 y 3,000 trabajadores mexicanos se hallan en huelga contra los japoneses, según las declaraciones hechas ayer por Fukami, siendo los Condados de Los Angeles y Orange los más afectados por el movimiento.
>
> **MAS APOYO A LA HUELGA EN LA CIUDAD DE MEXICO**
>
> El Sindicato Nacional de Redactores de la Ciudad de México, por gestiones hechas en la capital de la República por el representante del Frente Unido de Trabajadores, de Los Angeles, tomó importantes acuerdos en favor de la huelga de los mexicanos en California, anunciando que dará toda su cooperación al Comité General Pro-Huelga que lucha aquí por el mejoramiento del trabajador mexicano.
>
> En un boletín enviado por la directiva del Frente Unido de Trabajadores establecido aquí en el 1526 al Este de la Calle Cuatro, al Comité General Pro-Huelga, al Consulado de México y a LA OPINION,

FIGURE 6. Statement of Japanese immigrants in Mexicali, June 1933. SOURCE: *La Opinión*, June 30, 1933.

The Mexicali Japanese even donated $500 (approximately $9,980 in 2020) for strikers to quell anti-Japanese sentiment in Mexico more effectively. Fukushima later reported to Tokyo that Japanese residents published the pro-strike statement and made donations under pressure from a local Mexican lawyer called Edmundo Guajardo. After Calles demonstrated his support for Mexican strikers in Los Angeles, Guajardo organized an anti-Japanese donation committee calling local

Mexicali leaders for support in fundraising and a boycott in Mexicali. According to Fukushima, on June 27, a Mexican merchant suspended his business with Japanese merchants in concert with the anti-Japanese campaign in Mexicali.[80] Throughout the strike in Los Angeles and its unexpected repercussion in Mexicali, Fukushima stayed well informed by Japanese immigrants in Mexicali and maintained a sympathetic attitude toward them. This close relationship was partly because Japanese immigrants in Mexico were loyal to the Japanese government that provided protection, knowing that Chinese immigrants had suffered harsh discrimination because they lacked the Chinese government's protection in Mexico.[81] In addition, President Rodríguez was known as an anti-Chinese politician through his career as the governor of Baja California Norte from 1923 to 1930, while Calles was from the state of Sonora where anti-Chinese sentiment was strong and where his son Rodolfo Elías Calles, while governor, ordered the expulsion of Chinese residents in 1931. Jason Oliver Chang argues that anti-Chinese racism was indispensable for the creation of Mexican nationality as racially *mestizo*.[82] Although the expulsion of Japanese residents did not seem to be an indispensable policy for Rodríguez as will be briefly mentioned in chapter 5, anti-Japanese sentiment certainly gave an opportunity for local and national Mexican leaders to fuel Mexican nationalism on both sides of the US-Mexico border during the El Monte strike. Further, it was imperative for Mexicali Japanese to prevent the anti-Chinese movement from igniting racist attacks against Japanese residents.

On the other hand, some Mexicans criticized the anti-Japanese campaigns. Before the publication of the pro-strike statement, a newspaper circulated in Tijuana, *El Hispano-Americano*, ran an editorial questioning the anti-Japanese boycott in Mexico. It asked, "What responsibility corresponds to the Japanese rooted in Mexico, who had nothing in common with the Japanese farmers of California other than their nationality and had not intervened in the conflict between Mexican pickers and *patrones amarillos* [yellow employers] in the said state?" Anti-Japanese sentiment was not strong in Tijuana, presumably because the city lacked much of a Japanese population. This editorial did little to decrease the anti-Japanese pressure in Mexicali, ninety miles east of Tijuana.[83]

Mexicali Japanese cotton farmers were also a middleman minority in Mexicali who leased lands from an American company and hired Mexican workers. What is significant about their actions during the El Monte strike is that they revealed the inability of their middleman-minority position in Mexicali to maintain transborder ethnic solidarity, when their economic interests contradicted those of their co-ethnics in the north. As an Asian minority among the Mexican majority, the Mexicali Japanese faced growing anti-Japanese sentiment backed by rising Mexican nationalism and antipathy toward Japanese expansion in Asia during the 1930s. Anti-Japanese Mexican nationalism fueled by the El Monte strike made the socioeconomic position of the Japanese in Mexicali even more precarious and urged them to break their ethnic solidarity with the compatriots in Los Angeles, if only briefly. In such an unexpected way, Mexicali Japanese played a role in heightening the interethnic tension in Los Angeles by taking an extremely pro-Mexican stance despite their commonalities in race, class, and nationality.

Los Angeles Japanese did not publicly discuss the pro-strike actions by the Mexicali Japanese as a major problem. During the strike, in contrast with *La Opinión*, the *Rafu Shimpo* did not openly discuss the pro-strike statement and donations made by Japanese immigrants in Mexicali. Instead, the *Rafu Shimpo*'s correspondent in Mexicali emphasized the difficulty that fellow Japanese immigrants were facing there. It reported that Japanese immigrant leaders in Mexicali visited the local Mexican chamber of commerce to declare that they had nothing to do with the El Monte strike and to ask for help to stop the anti-Japanese campaign.[84] The *Kashu Mainichi* did not discuss the statement and donation in its major Japanese-language sections, but shortly mentioned, "the strike problem of Mexican workers in Japanese farms has come to influence not only [Japanese in] Southern California, but also Japanese in the state of Arizona and even Mexico." The *Kashu Mainichi*'s one-page English section, however, reported the anti-Japanese boycott in Mexicali and mentioned, if briefly, the Mexicali Japanese statement that had appeared on *La Opinión*, as it wrote "*La Opinión* carries telegrams from Japanese residing in Baja California, Mexico, protesting the actions of Japanese berry growers to the Mexican authorities. It seems that there was an old wheeze about 'self-preservation being the first law of nature.'" Even this English article intended for Nisei readers did not reveal the details of the stringent situation faced by the Mexicali Japanese community due to the El Monte strike.[85]

Ordinary Japanese immigrants in Los Angeles were unlikely to know the details of anti-Japanese actions such as boycott and fundraising campaigns in Mexicali since the *Rafu Shimpo* and *Kashu Mainichi*, their major information sources, did not report on them or, if anything, mentioned them only briefly, although immigrant leaders might have known them through their connections with the Japanese consulate in Los Angeles and immigrants in Mexicali. Nor did Japanese diplomatic correspondence report any case of the anti-Japanese actions in Mexicali being publicly discussed and problematized in the ethnic Japanese community in Los Angeles. The absence of public discussion about the controversial actions by Mexicali Japanese implies that such actions were too disturbing for the Los Angeles Japanese community when the strike was an ongoing problem. Meanwhile, Japanese farmers in Los Angeles maintained their uncompromising stance, which could only exacerbate the situation of Mexicali Japanese. In short, each ethnic Japanese community in the borderlands attempted to secure their respective socioeconomic position as a middleman minority even at the cost of transborder ethnic solidarity, revealing the situational and fluid nature of ethno-racial relations in the borderlands context.

By the end of June, 1933, anti-Japanese sentiment, first generated in El Monte, traveled across the US-Mexico border and resulted in the interethnic tension between Japanese and Mexican residents in Mexicali. We could understand anti-Japanese sentiment found in both Southern California and Mexico as an important aspect of hemispheric Asian American history, a framework that historian Erika Lee applies to anti-Chinese sentiment in the Western Hemisphere.[86] Yet, we can better understand the expansion of anti-Japanese sentiment generated by the El Monte strike as a historical process that contributed to the making of transpacific borderlands because anti-Japanese sentiment in the US-Mexico borderlands forced the Japanese government to handle the volatile situation through its transpacific diplomatic network. As demonstrated in their frequent diplomatic exchanges, Japanese government officials in Japan, Mexico, and the United States could no longer ignore anti-Japanese sentiment circulating in the US-Mexico borderlands, since it could result in further restriction on the land use by Japanese farmers and in larger criticism against Japanese expansion in Asia.

THE SETTLEMENT OF THE STRIKE AND UNSOLVED PROBLEMS IN TRIRACIAL LOS ANGELES AGRICULTURE

While Japanese diplomats were increasingly concerned about the impact of anti-Japanese sentiment spreading in the US-Mexico borderlands, the situation remained precarious. On July 2, Hori, the minister of the Japanese Legation stationed in Mexico City, reported to both Uchida in Tokyo and Satō in Los Angeles that there was a rumor that Chinese residents in California were providing financial support for Mexican strikers and making contact with local newspapers in Mexico to turn anti-Chinese sentiment into anti-Japanese sentiment.[87] Although both Hori and Japanese merchants in Mexico believed the rumor to be false, Japanese diplomats in the US-Mexico borderlands still paid careful attention to the situation, since ethnic Chinese in the United States were protesting strongly against Japan's aggression in China.[88] Japanese farmers had not wavered in their stance toward Mexican strikers in Los Angeles, but without an agreement, the strikes could continue year after year, which neither party wanted. The remaining question was whether Los Angeles Japanese would understand the nature of the strike as a problem that would hurt not only local Japanese-Mexican relations but also international relations involving Japan, Mexico, and the United States. This trinational situation was something that urged Los Angeles Japanese farmers to find a way to defy, if only slightly, the existing racial and class boundaries in order to solve the strike.

After the failure of the first round of negotiations in late June, Thomas Barker, the chief of the Division of Labor Statistics and Law Enforcement of the California State government, was in charge of mediating a settlement by the order of

Governor Rolph. On July 3, with the assistance of Barker, the Japanese and Mexican consuls held a meeting to discuss a solution with the representatives of both Japanese farmers and Mexican farmworkers. Willing to settle the strike, the farmworkers' representatives made a compromise and demanded twenty-five cents an hour, ten cents lower than the initial demand. Japanese farmers maintained that they could not pay more than seventeen cents an hour due to the decline in crop prices. Attempting to broker concessions from both sides, Barker proposed twenty cents an hour until August 15. Although the Mexican side finally agreed to Barker's proposal, the Japanese refused the compromise.[89]

Two days later, Satō, feeling a responsibility to persuade Japanese farmers to reconsider, summoned the leaders of farm communities to the consulate building. At this meeting, Satō explained to them that the strike had become an international problem, generating serious anti-Japanese sentiment in the northern part of Mexico, increasing the possibility of a boycott against Japanese merchants in Mexico City, and giving Chinese residents in Mexico a chance to direct anti-Chinese sentiment against the Japanese. Then he urged Japanese farmers to make an agreement or else they would need to bear responsibility for the ongoing international conflicts. Responding to Satō, the farmers decided to end the strike for the moment, by agreeing to increase wages to 17.5 cents, a mere half-cent higher than their previous deal. While not totally convinced about the settlement and still concerned about their difficult economic situation, the Los Angeles Japanese finally came to understand the nature of the El Monte strike as a serious international problem that went beyond a local conflict and that could affect diplomatic relations involving three Pacific Rim nations.[90]

The next day, July 6, the Japanese side again met with their Mexican counterparts. Like the previous meeting, state government officials such as Barker attended in order to mediate the negotiation. After several hours of deliberation, both sides finally reached a deal that consisted of three agreements. First, Mexicans working a minimum of six nine-hour days per week would be compensated $1.50 a day and twenty cents an hour for overtime. Second, temporary farmworkers working less than six days a week would receive a flat rate of twenty cents an hour. Third, the Japanese had to re-employ the strikers without discrimination. The deal, effective immediately, was applicable until August 15 when both sides would discuss an extension if it was deemed necessary. The agreement did not specify names of crops so that it seemed to apply to all farmworkers working under Japanese farmers. It was signed by the representatives of Japanese farmers such as Fukami and Katsuma Mukaeda (respectively general secretary and president of the Central Japanese Association of Southern California) and those of Mexican farmworkers such as Flores (general secretary of the UCOM) and Manuel González (representative of San Gabriel Valley Mexican workers), and witnessed by Japanese consul Satō, Mexican consul Martínez, and approved by chief Barker.[91]

After this final agreement, Barker commented to the *Los Angeles Times*, "neither workers nor growers are satisfied with the agreement made.... If the conditions of the workers and growers in this important industry are to be improved materially, there must be a decided increase in commodity prices [so that producers would gain more and pay more to farmworkers]." He gave a relatively fair observation of the settlement, although he did not touch upon the responsibility of white landowners for the interethnic conflict and the fact that the Japanese buffered between landowners and strikers. His comment appeared at the bottom of page seventeen, where few would read it. This placement shows the *Los Angeles Times*' anti-union stance and provides a strong contrast to the significant and substantial article on the settlement that appeared in *La Opinión*.[92]

Interestingly, although strikers gained far less than their initial demand of thirty-five cents an hour, *La Opinión* celebrated the agreement as a victory for Mexican farmworkers, devoting three pages, including the front page, to the labor agreement. It emphasized the contribution of the Mexican government and particularly Calles to their alleged victory, obscuring the fact that farmworkers actually gained little. The newspaper claimed that farmworkers succeeded in making Japanese farmers accept the major part of their demands. Although the deal was not a complete victory for the Mexican side in terms of wages, it was significant that the Japanese farmers had to make their compromise as part of a tri-national negotiation, not as a mere local agreement they could easily ignore. Furthermore, in his comments to *La Opinión*, Flores emphasized that one of the largest triumphs of the agreement was that the Japanese would not employ Mexicans who had served as strikebreakers, which the official document of the agreement did not clearly mention.[93] In fact, Japanese farmers did not need many Mexicans after the harvest season and continued to employ their compatriots and other non-Mexican workers who helped them during the strike.[94] In the consular report, Mexican consul Martínez did not emphasize the final agreement as a victory, but appreciated Governor Rolph for his intervention and Barker and his colleague for their "impartial behavior."[95]

From the viewpoint of the Japanese side, the agreement was quite similar to the proposal offered by the Japanese farmers, since $1.50 a day for nine hours of work was equivalent to 16.6 cents an hour. Even if farmworkers worked overtime, their average wages would be about seventeen cents an hour. On July 18, Satō reported to Tokyo, writing that the agreement had "almost no impact" upon Japanese farmers and that they were satisfied with the result because it did not amount to much of a change.[96] In addition, the strike strengthened solidarity among the Japanese farmers and helped them understand the importance of ethnic associations.[97] The *Rafu Shimpo* also emphasized that in fact Japanese farmers had to pay 16.6 cents an hour by the final agreement and regarded the deal as "favorable for fellow farmers."[98] The *Kashu Mainichi*'s publisher Sei Fujii posted an English commentary on the final agreement. Fujii praised both Japanese and Mexican parties for achieving "a friendly settlement," yet hoped that Mexicans would understand that Sato and Mukaeda "uttered not a single word hurting the Mexican people or their country. Their attitude was that of sympathetic friends considering the best interest of all the parties concerned." On the other hand, since the *Kashu Mainichi*, particularly Fujii himself, took a more understanding attitude toward Mexican strikers, he implicitly criticized *La Opinión* and its rival paper the *Rafu Shimpo*, stating that, "some pretty strong articles had appeared on some of the daily newspapers due to their over-zealousness to uphold the side of their own people. . . . The newspapers could render more valuable and prais[e]worthy services in a case of this kind by taking a stand of a disinterested arbitrator and by temporarily withholding criticism."[99]

However, their ethnic community also faced the problem of how to understand the anti-Japanese actions taken by Japanese residents in Mexicali, which seemed to divide the bonds of the overseas Japanese population in the US-Mexico borderlands. One week after the final agreement, two leaders of the Japanese Association of Mexicali came over to Los Angeles to explain their struggle during the strike. Visiting the Japanese consulate, the Central Japanese Association of Southern California, and the *Rafu Shimpo*'s head office, they described their "delicate position" in Mexicali: "We did not want to take any action that would hurt your feelings since we owe a lot to the fellow Japanese in Southern California. However, we could not help but take that attitude, being stuck in a difficult situation and facing the dilemma."[100] By a "dilemma" they referred to their relationship with the Japanese in Los Angeles on the one hand and anti-Japanese sentiment in Mexico on the other hand.

The apology of Mexicali Japanese tells us that their cooperation in the Mexican nationalist campaign during the strike was not sincere but rather strategic, but this does not mean that Los Angeles Japanese were able to discuss openly what was happening in Mexicali during the strike. Even after the Mexicali Japanese came to apologize, the *Rafu Shimpo* only vaguely reported, "the fellow Japanese in that region [Mexicali] took an action that somewhat hurt the feelings of the Japanese in Southern California" without clearly explaining their pro-labor statement or their donation for Mexican strikers.[101] In short, the chasm between Los Angeles Japanese and Mexicali Japanese during the strike was temporary but serious.

The Japanese consul Satō, in his summary report about the strike submitted to Tokyo in mid-July, blamed the local Mexican labor union for "threatening and coercing" Japanese residents in Mexicali to support the strikers. While criticizing the Mexican side, he paid little attention to the fact that poor working conditions of Mexican farmworkers in Japanese farms in Los Angeles caused anti-Japanese sentiment in Mexicali in the first place. Probably, Satō's one-sided judgment about the actions of Mexicali Japanese came from his nationalism as well as skepticism about the triangular relationship between the strike leader Flores, the Mexican

> La Sociedad Japonesa de Ensenada, lamenta el conflicto existente entre trabajadores mexicanos y japoneses en Los Angeles, Cal.
>
> La Sociedad Japonesa de esta Municipalidad, nos hizo ayer, para su publicación, las siguientes declaraciones:
>
> "Que han estado enterándose con interés por medio "de la prensa sobre el conflicto huelguístico que llevaron "a cabo los trabajadores mexicanos en contra de los agri- "cultores capitalistas japoneses, en el Condado de Los "Angeles, California."
>
> "Que felizmente y a última hora se ha sabido que "entre ambas partes han llegado a un buen entendimien- "to."
>
> "Que desean sinceramente que ésto se confirme para "que dicho movimiento concluya pronto y satisfactoria- "mente, a fin de que la amistad franca y leal que desde "tiempo inmemorial ha existido entre mexicanos y japo- "neses, no vaya a resentirse."

FIGURE 7. Statement of Japanese immigrants in Ensenada, July 1933. SOURCE: *El Faro*, July 8, 1933.

consul Martínez, and the former president Calles. In other words, Satō's report left the impression that Japanese subjects in the United States and Mexico maintained their transborder ethnic solidarity.[102]

The borderlands situation was, however, not that simple. Two days after the final agreement, Japanese immigrants in Ensenada, Baja California, posted a statement on a local newspaper, *El Faro*, showing their lament over the Japanese-Mexican conflict in Los Angeles. They wrote, "We sincerely desire that this [final agreement] will be confirmed and thus the said [labor] movement will conclude soon and satisfactorily, so that the frank and faithful friendship that has existed since time immemorial between Mexicans and Japanese will not deteriorate." At the same time, although the El Monte strike did not affect the Ensenada Japanese directly, their statement shows that they were also under the pressure of Mexican nationalism growing in Baja California, since they described Los Angeles Japanese farmers as "Japanese agricultural capitalists" in tune with Mexican strikers' perspective (Figure 7).[103]

Meanwhile, Fukushima, the Japanese diplomat stationed in Tijuana, had an uneasy feeling about what happened to the Mexicali Japanese since he had been observing their situation closely. Fukushima also sent a ten-page summary report to Tokyo and explained: "I think that the stringent situation in Mexicali forced the Japanese residents to take such difficult actions. But it is not desirable for Japan's overseas subjects to get extremely upset and overlook negative consequences of their myopic and desperate behavior [in supporting Mexican workers]. If they do, it will be difficult [for them] to make sound progress and development as a *daikokumin* [member of the great nation], which I would deeply deplore. Thus, I gave cautions to the leaders of the Japanese Association [of Mexicali]."[104]

The report shows Fukushima's sympathy to Japanese residents in Mexicali who found themselves torn between the politics of Southern California and Baja California. However, this ended up with a nationalistic conclusion that Japanese should act as a *daikokumin*, while the same time ignoring the structural causes of the strike rooted in the triracial hierarchy in Los Angeles agriculture. When Mexican nationalism divided Japanese ethnic solidarity in the borderlands, Fukushima could only appeal to Japanese nationalism to prevent such an unexpected situation from happening again in the future.

Four years after the strike, however, the Mexicali Japanese community would face a much more difficult situation that devastated their agriculture and livelihood. During the presidency of Lázaro Cárdenas, Mexican nationalism swept across the country and expelled many Japanese farmers from their cotton farms due to the development of the *agrarista* movement for agrarian reform. In 1937, Cárdenas promoted radical land reform that would divide large-scale farmlands into small parcels called *ejidos* and distribute the lands to Mexican citizens, in the belief that the *ejido* was fundamental for the country's economic progress. This policy reflected an agrarian ideal ingrained in the Mexican Revolution, although it benefited Mexican farmers unevenly by allocating more resources to the northern part than the southern and central parts of the country. The land reform affected the Japanese community because it forcibly divided the land owned by the Colorado River Land Company that leased lands to the Japanese cotton farmers in Mexicali. In the late 1930s, there were more than twenty large farms cultivated by the Japanese in Mexicali. For example, a ranch worked mainly by the Katagiri brothers had two tractors and hired two hundred Mexican pickers. The *agrarista* movement confiscated approximately six thousand acres from Japanese farmers, one sixth of the total Japanese cotton farmland, forcing many to give up farming, switch to commercial business, leave for other places to continue cotton farming, or even return to Japan. Nevertheless, the majority of former Japanese lands distributed as *ejidos* remained unplanted because the Mexican government left unskilled Mexican farmers without providing them with enough farming knowledge and tools. Although Mexicali Japanese were still able to lease land, the *agrarista* movement led to an unforgettable tragedy, which would soon be overwhelmed by an even larger tragedy during the Pacific War.[105]

After all, the economic structure of Los Angeles agriculture did not change, preserving the intermediate position of Japanese tenant farmers between white landowners and Mexican farmworkers. Over the course of the El Monte strike, the Japanese and Mexican governments played a direct role in the interethnic conflict for the sake of themselves, drawing a clear line between the Japanese and Mexican sides. Although Japanese farmers faced anti-Japanese laws and had economic difficulties during the Depression, they thrived in the 1930s in collaboration with white landowners.[106] Life was not easy for the Japanese farmers, in that they, like Mexicans, were under residential and occupational discrimination, but their economic position was an integral component of the white agribusiness of Los Angeles, supported by landowners, business leaders, and government officials. Four years later, Clements, the manager of the Chamber's Agricultural Department, commented that the Chamber had "done a good deal of work for the Japanese in order to save ourselves."[107]

Nevertheless, Clements's comments did not fully represent the attitude of the Chamber of Commerce regarding the Japanese-Mexican conflict in 1933. A month after the final agreement of the strike, the assistant secretary of the Chamber of Commerce, F. L. S. Harman, sent a letter to Clements, writing, "I realize that much of the work to be done in this section [agriculture] can best be done by Mexican and Japanese labor, but if we are going to be continually hounded by these foreigners and held up by strikes, it is about time we threw them all out of the country. . . . Personally, I am not very much in sympathy with playing much with either the Mexicans or the Japanese."[108] Harman's comment reveals the vulnerable position of both Japanese and Mexican residents, whom the dominant white society perceived and treated as dispensable foreigners despite the fact that they were indispensable to Los Angeles agriculture. This proves Satō's concern that the strike, although launched at the local level, could generate a larger problem that would affect international relations and the entire Japanese communities in the US-Mexico borderlands.

Witnessing the surge of strikes including the El Monte strike in 1933, California white farmers became increasingly concerned and fearful about the agricultural labor movement. In the following year, they organized the Associated Farmers of California, an anti-labor organization. California business leaders were behind the foundation of the Associated Farmers, which secretly received funds from organizations such as the California Packing Corporation, the Southern Pacific Railroad, the Santa Fe Railroad, the Industrial Association of San Francisco, and so forth. After the turbulent year of 1933, California agriculture was destined to witness more conflicts between better organized anti-labor agribusiness and more strongly motivated farmworkers in the era of the New Deal.[109]

The El Monte strike of 1933 evolved from a local Japanese-Mexican conflict into an international problem in which anti-Japanese sentiment traveled across the US-Mexico border, merged with Mexican nationalism, and forced Japanese residents in Mexicali to issue an unexpected pro-strike statement against their fellow Japanese in Los Angeles. This event drew the closer attention and involvement of both Japanese and Mexican governments through their consulate networks in Japan, Mexico, and the United States, strengthening the character of the US-Mexico borderlands as transpacific borderlands in which the triracial hierarchy of Los Angeles agriculture intersected with international relations of three Pacific Rim countries. In this context, the transborder anti-Japanese sentiment trumped Japanese ethnic solidarity across the border and thereby made Japanese diplomats and farmers in Los Angeles understand the international dimension of their local conflict and the necessity for the settlement. Japanese immigrants in Mexico faced pressures of Mexican nationalism in the guise of anti-Japanese sentiment and thus chose to identify publicly with Mexican nationalists rather than co-ethnics in the north despite their commonalities in race, class, and nationality. In other words, while the racial, class, and national boundaries were intensified by the El Monte strike in the local context of Los Angeles agriculture, these boundaries proved to be quite fluid and unstable in the transnational context of the US-Mexico borderlands as shown in the pro-Mexican support of Mexicali Japanese and its influence on the settlement of the strike.

After the settlement of the El Monte strike, the problems of poor labor conditions among Mexican farmworkers existed untouched. At the same time, anti-Japanese sentiment remained in the US-Mexico borderlands, as imperial Japan continued its expansionist policy in East Asia. Los Angeles was on the path to another large-scale strike by Mexican farmworkers in 1936 against the Japanese: the Venice Celery Strike of 1936. The next chapter will examine the Venice strike by focusing more on internal divides within the respective Japanese and Mexican communities in Los Angeles County and Japanese-Mexican interethnic alliances born out of such internal divides. This is another story of the *transpacific workplace* and its possibility of nurturing mutual understanding beyond racial and class differences.

4

Ethnic Solidarity or Interethnic Accommodation

The 1936 Venice Celery Strike

The El Monte Berry Strike of 1933 did not improve the working and living conditions of Mexicans hired by Japanese tenant farmers, although it did have local and international repercussions in the transpacific US-Mexico borderlands. Its international repercussions functioned to fuel nationalism in the respective ethnic communities, which ironically set aside the plight of Mexican farmworkers. The economic depression continued well into the mid-1930s keeping the lives of ethnic Mexicans difficult and giving them reasons to claim their rights as workers. In April of 1936, Mexican workers decided to go on another large-scale strike against Japanese farmers in Venice in Los Angeles County, which would be later remembered as the Venice Celery Strike.

The Venice strike was very different from the El Monte strike. In contrast to the El Monte strike that evolved into an international conflict in which the Japanese consulate worked closely with Japanese farmers, the Venice strike essentially developed as a local problem. Japanese farmers created a new organization to fight sternly against Mexican strikers, and the Japanese consulate let them handle the strike without actively taking part in it. The Venice strike, however, became a significant stage in which some Issei leaders came to accept a new regime of American business and labor norms of the New Deal period that was more sensitive to interethnic harmony. In 1935, a year before the Venice strike took place, the US government enacted the National Labor Relations Act or Wagner Act that recognized workers' rights to organize into trade unions and engage in collective bargaining. Although this New Deal law did not cover agricultural workers, it empowered the whole labor movement from the mid-1930s, and farmworkers began to increasingly demand labor recognition.

Historian Yuko Matsumoto has explored the Venice strike from the perspective of the ethnic Japanese farming community by analyzing mainly two ethnic Japanese newspapers, the *Rafu Shimpo* and the *Kashu Mainichi*. She points out that the class hierarchy and tension within the ethnic Japanese community surfaced during the Venice strike but that the strike did not result in the formation of class consciousness beyond ethnic differences between Japanese and Mexicans in Los Angeles.[1] But a further analysis of the strike based on diplomatic and Spanish-language sources, in addition to ethnic Japanese newspapers, shows us that the Japanese-Mexican relationships during the strike were much more complicated. The Venice strike was not simply an episode about the failure to form an interethnic class consciousness but rather about the development of interethnic understanding beyond both racial and class differences, which this chapter will highlight.

The dramatic change of the American political atmosphere symbolized by the Wagner Act affected how the Venice strike developed, resulting in internal divides among Japanese tenant farmers and complicating the triracial hierarchy of Los Angeles agriculture. In the El Monte strike of 1933, a division in the ethnic Japanese community appeared at the international level between Los Angeles Japanese and Mexicali Japanese who faced Mexican nationalism and anti-Japanese sentiment fueled by Mexican politicians such as Calles. In the Venice strike of 1936, a different division appeared at the local level within Los Angeles County. Anti-labor farmers, representing the mainstream Japanese community, vehemently opposed union recognition and stressed the importance of ethnic Japanese solidarity within the framework of the triracial hierarchy. On the other hand, pro-labor Japanese farmers entered the stage and understood the importance of union recognition and the need for interethnic cooperation with ethnic Mexican residents, a move that challenged the existing power structure of the triracial hierarchy in Los Angeles agriculture.

By exploring the understudied Venice Celery Strike, this chapter examines how the Japanese-Mexican interethnic conflict in Los Angeles farmland forced Japanese immigrants to reconsider their position in the multiethnic society and created unexpected Japanese-Mexican alliances in both anti-labor and pro-labor camps. This is augmented through documenting the internal divides of the ethnic Mexican community. Although Japanese farmers could eventually get through the strike without recognizing the Mexican labor union, the Venice strike demonstrates an aspect of the *transpacific workplace* that unsettled the racial and class boundaries, prompting efforts of mutual understanding from the Japanese side and forcing them to choose between ethnic solidarity and interethnic accommodation. More importantly, the Venice strike shows us that Japanese immigrant nationalism served as a basis of their understanding of interethnic accommodation with both white Americans and Mexicans, rather than simply incorporating the white supremacist view on other nonwhite groups such as ethnic Mexicans.[2]

UNION RECOGNITION AS A HOPE OR A THREAT: ENTERING A NEW PHASE OF THE JAPANESE-MEXICAN CONFLICT

In the mid-1910s, a few Japanese farmers moved into the Venice area, a Pacific Coast region of Los Angeles County, and began to grow sugar beets and celery. They developed a productive way to grow celery in a glasshouse and transplant them to the field. This made it possible for Japanese farmers to harvest celery earlier than usual and become major celery producers in the United States. By the 1920s, an ethnic Japanese farming community had fully developed in the Venice area, selling their produce in Los Angeles and shipping it to the East Coast. In the mid-1930s, about 146 ethnic Japanese families, or 5 percent of all 2,895 Japanese farming families in Southern California, were growing celery in Venice.[3] The Venice area was also a *transpacific workplace* where Japanese farmers relied on Mexican workers for harvesting crops.

As early as July 1935, Mexican farmworkers in Los Angeles County began to demand from Japanese farmers an increase in wages and other improvements in their working conditions. But Japanese farmers were not willing to agree with Mexican workers, arguing that the economic situation had not been improved due to the depression. As the Mexican consulate in Los Angeles reported to the Mexican Ministry of Foreign Affairs, Mexican workers wanted to have "talks with the Japanese in the presence of the 'Regional Labor Board' to try to sign a more favorable agreement." Although the Wagner Act was not designed to protect the labor rights of agricultural workers, the enactment of the Wagner Act and the presence of the Regional Labor Board encouraged the Mexican labor movement vis-a-vis Japanese farmers.[4] Even before the enactment of the Wagner Act, there were expectations among officials of New Deal organizations such as the National Recovery Administration that labor rights of farmworkers should be protected like those of industrial workers.[5] Since the Japanese continued to refuse negotiations with their Mexican counterpart, on April 17, 1936, three hundred Mexican celery workers went on a strike against Japanese farmers in the Venice area. Mexican strikers demanded that Japanese farmers accept three conditions: (1) Workers in Japanese farms should be composed of more than 90 percent members of labor unions; (2) Japanese farmers should increase wages from twenty-two cents (approximately $4.11 in 2020) to thirty-five cents an hour for relatively easy work and forty cents an hour for more demanding work such as picking celery. In addition, wages for overtime work should increase by 50 percent; (3) Japanese farmers should pay male and female workers equally. Japanese farmers immediately rejected their demands and showed strong opposition against union recognition and the idea of setting up a percentage of union workers in their farms. They believed that union recognition could devastate Japanese agriculture and thus the

Venice strike was a "scheme of red elements" to take control of Japanese agricultural business.⁶

A Mexican labor union, la Confederación de Uniones de Campesinos y Obreros Mexicanos (CUCOM), took charge of organizing Mexican strikers in the Venice strike. The CUCOM was established right after the El Monte strike of 1933 in order to continue the Mexican labor movement in Los Angeles and other areas in Southern California. The leader was Guillermo (William) Velarde, who served as the undersecretary of the Mexican union, la Unión de Campesinos y Obreros Mexicanos (UCOM), which organized Mexican workers during the El Monte strike. When the El Monte strike ended without substantial gains for Mexican workers, Velarde remained frustrated about the compromising stance of the Mexican consulate and the union secretary Armando Flores. Three years after the El Monte strike, the Venice strike gave an opportunity for Velarde to become a strike leader and seek revenge against the Los Angeles agribusiness establishment in which white landowners and Japanese farmers were allied. Velarde organized the Venice strike not simply as a Mexican campaign but as a multiethnic one; from the beginning, the strike included support from Japanese, Filipino, and white American labor activists. One non-Mexican activist was Lillian Monroe, a well-known labor organizer and former Communist, whose presence particularly alarmed Japanese farmers.⁷

The Venice strike rapidly expanded to other areas of Los Angeles County such as San Pedro, Wilmington, Dominguez Hills, Artesia, El Monte, Belvedere, and the San Fernando Valley. On April 19, a delegation of strike leaders, mostly Mexicans, visited the office of *La Opinión* and criticized the Japanese celery farmers for not having "the least desire to improve our situation." The delegation consisted of multiethnic members including Velarde as the Mexican leader and a Japanese leader named Kōken Ishida, who was in charge of negotiating with Japanese farmers on behalf of Mexican workers. On the other hand, they strongly denied their cooperation with Monroe, despite her actual involvement in the strike. As was the case in the El Monte strike, strike leaders wanted to avoid anti-Communist criticism from both Japanese and Mexican communities, explaining, "We want to deny the story that Lillian Monroe, described by the police as a Communist leader, is leading our movement."⁸

Japanese farmers had been on alert against Mexican strikes since unionizing efforts became increasingly active in California in the mid-1930s because of the enactment of the Wagner Act. To prevent strikes against Japanese farmers, they founded the Southern California Farm Federation (Nanka Nōkai Renmei, hereafter Nōkai Renmei) as a member of the Associated Farmers of Los Angeles County, an anti-labor organization of farmers established in late March of 1936. Nōkai Renmei set up their office on San Pedro Street in Little Tokyo, in downtown Los Angeles, and about sixteen hundred Japanese farmers joined the organization.

The Nōkai Renmei leadership started up with ten Japanese immigrant leaders and one Nisei. Shin'ichi Katō, the manager of Nōkai Renmei, became responsible for leading Japanese farmers and negotiating with Mexican strikers.[9] The establishment of Nōkai Renmei was a sign of strong ties between Japanese and whites in local agriculture, since their parent organization, the Associated Farmers of Los Angeles County, consisted mostly of white farmers and business officials including George Pigeon Clements, the manager of the Agricultural Department of the Los Angeles Chamber of Commerce.[10] When the CUCOM first demanded that Japanese farmers should hire union members in late March of 1936, Nōkai Renmei held a meeting and reaffirmed their uncompromising stance against labor unions. They considered that the Venice strike was particularly dangerous because this strike gave the highest priority to union recognition unlike previous strikes that simply demanded pay increase. Nōkai Renmei leaders understood that "unions serve as a castle wall to defend workers from the abuse of capitalists" but they stressed that Japanese farmers were not capitalists because "only 20 or 30 percent of the entire Japanese farming population might belong to the capitalist class but the remaining 70 or 80 percent must be regarded as workers" who could make ends meet only by making their family members work in the field. They feared that unionizing efforts could take power from Japanese farmers in controlling wages and eventually result in the "demise of our business." Since losing their agricultural business seemed nearly identical to losing their ethnic community itself, the Japanese-Mexican conflict in 1936 appeared to Japanese farmers almost as an existential emergency.[11]

The Los Angeles Chamber of Commerce paid close attention to the development of the strike. As in the El Monte strike, the Chamber of Commerce was firmly supportive toward Japanese farmers, an integral part of white agribusiness in Southern California. As early as in March 1936, Nōkai Renmei appealed to the Chamber of Commerce that the CUCOM was preventing farmworkers from picking celery in Japanese farms and working with other unions such as the Japanese Farm Workers Union of California (JFWUC), the Agricultural Industrial Workers Union of America (AIWUA), and the Filipino Federated Workers Union (FFWU). Nōkai Renmei also reported the names of individuals leading these unions such as Velarde and Juan C. Avila of CUCOM, Masato Deguchi of JFWUC, Lillian Monroe of AIWUA, and C. D. Monsalves of FFWU.[12]

Within a week after the outbreak of the strike, a violent incident took place in Venice. On April 24, strikers, mostly Mexicans, came to prevent other Mexicans and Filipinos from working in a celery farm owned by a Japanese farmer Kazuo Nishi. The *Rafu Shimpo* reported that strikers threatened workers with knives so that the local police authority quickly arrived at the scene and used tear gas bombs against strikers.[13] While the *Rafu Shimpo* emphasized the violence committed by strikers, *La Opinión* reported the incident with sympathy toward Mexicans.

With a front-page headline that read "8 Mexican Strikers of Venice, Injured in a Mutiny," *La Opinión* described that a group of vigilantes "attacked workers provoking a havoc that was about to culminate into a tragedy." According to the official statement of the Los Angeles Police Department, three hundred Mexicans participated in the incident and various strikers were armed with iron tubes, stones, and sticks. Some strikers even tried to set some houses on fire. The police explained that this was why they had to use tear gas bombs to calm down the situation and added that strikers were working together with Communist activists. Strikers denied the story told by the police when interviewed by *La Opinión*. They claimed that police officers harassed strikers on behalf of Japanese farmers. Again, the CUCOM strongly denied the involvement of Communists, arguing, "What the police intends . . . is to discredit the [labor] movement, calling us Communist." Another CUCOM member Blas Piñon also told *La Opinión*, "Various workers became victims by [the attack of] vigilantes" as they urged their coworkers to abandon their work.[14]

On the same day, Nōkai Renmei held a meeting where representatives of thirty-five Japanese organizations attended and exchanged opinions with white Americans involved in Los Angeles agriculture. Japanese leaders demonstrated their concern that some strike organizers were Japanese. An elderly Issei in Lomita told the *Rafu Shimpo*, "We can't help but deplore that there are some [Japanese] radicals who make their compatriot farmers suffer."[15] They also made clear the importance of defending Venice celery farmers, because otherwise the strike could develop and expand all over the county. Therefore, they called for support from other major Japanese organizations such as the Central Japanese Association of Southern California (Nanka Chūō Nihonjin Kai), which played a major role in defending Japanese interests in the El Monte strike. Responding to the Nōkai Renmei's call for support, Japanese farmers in Los Angeles County and Orange County began to send groups of temporary workers to pick celery in Venice. These groups were called *giyūdan* (volunteer corps) and organized mainly by young Nisei in several Japanese farming communities such as San Fernando, Burbank, San Gabriel, Montebello, Norwalk, Downy, Compton, Dominguez Hills, Hawthorne, Gardena, and so forth.[16] In the El Monte strike, Nisei students helped harvest crops for their parents. Three years later in 1936, Nisei were more organized probably because the strikers' demand for union recognition posed a larger threat to the Japanese farming community and because Nisei, now three years older, had taken on more responsibility for their family farms.

The busiest season for Venice celery farmers was from late April to late May when they needed about 150 workers to harvest and export their crops to the East Coast, although the harvest itself would continue until August. The strike took place in this peak period for harvest, so that the *giyūdan* workforce played a critical role for the Venice farmers to keep operating.[17] Another likely reason

FIGURE 8. Japanese *giyūdan* workers helping harvest celery in Venice, 1936. SOURCE: *Rafu Shimpo*, April 28, 1936.

the *giyūdan* was organized during the Venice strike but not during the El Monte strike is that the former caused a more serious labor shortage.[18] On April 28, more than sixty *giyūdan* workers arrived in Venice from other areas, and on later days, the *giyūdan* continued to provide labor to Japanese celery farms in an emergency (Figure 8). What helped *giyūdan* workers enter and work at Japanese farms was the protection provided by the Los Angeles County Sheriff's Department.[19] On May 1, the Associated Farmers of Los Angeles County sent a letter to the Los Angeles Sheriff Eugene Biscailuz and praised the department for "the splendid work done by officers of your department in maintaining peace in the Venice celery area during recent disturbances fostered by radical agitators."[20] Just as seen in the El Monte strike, Mexican strikers were fighting against the whole structure of Los Angeles agribusiness operated by Japanese farmers, controlled by white agribusiness leaders, and protected by the local police authority.

Around the same period, Japanese celery farmers in Venice faced a serious trouble. A white landowner named Mesmer, who had been rather sympathetic to Mexican workers, suddenly signed a contract with the CUCOM to pay thirty cents an hour and recognize the union, so that fourteen Japanese farmers who grew celery on Mesmer's land followed the landowner to comply with the contract. For Japanese farmers squaring off with strikers, the action taken by the fourteen farmers was "a big shock" and "a betrayal." Soon after, the CUCOM began to send workers to the Mesmer ranch, while major Japanese organizations such as the Central Japanese Association of Southern California, the Los Angeles Japanese Association (Rafu Nihonjin Kai), and the Central Industrial Association of Southern California (Nanka Chūō Sangyō Kumiai) stepped in to make the fourteen Japanese farmers revoke the contract with the CUCOM. Due to intervention by the three major Japanese immigrant organizations, the fourteen farmers in the Mesmer ranch came to reach a reconciliation that would remove the influence of the CUCOM.[21]

Although *giyūdan* workers played an important role in maintaining the operation of celery farms, Venice Japanese farmers knew that they could not depend on the *giyūdan*'s help forever because other Japanese farming communities needed labor for the harvest of their own crops. Venice farmers needed to develop a new strategy to maintain a certain number of Mexican laborers in their fields. What they invented was a card registration system that would require Mexican pickers who would not participate in the strike to carry a badge corresponding to his or her member card kept by the Venice Industrial Association, an association of Japanese farmers in Venice. With this card, farmers could distinguish reliable Mexican workers from others who might be CUCOM members. It was also useful for Mexican workers since they could get a job more easily than others not registered in the system. In fact, this system functioned even better than Japanese farmers expected. By May 9, thanks to the card registration system, Venice farmers could keep enough Mexican workers to harvest the rest of the celery and thereby allow *giyūdan* workers to return to their respective communities. The effectiveness of the system even reached outside the Venice area, since Japanese and white farmers in other areas began to accept the same card system when they hired Mexican workers.[22] In a sense, Japanese farmers forged an effective immigrant-made immigration policy to control the type of foreign workers entering their farms in multiethnic Los Angeles County.

At the same time, in the larger context of labor-management conflicts in California agriculture, the Nōkai Renmei's anti-labor measure can be understood as part of the strategy adopted by the Associated Farmers. In 1934 in Contra Costa County, when farmworkers demanded an increase of wages and picketed the roads and orchards, seventy-five growers formed a local branch of the Associated Farmers and broke the strike. Strike leaders were arrested and strikers sent outside the county. After this incident, the Associated Farmers of Contra Costa County introduced a new measure to register and control farmworkers, while preparing gas bombs to use in case of an emergency. They made all migrant workers register with their central labor bureau in advance and shared information about workers with other informers in order to hire only pre-registered workers with no records of troublemaking.[23] Although the Nōkai Renmei's policy was unique in registering Mexican farmworkers with cards that could be used widely in Los Angeles County, it certainly operated within the statewide anti-labor strategy taken by the Associated Farmers against the labor movement.

Mexican strike leader Blas Piñon claimed that by April 24, five thousand workers, including Japanese and Filipino workers, had joined the strike throughout Los Angeles County. However, he probably exaggerated the number, since Japanese farmers affiliated with Nōkai Renmei usually hired from three to four thousand workers in total.[24] Nevertheless, the strike was affecting the whole Japanese farming population in Los Angeles County. One such place was El Monte in the San Gabriel Valley, the very region that saw the outbreak of Japanese-Mexican conflict three years earlier. Japanese immigrants in El Monte took the Venice strike very seriously because of their "bitter experience in the large strike" of the recent past. On May 2, 1936, when the berry harvest was at its peak, a group of twenty-seven Japanese youth in the San Gabriel Valley founded a Japanese vigilante group named Seinen Seigidan (Youth League for Justice) to protect Japanese farms from Mexican strikers. The Seinen Seigidan elected vigilante leaders to protect eight sections in the area and consulted with the Sheriff's Department about their activities. By May 8, Japanese farmers in El Monte had distributed fliers that read "No Trespassing" in English and Spanish to display at their berry farms. An editor of the *Rafu Shimpo*, Yoneo Sakai, also mentioned the El Monte strike when describing the Venice strike as a different kind of conflict because the CUCOM demanded union recognition.[25]

On May 1, Mexican consul Ricardo Hill and Edward H. Fitzgerald, an official of the US Labor Department, visited Nōkai Renmei and discussed Mexican workers' demands with Katō and other Japanese leaders. But the Japanese side was determined to reject any condition that would make them recognize unions. In fact, Hill's presence made Japanese farmers reluctant to negotiate with the Mexican side because they knew well that Hill was active in supporting Mexican strikers in the El Monte strike as the vice-consul of the time. To make clear Hill's intention in the Venice strike, on May 7, *Rafu Shimpo* reporters visited the Mexican consulate and interviewed Hill about the ongoing interethnic problem. In the interview, Hill encouraged Japanese farmers to have more constructive conversations with Mexican strikers and denied the participation of radical agitators in the CUCOM. Hill said, "First of all, I want to tell you that I worked at the Mexican Legation in Tokyo from October 1923 to June 1924, which made me favor Japan even more. I have held deep respect for Japan and its people since I was young." And he continued, "I deplore this strike in terms of Japan-Mexico friendship and strongly hope that the strike will be solved as soon as possible. But that goal will not be achieved unless the representatives of Japanese farmers meet with the representatives of Mexican workers."[26]

Although Hill publicly supported Mexican strikers at the local level, the Mexican government in Mexico City did not play a significant role in the Venice strike.

In the El Monte strike, Calles openly criticized the Japanese and funded Mexicans to gain public support for the Mexican government under his influence. Unlike Calles, Lázaro Cárdenas who assumed the presidency in 1934 did not need to take advantage of the situation of Mexican workers in Los Angeles to garner public support in Mexico, most likely because he already had strong support from the Mexican working class. As a result, this time the CUCOM lacked donations from Mexico and thus needed to hold fundraising events in Los Angeles. On May 1, the CUCOM held an event celebrating May Day in downtown Los Angeles. While criticizing Japanese farmers, they called for donations from which the CUCOM would provide material support for the families of Mexican strikers. *La Opinión* also explained the lack of financial sources for Mexican strikers. The immigrant press wrote, "During the past movement [in the El Monte strike] General Plutarco Elías Calles who then lived in El Sauzal, Baja California, contributed a large sum that reached several thousands of dollars" to support Mexican strikers. But the CUCOM "is in a grave situation since economic resources are exhausted" due to the lack of donations.[27]

Since the Mexican government in Mexico City did not intend to make the Venice strike an international problem, the Japanese consulate opted to remain silent and wait for the conflict to end with time. However, the lack of the Japanese government's involvement did not mean that the Venice strike was less complicated and easier to solve than was the El Monte strike. It was in fact more difficult to resolve because the social climate for the labor movement in the United States was very different before and after 1935. The Venice strike took place after 1935, the year when the US government enacted the Wagner Act. As mentioned earlier, the law excluded agricultural workers from its protection. In fact, a Los Angeles local office of the National Labor Relations Board (NLRB) commented on the Venice strike in their internal report, writing, "We are taking no part in this controversy."[28] Yet the changing social mood for the labor movement surely helped agricultural workers put priority on making their employers recognize unions. In fact, some Japanese farmers in Southern California had already succumbed to the pressure of Mexican union workers before the Venice strike took place. For example, in August of 1935, Japanese farmers in the San Diego area signed a contract with a Mexican union called the Union of Laborers and Field Workers. They agreed that "at least sixty (60%) percent of all field workers employed and working at any one time shall be members of The Union of Laborers and Field Workers" and that Japanese farmers preserved the right to fire unsatisfactory union workers but "any vacancy created by such discharge shall be filled only by members of the Union [of] Laborers and Field Workers." This agreement was made by Japanese leaders I. Kawashima and Eyno Kawamura and Mexican leaders Martín Omendaiz, J. C. Espinoza, Miguel Delgado, Juan D. Gonzáles, and Antonio Del Buono.[29] In addition, when the Wagner Act was enacted, the Mexican consulate in Los Angeles reported about it in relation to the conflicts between Mexican farmworkers and Japanese farmers in Southern California. They wrote, "The project of the Wagner Act was finally approved by the US Congress and signed by President Roosevelt. This law, as it has already been informed, regulate[s] the relations between workers and industry people" and "[Mexican] farmworkers in Los Angeles County [were] demanding an increase of wages and other improvements in working conditions."[30] Given that Mexican strikers had successfully negotiated with Japanese farmers in San Diego, it is understandable that Venice strikers hoped and insisted that Japanese operators should hire union Mexican workers.

Meanwhile, in Los Angeles County, Japanese labor activists, who did not play a major role in the El Monte strike, demonstrated their support for Mexicans in the Venice strike. In early May of 1936, they distributed fliers written in Japanese to criticize Japanese farmers in Venice and urge the ethnic Japanese community to support Mexican workers. They denounced Katō as a *haori goro* (well-dressed bully) who "intends to harm the relationship between farmers and workers and works hard to leave celery to rot in the Venice area" and asserted that if ethnic Japanese residents did not cooperate with strikers, "it will darken the future of the whole Japanese community living abroad [outside Japan]."[31] On May 2, Kōken Ishida, the chairman of the Japanese Farm Workers Union of California, visited the *Rafu Shimpo* headquarters to explain why he was supporting Mexican strikers as a labor activist. He said, "First of all, Japanese farmers wrongly believe that a few Japanese Communists are playing a central role in this strike and radicals were involved. But there are only three Japanese who work at the strikers' headquarters, me and two other secretaries of the Japanese Farm Workers Union of California, Deguchi and Ōi. We are neither reds nor radicals."[32] Ishida had lived in the United States for seventeen years and worked mostly in agriculture. Interestingly, Ishida himself was a farm operator in Orange County who cultivated tomatoes on 120 acres of land and hired Mexican farmworkers. Based on his experience as a laborer and a farmer, he tried to persuade Japanese farmers in Los Angeles that an immediate settlement of the strike was beneficial for both Mexican workers and Japanese farmers:

> Some [Japanese] people fear unions as a demon or snake and consider that recognizing unions would result in the demise of their business, but that is a huge misunderstanding since workers need farmers to make their living and they know it very well.... Despite the fact that strikers hope to meet and talk with the leaders of Japanese farmers to clear misunderstandings and solve the problem, Japanese farmers stubbornly reject their proposal and try to repress the strike. I am deeply sorry for this situation because Japanese farmers need Japanese, Mexican, and Filipino workers. Workers are human beings.... Until now, Mexican workers had felt greater respect for the Japanese than they did for whites and spent most of their income at Japanese-operated shops. But how would they feel now?[33]

A year earlier in Orange County, Mexican farmworkers demanding that Japanese farmers should provide better working conditions succeeded in reaching an agreement with the Japanese. That a Japanese farmer from Orange County was organizing the strike in Los Angeles was a disturbing fact for Japanese farmers in Los Angeles. Yet what disturbed them even more was the fact that many Japanese farmers in Los Angeles County had begun to show sympathy toward Mexican union members during the Venice strike, which was not the case in the El Monte strike. Nōkai Renmei leaders became increasingly concerned about the growing division within the Los Angeles Japanese farming population regarding how to confront and solve the interethnic labor conflict. Feeling pressure to explain more carefully about their uncompromising stance toward strikers, Katō wrote a series of articles to the *Rafu Shimpo* between May 4 and 6 in which he asserted: "What was made against the [farmers'] will is the current Japanese-Mexican wage agreement in Orange County. . . . I want to make clear one important fact. It is not that only a small group of [anti-labor] Japanese farmers are trying to push through their cause. We have been following the collective will of farmers. . . . Making a compromise is to weaken our solidarity, which makes it impossible to win the fight that we should be able to win."[34] Nōkai Renmei represented the majority of Japanese farmers in Los Angeles and the Japanese consulate regarded them as the leading ethnic organization in the Venice strike. However, Katō's explanation ironically reaffirmed that many other Japanese suspected that only a small number of leaders like himself were leading the Japanese community in the wrong direction at a time when unionization and collective bargaining became a legitimate right protected by the US government. In the El Monte strike, a division within the ethnic Japanese community appeared between Los Angeles Japanese and Mexicali Japanese who faced Mexican nationalism merged with anti-Japanese sentiment.[35] In the Venice strike, a different division appeared within Los Angeles County and separated anti-labor farmers who stressed the importance of the ethnic Japanese solidarity from pro-labor farmers who understood the need for interethnic harmony with ethnic Mexican residents. In other words, Los Angeles farmland as a *transpacific workplace* forced the Japanese to consider which was more important for the future of the Japanese community, ethnic solidarity or interethnic accommodation.

To prove the existence of a growing number of pro-labor Japanese farmers, on May 13, *La Opinión* cheerfully reported that Mexican strikers in the Gardena area "reached an agreement" with Japanese farmers and "accomplished a partial triumph yesterday." The Gardena area was one of the major concentrations of ethnic Japanese residents in Los Angeles County. Velarde told the press that a group of Gardena Japanese farmers had agreed to increase wages of about fifty workers from 22.5 cents to 35 cents an hour. Since there were still about two thousand workers engaged in the strike, Velarde stated, "The movement continues with all intensity and fieldworkers are actually backed by the moral and financial supports from fifty-two organizations including the American Federation of Labor.... In a short time, we will reach a definitive solution."³⁶ Indeed, it was a partial victory since Velarde's goal was to make Japanese farmers recognize his union. The *Rafu Shimpo* did not highlight this agreement, probably because they needed some time to confirm it or simply wanted to downplay the fact, but it is clear that anti-labor Japanese farmers knew that the strike was spreading far outside the Venice area by this time.³⁷ Later in May, pro-labor Japanese farmers of the Gardena area would take another significant step to settle the strike: union recognition. Since anti-labor farmers represented by Nōkai Renmei feared that union recognition was a stepping stone toward the demise of the whole of Japanese agriculture in the region, the Gardena agreement posed a serious threat and blow to their ethnic solidarity.

The Japanese-Mexican conflict in 1936 had created a division that made both anti-labor and pro-labor Japanese farmers reconsider the role they should play as a minority in the multiethnic and multiracial Los Angeles society. Ishida urged anti-labor Japanese farmers to make an agreement with strikers, saying, "Since I am a Japanese who shares the same blood [with you all], it is my personal desire that Japanese farmers should solve the problem to avoid a considerable loss." On the other hand, Katō denounced pro-labor Japanese farmers, "If you have a good faith as fellow Japanese, you, a minority group of people [in the ethnic Japanese community], should neither collaborate with radicals of other races nor engage in activities against our national unity that agitate Mexicans and Filipinos and make only Japanese farmers suffer. You should back out of this conflict and show good faith."³⁸ Both Ishida and Katō stressed the importance of their blood ties and of nationalism, concepts deeply connected to their sense of immigrant nationalism and ethnic solidarity. However, they had different understandings about the path Japanese immigrants should take in Los Angeles. For most Japanese determined to confront Mexican strikers, what it meant to be Japanese was to put priority on ethnic Japanese solidarity over interethnic accommodation and regard agriculture as the core of their solidarity and future prosperity. On the other hand, for those Japanese considering a possibility of hiring Mexican union workers, what it meant to be Japanese was to see the importance of coexisting with other ethnoracial minorities and thus to regard agriculture more as a multiethnic project in Los Angeles. The division within the ethnic Japanese community made the racial and class boundaries in the triracial hierarchy of Los Angeles agriculture fluid and unstable.

In the mid-1930s, therefore, the farmland of Los Angeles, a site of transpacific intersection of Japanese and Mexican immigrants, triggered a serious interethnic conflict that challenged the existing concept of "solidarity" in the Japanese immigrant community and saw a gradual development of their understanding for interethnic accommodation with Mexican workers.

INTER-JAPANESE DIVIDE AND GROWING SUPPORT FOR MEXICANS

By mid-May of 1936, strike organizers had moved their new headquarters from Venice to Harbor City, about twenty miles south of downtown Los Angeles. In Venice, the card registration system introduced by Japanese farmers proved quite effective to keep Mexican picketers away and workers in their celery farms.[39] The strike itself, however, was expanding and targeting the South Bay area of Los Angeles such as Lomita, San Pedro, and Dominguez Hills, where many Japanese farmers and their families lived. In Lomita, more than one hundred picketers appeared in Japanese farms. In San Pedro, more than one hundred picketers came to Japanese farms in about fifty cars and trucks in total and interrupted the operation of Mexican workers including women and children. Sheriff officers rushed to the scene and arrested a Filipino leader and forty-seven protestors. The strike affected the urban area of Los Angeles as well. Strike organizers marched and distributed fliers in downtown Los Angeles to criticize Japanese farmers, as shown in Japanese hotel owner Noboru Murakami's diary record of one of the strikers' marches. Some fliers were written in Japanese to call for wider support among Japanese residents. One of the fliers denounced Japanese farmers, "Why can't you raise our wages when you provide police officers with money [to protect Japanese farms]? Why can't you recognize our union when we recognize farmers' associations?"[40]

Meanwhile, feeling the need to settle the conflict, Nōkai Renmei leaders and strike organizers had begun to set formal meetings to discuss working conditions on Japanese farms. On May 14 they held the first meeting. While Katō, Naonori Mibu, Seijirō Kai, and Kengorō Nakamura represented anti-labor farmers, those who represented strikers were not only Mexicans such as Velarde but also Japanese activists such as Ishida and Deguchi. Filipino and white members also attended the meetings to support strikers.[41] Although Japanese consul Hori did not take part in the conflict as mentioned earlier, a week before the meeting he recommended Katō to meet with Velarde to discuss the solution for the conflict, leading them to meet on May 7.[42] Hori's recommendation would not be the major reason Katō decided to talk with the Mexican side. Rather, Katō wanted to use these opportunities to demonstrate Nōkai Renmei's uncompromising stance toward the strikers.

Negotiations between the two sides carried on for four consecutive meetings from May 14 to 22. The strike leaders softened their demands but still demanded that 60 percent of workers in Japanese farms should be union members and paid 30 cents an hour, while Nōkai Renmei provided a counter proposal that they would pay 22.5 cents an hour for long-term workers, 25 cents for relatively easy harvest, and 30 cents at most for more complicated work like harvesting celery.

Although the strike leaders gave ground regarding wages and said that they would agree to farmers being paid 27.5 cents an hour for harvesting crops apart from celery, they did not withdraw their demand for union recognition. Union recognition, however, was the last thing that anti-labor farmers could agree to.[43] On May 22, after their negotiations broke down, Velarde visited the *Rafu Shimpo* headquarters with twenty other strike organizers consisting of Mexican, Filipino, and Japanese members including Ishida and Deguchi. Frustrated by the failure of the negotiations, Velarde told the *Rafu Shimpo*, "I'm a member of the Democratic Party in the sixty-seventh district and got support from the American Federation of Labor, which is critical of the leftists, for this strike. For this reason, I think you understand that I am not a Communist. I've told [Nōkai Renmei] that I want them to sign an agreement with us, let's say for four months, to see if unions are such a horrible thing as they think. Since Mexican workers know well about the difficult situation faced by Japanese farmers, they won't make an outrageous demand."[44] From the perspective of most Japanese farmers in Los Angeles, union recognition was an outrageous demand. So why did Velarde adhere to union recognition, which made it almost impossible to draw concessions from Nōkai Renmei? Nōkai Renmei leaders speculated that it was because some Japanese farmers in the Gardena area, a major Japanese farming region in Los Angeles County, had begun to show sympathy toward strikers and the idea of union recognition. Given this gradual change in the attitude of some Japanese farmers, there seemed to be a chance for strikers to win the conflict.[45]

In addition, unlike the El Monte strike, the California State government offered only limited assistance for both the Japanese and Mexican sides. Again, the reason was because strike organizers demanded union recognition. At one of their negotiation meetings, strike leaders proposed that they would ask Thomas Barker, the state government mediator who played an important role in the agreement at the end of the El Monte strike, to mediate the Venice conflict. Nōkai Renmei leaders agreed on this idea. However, Barker replied that it was not him but interested parties who should discuss union recognition, while he could only offer some help regarding wages.[46] Barker also thought that Japanese and Mexican immigrants could solve the Venice strike through a contract agreement just like they did in the El Monte strike. On May 22, Barker told the *Rafu Shimpo*, "I should maintain a fair stance for both parties from an objective point of view [as a third party]. This strike reminds me of the berry strike that happened three years earlier. At that time, Mr. Mukaeda, the former president of the Central Japanese Association of Southern California, mediated the conflict to reach an agreement that I think was a quite fair and appropriate document." He also added his opinion that reaching an agreement with union leaders would not necessarily mean that Japanese farmers had to hire union workers, although anti-labor Japanese farmers could not accept such an idea. The Japanese side invited Barker to the fourth meeting between farmers and strikers, but he declined the invitation for the same reasons mentioned above.[47]

The *Rafu Shimpo* was basically supportive of Nōkai Renmei unlike the *Kashu Mainichi*, but also provided its readers with various opinions sympathetic toward Mexican strikers. One day after the Japanese-Mexican negotiation ended in failure, a prominent Japanese immigrant Shōji Nagumo, a well-known leader of Japanese gardeners in Los Angeles, contributed his opinion regarding the strike. On the *Rafu Shimpo* article, he wrote, "By observing the actual living conditions [of Mexicans], they are very impoverished. Since they suffer lives more difficult than that of fellow Japanese farmers, they are in a situation in which they cannot lower the level of their lives anymore."[48] Nagumo was well educated and able to speak Spanish because he had hired Mexican workers since the 1920s, which seems to have helped him better understand the situation of ethnic Mexican neighborhoods. Represented by Nagumo, Japanese gardeners were supportive of Mexican strikers during the Venice strike, although such a pro-labor stance was not dominant in the whole ethnic Japanese community. By shedding light on the prewar history of Japanese gardeners in Southern California, Nobuya Tsuchida argues that the Japanese gardeners could take a pro-Mexican stance during the Venice strike because they depended almost exclusively on white customers, not Japanese patrons. More importantly, "the ambiguous class position of gardeners, between labor and the petite bourgeoisie, seems in this instance to have led to their identification with, and support of, the workers."[49] While Nōkai Renmei leaders sometimes claimed that "farmworkers earn more income than farmers do," Nagumo's observation was important evidence that Japanese immigrants were not that naïve to believe such awkward claims by Nōkai Renmei.[50]

Without making any progress in negotiating with the Mexican side, an increasing number of Japanese farmers began to criticize Nōkai Renmei for not quite representing them. This forced Katō to convey his intention to step down as the manager of Nōkai Renmei at their meeting on May 20. About sixty representatives of Japanese agricultural associations in Los Angeles County attended the meeting and persuaded Katō to stay in his position, since they were in line with Katō unanimously and firmly against union recognition. To make clear their solidarity, they even issued a resolution to acknowledge that "the contribution [made by Katō] has been huge."[51] But the criticism against Nōkai Renmei did not stop. Another ethnic Japanese newspaper *Kashu Mainichi*, whose editor-in-chief was Sei Fujii, represented small-scale tenant farmers who were increasingly frustrated about the leadership of Nōkai Renmei and wanted to handle the strike independently in each farming community without the authoritative instruction of Nōkai Renmei.[52] Fujii supported the small-scale farmer's position, writing that they could maintain production only by the help of their family members and should not bear the burden of providing financial support for anti-labor measures protecting larger-scale farmers.⁵³ Thus, the rivalry of these two newspapers represented this subtle class difference among Japanese farmers, although the *Rafu Shimpo* represented the mainstream position of Japanese farmers who supported Nōkai Renmei.⁵⁴

The labor-friendly *Kashu Mainichi* introduced an article in its English section written by a Japanese American woman who criticized the anti-labor attitude of Japanese farmers. She wrote anonymously, "I, as a farmer's daughter, cannot remain silent and see the present strike continuing and doing damage to the crops which are now ready to be harvested. Why don't the farmers and those interested in their welfare wake up to the fact that there is no danger in getting together with the union people and hear their point of view?" The fact that she chose to be anonymous indicates that the dominant opinion of the ethnic Japanese community was in favor of Nōkai Renmei. Although it is likely that Nisei were less antagonistic toward the strikers' demand for union recognition than Issei farmers, there was not a clear generational difference since many Nisei engaged in the collective campaign of *giyūdan* to work voluntarily on the farmland during the strike. Further, the English sections of both the *Rafu Shimpo* and *Kashu Mainichi* reported the cooperation of Nisei. A clearer line could be drawn between the two papers regarding how they reported the strike. For example, even when the farmer's daughter mentioned above contributed her pro-labor essay, she did it in response to Fujii's appeal. The *Kashu Mainichi* also published a Gardena Issei's opinion sympathetic to Mexican workers. An Issei named Juzō (or Toshizō) Ōta complained that a few Japanese farmers had used abusive language about workers at a meeting of Nōkai Renmei and demanded that Nōkai Renmei "change their attitude to a more compassionate one and demonstrate their will for a settlement."⁵⁵ From the perspective of historical analysis of Japanese-Mexican relations, a more important question to draw from Ōta's article is whether any "compassionate" voice could emerge from the leadership close to Nōkai Renmei, because such a voice might have been able to make many Japanese farmers realize the importance of understanding Mexicans as fellow minority residents in the white-dominant society despite class and racial differences.

Observing the deadlock between strikers and farmers, Mexican consul Hill began to wonder whether Mexican strikers should stay away from non-Mexican labor activists and negotiate independently with Japanese farmers to make more rapid progress toward settlement. Since Japanese farmers and Mexican strikers signed an agreement a year earlier in Orange County, Hill considered whether he could take the Orange County's Japanese-Mexican agreement as a model to solve the problem in Los Angeles. He then asked Lucas Lucio, the consulate's representative in Orange County, and Masami Sasaki, a prominent Japanese immigrant in Huntington Beach in Orange County, to set up meetings between Hill and Nōkai Renmei starting from May 22. Since Hill wanted to draw on the Orange County agreement, Nōkai Renmei agreed to appoint Sasaki as a negotiator on behalf of Japanese farmers. May 22, the day when the first meeting of Hill and Sasaki was held, happened to be the day of the failed meeting between the CUCOM and Nōkai Renmei, meaning that Hill was working separately from Velarde during the Venice strike.[56] On the other hand, Lucio was a publisher of a weekly Mexican immigrant paper *El Nuevo Mundo* that put emphasis on the importance of the Mexican consulate and reiterated the danger of radicalism. While Velarde represented the hardline of the radical labor movement, therefore, Lucio attempted to settle the labor conflict through the mediation of government agencies.[57] Nōkai Renmei thought it worth meeting independently with Hill and hoped to reach a Japanese-Mexican agreement without union recognition.

While the negotiation continued between the Mexican consul and Japanese farmers, the strike itself was expanding and became increasingly violent. Since strike organizers moved their headquarters, Japanese farmers in Dominguez Hills, only about five miles from the CUCOM headquarters in Harbor City, were on high alert and mobilized their family members to get their harvest done. Otokichi Kuwahara, the leader of Japanese farmers in Dominguez Hills who immigrated to California from Kumamoto Prefecture in 1902, told Japanese American children who attended a local *kendō* (Japanese fencing) club, "Now we Issei have been struggling to break through this strike without enough sleep at night. So you Nisei need to get up at five a.m. and help us for a couple of hours before going to school. You also need to help us after coming back from school as you usually do."[58]

The expansion of the strike in Dominguez Hills resulted in a bloody encounter between Mexican strikers and strikebreakers that took place on Japanese farms in Dominguez Hills on the morning of May 25. *La Opinión* reported this incident as front-page news based on their interview with the police and the CUCOM. According to the police report, more than twenty people were injured because the encounter involved the use of rifles and bladed weapons. In the afternoon, the police authority arrested about forty strikers, most of whom were Mexican, for the incident. Three Mexican strikers named Mike Pulido, Joe Delgado, and Bernardo Lucero were arrested by the police but were also brought to the hospital to receive treatment such as the removing of pellets from their body. The police report did not mention who opened fire on the Mexicans but gave an impression that Mexican picketers and workers caused a bloody incident anyway.[59] The *Rafu Shimpo* also reported the incident in Dominguez Hills with the names of farmers attacked by picketers, while mentioning other violent encounters in the nearby Compton area and other areas in the San Gabriel Valley. In Dominguez Hills, the police also arrested Lillian Monroe who had been involved in the Venice strike from the beginning. Although Monroe was released shortly after her arrest, the Japanese immigrant press described her as the "Red queen who masterminds the agricultural strike." The Japanese labor activist Deguchi was also arrested.[60]

Right after this violent incident, about 150 Japanese residents in Dominguez Hills held an emergency meeting and approved resolutions: (1) that they would support Nōkai Renmei as much as possible, (2) that they would ask the Japanese consulate for protection, (3) that they would request the police authority to raise the level of vigilance, and (4) that they would gather donations for the safety of their farms. As this reflects, the incident resulted in hardening the attitude of Japanese farmers in Dominguez Hills.[61] Even the *Kashu Mainichi*, which was labor-friendly in comparison with its rival *Rafu Shimpo*, criticized the Mexican side regarding the bloody encounter in Dominguez Hills. It wrote, "We understand and sympathize with rational agricultural strikes since the majority of fellow [Japanese] farmers were once in the position of laborers.... Yet the eruption of violence in Dominguez Hills this time cannot be accepted with such farmers' sympathy. We are truly infuriated by their inhuman action."[62]

In *La Opinión*, the CUCOM provided their version of what happened in Dominguez Hills on May 25 and criticized police officers and Japanese farmers armed with rifles for attacking Mexican strikers. It would have caused a serious international problem that both Japanese and Mexican consulates had to deal with if some Japanese national injured Mexican nationals with a deadly weapon. In fact, neither the Japanese nor Mexican consulates took prompt action on this incident, indicating that no Japanese opened fire against Mexicans. For this reason, it is most likely police officers did so. No matter who actually injured Mexican strikers, the CUCOM criticized Japanese farmers and said that "workers have decided to stay strong, despite accidents and injustices in which they became victims, while suffering and risking their lives to improve their conditions. Unfortunately, no [Japanese] hear us when we ask for a piece of bread for our children and avoid misery in which we live."[63]

Interestingly, this CUCOM's message revealed a weakness of their campaign as well, since they claimed, "Through this pro-labor general committee, we make a call for all workers in El Monte, San Gabriel, and surrounding neighborhoods and ask them not to hinder this movement of their own brothers of *raza*."[64] In other words, there *were* Mexicans who did not follow the order of the CUCOM. Being aware of this problem, the CUCOM worked hard to strengthen the solidarity of Mexican workers by holding daily meetings from May 26. At the Zaragoza hall in Hicks Camp, the Mexican barrio in El Monte, the CUCOM screened a movie about the "huelga del 33" (El Monte strike) to raise morale to fight against the Japanese.[65] Although the El Monte strike did not much improve working and living conditions of Mexican farmworkers, it had already become such an important part of local Mexican American history that the CUCOM could use it to strengthen ethnic Mexican solidarity. Yet the solidarity of *raza* was not guaranteed because many Mexican workers could not keep up with the prolonged strike. Ironically, the Venice strike was not successful in the San Gabriel Valley, which included El Monte. As mentioned earlier, ethnic Japanese residents, particularly youth, were proactive in protecting their farms in the valley. Japanese American youth there, both male and female, held a meeting and confirmed that they could contribute to the "development of the national spirit" and protection of Japanese agriculture. In addition, many Mexican workers including women continued to work for the Japanese, while local sheriff officers prevented Mexican picketers from influencing those workers. For example, on May 19, about 110 strikers tried to force Mexican workers to leave Japanese berry farms in the El Monte area, prompting sheriff officers to quickly respond and remove picketers from Japanese farms. Another case took place on May 28 when about fifteen Mexican picketers arrived at berry farms and Katō happened to confront them. At that time, sheriff officers arrested thirteen picketers, while another three escaped the scene.[66] About a week later in the county court, seven arrested Mexicans were sentenced to 180 days in prison for interrupting harvest and trying to kidnap workers. Another five picketers were also convicted of assault or assisted assault against a Japanese farmer. Although picketers continued to appear after this guilty verdict, with the support of the Sheriff's Department Japanese farmers in the San Gabriel Valley could maintain a necessary number of Mexican workers.[67]

However, in late May, Nōkai Renmei had unwelcome news. On May 28, a group of more than fifty Japanese farmers in the Gardena area led by a Nisei named Bob Ueda, met with Velarde and signed a contract to raise wages to 27.5 cents an hour and recognize the CUCOM. What was more important was that this contract required that 60 percent of their workers should be members of the CUCOM. *La Opinión* celebrated the deal with the headlines "Victories of Pickers" and "The Japanese Bow to CUCOM." Their contract would benefit nearly three hundred Mexican workers in areas such as Walteria, Harbor City, Lomita, and Torrance, although Velarde claimed that another two thousand workers were still on the strike in Los Angeles County. After signing the contract with Ueda, Velarde told Mexican workers to come to the CUCOM's headquarters in Harbor City to obtain identification cards for union membership, which happened to resemble what Venice Japanese farmers did to hire nonunion Mexican workers.[68]

The *Rafu Shimpo*, on May 29, touched upon this shocking development by quoting a local newspaper, *Los Angeles Daily News*, that reported about fifty Japanese farmers signed a contract and recognized the CUCOM. But the *Rafu Shimpo* described it as a rumor based on an unreliable explanation given only by the CUCOM.[69] The *Kashu Mainichi* also reported the alleged agreement but did not immediately downplay it as a rumor. It explained that its reporter was investigating the event, while its English section mentioned it in a very short article of thirty-three words.[70] In the morning of the next day, Katō visited the Gardena Valley area including Harbor City, Torrance, and Lomita, with another two Nōkai Renmei leaders to ask Katsuichi Inoue, who represented the local

Japanese association, about the contract made by Ueda. Inoue told them that he had no idea about the alleged contract signed by fifty farmers but was surprised to know the fact that "the Nisei" signed independently. In the afternoon, Inoue held a meeting with about thirty Japanese leaders of the area and reaffirmed their support for Nōkai Renmei. While Nōkai Renmei negotiator Sasaki confirmed that four farmers including "the Nisei" signed the contract with the CUCOM, Nōkai Renmei and *Rafu Shimpo* basically dismissed it, at least publicly, as a trivial matter and did not even mention the name of Bob Ueda.[71] The *Rafu Shimpo*'s English section simply repudiated the deal claimed by the CUCOM as "a large fabrication" and belittled the fact by explaining that "only three independent growers and one nisei land leaser, who had signed because their conditions forced them, listed with the union."[72]

Nōkai Renmei leaders hastily made a visit to the Gardena Valley area to investigate the influence of strikers. The leaders speculated that those Japanese led by Ueda did not suffer labor shortage since most were small tenant farmers who would not depend much on Mexican workers. Based on this assumption, they concluded that these Gardena farmers signed the contract as they were influenced by pro-labor sentiment not by their desperate need for Mexican labor, without understanding that Nōkai Renmei's rather insensitive attitude toward small-scale farmers was a major reason why some other farmers wanted to act independently. Around the same time, Mexican consul Hill suddenly became reluctant to meet with Nōkai Renmei and abandoned his own settlement plan. Hill's change of heart made Nōkai Renmei leaders suspect that there must be considerable relations between Ueda and Hill, as they argued that "now Hill says that we do not have to model after the agreement in Orange County, clearly because a group of Japanese farmers in Gardena began to sign for union recognition."[73]

Meanwhile, almost forty days after beginning of the Venice strike, it was becoming increasingly difficult for Mexican strikers to live without work. In early June, a Mexican American strongman David Benítez organized as many as nine hundred Mexican workers, who once belonged to the CUCOM, to seek for a different solution. Benítez, who was originally from Arizona, was working to support Mexican workers in the El Monte area as part of the CUCOM's campaign. However, he came to believe that it would be better to pursue independent negotiation with Nōkai Renmei without other non-Mexican unions. Benítez visited Japanese leaders including Katō and demanded that Japanese farmers pay twenty-five cents or more for ordinary work and thirty cents for more expensive crops such as celery, that Japanese farmers should hire workers regardless of their union membership, and that the contract would be valid for one year. In short, Benítez did not demand union recognition itself, as he did not set the percentage of union workers to be hired by Japanese farmers. He also submitted signatures of nine hundred Mexican workers and told that the number would soon reach fifteen hundred. Facing an

FIGURE 9. Japanese and Mexican representatives signing a provisional agreement, 1936. Shin'ichi Katō (left) is watching David Benítez (second left) adding his signature.
SOURCE: *Rafu Shimpo*, June 9, 1936.

emergency in the Gardena area, Nōkai Renmei welcomed the proposal of Benítez.[74] Although Nōkai Renmei leaders were concerned of the possibility that the campaign led by Bob Ueda would spread to other areas, most Mexican workers had already returned to Japanese farms. Nōkai Renmei expected that the contract with Benítez could help prevent the increase of pro-labor and pro-union farmers.

On June 7, Nōkai Renmei and Benítez made a provisional agreement, which on the next day *La Opinión* reported as front-page news stating, "1,500 Pickers Destroy the Strike; They Abandon CUCOM." Mexican workers led by Benítez could not continue their struggle as members of the CUCOM because "their families find themselves in an urgent situation." Benítez signed a contract with Japanese leaders such as Katō, Masajirō Kai, and Yemon Minami to end "one of the gravest labor conflicts in the history of Mexican organizations in the United States" (Figure 9). The signers announced, "Last night the strike of workers in vegetable fields ended peacefully and all Mexican farmworkers who want to work can get all the information at the office of the Federated Farmers Association of Southern California [Nōkai Renmei]." The Nōkai Renmei negotiator Sasaki looked at the *La Opinión* article and appreciated "the most influential newspaper among Mexicans" for encouraging Mexican workers to visit the Nōkai Renmei office to work. As reported by *La Opinión*, the separation of 1,500 Mexican workers must have been "a harsh attack" for Velarde and the CUCOM, who had been leading Mexican strikers by that time. Mexican consul Hill gave no comments on the action taken by Benítez when the *La Opinión* interviewed him.[75] Probably Hill was not behind Benítez, since Lucas Lucio, the Mexican consulate representative in Orange County who worked closely with Hill, visited the *Rafu Shimpo* headquarters to criticize Benítez immediately after the signing.[76] Yet, white agribusiness leaders and Japanese farmers in the El Monte area might have put some pressure on Benítez, who was an ethnic Mexican well trusted by white Americans according to Nōkai Renmei.[77]

Although it is not clear what kind of power was behind Benítez, a division within Mexican workers was evident just like that within Japanese farmers. While the CUCOM led by Velarde put priority on union recognition, many Mexican workers led by Benítez cared about their wages and employment more than union recognition. Both groups of Mexican workers wanted to live in Los Angeles permanently securing their job and sustaining their families. Again, Los Angeles farmland as a *transpacific workplace* made them think about which was more important to survive in Los Angeles, union recognition in multiethnic cooperation or more stable employment, if only temporarily, in a bilateral Japanese-Mexican negotiation. It would be inaccurate to describe the compromise made by Mexican workers led by Benítez simply as a result of mutual understanding, given the unequal economic relationship between Japanese farmers and Mexican workers. But it was certainly a result of interethnic negotiations where both the Mexican and Japanese sides met and explained their respective situations.

Although losing most union members, Velarde did not stop organizing workers, since he had succeeded at least in part of the Gardena area. In mid-June, the *Los Angeles Times* reported that more than one hundred small Japanese farmers in Gardena signed a contract with Velarde and exaggeratedly explained, "Such is being advocated by Sei Fujii . . . in opposition to the great majority of the Japanese growers, numbering more than 1600, who are in the Southern California Farm Federation [Nōkai Renmei]." The *Rafu Shimpo* simply cited and repeated the *Los Angeles Times*'s report, characterizing the union movement as encouraged by Fujii.[78] Likewise, Ueda continued to be active in persuading Japanese farmers to recognize the CUCOM. Nōkai Renmei leaders were concerned that the pro-labor campaign by some Gardena Japanese could give a negative impression to white farmers who were resisting the labor movement in Southern California and "damage a good situation in recent years in which amicable relations [between Japanese and white farmers] are being made in this industry." The anger of anti-labor Japanese was not only triggered by their class interests but also by their racial understanding about Japanese and Mexicans. When they criticized Japanese labor activists who took part in organizing the Venice strike, they asserted that "it is outrageous that they agitate ignorant Mexican workers to take violent actions and afflict Japanese farmers who share the same blood and nation." For anti-labor Japanese leaders, Mexican strikers were wrong because they were "ignorant" and pro-labor Japanese were bad because they betrayed racial and ethnic solidarity.[79]

From the perspective of pro-labor farmers like Ueda, Mexican workers were not ignorant at all, and Japanese farmers should think beyond racial and ethnic backgrounds. In an interview conducted by the *Kashu Mainichi* in early July, Ueda explained the reason why he came to hire union members. Although he did not deal with Mexicans who seemed violent to him at first, he realized that the union's demands were not irrational after negotiating with Velarde. Ueda asked Velarde to accept the wage of twenty-five cents per hour, leave Ueda's neighbors and relatives or those small farmers who needed only a few workers free from the union contract, and let him keep nonunion old or resident workers who could not go anywhere. Velarde accepted all these conditions and added that Ueda could fire union workers if they were lazy. Thus, Ueda signed a contract with the CUCOM. Ueda said, "There has been no trouble for more than a month. I recommend what I believe is good to others. At first, I was afraid of the union, but now I am not afraid at all. I am pleased [with the union] since it is actually convenient." Given that Ueda's interview neither showed any generational factor in his decision to work with the Mexican union nor appeared in the *Kashu Mainichi*'s English section, Ueda's position would not be representative among Nisei readers. Yet his interview shows that Japanese farmers like Ueda, if a minority, did not have the anti-labor phobia that the union recognition would automatically lead to the demise of ethnic Japanese agriculture.[80]

In order to ease and end agricultural conflicts, it was important for pro-labor Japanese to build amicable relationships between Japanese farmers and Mexican workers. As seen in the Venice strike, multiethnic Los Angeles saw class and race intersect each other generating multiple relations between Japanese and Mexicans. Anti-labor Japanese and white farmers worked together based on their common class interests. Their Japanese-white alliance helped maintain the white dominant agriculture of Los Angeles in which nonunion Mexican workers would fit as an indispensable element. On the other hand, pro-labor Japanese farmers and Mexican strikers helped each other, envisioning an interethnic and interracial harmony beyond their racial and class status.

Agriculture had been the most important industry for Japanese immigrants to build their ethnic solidarity and survive the hostile Los Angeles society, which was true until the Pearl Harbor attack. But a close look at the Venice strike gives us a new understanding. In the mid-1930s, due to the heavy dependency of Japanese agriculture on ethnic Mexican workers, the growing labor movement particularly after 1935 in the United States, and the lack of the Japanese government's involvement, the Venice strike forced ethnic Japanese residents to question the premise of the ethnic Japanese solidarity within the triracial hierarchy in Los Angeles agriculture and some Japanese like Gardena farmers began to envision a possibility of interethnic accommodation in the *transpacific workplace* where Japanese and Mexican immigrants had come to settle and work together.

NEW DEAL TWIST OF JAPANESE IMMIGRANT NATIONALISM AND INTERETHNIC ACCOMMODATION

The split within Japanese farmers alarmed white agribusiness leaders who had been working closely with Nōkai Renmei and the police authority to suppress the labor movement more severely, while they knew that the strike had been basically unsuccessful in Los Angeles County. On June 11, 1936, the executive secretary of the Associated Farmers of Los Angeles County, Arthur Clark, wrote a report on the Venice strike to the Board of Direction of the Associated Farmers, which was shared by the Los Angeles Chamber of Commerce. Clark believed that radicalization of the Mexican labor movement resulted in the division of anti-labor and pro-labor Japanese farmers:

> A very critical situation has developed in agricultural labor during the past few weeks.... The spear head of the attempt [of strikers to make growers recognize unions] was in the celery and vegetable harvests locally where old line Mexican unions of no particular size or strength in past years were taken over by militant, radical organizers of the San Joaquin Valley apparently with the full support of Ricardo Hill, local Mexican consul. This strike, as far as delaying or interfering with the harvests was concerned, was a complete failure, but because it was directed against *Japanese growers who now find themselves divided*, some progress has been made toward accomplishing the real purpose of the walkout, i.e. establishment of complete union recognition and the closed shop [Italics added].[81]

This report went on to state, "Because of the split up of Japanese growers some 100 Japanese have signed up with the union on what is referred to as a 60 per cent closed shop. There are between 1500 and 200[0] Japanese growers in this County and so the progress cannot be regarded as very favorable to the 'strikers,' but with silent support and approval of the local A.F. of L. the organizers are [bearing] away in their efforts to make further inroads into the Japanese growers." Since Nōkai Renmei was affiliated with the Associated Farmers of Los Angeles County, Japanese leaders such as Katō must have known that nearly one hundred Japanese farmers signed up with the CUCOM. While strike organizers were still active in Los Angeles County, they were also active in Orange County and could be mobilized to accomplish "complete unionization on closed shop principles of all farm labor here and throughout California." Thus, Clark's report warned, "United action by all farm labor employers, whether Japanese or American, is vitally necessary if this battle is to be won."[82]

To prevent further strikes by Mexicans, the secretary of the Los Angeles Chamber of Commerce A. G. Arnoll discussed the need to set up a "permanent board of strategy" against Mexican strikers in his letter to Clements sent on June 20. Arnoll's suggestion was to create "Mexican villages out in the agricultural districts where the mean labor supply can be housed and taken care of." Since many Mexican workers lived in the urban area of Los Angeles and commuted to agricultural areas, Arnoll thought that it would be easier to control Mexican workers if they were scattered and lived near different agricultural areas.[83] His idea reflected their typical understanding of Mexicans as foreigners who should and could be tamed through government or business policy. This type of understanding would be shared with many other Chamber of Commerce officials who regarded Mexicans as foreign labor to be controlled rather than people who deserved better wages and labor conditions.

At the same time, Chamber of Commerce officials were aware of the division within Mexican workers, as documented in Clark's report. They observed that "only a handful of the Mexicans actually at work want to belong to the union," because many continued to harvest crop despite "the known desire of Consul Hill that they stop work." Chamber of Commerce officials took the role of Hill seriously, while being aware that not only Mexican organizers but also non-Mexican leaders such as Monroe and Deguchi were involved in the expansion of the strike. However, the Chamber of Commerce also knew that the role of Mexican government officials was limited in the Venice strike because "a split between the followers of the present Mexican government [led by Cárdenas] and Calles has developed to further complicate the situation."[84] In other words, Hill could not receive similar support from the Mexican government in the Venice strike due to the absence of Calles. This lack of coherent support from the Mexican government helped the Japanese government stay away from the Venice strike in order to avoid transforming it into an international problem that might harm US-Japan relations, although the respective consulates were never able to give up their role in protecting and monitoring their citizens in Los Angeles. This absence of the consulates' active involvement was also an international factor that defined the Japanese-Mexican relations during the Venice strike.

By early June of 1936, the Venice strike was on the decline, as a contract was made between anti-labor farmers led by Nōkai Renmei and nonunion Mexican workers organized by Benítez. However, anti-labor Japanese farmers would not feel easy unless the strike completely faded away. Around this time, the labor movement in Orange County became increasingly active, which could unsettle the situation in Los Angeles.[85] Katsuma Mukaeda, the former president of the Central Japanese Association of Southern California who represented Japanese farmers during the El Monte strike and succeeded in signing a contract with Mexican strikers back then, was worried about the unsettled situation between

Japanese farmers and Mexican workers. Although Mukaeda continued to work for the association as the vice president, he was absent in Los Angeles when the Venice strike broke out, as he was visiting Japan and its overseas territories such as Korea and Manchuria. In mid-June, Mukaeda returned to Los Angeles and, as an advisor for Nōkai Renmei, immediately took action to settle the trouble especially with Velarde and Hill. Mukaeda knew Velarde and Hill well, since he negotiated with them to settle the El Monte strike. Then Mukaeda personally set up meetings with Velarde and Hill and reached an idea of how to solve the strike with the CUCOM.[86]

In the Venice strike, Mukaeda made serious efforts to make compromise with the Mexican counterpart. However, it did not mean that he was a cosmopolitan. He was a Japanese nationalist like many other Japanese immigrants were. He praised imperial Japan for its military and economic colonization of East Asia when he visited Korea and Manchuria. In his travel report that the *Rafu Shimpo* published in June 1936, Mukaeda wrote, "I became filled with a feeling of superiority as Japanese when I arrived at Busan [a major port city in Korea]. All Koreans were carrying heavy baggage by hand. People in the United States would use a truck to carry them. Now our train was heading to *Keijō* [Seoul]. I could see the hardships and fruits of *our rule* through the train window" (italics added). Inspired by Japanese compatriots building the empire in Korea and Manchuria, Mukaeda reaffirmed his mission to "work hard for amicable US-Japan relations" despite or because of the possibility that the United States might "misunderstand" Japanese diplomacy in East Asia.[87] With this hope and determination in his mind, Mukaeda began to solve the Japanese-Mexican conflict during the Venice strike. Mukaeda's view on interethnic conflicts demonstrates that Japanese immigrant nationalism could take a multiethnic and accommodationist position to make compromise with Mexicans rather than simply incorporating the white supremacist view to look down on Mexicans and reinforce the racial and class boundaries of the triracial hierarchy in Los Angeles. Japanese immigrant nationalism and ethnic solidarity were compatible with labor multiculturalism in the 1930s when their economic interests were challenged. It is also significant that Mukaeda, a widely respected community leader, showed such a nationalist-cum-multiethnic view given the changing understanding of labor rights in mid-1930s Los Angeles.

On July 6, Mukaeda submitted his proposal to Nōkai Renmei. The proposal said that Japanese farmers should negotiate only with the CUCOM, that the CUCOM should be regarded as a negotiation agent, that the contract would be valid for one year, that wages should be from twenty-five to thirty cents an hour, that a mediation committee should be set up when it was necessary, that the CUCOM should nullify any previous contracts, and that Japanese farmers should hire Mexicans regardless of their membership in the union. In terms of wages, this was similar with the contract signed between Nōkai Renmei and Benítez. Yet

Mukaeda's proposal would prevent the CUCOM from setting up the percentage of union workers at Japanese farms and nullify the contract signed between the CUCOM and the group of Gardena farmers organized by Ueda. Soon after, however, the CUCOM disagreed with Mukaeda's idea and insisted that Japanese farmers should sign a contract not only with the CUCOM but also with other non-Mexican unions and that the contract should be valid for nine months. In addition, the CUCOM removed the provision that would nullify previous contracts, as they wanted to keep the deal with Gardena Japanese farmers, while adding another provision that allowed union representatives to check the fulfilment of the contract without interrupting workers.[88]

Figuring out a middle ground for compromise, Mukaeda revised his original proposal based on the CUCOM's demands. On July 8 when Mukaeda visited Velarde, they agreed on the revised proposal, and on the next day, the state government mediator Thomas Barker and Hill agreed on their provisional agreement. The provisional agreement was a product of a trusting Japanese-Mexican relationship between Mukaeda and Velarde, as seen, for example, in the provision that Mukaeda agreed to allow union representatives to enter Japanese farms as a partner for the appropriate implementation of the agreement.[89] Since the provisional agreement did not use the term "closed shop" or mention the percentage of union workers to be hired, Mukaeda gained support from the Los Angeles Chamber of Commerce that regarded it as "the best contract for both labor and management." When Mukaeda explained the importance of this provisional agreement, he appreciated Velarde for "understanding the position of Japanese farmers well and persuading hard-liners in his union not to oppose."[90] As one of the most prominent immigrant leaders in the Los Angeles Japanese community, Mukaeda knew the importance of their ethnic solidarity and economy. At the same time, he also came to understand the importance of building trusting relations with ethnic Mexican workers, without whom Japanese agriculture in Los Angeles could neither survive nor strive. In the three years since the El Monte strike, Japanese-Mexican labor relations did not improve much. But there was certainly a growing understanding among Japanese immigrants for cooperating with Mexicans as well as white Americans.

On July 11, Nōkai Renmei held a meeting to discuss Mukaeda's revised proposal but politely disapproved it while showing gratitude for his efforts. Nōkai Renmei disapproved his proposal because a nine-month contact would be invalid before the next year's harvest and because letting union representatives into Japanese farms could result in an increase of union workers even though the contract did not set the percentage of union workers. At the same time, white landowners had demonstrated a stern attitude toward labor unions and made it even more difficult for Japanese farmers to negotiate with the CUCOM. White landowners in San Pedro and Dominguez Hills made a statement that they would not lease lands to Japanese farmers who had signed a contract with any labor union. On July 13, Nōkai Renmei and the CUCOM were supposed to sign a contract based on Mukaeda's revised proposal.[91] But without the approval from Nōkai Renmei leaders, the Japanese and Mexican sides could not reach the agreement. CUCOM leaders denounced Japanese farmers for "trying to deceive workers" and called Mexican workers not to fall into "traps" set up by the Japanese.[92]

Meanwhile, since early June, the CUCOM was gradually shifting their focus from Los Angeles to Orange County where Mexican strikers were fighting against white citrus farmers. Just like anti-labor Japanese farmers in Los Angeles County, white citrus farmers maintained an uncompromising stance with support of the local police authority.[93] White farmers were skeptical that Mexican consul Hill was promoting the strike in Orange County. They sent a petition to the US Labor Department for investigating the role of Hill in the Orange County strike. Hill immediately refuted their allegation and explained his position by saying, "I have always thought of complying honestly with my obligation, as the representative of my government and of ordinary Mexican citizens, to actively intervene in controversies" involving Mexican citizens.[94] On July 14, one day after the disapproval of Mukaeda's revised proposal, the Orange County Sheriff's Department arrested Velarde as well as another Mexican strike leader, J. Espinosa, and Fred West, a local representative of the American Federation of Labor on charges of "vagrancy." Velarde, Espinosa, and West were held on $1,000 bond (approximately $18,700 in 2020) each. *La Opinión* reported that Logan Jackson, the Orange County Sheriff, had given a "shoot to kill" order regarding strikers, while Edward H. Fitzgerald, a US Labor Department official, criticized Jackson, saying that any tragedy caused by such an order would provoke a "very serious" international conflict.[95]

On July 16, Velarde was released but could not regain the leadership of the labor movement in Orange County because other Mexican leaders such as Lucas Lucio had come to play a larger role in negotiating with white citrus farmers.[96] In contrast to Velarde, who believed in the importance of union recognition and cooperation with non-Mexican workers, Hill and Lucio focused more on wages and nondiscriminatory treatment for Mexicans without insisting on union recognition. On July 25, Orange County citrus farmers and Mexican workers reached an agreement thanks to the support of the Mexican consulate in Los Angeles. While citrus farmers in Orange County used to pay six cents per box without hourly wages, the new agreement required them to pay twenty cents an hour and three cents per box in excess of thirty boxes daily. However, union recognition was not included in the agreement.[97] In short, the CUCOM and Velarde lost in both Los Angeles and Orange Counties, and were followed by less demanding negotiators who subsequently succeeded.

Back in Los Angeles, the strike was over by this time. On August 18, Japanese consul Hori sent a report to the Ministry of Foreign Affairs of Japan in Tokyo and explained that "the strike faded away on its own." He attached a detailed report about the Venice strike written by Nōkai Renmei.[98] During the strike, Hori stayed away and even traveled to the East Coast.[99] He must have been happy about the fact that the strike ended in Los Angeles without his involvement. The US government was not involved in the Venice strike, either. The NLRB simply did not deal with agricultural workers but hoped that there would not be serious labor disputes. Particularly their regional branch office in Los Angeles was looking forward to the end of the Venice strike. On July 10, a weekly report of the NLRB regional office celebrated the agreement between Japanese and Mexican representatives. Although this agreement was still an unofficial one between Mukaeda and the CUCOM, the NLRB regional office mistook it for the final contract signed between Nōkai Renmei and the CUCOM. The report wrote, "We are pleased to report that the Los Angeles County Vegetable Workers strike ended today with a signed agreement between the Mexican union and the Japanese Associations. This agreement is to continue for a period of nine months and grants the workers a slight increase in wages, a few concessions in regard to hours but does not recognize a closed shop."[100]

In addition to the fact that their observation was wrong, Towne Nylander, the director of the Los Angeles Regional Labor Board, a local branch of the NLRB in Los Angeles, did not take the Japanese-Mexican conflict very seriously. One year after the Venice strike, Nylander wrote about Mukaeda and the Japanese-Mexican conflict in a letter to his colleague. Nylander said, "Makaidam [Mukaeda] . . . is a graduate of the University of Southern California, General Manager of the Central Japan Association, and understands English just as well as you and I do, but when forced into a corner resorts to that most irritating trait of the Japanese—pretending not to understand. Makaidam will play ball, however, if a strike actually threatens but he will bluff right down to the very last minute and in several cases in the past the Mexicans have moved too fast for him and have actually struck before he could make the concession that he was prepared to make from the very beginning. If you have plenty of time I think you will enjoy this Mexican-Japanese problem."[101]

On the contrary, Mexican consul Hill was working hard for the sake of Mexican workers. Although he did not adhere to union recognition and intended to exclude radicals from the labor movement, white farmers and agribusiness leaders were frustrated by the "subversive activities" of Hill and wanted him out of Los Angeles. Arthur Clark, the executive secretary of the Associated Farmers of Los Angeles County, misunderstood the role of Hill and believed that he purposefully teamed up with Velarde and Monroe to organize workers for "interfering with a purely domestic problem." Likewise, the Associated Farmers of Orange County was dissatisfied with Hill regarding him as a pro-union leftist. By October, Hill had left the Mexican consulate in Los Angeles to work as a deputy in the Federal Chamber of Deputies in Mexico. Clements welcomed Hill's resignation and believed that the Mexican government removed him in order to avoid international conflict. In November, when new consul Renato Cantú Lara arrived at Los Angeles, Clark and Clements contacted his vice-consul and made sure that Lara should "adhere strictly to his consular work" and work closely with local agribusiness leaders and farmers, unlike Hill, who "made the grave error of not recognizing his limitations."[102]

Resisting the strike of Mexican workers, Japanese farmers built stronger relations with white landowners and agribusiness leaders, as they believed that "Japanese and Americans are firmly tied together not merely through words but through agriculture."[103] Most Japanese farmers and white landowners demonstrated an uncompromising stance against union recognition. However, the question that the Venice strike forced Japanese farmers to consider was not simply about union recognition but also about how to survive as a minority in white-dominant and multiethnic Los Angeles. The Venice strike helps us understand how Japanese farmers negotiated a Los Angeles society divided by race and class and how they could make Japanese agriculture sustainable for years to come. While anti-labor Japanese farmers drew a clear line between themselves and ethnic Mexicans in order to maintain ethnic Japanese solidarity, pro-labor farmers regarded the Japanese-Mexican relationship as a mutually dependent and indispensable component in Japanese agriculture that would necessitate some kind of interethnic accommodation such as hiring a definite number of union members.

Mukaeda's position was in between these two groups. By employing his personal networks with Mexican and white American key persons, he urged Japanese farmers to recognize the CUCOM while preventing the Mexican side from pre-determining the percentage of union workers to be hired. Although his efforts did not materialize, it is important that by the mid-1930s Issei leaders like Mukaeda had come to recognize the importance of inter-minority cooperation in white-dominant and multiethnic Los Angeles. In other words, Los Angeles, a *transpacific workplace* located in the US-Mexico borderlands, provided a space for Japanese immigrants to understand the importance of both ethnic solidarity and interethnic accommodation. In fact, as the vice president of the Central Japanese Association of Southern California, Mukaeda continued to work for the final settlement of the Venice strike and finally succeeded in reaching an agreement between Nōkai Renmei and the CUCOM in April 1937. Both the Japanese and Mexican sides signed a contract with important provisions such as the recognition of the CUCOM and other unions as agents for collective bargaining and the payment of a minimum wage of thirty-five cents per hour for celery pickers and thirty cents per hour for all other farmworkers. The agreement was made between representatives of Japanese farmers, the Mexican consul, and the California State Labor Commissioner's office, and then ratified by the unions such as the CUCOM, the Filipino Federated Workers Union, and the Japanese Farm Workers Union.[104]

As a leader of the ethnic Japanese community, Mukaeda had his own view about how to survive a white-dominant and multiethnic Los Angeles society and made efforts to foster mutual trust with both white Americans and Mexicans. On the night of December 7, 1941, when Japan attacked Pearl Harbor, however, Mukaeda was arrested by US authorities because he was a community leader, no matter what he had been doing in his beloved city of Los Angeles. As he recalled later in the 1970s, however, "Whenever troubles, came, or maybe when troubles were coming up, I always settled them or stopped them." During the war, Mukaeda served his community as the spokesman of his camp and worked to make the living conditions of ethnic Japanese internees within the camp more comfortable.[105]

There was a top-down belief among some New Deal bureaucrats that recognizing labor organizations was indispensable for the federal government to effectively manage and control labor.[106] What was significant about the Venice strike is that some Japanese farmers, who did not have such a belief, came to understand the importance of union recognition during the New Deal period and the need for mutual understanding and interethnic harmony with ethnic Mexican residents, thus challenging the existing norm of the triracial hierarchy. Nevertheless, the majority of Los Angeles farmers, who were vehemently anti-labor, could go through the strike without recognizing the Mexican labor union. One of the places that demonstrated the strongest alliance between Japanese farmers and white landowners was Dominguez Hills. However, this does not mean that they were simply pro-business and anti-Mexican. In the last two chapters, we will examine the impact of Japanese removal and internment on Los Angeles agriculture and Japanese-Mexican relations. Japanese removal wiped away Japanese-Mexican relations from the triracial hierarchy as well as the transborder ethnic Japanese community. Yet, by focusing on the Dominguez Hills area, we can see that the events of World War II could not completely remove mutual trust between Japanese tenant farmers, white landowners, and Mexican workers.

5

Japanese Internment as an Agricultural Labor Crisis

Wartime Debates over Food Security versus Military Necessity

On the morning of December 7, 1941, Kumezō Hachimonji, a Japanese immigrant and owner of a seed and fertilizer shop in El Monte, woke up as usual and tended his field in shirt sleeves. The sun was shining brightly. At about 2 o'clock in the afternoon, Jim, his trusted employee came to his shop. He came by the back gate and did not look well. In his diary, Hachimonji wrote, "[Jim] came this time with a kind of smile on his face—as if he had [a] mask on." When Hachimonji said "Hi," Jim calmly told him, "You know [that the] Japanese [are] bombing Hawaii, now." Hachimonji responded, "What? No. What do you mean? It can't be true. Maybe [some] American aviator dropped bombs on Honolulu by mistake or something." Jim said, "Well, . . . Go in and listen [to the] radio." Hachimonji listened to the radio and realized that it was true. For him, it was "a peal of thunder out of a clean sky." Two days later, Hachimonji wrote in his diary that he wanted to transfer his properties to his US-born children in the event that he was arrested as an enemy alien. He hoped that his diary would serve as a legal document, although he was not sure whether he was legally able to transfer his properties to his children in the first place. Yet, Hachimonji anticipated that "the government would tolerate it [property transfer] so that my US-born children could operate [my shop] to make their living."[1] His diary shows that he had no idea that the government would mercilessly remove the entire ethnic Japanese population, both Japanese immigrants and their US-born children, altogether from the Pacific Coast.

Japanese Internment marked a key moment in US racial history by inflicting a grave injustice on Japanese immigrants and Japanese American citizens. Previous studies of Japanese Internment have meticulously examined the decision-making processes that led to the forced removal of the ethnic Japanese population in the contexts of anti-Japanese racism, wartime hysteria, and political tension among different governmental agencies.[2] From the agricultural perspective, however, internment resulted in the sudden loss of Japanese farmers, triggering a serious labor shortage in California, where vegetable production was an integral part of wartime food security.[3] The ethnic Japanese in California were economically very important, just like their co-ethnics in Hawai'i who were not interned because of their economic importance in the islands.[4] This chapter examines the economic impact of Japanese Internment on California agriculture and political debates over food security versus military necessity by highlighting the reactions of California's farming communities, the federal government, the California State government, particularly Governor Culbert Olson, and the attitudes of Japanese immigrants living in Los Angeles to such debates before the implementation of the mass removal. As detailed in previous chapters, Los Angeles farmland developed as a *transpacific workplace* with the unique triracial hierarchy in which Japanese farmers, Mexican workers, and white landowners interacted with one another. The disappearance of Japanese farmers brought an end to this triracial relationship in Los Angeles agriculture and thus produced a serious problem of how to keep Japanese farms operational without the Japanese.

In such an emergency, local officials of the US Department of Agriculture (USDA) and Governor Olson attempted to keep the ethnic Japanese within the borders of California, portraying them as important contributors of labor and as trustworthy people. Despite growing anti-Japanese sentiment, Olson continued to hold his idea of using ethnic Japanese agricultural workers on California farms, while ethnic Japanese residents were rather appreciative of the governor's attitude toward them during the war. What was more important in terms of Japanese-Mexican relations was that this period saw the linkage between Japanese Internment and the Bracero Program, as the importation of Mexican workers emerged as a potential solution for the loss of ethnic Japanese agricultural labor in California. By explaining these processes based on state and federal government documents, records of congressional hearings, and the Japanese immigrant press in Los Angeles, this chapter demonstrates that Japanese removal prompted voices sympathetic to the ethnic Japanese population that questioned the necessity of the racist and full-scale implementation of mass evacuation and eventually led to a growing demand for Mexican farmworkers, while generating a serious labor crisis that would endanger wartime food security.

Food security is often an overlooked subject in the study of Japanese Internment, as its legal and military aspects tend to be foregrounded. By looking at the Japanese Internment from an agricultural perspective, we can deepen our historical understanding of this tragedy through the lens of interethnic relations, which takes into account, for example, the resistance of white leaders such as Olson to full-scale internment and the substitution of Mexican workers provided to replace

Japanese agricultural labor. Consideration of these understudied realities may shift the narrative of Japanese Internment from an almost exclusive focus on the ethnic Japanese population to inclusion of non-Japanese populations who also experienced the impact of Japanese Internment. Seen from this perspective, Japanese Internment is not simply an ethnic Japanese experience but rather an integral part of the racial and economic history of California, a region characterized by a uniquely diverse population and economy.

JAPANESE AGRICULTURE IN WARTIME CALIFORNIA

After Japan's surprise attack on Pearl Harbor on December 7, 1941, the US government declared war on Japan, and thus Japanese immigrants became enemy aliens in the United States. After ten weeks, President Franklin Delano Roosevelt signed Executive Order 9066 providing a legal basis for the mass removal of Japanese immigrants (Issei) and Americans of Japanese ancestry (US-born citizens) from the Pacific Coast of the mainland United States. As far as agriculture was concerned, US agricultural officials faced two contradictory tasks created by the Pearl Harbor attack: keeping Japanese farms operational for the Food-for-Freedom program while also removing the Japanese from their farms. Eventually, the War Department and USDA reached a compromise by keeping Japanese farms functioning yet without the Japanese. However, before putting this compromise into action, local USDA officials in California had to handle a messy situation caused by the Treasury Department's freezing of Japanese bank accounts immediately following the Pearl Harbor attack.[5] Around that time, Japanese farmers produced from 35 to 50 percent of the vegetables grown in California, and California's vegetable harvest constituted between one- to two-thirds of the country's vegetable production. About 5,000 ethnic Japanese farmers operated 175,000 acres of California farmland, constituting more than half of the total California farmland devoted to vegetables.[6] In Los Angeles County, the number of Japanese-operated farms increased from 531 in 1910 to 1,523 in 1940 operating 28,670 acres.[7] In 1940, the ethnic Japanese population in Los Angeles County was 36,866, representing 39 percent of the Japanese population in California and, more importantly, 29 percent of the entire Japanese population in the mainland United States. In Los Angeles County, about 28 percent of the total 17,005 employed ethnic Japanese were engaged in agriculture and about 90 percent of Japanese farmers were tenants. Ethnic Japanese farmers dominated the county's production of at least seventeen crops, including celery, peas, spinach, beets, broccoli, radishes, peppers, snap beans, strawberries, cauliflower, and lettuce.[8]

The Treasury Department's action to freeze Japanese immigrants' bank accounts halted the distribution of Japanese-grown vegetables and forced three major produce markets on Seventh, Eighth, and Ninth Streets in downtown Los

Angeles to suspend their operation. On December 8, about two hundred people—Japanese, Chinese, and white Americans—working at these markets held a joint meeting about the wartime emergency and affirmed the necessity of resuming their market operation based on the understanding that the suspension of vegetable distribution would cause a serious inconvenience for consumers living in Los Angeles County and other neighboring counties. Issei merchants decided to hand over their stored vegetables to the companies run by white American or Japanese American merchants so that they could prevent the vegetables from going rotten.[9] In downtown Los Angeles, the Treasury Department's action made Japanese immigrants feel uneasy about their assets, as many "rushed into" a bank to withdraw money only to find out that the bank allowed only Nisei, US-born children of Japanese immigrants, with birth certificates to withdraw money. Like the produce markets, most Japanese-operated shops in Little Tokyo were closed because "banking transactions by Issei were prohibited." Although the Japanese immigrant newspaper *Rafu Shimpo* expected the US government to alleviate the restriction on behalf of "bona fide Issei," the immediate reaction of the Treasury Department to the Pearl Harbor attack certainly created a financial crisis in the daily lives of ethnic Japanese residents in Los Angeles County.[10]

This situation, which unfolded right after the Pearl Harbor attack, was troubling not only for Japanese farmers and merchants but also for the USDA because it could jeopardize wartime food security. During World War II, the USDA promoted the Food-for-Freedom program that sought to increase food production as a home-front war effort against the Axis Powers. In a program pamphlet published in November 1942, Secretary of Agriculture Claude R. Wickard explained, "Our farm recourses must be used toward but one end—Victory" and "Not only must we keep our own soldiers strong physically by producing the food they need, but we must back them up in another way by keeping workers in our war factories well fed."[11] Local officials of the USDA took the suspension of Japanese agriculture seriously because it could impede their wartime efforts under the Food-for-Freedom policy. On December 10, Dave Davidson, chairman of the California USDA Defense Board, sent a letter to representatives of County Defense Boards, warning, "All resources of alien Japanese are frozen. This is creating a serious problem in the Food-for-Freedom program in areas where alien Japanese are employed." The State and County Defense Boards were established by the USDA in July 1941 and later changed to War Boards in January 1942. Their goal was to "help farmers produce commodities needed in the war" in cooperation with other war agencies in the field. Davidson asked the county representatives to make sure that "employers should be advised verbally not to hire other labor to replace alien Japanese." It was most likely because white landowners would possibly terminate contracts with Japanese farmers and hire non-Japanese workers as their new tenants if the Japanese could not pay for land lease, given the situation that "all payments by check and cash to enemy aliens [are] stopped." Davidson also informed them that the Treasury Department was about to modify their anti-Japanese measure regarding Japanese assets. In his correspondence, Davidson showed no prejudice or antipathy against the Japanese but instead stressed that "Japanese should not be disturbed as to their safety."[12] In Davidson's understanding, the suspension on Japanese immigrants' economic activities generated concerns not only about the Food-for-Freedom program but also about the socioeconomic safety of ethnic Japanese residents.

On the next day, the Treasury Department decided to partially unfreeze Japanese assets so that the immigrants could sustain a minimum level of living. With this modification, the Treasury Department approved Japanese immigrant withdrawals up to $100 (approximately $1,760 in 2020) per month by showing a notarized affidavit to designated banks.[13] Yet, this measure did not restore the normal operation of Japanese agriculture because Japanese farmers were still unable to receive payment for their produce directly from merchants at wholesale markets. The Central Industrial Association of Southern California (Nanka Chūō Sangyō Kumiai), an ethnic Japanese organization consisting of both producers and merchants to adjust shipping and control market prices of their produce, claimed, "Due to the outbreak of war between Japan and the United States, Japanese Issei are not able to receive payment for their produce so . . . they could not make their living. . . . This is a serious problem in terms of national defense. In time of war, the shortage of food, particularly fresh vegetables, will affect the spirit of soldiers in the war front and that of people in the home front."[14] Before the Pearl Harbor attack, it was not uncommon for Japanese immigrants to express their national and racial pride for Japan, directly or indirectly supporting Japanese imperialism. After the attack, in contrast, they found themselves in an emergency situation in which they needed to explain that Japanese agriculture was an important part of the war effort for the United States to fight *against* Japanese imperialism.[15] The sudden shift of the immigrants' attitude toward Japanese imperialism was a necessary move for them to survive in the wartime political environment.

Meanwhile, the Treasury Department came to understand the importance of Japanese agriculture in the West Coast economy and the necessity of letting money flow between Japanese farmers and the Los Angeles wholesale markets. Under government control, Japanese farmers were allowed to receive payment for their produce from the banks designated by the government but required to bring bills to prove their expenses for growing their crops in order to receive the payment. On December 13, Japanese farmers resumed shipping operations for their vegetables. Yet some farmers were reluctant to ship their vegetables because they were not able to receive the cash payment directly from merchants at the markets. The *Rafu Shimpo* warned that reluctance to ship vegetables could be seen as an act of sabotage and encouraged farmers to ship as many as possible "in line with the national defense policy." With Japanese assets partially unfrozen, Japanese shops in Little Tokyo such as grocery stores, restaurants, and barber shops began to reopen, advertising the end-of-year sales.[16]

Nevertheless, the USDA was still concerned about whether unfreezing the Japanese assets would really restore the living and working conditions of Japanese farmers. In late December, P. A. Minges, a specialist on truck crops at the California Extension Service of the USDA, conducted a survey of ethnic Japanese farmers between December 19 and 24. Minges collected information from eleven California counties: Yolo, Fresno, Tulare, Kern, Los Angeles, Riverside, Imperial, Orange, Santa Barbara, San Luis Obispo, and Monterey, by working with local farm advisors and conducting interviews with people who knew Japanese farming conditions well and, in some cases, with Japanese farmers in person. Minges wanted to find out if Japanese farmers could resume shipping after December 15 and if they were willing to stay in their business and continue farming in the coming years as usual. According to his survey, "Practically all Japanese farmers indicate that they are going ahead with present crops and are planning to continue in the future as usual." Some farmers had already signed contracts for larger acreages for the next year. Yet, Minges observed that "the Japanese realize they are on the spot and their optimistic outlook may not be entirely sincere," assuming that Japanese farmers had signed new contracts to prevent landowners from replacing them with American farmers who "are anxious to get control of the land now operated by Japanese."[17]

While appreciating the likelihood that unfreezing Japanese assets "greatly benefitted the truck crop growers," Minges identified four problems that Japanese farmers could face. First, Japanese-operated banks were still closed, preventing money saved in those banks from flowing for Japanese agriculture, while American banks would likely stop making loans to Japanese farmers due to increasing public antagonism toward them. Second, non-Japanese farmworkers began to refuse to work for the Japanese. Minges mentioned particularly that "Filipinos have definitely quit [on] the Japanese. In some sections, other races have also refused to work for the Japanese." Minges carefully observed that "Japanese farmers may be able to obtain more Japanese labor than usual, because many Japanese are losing their jobs in town and will therefore be available for farm work," although this situation would depend on "public opinion and on the progress of the war." Third, white landowners might remove Japanese farmers who used the names of their US-born children to lease lands, despite the fact that it had long been practiced by Japanese farmers and tacitly approved by white landowners, agribusiness leaders, and local governments. War hysteria could easily turn such a practice into evidence of the dishonesty of Japanese farmers, as "in some sections there apparently is much agitation for landowners to do this very thing [to remove Japanese tenants]." In his survey, Minges maintained, "there is nothing to prevent landowners to refuse to lease land to American-born Japanese.... Since 90 to 95 per cent of the land operated by Japanese is leased, the refusal of landowners to renew leases could be serious." In this regard, the situation had already become serious in Salinas and the Imperial Valley. He suggested that "one solution for this situation may be for Americans to take over the land and then to hire the replaced Japanese [tenant farmers] as farm laborers."[18] Even if landowners canceled lease contracts with Japanese tenants, Minges felt that it was important to guarantee the employment of Japanese immigrants. Similar to how Davidson stressed the need for their economic security, Minges was also concerned with how to maintain the economic safety of Japanese farmers in the heightened racial climate of the weeks following the Pearl Harbor bombing.

Finally, Minges pointed out that the fundamental problem was anti-Japanese sentiment, which was particularly strong in the areas where Japanese farmers dominated the production and distribution of vegetables. Minges also mentioned that some informants "expressed the opinion that the Japanese may attempt to sabotage their crops" to support Japan's war effort. However, he simply dismissed such a claim, arguing, "Such an occurrence [of sabotage] is to be doubted on the grounds that most Japanese are interested in self-preservation and money, and are not likely to jeopardize their own well-being or their pocketbook." He also expressed concern that "some rumors are around that this discrimination [against the Japanese] is already occurring and that it may become a serious problem with the shipment to the eastern United States."[19] Japanese immigrants had been legally regarded as aliens and were politically categorized as enemies of the United States due to the outbreak of war. Nevertheless, they were also important participants in California society due to their economic impact as resident farmers. Minges did not overlook this socioeconomic aspect of Japanese farmers. His survey demonstrated the importance of Japanese agriculture in California and a hands-on understanding of Japanese farmers as a group of permanent residents who had long been working hard to make their living in California. From this perspective, sabotage was the last thing they would do because they did not want to jeopardize their "pocketbook," let alone the national security of the United States.

Minges's observation was also correct because Japanese immigrants were well aware that any suspicious activities would do great harm to the entire ethnic Japanese community. The day after the Pearl Harbor attack, the *Rafu Shimpo* issued two breaking news extras but voluntarily refrained from publishing the daily issue, considering it necessary to talk with the US government about how to continue their business before resuming their daily operation. The next day, on December 9, the immigrant press issued only the English section, mainly for English-speaking Nisei readers, and made clear their loyalty to the United States with a large headline on the bottom of the front page "We Are 100 Percent for The United States." After consulting with the federal government, the *Rafu Shimpo* resumed its main Japanese section on December 10, in which it posted a "warning to fellow Japanese in the United States." The message stressed that Japanese immigrants should understand their position as *"eijūsha* [permanent residents] who have moved and settled in the United States and benefit from living under the U.S. Constitution," exhorting them to demonstrate "one hundred percent" cooperation with the US government. On the next day, another message from the *Rafu Shimpo*, in a tone that was both careful but emotional, expressed alarm that "even if only one individual makes a rash action, that will throw all Japanese residents in the United States into the jaws of death and bring indescribably serious troubles to the whole Japanese immigrant society."[20] The Japanese American Citizens League (JACL) promptly formed the Anti-Axis Committee and began to censor Japanese immigrant newspapers.[21] When the US government prohibited Japanese immigration in 1924, the *Rafu Shimpo* had indirectly but openly criticized the United States on the front page by quoting Japanese newspapers that said, for example, "Americans are stupid people" or "We have learned the barbarity of Americans." However, in 1941, the immigrant press recognized the need for greater caution. The *Rafu Shimpo* explained that they were able to resume publication just because they lived in "the United States, a democratic country that secures the freedom of speech and publication." Yet there was no room for the ethnic Japanese community or its newspapers to exercise such freedom of speech.[22] Japanese immigrants knew that sabotage or any suspicious activity could seriously jeopardize not only their financial survival but also their very existence in California.

While the US government arrested 924 Japanese leaders in the mainland United States (and 367 in Hawai'i) in the three days following the Pearl Harbor attack, political pressure against Japanese farmers became increasingly heavy. Just as Minges anticipated, in January 1942, the California Senate unanimously adopted a resolution to "investigate any and all possible evasions of the Alien Land Laws and to prosecute to the utmost . . . any violations," clearly targeting Japanese immigrant farmers. Congressman Leland Ford of Los Angeles saw the whole ethnic Japanese community as a group of enemies and demanded an even more aggressive measure against them. In his letter to the secretaries of War and Navy as well as the FBI director, Ford claimed that "all Japanese, whether citizens or not, be placed in inland concentration camps."[23] Such a mass evacuation of ethnic Japanese residents could mean the sudden disappearance of Japanese farmers that could imperil wartime food security, since Japanese farmers had been an integral and indispensable part of California agriculture. Along with the intensification of anti-Japanese sentiment, prominent leaders of the state and federal governments would soon join the political debates over food security versus military necessity.

One of those leaders was Governor Olson. Although he was the first democratic governor of California since 1899, he did not adopt the anti-Japanese position taken by the Democratic Party in the early twentieth century.[24] His actions show us a significant point of analysis in problematizing the political and economic dialogue that led to the mass removal of ethnic Japanese farmers. In the midst of intense anti-Japanese public sentiment, Olson neither strongly protested nor enthusiastically supported a policy of mass evacuation but took a more nuanced attitude. He was concerned with the intrinsic well-being of the ethnic Japanese community in California and aware of the negative impact that Japanese evacuation would wreak on the California economy. Five days after the Pearl Harbor attack, Olson sent a message to Japanese American citizens urging them to support the US government and continue working hard in any kind of production.[25] Many Nisei were engaged in agriculture. In Los Angeles County, 1,895 US-born Japanese Americans, 26 percent of the total employed US-born Japanese Americans in the region, were farmers, farm managers, or farmworkers.[26] Regarding Issei and other enemy aliens, on January 28, 1942, Olson issued a proclamation pursuant to the proclamation issued by President Roosevelt on January 14, which required all Japanese, Germans, and Italian aliens fourteen years of age or over to have identification certificates and register for identification, so that the state government could keep them under surveillance.[27]

At the same time, Olson developed an original plan that weighed the importance of Japanese agricultural labor for both the California economy and national food security. The governor's plan, which historian Roger Daniels calls the "California plan," was to relocate but still keep Japanese agricultural labor within the borders of the state of California, which Olson believed could solve both military and economic problems related to the ethnic Japanese population.[28] On February 2, Olson met with General John DeWitt of the Western Defense Command, Assistant Attorney General Thomas B. Clark, USDA official J. M. Thompson, and Adjutant General J. O. Donovan of the California State Guard to discuss "particularly this problem of the Japanese population" and develop "plans for protection against any menace to defense and civilian safety from the large population of Japanese within our borders." Two days later, Olson gave a radio speech in which he talked about the California plan discussed in the meeting. To the people of California, he explained that "general plans were agreed upon for the movement and placement of the entire adult Japanese population in California at productive and useful employment, within the borders of our State, and under such surveillance and protection for themselves.... Such plans, we believe, are the most feasible for meeting this problem, both from the standpoint of State and national defense and from the standpoint of fairness to the Japanese people themselves." While touching upon "the possibility of sabotage and organized fifth column Japanese activities," Olson clearly stated, "To lose the benefit of this Japanese labor in agricultural production would be a serious loss to our war economy."[29] While California's location on the Pacific Coast made it vulnerable to the Japanese Empire, the removal of Japanese immigrants could be a great risk to the food security at the home front.

Olson's radio speech—publicly acknowledging the importance of Japanese agriculture and not calling for relocation to inland areas outside of California—was favorably received by Japanese immigrants. On February 5, the *Rafu Shimpo* covered Olson's radio speech about the California plan. The *Kashu Mainichi*, another Japanese immigrant newspaper, also reported it and his plan to provide surveillance and protection for Japanese residents so that they could continue to engage in agriculture and other works. On the next day, the *Rafu Shimpo* highlighted Olson's position in an article entitled "Governor Olson opposes the evacuation of Japanese to inland areas, considerable influence on the food problem," reporting that Olson explained that the loss of Japanese farmers meant "a serious loss to our war economy."[30] On the same day, Olson invited Nisei representatives of the JACL and the ethnic Japanese media to his State Capitol office in Sacramento, where he spent two hours explaining to them how the state government would handle the situation of ethnic Japanese residents. Attending the meeting were three writers of the *Rafu Shimpo* including Akira Komai, the eldest son of Toyosaku Komai, the president of the *Rafu Shimpo* who had been arrested by the FBI after the Pearl Harbor attack. Olson told them that it was difficult to distinguish the loyal from the disloyal among Japanese immigrants, which "makes it embarrassing for loyal American Japanese, and it might have more tragedy if there is indiscriminate treatment of all persons of the Japanese race." He added that he had learned of the presence of Japanese engaged in sabotage or fifth columnist activities through his communication with DeWitt and other federal government officials. While acknowledging that the ethnic Japanese were "law abiding" and "industrious," Olson demanded that both Issei and Nisei support the US war effort by voluntarily leaving the militarily important areas designated by the War Department.[31]

However, Olson explained the state's middle position to the Nisei leaders in a careful manner. According to the *Rafu Shimpo*'s report in its English section on their meeting with Olson, he gave a more nuanced explanation. Olson told them to be ready to leave the militarily important areas, "EVEN THOUGH YOU AND I MIGHT BE SURE THAT THERE WOULDN'T BE ONE JAPANESE IN THAT AREA WHO WOULD BE DISLOYAL. There would still be suspicion in the minds of the people in that area." The *Rafu Shimpo* printed Olson's explanation in capital letters to emphasize its importance for the ethnic Japanese community. Regarding where Japanese evacuees would go, Olson told them, "There will definitely be movement to places where the Japanese can be employed in producing goods and engaging in other activities OUTSIDE the combat areas."[32] Although the *Rafu Shimpo*'s description of what Olson said might not completely be the same with what he actually said, it did not change the significant fact that Olson took time to meet with the Nisei leaders in person to discuss the wartime situation. What is even more significant is that Olson did not treat all the Japanese as a faceless group of an enemy race and that he suggested a possibility of employment "outside the combat areas," which actually meant "somewhere in California outside the combat areas" in line with Olson's California plan.

The USDA was a proponent of the California plan.[33] On the same day Olson discussed the California plan with General DeWitt, Roscoe E. Bell, secretary of the California Agricultural (Land Use) Planning Committee of the USDA Bureau of Agricultural Economics, sent a letter to its local representatives of the County Farm Labor Subcommittees in California about "the possibilities of using enemy alien evacuees." The USDA letter asked its local representatives four questions: (1) "Which of the three nationalities (Japanese, Italians, and Germans) are now members of your communities in sufficient numbers so that immigration of evacuees would not cause serious problems?" (2) "Are there any possibilities of housing these individuals with people now resident in the community?" (3) "Can you rally public support for an evacuation of enemy aliens into certain areas in your county?" (4) "What is your estimate of the number of people that could be handled by the various communities in your county?" The USDA bureau described the use of enemy alien labor as a war effort that agricultural communities could make, explaining that "an opportunity is provided for certain areas to build up a local reservoir of labor required to harvest the agricultural crops so vitally needed for defense." Furthermore, he counseled, they had to recognize "the need for increased food production and the utilization of all available sources of labor in that production." In addition, the letters gave the impression that the California plan had already been in progress with support from other government agencies, as they advised, "It is important, also, to emphasize that the FBI will have investigated the aliens and that they will be under observation."[34]

By February 7, 1942, Bell had hastily collected the answers from the representatives of twenty-five counties: Lassen, Tehama, Glenn, Butte, Yuba, Sutter, Colusa, Sacramento, Yolo, Solano, Placer, El Dorado, San Joaquin, Stanislaus, Merced, Madera, Fresno, Kings, Tulare, Kern, Lake, San Benito, San Bernardino, Riverside, and Imperial. Bell created a report based on the survey and, on February 11, sent it to the California USDA War Board. According to the report, the county representatives in general showed "a willingness on the part of local people to cooperate with the Federal Government in any evacuation plans undertaken." Regarding Japanese enemy aliens, the report explained that "in a few counties there was very strong anti-Japanese feeling" and that "the anti-Japanese sentiment was stronger than the anti-Italian and anti-German sentiment." For example, counties in Southern California such as San Bernardino, Riverside, and Imperial either wanted no enemy alien labor or did not reply by the deadline. On the other hand, "In some counties a preference was expressed for Orientals because of their ability to do certain kinds of labor," as Japanese immigrants had been known as skilled farmers for decades. In fact, counties in Northern or Central California such as Glenn, Sutter, Colusa, Solano, Placer, San Joaquin, and Tulare Counties regarded the Japanese acceptable for their respective communities. Thus, Bell explained, "Willingness to use approximately 10,000 Japanese was expressed."[35] What this USDA report clearly tells us is that California was not unanimously anti-Japanese after the Pearl Harbor attack and some counties even needed and wanted Japanese immigrants for the harvest of their agricultural crops. At the time, the California plan was considered feasible, and the fear of the "yellow peril" was not dominant in California, because both Japanese immigrants and agricultural communities in California could agree on the plan.

Like the ethnic Japanese in Hawai'i, their co-ethnics in California were equally very important in terms of the local economy and thus their removal was similarly problematic during the war. For the USDA officials and Olson, agricultural necessity for the local economy and national food security was as important as military necessity. Furthermore, their documents help us understand that they shared a certain level of sympathy toward the ethnic Japanese based on their awareness about the importance of Japanese agriculture in California and their understanding of the ethnic Japanese as resident farmers. With this understanding, their attempt to maintain food security by keeping the Japanese within the borders of California would invigorate the political debates over enemy aliens, challenging the racist policy of mass evacuation that deemed the ethnic Japanese as a faceless group of undesirable and expellable people.

ALLEGED MILITARY NECESSITY VERSUS REAL ECONOMIC NECESSITY

While DeWitt indicated that the California plan was acceptable after discussing it with Olson and USDA representatives, Army officials such as Provost Marshall General Allen W. Gullion and his assistant Karl R. Bendetsen were pressing the War Department to implement the mass evacuation of ethnic Japanese residents, both aliens and citizens. Gullion warned Assistant Secretary of War John McCloy that the United States might "very possibly lose the war" unless the US government took a stern measure regarding ethnic Japanese residents and that "the danger of Japanese inspired sabotage is great." Their stance was supported by anti-Japanese politicians and newspapers suspecting that ethnic Japanese residents would engage in fifth columnist activities. On February 10, a committee organized by the joint delegation of Congress members from western states approved a resolution calling for the evacuation of enemy aliens and citizens from the coastal area.[36] Los Angeles business leaders were also part of the anti-Japanese campaign. The Los Angeles Chamber of Commerce played an active role in crafting the evacuation ideas in cooperation with anti-Japanese congressional members. The Chamber's teletypewriter contained a message that Wayne Allen, chief administrative officer of Los Angeles County, wanted to send to a leading proponent of Japanese removal, Leland Ford: "Japanese Daily News [presumably the *Rafu Shimpo*] still publishing according to their own admission. Thought you might be interested in this for use on radio or press release."[37]

In the 1930s, the Los Angeles Chamber of Commerce was a business partner of Japanese farmers in order to suppress the labor movement of Mexican farmworkers. However, the Chamber quickly altered its stance in wartime when Los Angeles could expect to enjoy the rapid growth of defense industries and its lands were "in a transition period" from agriculture to other industries and urbanization. In this context, Mexicans ceased to be regarded as undesirable strikers but instead became regarded as desirable substitute farmworkers who could replace Japanese evacuees in remaining agricultural lands. The utilization of Mexican workers would soon become a central subject in the political debates over food security versus military necessity generated by the possibility and eventual implementation of Japanese removal. In March, when the manager of the Chamber's Agricultural Department, Howard B. Miller, discussed before Congress the availability of substitute workers who would go into former Japanese farms, he mentioned, "the Japanese are rather large employers of Mexican labor" and that the operation of Japanese farms are conducted "in a considerable degree by employment of Mexican and other labor," implying that Mexicans could be substitute workers and keep Japanese farms operational.[38]

Mainstream media coverage on Japanese military activities in Asia and Japanese residents in the United States, such as Walter Lippmann's piece entitled "The Fifth Column on the Coast," fueled anti-Japanese sentiment, turning public opinion increasingly in favor of mass evacuation. As historian Greg Robinson argues, President Franklin D. Roosevelt certainly lacked empathy for the Japanese. On February 19, he issued Executive Order 9066 empowering the Army to execute the mass removal of the ethnic Japanese population. Although the Justice Department had resisted the idea of evacuating Japanese American citizens on constitutional grounds, by mid-February, its resistance ceased. The ethnic Japanese community of Los Angeles had no choice but to follow the executive order, but some expressed their frustration. For instance, in Little Tokyo, Japanese immigrants showed their anger by casting contemptuous eyes, spitting on the street, and even vandalizing patrolling cars. The *Rafu Shimpo* strongly criticized such countrymen as "molesters who don't know their place."[39]

The issuance of Executive Order 9066, however, did not mean that the California State government gave up the California plan. In fact, Olson continued to promote the plan and even explained it before anti-Japanese organizations. On February 20, Olson visited Los Angeles and gave a speech on the state's position on national defense before local members of the American Legion. The American

Legion was an organization of veterans who fought in World War I; it was one of the anti-Japanese organizations that promoted the nativist movement for the enactment of Japanese Exclusion in 1924. In January 1942, the American Legion's national commissions on war effort unanimously adopted a resolution calling for the mass evacuation of all enemy aliens from the Pacific Coast.[40] At the meeting in Los Angeles, Olson praised the American Legion as "perhaps the only group of citizens" with "a realistic conception of our problem" in the war and discussed the importance of the California State Guard newly organized in 1941. Then, Olson moved on to rearticulate the effectiveness of the California plan by quoting his own radio speech made on February 4, 1942, repeating that to lose Japanese agricultural labor would mean "a serious loss to our war economy." And he stressed that the Army, the Department of Justice, the Department of Agriculture, and the State of California will "determine upon specific plans for comprehensively locating and regulating the activities of our adult Japanese population for the duration of the war" outside the combat zone along the West Coast but "within the borders of our State."[41] Even after the Army took control of the Japanese issue, Olson confidently clarified his policy before this patriotic and anti-Japanese organization, hoping that the California plan could be implemented in cooperation with the Army and the USDA.

In the context of the wartime emergency, however, the governor of California could do only so much to resist the decision of the federal government, particularly the Army. Two days after the issuance of Executive Order 9066, the House Select Committee Investigating National Defense Migration, the so-called Tolan Committee, began hearings to discuss the possibility of the mass removal of ethnic Japanese residents from the West Coast. On March 6, Olson gave his testimony and agreed with the racist idea that the Japanese should be examined as a group, while Germans and Italians should be examined as individuals. He eventually supported mass evacuation. Yet, for exploring the relationship between Japanese removal and food security, it is important for us to carefully observe his testimony. There were three reasons why Olson agreed with the mass evacuation of the Japanese at the Tolan Committee. First, as he had already told Nisei leaders, it was difficult for "the average Caucasian" to distinguish the loyal from the disloyal among the Japanese, which Olson described as "a most unfortunate disadvantage." Second, "representatives of the Japanese-American population," presumably JACL representatives, "professional men, businessmen, farmers, and publishers ... were in good faith when they said whatever program is decided upon with regard to the removal of the entire Japanese population from any area in California or from the State, they would follow," which did not contradict what the *Rafu Shimpo* urged their community members to do. Finally, local communities in California refused to accept Japanese evacuees as of March 1942, although Olson wanted to "put these evacuated Japanese people in the State, so as to utilize their manpower in productive effort during the war, and their contribution to our agricultural production." As mentioned earlier, in December 1941 the USDA conducted a survey regarding where Japanese agricultural labor could be relocated within California and several counties showed a willingness to accommodate Japanese evacuees. In February 1942, at Olson's request, the State Department of Agriculture was conducting another survey and its result turned out to be quite different from the previous survey. The February survey could find no county willing to accept large numbers of Japanese evacuees, reflecting the rapidly growing anti-Japanese sentiment in California in the few months since the Pearl Harbor attack, during which the Japanese military expanded its control in East Asia, defeating the US military in the Philippines and the British military in the Malay Peninsula. Tulare County, for example, indicated a willingness to accommodate Japanese evacuees in December 1941 but switched its position in February, rejecting the relocation of the Japanese to the county—a significant change of public opinion that made the California plan look unfeasible. The Tulare County hospital even ordered a Japanese doctor fired simply because of his national origin.[42]

At the Tolan Committee, Olson's testimony was not only about his concerns about California's economy and wartime food security, but it demonstrated his sympathy toward ethnic Japanese residents in California confronting a very difficult situation in the aftermath of the Pearl Harbor attack. Olson stressed the importance of understating the feelings of ethnic Japanese residents who faced an extremely difficult situation in which their country of ancestry attacked their country of permanent residence. Olson was "hoping that it will be your [the Tolan Committee's] recommendation that States ... cooperate so as to help the movement of these evacuees in a way to maintain, as near as possible, their normal lives; to have them made self-sustaining and avoid any injustices and the consequences of prejudices against them." While Olson "would yield largely to the judgement of the Department of Justice and the F.B.I. and the military" with respect to the removal of Japanese enemy aliens, he mentioned that Japanese evacuation "presents a problem" since "there are a great many whom we shouldn't treat as alien enemies, although so classified, because of their lack of citizenship" and "the trouble about that is, as I say, too many people will conclude that every Japanese is a fifth columnist, no matter what may be in his heart." He even confessed that if Japan attacked California, "I would feel sorry for any Japanese loyalist inside because I am just afraid that he would suffer even if he were innocent."[43] In other words, the triumph of military necessity over food security in the political debates regarding the ethnic Japanese population as seen at the Tolan Committee did not mean that Olson reconciled himself with the idea of mass removal. He did not change his mind. As he told the representatives of Japanese Americans in person in February, Olson continued to express his concern about the situation of ethnic Japanese residents during the war, no matter whether his California plan was adopted or not. Although it is fair to argue that Olson's war effort to keep Japanese labor within California was primarily based on his economic concerns, it is important to shed light on his sympathetic words and actions toward ethnic Japanese residents in order to avoid the simplistic conclusion that California's policy regarding the ethnic Japanese during the war was only based on racism and wartime hysteria.

The *Rafu Shimpo* did not translate Olson's sympathetic words for the Japanese in detail and thus reported his testimony with the impression that he was not particularly anti-Japanese but still pushing for mass evacuation. The *Rafu Shimpo* might have wanted to minimize Olson's sympathy to avoid sounding as though the ethnic Japanese community was resisting the idea of mass evacuation. On the other hand, the *Kashu Mainichi* reported his testimony in detail and translated it including his words, "I am just afraid that Japanese would suffer even if they were innocent." In line with the federal government's plan for mass evacuation, the *Rafu Shimpo* and the *Kashu Mainichi* reported that Olson urged other states to accept Japanese evacuees because "It is our baby, all of us—the United States of America."[44]

In contrast, the *Rafu Shimpo* was critical of Los Angeles mayor Fletcher Bowron, who fueled anti-Japanese sentiment, although he had demonstrated a rather friendly attitude toward the ethnic Japanese population before mid-January of 1942. Bowron became increasingly concerned about the large Japanese population in Los Angeles, particularly on Terminal Island, an economically and militarily important site located in Los Angeles Harbor. On February 5, Bowron made his first public statement in favor of mass removal, and about a week later, gave a Lincoln Day address in which he stated, "If Lincoln were alive today, what would he do[?] . . . Lincoln, the mild-mannered man whose memory we regard with almost saint-like reverence, would make short work of rounding up the Japanese and putting them where they could do no harm." The *Rafu Shimpo* reported it with a headline that said "Mayor Bowron Dwells on Relocation" along with another article about the evacuation order to ethnic Japanese residents in Terminal Island.[45]

At the Tolan Committee, Bowron gave his testimony, assuring the city's full cooperation for the Army with respect to the evacuation of the Japanese. He dared to say, "I first want to make it clear that my position relative to the Japanese population here in our midst is not by reason of any racial or other prejudice. . . . The Japanese have caused very little trouble. They are law abiding and industrious and cooperative," but continued, "As I look back on some events after the 7th of December, I am quite convinced that there was a large number of the Japanese population here locally who knew what was coming." Bowron's racial prejudice was clear, although the aggression of the Japanese military in Asia and the increasingly hostile public opinion could have influenced his attitude. Furthermore, regarding food security, Bowron downplayed the economic impact of Japanese removal on the city's food supply and distribution, making a rather optimistic assumption, "There are others who could describe that much better than I.... Necessarily, it will quite seriously affect the fresh vegetable supply for this large populous area. However, I think our people will be glad to adjust themselves to wartime conditions." As shown in his testimony, the ethnic Japanese residents were not part of "our people" in Bowron's mind.[46] His hypocritical stance aroused Nisei to anger. After his testimony at the Tolan Committee, Togo Tanaka, a Nisei editor of the *Rafu Shimpo*'s English section, wrote an open letter to Bowron and criticized him, contending, "You have been the spearhead of press publicity for uprooting us from the only home we know. Yet, before the Tolan Committee . . . you consistently referred to the responsibility of the Federal government. In a word, you passed the buck."[47] For the ethnic Japanese community of Los Angeles, Olson appeared more understanding and clearly different from Bowron, although both eventually agreed on the mass evacuation of the entire Japanese population. The testimonies of Olson and Bowron reflect the debates over alleged military necessity versus real economic necessity.

MEXICAN WORKERS AS A SOLUTION FOR THE JAPANESE REMOVAL

Even after the Tolan Committee hearings, the loss of Japanese agricultural labor remained a serious problem for California agriculture with no clear solution. At the Tolan Committee, Olson answered the question regarding who would operate former Japanese farms, arguing that Japanese removal "will eliminate the possibility of having the benefit in agricultural production of the labor of the Japanese during this war period. We are going to have some labor problems, I believe, in agriculture." Olson gave the committee a stereotypical explanation that "the Japanese are peculiarly fitted" to pick vegetables in a stooping posture, and "they have been a large part of it," while Mexicans and Filipinos were also "adaptable to do that." Although Olson believed that Japanese farms should be worked by new tenants, he thought it doubtful that "there will be sufficient manpower in certain classes of agricultural work." For example, in Salinas, landowners were worried about the lettuce harvest because they could not find enough Filipino workers. Many Filipinos had been enlisted into the Army or were leaving to do more profitable work in the rapidly growing defense industries.[48]

In April 1942, the *Los Angeles Times* reported on the Japanese evacuation from the local harbor areas, which the Army considered the "most vulnerable to sabotage and espionage," embracing the areas of San Pedro, Long Beach, Wilmington, Redondo Beach, Torrance, Signal Hill, and Hynes. These areas included many war industry sites such as shipyards, naval installations, oil fields, the steel production center of Torrance, and the new aircraft factory at Long Beach. The *Times* noted that "most of the affected Japanese are farmers." By that time, out of the more than twenty-five thousand acres of Los Angeles County farmland operated by the Japanese, one-third had been put under the control of the authorities to transfer the lands to "American owners going into production." By August 18, 1942, the US government had expelled all the ethnic Japanese residents, both aliens and citizens, from California except for those relocated to the remotely located Tule Lake and Manzanar camps and others supervised in hospitals and prisons. However, many of the Japanese farms were abandoned without being managed by new operators. One example was a two-thousand-acre tomato farm in Palos Verdes Estates in Los Angeles County. The *Los Angeles Times* reported later in September that the farm's tomatoes "may never reach the United States Army, contract canneries or city markets unless there is some vital change in the labor outlook," to the extent that the situation "became a do-or-die campaign among civic leaders today." Although local high school students helped pick the tomatoes, the farm still lacked the manpower for the peak of the crop season. To make matters worse, motorists picked the apparently abandoned tomatoes. As for this situation, non-Japanese growers also announced that the problem was "virtually out of control."[49]

While many Japanese farms were destined to remain unattended, Olson came to have a more optimistic view on how to maintain agricultural labor in California. Rapidly changing dynamics of international relations around the Pacific Ocean and across the US-Mexico borderlands created a possibility of importing a large number of Mexican agricultural workers. The Pacific War between the United States and Japan resulted in a closer hemispheric cooperation between the United States and Mexico. In May of 1942, the US and Mexican governments began to discuss the importation of Mexican agricultural workers into the United States. This binational measure, later known as the Bracero Program, would bring Mexican workers to the United States starting in the summer of 1942, awarding 4.5 million work contracts by 1964 when the program was terminated. With this wartime collaboration, the US government intended to solve the wartime labor shortage in agriculture and the Mexican government sought to regulate the northward migration of its citizens.[50]

Olson hoped that the importation of Mexican workers, or braceros, could replace his California plan. On July 2, 1942, Olson made a radio speech entitled "Mexican Labor" in which he argued that the importation of Mexican workers might solve the agricultural labor crisis created by Japanese Internment. Olson touched upon negotiations "conducted between the secretary of state of the United States and the Mexican government to ascertain whether Mexico will approve a plan for bringing Mexican laborers into this country to be employed on the farms for the duration of the war. Representatives of growers have been urging such a program in Washington." Olson reported that he had demanded in his telegram to the War Manpower Commission that the federal government take the responsibility for recruitment and transportation of Mexican workers. Yet, even at this stage, he mentioned his California plan, explaining its advantages and the difficulties that prevented its implementation. He said, "It was then [re]cognized that if the Japanese could [be] employed in the performance of [ag]ricultural work, under appropriate [re]gulations and control of their movements, [tha]t would serve the economy of the [nat]ion, avoid the appropriations of [hun]dreds of millions of dollars for [the]ir maintenance in Assembly Centers, [and] solve the agricultural labor problem [in] California. But the natural antipathy [of] having Japanese in the presence of [any] community under any condition was manifest." Olson pointed out that despite the economic importance of Japanese agricultural labor, rapidly growing anti-Japanese sentiment in California made it very difficult to implement his California plan, saying, "an entire change of [dis]position and sentiment on the part [of] the farmers and employers of farm [lab]or in California would be needed for the employment of Japanese."[51]

Then, Olson stressed that Japanese evacuees could have stayed and worked in California farms under continuous surveillance that would have made it impossible for Japanese evacuees to participate in sabotage or fifth columnist activities. He closed his radio speech by touching upon the importation of Mexican workers:

> Such an effort to [util]ize this vast reservoir of manpower [would] undoubtedly be aided and assisted [by] that proportion of the Japanese people [them]selves, who undoubtedly have an [undi]vided loyalty to our country and ... [as] thousands of Japanese now serving in [the] United States Army and fighting [agai]nst the Japanese power. If the farm labor shortage could be [supp]lied without the importation of foreign [labo]r, we would avoid all of the problems, [dela]ys, difficulties and expense which [such] importation would entail. But with [the] uncertainty that any other solution [may] be found, efforts will continue to [make] available such Mexican labor as shall [be] found needed to save the crops of California. I thank you and bid you good night.[52]

Olson's radio speech was not only about his hope for the Bracero Program. It was also about his belief that the California plan was feasible because of the loyalty of ethnic Japanese residents as well as his implicit criticism of uncompromising anti-Japanese sentiment that made it impossible to keep Japanese farmers in California. In fact, after this radio speech, Olson met with DeWitt to discuss his idea of using evacuated Japanese people as emergency farm laborers. DeWitt simply declined Olson's idea, telling him that the use of evacuated Japanese as farm workers would contradict the ongoing evacuation program adopted as a military necessity. In fact, ethnic Japanese evacuees engaged in farming to feed themselves at their camp sites including Tule Lake and Manzanar. In 1943, the total amount of vegetables that Japanese evacuees produced and consumed at each of ten camps, officially known as "relocation centers," was estimated to be more than forty-three million pounds. However, they were not allowed to work as emergency farm laborers in regular California farms as Olson hoped. In addition, proposing the use of the evacuated Japanese made Olson look weak or soft on enemy aliens, as a *Los Angeles Times* writer criticized Olson for his proposal, saying, "We don't need the Japs. . . . In fact the Governor had better quit fooling around with the Army." At this time, Olson regarded Mexicans as a possible source of emergency farm labor but was not sure if the importation of Mexican workers could really solve the "still serious" situation on California farms.[53]

As the situation worsened, in August 1942, Olson sent a telegram to President Roosevelt urging him to bring in Mexican workers as quickly as possible. Olson explained the serious situation of California agriculture in which crops were "wasting and spoiling," even though "every possible use is being made of all local supplies of labor." Olson contended, "We must have help now," and asked President Roosevelt "to immediately put an end to the current academic debates in Washington on this subject. Send recruiting teams into Mexico and send someone to California with full authority [to] handle this matter now in a direct practical fashion." And he added, "Matter has been delayed to the point of negligence and will have serious effect upon our entire war effort." About a week later, Secretary of Agriculture Wickard responded to Olson, writing, "Final agreements are being made to supply Mexican farm labor to California farms where domestic labor cannot be obtained."[54] Around this time, the Bracero Program began to bring Mexican workers from south of the US-Mexico border.

The importation of Mexican workers was one of the wartime policies born out of US-Mexico wartime collaboration. Mexicans not only worked in farmlands in the United States but also served as soldiers in the US Army. The number of Mexican citizens serving in the US Army reached nearly fifteen thousand during the Pacific War. This remarkable collaboration that incorporated Mexican manpower into the US war effort was promoted by Mexican president Manuel Ávila Camacho. In October 1942, Ávila Camacho announced that Mexican residents in the United States were allowed to enlist in the US Army because "Mexico is a member of the Allied Nations and we are obligated to contribute decisively to the triumph of Allies over Germany, Italy and Japan."[55] Ávila Camacho became president in 1940 and contrasted with the former president Lázaro Cárdenas who nationalized the oil industry that had been largely controlled by American, British, and Dutch owners. Ávila Camacho's predecessor galvanized the Mexican people in his nationalist policies but also exacerbated already tense diplomatic relations with the United States. In contrast, even before the Pearl Harbor attack, Camacho welcomed foreign investment and strengthened its alliance with the United States partly because he needed to gather recourses to suppress anti-Camacho protests in Mexico. In his inauguration speech, Camacho emphasized, "Nothing divides us in this America of ours. Any differences that may exist between our peoples are overcome by a lofty desire to secure the permanence of a continental life of friendliness based on mutual respect and the victory of reason over brute force, of peaceful cooperation over mechanized destruction."[56]

US-Mexico wartime collaboration even made Japanese Internment a transnational project that developed in the US-Mexico borderlands. After the Pearl Harbor attack, Ávila Camacho promptly responded to the request of the US government regarding ethnic Japanese residents in Mexico. In early January 1942, more than a full month before the issuance of Executive Order 9066, the Mexican government took action to relocate more than 2,700 ethnic Japanese residents in the US-Mexico borderlands to inland cities such as Mexico City and Guadalajara.[57] The relocated Japanese population was equivalent to about half of the entire population of Japanese nationals in Mexico.[58] In Ensenada, about sixty Japanese fishermen employed by the company of the former president Abelardo Rodríguez and politician Luis Salazar were able to stave off immediate removal thanks to the protection provided by the two company owners, who did not want to lose their economic interests. By March, however, the situation had turned against them as Lázaro Cárdenas, a popular former Mexican president who was now in charge of military defense in the Pacific Coast region, tightened anti-Japanese policy. These fishermen anticipated their eventual removal and voluntarily resigned from the company to relocate to Mexico City, leaving no Japanese immigrants and their descendants, except the children of a Japanese father and a Mexican mother, in Baja California.[59] The Japanese removal in Mexico was also the Mexican government's response to mounting anti-Japanese sentiment in the country following the Pearl Harbor attack, which made Mexican elites and workers increasingly fearful about possible Japanese espionage and invasion.[60] In sum, alleged military necessity brought about the forcible removal of the West Coast's ethnic Japanese farming population and gave rise to the importation of Mexicans to solve the pressing economic problems and relieve concerns over wartime food security.

When Japanese immigrants in Baja California heard the relocation order, they held emergency meetings and gathered about ten thousand pesos and, with that money, attempted to persuade the local government of Baja California to let them stay in the region. They failed and learned that the US government was behind the Mexican government's relocation order. Japanese immigrants in Baja California had no choice but to leave the region except for their Mexican wives and their children, who were allowed to stay. On January 2, 1942, the first group of twelve ethnic Japanese residents and a Japanese diplomat named Miyazawa left Mexicali for Guadalajara. One of them, Mitsu Ichikawa, later recalled her experience of Japanese removal from Mexicali. She immigrated to Mexicali in 1924 as a *yobiyose* to live with her husband Yonezō Ichikawa, owner of a soda water factory and a board member of the local Japanese association. Before leaving Mexicali, the Ichikawa family and others in the same group asked Miyazawa why they were the first to leave. According to Mitsu Ichikawa, Miyazawa answered, "If you don't leave, the United States would invade Mexico. To order other Japanese to leave, I want leaders of the Japanese community to leave first."[61]

On the same day when Miyazawa, Ichikawa, and other Japanese left Mexicali, *La Opinión* reported that the Mexican government had ordered all the Japanese in Baja California to "move to the country's inland without loss of time" as a measure to "remove the niponés [Japanese] from the coast where they could signal to enemy ships and planes, or dedicate themselves to fifth column activities to help the soldiers of their empire to disembark at the Mexican territory."[62] On the following day, *La Opinión* ran articles that showed the paper's favorable attitude toward the Mexican government's policy regarding the war and immigrants in Mexico. An article on the front page was about Lázaro Cárdenas. On January 2, he responded to the press in Ensenada and explained that he had "visited almost all the coastal area [of Baja California] under my command and found nothing abnormal" and that "there are no submarine or air bases along the Mexican coast of the Pacific Ocean." Meanwhile in Mexico City, the Mexican Ministry of the Interior conveyed a memorandum to its officials about the plan to create "migratory stations" as "concentration camps for those undesirable foreigners," who could be profiled with the archival data of "many wicked foreigners." Although the ministry did not mention Japanese immigrants as their main target for the "concentration camp," it clearly demonstrated that the Mexican government had begun to take tighter control of foreigners during the war. In addition, *La Opinión* demanded that ethnic Mexican residents in Los Angeles should support the US government war efforts. The paper placed an advertisement of US war bonds and wrote, "LA OPINION encourages all the American citizens of Mexican origin to support the [US] government, purchasing bonds and defense stamps, and makes the same call to Mexicans in general, residents of this country, as a demonstration of sympathy towards the great nation that has given them hospitality."[63]

The experience of the ethnic Japanese in Baja California had already been at the mercy of international relations between the United States and Japan. As detailed in chapter 1, the Immigration Act of 1924 nullified the Gentlemen's Agreement and helped develop the ethnic Japanese community in Baja California and the transborder ethnic Japanese community in the US-Mexico borderlands. Eighteen years later, the Pacific War brought an end to this community's existence due to the binational implementation of Japanese removal from both sides of the US-Mexico border. The large space vacated by the ethnic Japanese population in the US-Mexico borderlands was soon to be filled again with Mexican residents and Mexican cross-border migrants such as braceros. The history of the transborder ethnic Japanese community seems to have disappeared from public memory.

The wartime experience of the ethnic Japanese population teaches us not only how racism resulted in their mass removal but also how Japanese immigrants' everyday activities as farmers mattered in terms of wartime food security and the productivity of California agriculture. After the Pearl Harbor attack, local USDA officials in California and Governor Olson attempted to keep the ethnic Japanese farming population within the state in order to assure wartime food security and California's agricultural economy. They regarded the Japanese as an important source of labor but also as trustworthy people who should be allowed to stay in California under surveillance. Some local farming communities demonstrated their willingness to accommodate the evacuated Japanese as agricultural workers. Along with growing anti-Japanese sentiment fueled by the Japanese military aggression in East Asia, the alleged military necessity for Japanese removal sidelined the argument stressing the importance of Japanese agricultural labor to wartime food security, as seen at the Tolan Committee hearings. Finally, the importation of Mexican farmworkers through the Bracero Program brought hope to California agriculture once Japanese removal became inevitable, ending the debate over food security versus military necessity.

Race, not nationality or loyalty, was the most powerful driving force of Japanese Internment. At the same time, it was one of several significant factors in wartime debates regarding people of Japanese ancestry, as Japanese Internment generated serious debates over food security versus military necessity, which in turn led to a growing demand for Mexican farmworkers. Economic and social roles played by the Japanese agricultural community functioned to affect the California State government and build resistance against the merciless and overtly racist policy of removing all ethnic Japanese residents, whether US citizens or not, from their homes. More importantly, like the economic necessity that prevented the full-scale internment of the ethnic Japanese population in Hawai'i, there was a similar economic necessity regarding their co-ethnics in California. Nevertheless, such an economic necessity was attenuated by the Bracero Program in the context of the hemispheric wartime collaboration between the United States and Mexico, thus contributing to the mass removal and internment of the ethnic Japanese population from the Pacific Coast region. By looking at Japanese Internment as an agricultural labor crisis in California, we can understand it as not solely about race but also about economics in wartime, multiethnic California, in which ethnic Japanese and Mexican immigrant workers' experiences were interwoven.

6

Enduring Interethnic Trust in Rancho San Pedro

The Bracero Program gave hope for people like Governor Olson, who were concerned about the agricultural labor shortage in California after Japanese Internment. Nonetheless, the program was designed to provide temporary foreign workers, not tenant farmers. Many white landowners in Los Angeles County needed tenant farmers who could take diligent care of their farmlands. Since they had built stable and trusting relationships with Japanese tenants for the past decades, it was not an easy job for landowners to find tenants like Japanese farmers. To support such landowners and keep former Japanese farms operational without the Japanese, as early as in March 1942, the US Department of Agriculture (USDA) assigned the Farm Security Administration (FSA) to find non-Japanese tenant farmers and provide them with loan finance.[1] Landowners in the region, including the Dominguez Hills area and other neighboring areas in Los Angeles County, known as Rancho San Pedro (see Map 2), were no exception and remained concerned about the replacement of tenant farmers. During the Venice Celery Strike of 1936, Japanese farmers and white landowners in Dominguez Hills banded together in a demonstration of a strict and uncompromising stance against Mexican strikers. This situation was dramatically altered by the Pacific War, turning Mexican workers into hopeful replacement candidates for land tenancy in the area. Wartime experiences of the ethnic Japanese, ethnic Mexicans, and white landowners in Rancho San Pedro detail the impact of Japanese Internment on a local agricultural community and tell us an untold story of the triracial interethnic relations that continued even after the removal of the Japanese from Los Angeles County.

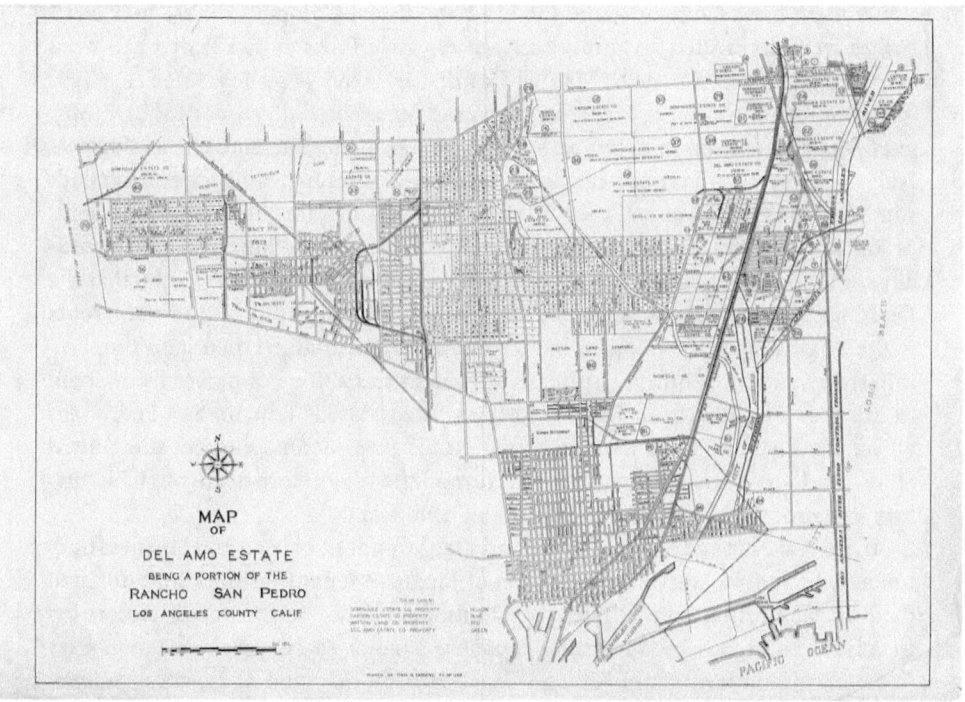

MAP 2. Rancho San Pedro, 1937. Courtesy of Special Collections, Gerth Archives and Special Collections, CSU Dominguez Hills.

TRIRACIAL AGRICULTURE IN AN OLD SPANISH RANCHO

Rancho San Pedro was a site of the original Spanish land grant located in the southern part of Los Angeles County overlapping mainly with today's Torrance, Carson, and the Wilmington area of Los Angeles. In Rancho San Pedro, Japanese immigrant farmers began to increase in the mid-1910s.[2] One example of this early Japanese tenant farming economy is the story of a Japanese immigrant named Masakichi Kuwahara. Kuwahara came to the United States in 1919 and settled in Rancho San Pedro despite the restrictions imposed under the Gentlemen's Agreement of 1907–1908. He could enter the United States legally as a *yobiyose* son of a Japanese farmer working in Rancho San Pedro.[3] Later Japanese farmers began to grow other crops such as cauliflower, cabbage, celery, and beans. Those Japanese farmers leased their farmlands from four local real estate companies in Rancho San Pedro: the Dominguez Estate Company, the Carson Estate Company, the Watson Land Company, and the Del Amo Estate Company. These four companies were connected as family companies, since Rancho San Pedro had been owned by the descendants of Manuel Domínguez, who was a Los Angeles mayor in the nineteenth century. In 1784, a veteran Spanish soldier Juan José Domínguez was granted the land by the Spanish government. The land ownership was taken over by Dominguez's nephew Cristóbal Domínguez and later Cristóbal's son Manuel. When Manuel died in 1882, more than twenty-four thousand acres of Rancho San Pedro were divided by his six children, all daughters, and eventually came to be managed by the above estate companies. It is noteworthy that the Dominguez descendants, socially considered as whites and proud of their roots in the original Spanish colonization of California, maintained their land property into the twentieth century despite the turbulent transitions of power from Spain to Mexico, and then from Mexico to the United States.[4] Rancho San Pedro was where the histories of settlers and immigrants from Spain, Mexico, the United States, and Japan merged together and turned the region into a site of global history and profitable farmland in Southern California.

These real estate companies preserved a large amount of legal and business documents, including land lease contracts of Japanese tenant farmers, and donated them to California State University, Dominguez Hills, in the 1970s. According to various records related to ethnic Japanese tenants, there were more than sixty Japanese family farmers in Rancho San Pedro by the time of Japanese Internment. Before Japanese tenants were gone, the Dominguez Estate Company and the Del Amo Estate Company, respectively, created a list of forty-two and twelve Japanese tenant farmers who worked on lands leased until February 10, 1942. The Carson Estate Company also had the records of land lease contracts with at least fourteen Japanese tenant farmers who worked until the time of their evacuation. The majority of ethnic Japanese farmers in Rancho San Pedro leased small plots ranging from three to thirty acres, but some had larger lands of more than one hundred acres.[5]

Land lease contracts give us a detailed picture of how Japanese farmers leased lands under the name of their US-born children in order to circumvent the California Alien Land Law of 1920 and how the landowners provided them with assistance in that process. In February 1941, a Japanese family made a lease contract for two small lots under the name of Chieno Amate, probably the family's daughter, with the Carson Estate Company. In April, however, the company canceled this lease because her birth certificate had not been submitted. A little later, the Amate family tried to lease the same lots under the name of their son, Shigeru Amate. The company official in charge of processing the lease cooperated to change the tenant's name, writing to his colleague, "I have cancelled the lease for Chieno Amate and applied the $35.00 received March 10 from Chieno on the Shigeru Amate lease. Hope this is O.K." The lease contract was successfully made with Shigeru's birth certificate, proving his birth in Los Angeles on March 11, 1920, as a son of Japanese parents.[6] As demonstrated in these records, Japanese farmers and the companies made collaborative efforts for legal compliance under the restriction of the California Alien Land Law until the time when the US-Japan war began.

The Amate family's lease contract also illustrates another important fact, which was observed by the USDA specialist P. A. Minges in December 1941. Their lease covered one year from January 1 to December 31 of 1941. Before the lease would expire, Japan attacked Pearl Harbor on December 7. Yet, even after the outbreak of the war, the Amate family and the Carson Estate Company renewed the lease for another annual term from January 1 to December 31 of 1942. A company memorandum shows that the Amate family paid one half of their yearly amount of $75 (approximately $1,190 in 2020) for the lease on January 27, 1942, not knowing that they would be removed from their farms shortly after the payment. Finally, their lease was canceled on March 11 of that year due to the mass evacuation of ethnic Japanese people. Other Japanese farmers in Rancho San Pedro also renewed their leases after the Pearl Harbor attack.[7] Since the Japanese farmers and the real estate companies in Rancho San Pedro had trusting relationships to maintain the profitable use of lands for both parties, Japanese Internment was a problem not only for the Japanese but also for real estate companies and landowners.

Being aware of this difficult situation, in March 1942, the FSA created the Wartime Farm Adjustment Program. At the same time, Laurence I. Hewes Jr., regional director of the FSA in charge of the states of California, Nevada, Utah, and Arizona, sent letters to all district officials and field agents of the Wartime Farm Adjustment Program and announced that the FSA had been assigned "the vital emergency job of seeing that agricultural production continues on the lands of Japanese aliens and citizens." The primary purpose of the Wartime Farm Adjustment Program was "to supervise the fair disposition of alien agricultural lands and to assure continued production on those lands by aiding qualified farmers to take over the vacated land and obtain credit to operate." Hewes emphasized that "increased production under the Food For Freedom program is of vital importance to our military effort—affecting not only supplies for our Army but supplies being sent to Britain and Russia—keeping the Japanese lands in production is a basic war measure."[8] It revealed the pragmatic but contradictory nature of the US war policy toward the ethnic Japanese population, which regarded as military necessity both the removal of Japanese residents and the maintenance of Japanese farms. The US government that violated the human and civil rights of the ethnic Japanese population still needed the fertile farmland cultivated by Japanese farmers.

Earlier in March 1942, Hewes gave his statement and testimony at the Tolan Committee. Although he agreed that the agricultural problem caused by the Japanese removal would not raise questions about whether or not there should be an evacuation, he put importance on maintaining the Japanese farmlands "in order that vital food supplies needed for war purposes be maintained." And he disagreed that mass evacuation should be a permanent relocation of the ethnic Japanese because "it is to be assumed, I think, that most of them will desire to return to their former homes if possible or at least to the community in which they have formerly lived and worked and which they know." His remark, in fact, echoed the sentiment of Japanese farmers, implying that Hewes was in favor of the return of the Japanese to California. The idea that the Japanese should be allowed to return was a reason why the FSA would work to "arrange for their operation [of former Japanese lands] under lease to nearby farmers," rather than finding new owners of the lands.[9] After all, what the US government wanted was the food grown on Japanese farmlands, not the ethnic Japanese residents themselves. Although the prevailing national sentiment was opposed to ethnic Japanese residents along the Pacific Coast, the FSA representatives, however discreetly, advocated for the return of ethnic Japanese farmers to California before the Tolan Committee.

WARTIME FARMS WITHOUT NEW TENANTS BUT MEXICANS

The Rancho San Pedro real estate companies faced the same problem of finding new tenants. John Victor Carson, a member of the Dominguez family and great-grandson of Manuel Domínguez who inherited Rancho San Pedro in the 1820s, was in charge of the management of family business, including farm operations. In 1972, Judson Grenier, professor of history at California State University, Dominguez Hills, interviewed Carson about his experience during World War II. Regarding the Japanese tenant farmers in the prewar period, Carson recalled, "We had a lot of Japanese gardeners [farmers], all scattered around," and "all of our land, being under irrigation, went into truck gardening, vegetable gardening. The Japanese were the only ones who would do it. So our farming operations went on pretty much as usual." However, "the second World War was different because the Japanese gardeners all got hauled out of here."[10]

Then the FSA began to find new tenants who would replace the Japanese. We can observe in land lease contracts how Japanese farms were taken over by non-Japanese farmers through the FSA. For example, a Japanese American tenant Tōru Horita leased a fifteen-acre piece of land known as "lease #3" (see Map 3) of the Carson Estate Company to use it for the period from July 1, 1941, to June 30, 1943. Horita was born in Compton in 1919 as a son of a Japanese farmer family. However, the Horita family was sent to a camp in 1942. On March 27, 1942, new tenants Kenneth Bruce Jones and his father J. D. Jones took over the "lease #3" through the FSA. On June 5, the FSA sent a letter to the Carson Estate Company informing it that the Horita family "gave Mr. Jones a Bill of Sale on all crops,

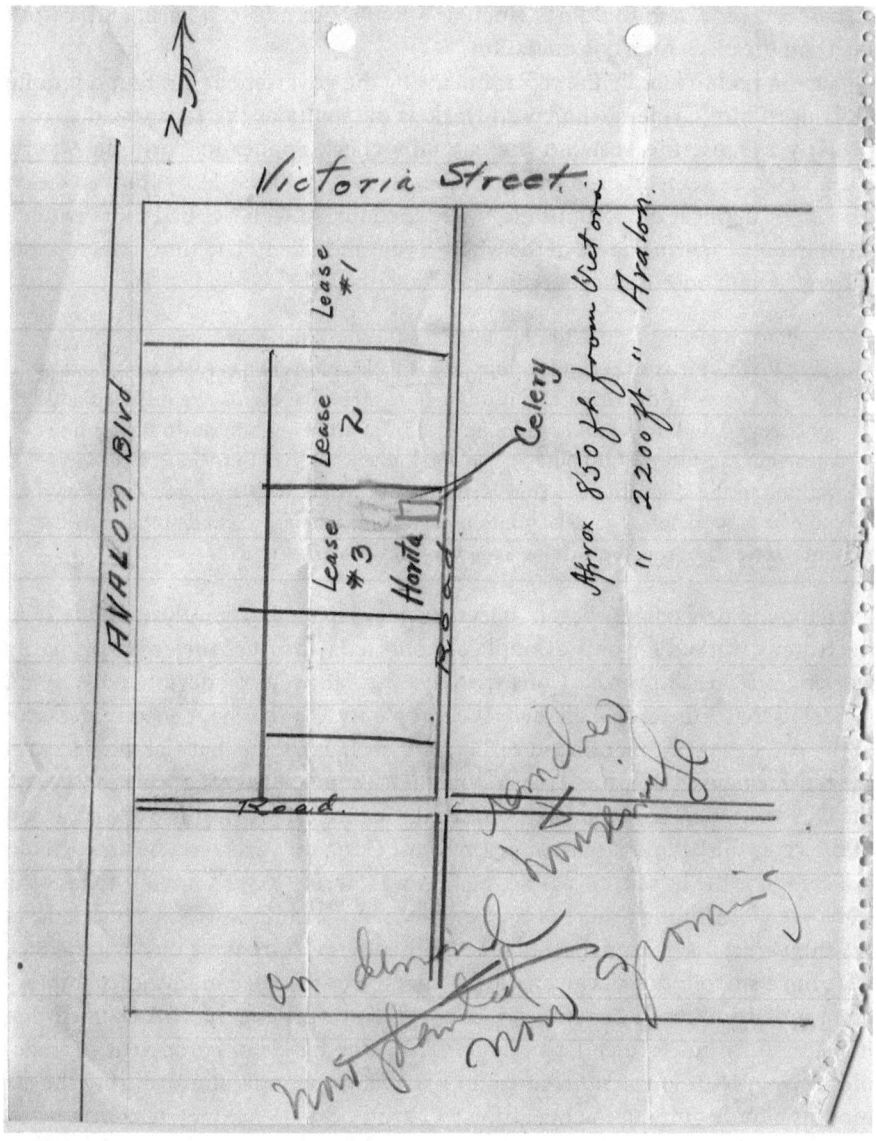

MAP 3. Horita and Haijima's farms in Rancho San Pedro. The Horita family farmed the land titled "lease #3," and the Haijima family leased the land titled "lease #2." This area is at the southeastern corner of Victoria Street and Avalon Boulevard. Courtesy of Rancho San Pedro Collection, Gerth Archives and Special Collections, CSU Dominguez Hills.

machinery, pipe, and buildings [such as a five-room house, a barn, and a work shed] on the place for a consideration."[11]

Carson had to handle the replacements by the government but found it quite difficult to hire farmers who could work as diligently as the Japanese did, particularly because the FSA did not carefully check applicants' farming experience. Later he remembered that experience, saying, "[The FSA] took anybody who made application. [Applicants] were the lousiest—oh, we had more trouble around here. I was in charge of the whole thing, and I had a bad time." Carson was frustrated with both FSA agents and new tenants, as he recalled:

> One day this government fellow [an FSA agent] came down to me and said, "I've got a man for this piece up here on Dominguez Hill, this ten-acre piece. He wants to take it." ... He gave me the name, and it was a guy I threw out the day before. He'd gone right around and in the other door. So I said, "Don't bring him down here. I don't want him. I just threw him out." ... Do you know what they were doing? They were working in the shipyards.... They went to work in the shipyards, and then they'd come back, work for a couple of hours, and go home. Then the next day, they'd do the same thing. The crops were dying and everything else.[12]

Even though new tenants began to lease former Japanese farms through the FSA, the tenants worked for only a couple of hours a day because they were primarily working in the shipyards. Consequently, the farms were devastated. Carson lamented that "[the crops] all died. We lost plenty."[13] What happened in the farm of the Amate family, mentioned earlier, tells such a trouble that Carson had with the replacements. After the Amate family was removed from Rancho San Pedro, the FSA sent a new tenant named William J. Cammack, providing him with a loan of $42.50 as the payment to the Carson Estate Company. However, Cammack did not complete the lease contract, so the FSA was "trying to get someone to take the lease over."[14] Although there is no evidence that Cammack was also working in the shipyards, it is reasonable to consider that the replacements through the FSA were not a smooth process given the fact that the war created many other employment opportunities in Los Angeles County.[15] Nevertheless, the FSA claimed that it successfully put former Japanese farms "in the hands of competent management ... without any serious interruption of farming operation" during the six months after beginning the operation.[16] Carson's experience clearly contradicted that conclusion.

While the new tenants such as Jones and Cammack were presumably white, there were Asian Americans who tried to replace the Japanese farmers in Rancho San Pedro. A Chinese American named John J. Wong tried to lease a 6.5-acre plot of land that was formerly cultivated by the Japanese family of Haruko Kurashige. The Carson Estate Company began the replacement process for Wong on May 19, 1942, but Wong did not sign the lease, since he "does not want it." A company memorandum written on June 24 says, "This Chinaman has not taken land, nor signed lease. Unable to locate him. Will lease it to someone else."[17] Regardless of the ethnicity, it was not easy for the local real estate companies to find the tenants who would stay and take care of the farms seriously after the removal of the Japanese. However, there was one group of people who eventually revitalized the Rancho San Pedro farmland: ethnic Mexicans, who had been farmworkers for decades in the region. Carson recalled that "they [Japanese] were replaced mostly by Mexicans."[18]

World War II had a great socioeconomic impact on the ethnic Mexican community in Los Angeles County, which was the largest concentration of ethnic Mexicans in the United States. In 1940 in Los Angeles County, Mexican residents, as foreign-born whites, numbered 59,260 and the whole ethnic Mexican population approximately 315,000.[19] The war triggered the rapid growth of defense industries and created job opportunities for residents and newly arriving domestic migrants to Los Angeles. In the hope of getting well-paying jobs, tens of thousands of ethnic Mexicans went westward to California from Texas, New Mexico, Colorado, and Arizona, while ethnic Japanese were forcibly relocated eastward to some of those same states. In around 1943 when defense production peaked, many Mexican residents were hired in the booming aircraft and shipbuilding industries. For example, about 12 percent of all Lockheed aircraft employees were Mexican Americans, 80 percent of whom were women working in assembly lines and as riveters. However, racial discrimination was still deeply rooted in US society despite the war against the Axis. When the war economy began to slow down, ethnic Mexican workers were the first to be dismissed.[20] Japanese Internment somewhat moderated anti-Japanese fear, but it then positioned ethnic Mexicans as a new target of racial hatred by the white majority, as most clearly demonstrated in the Sleepy Lagoon murder case in 1942 and the Zoot Suit Riots in 1943. The Pacific War heightened the racial tension between whites and Mexican Americans in Los Angeles by transforming the city's demography with the disappearance of the ethnic Japanese as well as the increase of domestic migrant workers, including Mexicans.[21] In the history of prewar Los Angeles, racial discrimination against Japanese and Mexicans were mutually constitutive and created in the context of local and international relations.

As far as Japanese-Mexican interethnic relations were concerned, the question is how the ethnic Mexican community in Los Angeles reacted to Japanese Internment. Since the ethnic Japanese and Mexicans interacted with one another in the urban and agricultural areas of Los Angeles County, Japanese removal could not go without influencing the ethnic Mexican community.[22] An Issei physician Toshio Ichioka had been serving the ethnic Mexican community in downtown Los Angeles and placing his clinic's advertisements on *La Opinión* since 1928 (a popular trend we looked at previously in chapter 2). His wife, Tsutayo, who was a Nisei, earned her medical doctor degree from the University of Southern California in 1938 and opened her own clinic in downtown Los Angeles in January 1942. While it was unfortunate for her to begin her business after Japan attacked the United States, the *Rafu Shimpo* ran an article about her clinic. At the same time, *La Opinión* wrote a larger article about her clinic with a picture of her face and introduced her as the "wife of doctor Toshio Ichioka, well known in our Colonia."[23]

Predictably Tsutayo's new clinic was soon shut down due to mass evacuation just like other Japanese shops in downtown Los Angeles. On April 19, *La Opinión* reported on close interactions between Mexicans and Japanese in Los Angeles County. It reminded the reader of the bitter experiences of Mexican strikers in the past, writing, "As for the relations between Mexicans and Japanese in this country, where our workers are concerned there is enough material for a long paragraph." On the other hand, regarding the Japanese evacuees, the article showed sympathy toward the Japanese: "The traditional 'mom-and-pop' store ... will pass for a long time into history, leaving behind a void in the soul of our people, since many of them speak Spanish, especially the children. And this may surprise you, the reader, but reciprocity obliges us to note that many Mexicans, especially in the border regions, speak Japanese."[24]

Nonetheless, *La Opinión* approved the government decision to relocate the Japanese as a military necessity and expressed their expectation for its positive impact on Mexican farmworkers: farmlands abandoned by Japanese evacuees.[25] On April 27, an editorial explained the work of the FSA and stressed "great opportunities" available for Mexicans with farming experience to become tenant farmers on former Japanese farms. On the other hand, it was not easy for Mexicans to do all the paperwork for land leases, because "the majority of us are, due to the lack of the perfect fluency of the English language, are averse to all the management that involves legal procedures." In El Monte, the very site of the large-scale Japanese-Mexican conflict in 1933 detailed in chapter 3, an ethnic organization named the Mexican Agricultural Society provided Mexican residents with necessary information for the ownership and lease of farmlands. Mexican residents could own and lease lands since they were legally regarded as white and eligible for citizenship. Mexican farmworkers were aware of the importance of owning or leasing farms instead of working as farmworkers through their bitter experiences in anti-Japanese strikes in the 1930s. *La Opinión*'s editorial concluded, "We hope that this opportunity presented today for the improvement of Mexicans can be utilized properly, since it means a flattering rise in their form of life, and a possibility for economic independence."[26] The Pearl Harbor attack and the subsequent removal of the Japanese brought an end to the triracial hierarchy in Los Angeles agriculture but created rare chances for Mexican farmworkers to fill in the socioeconomic spot formerly occupied by the Japanese.

In this context, the Rancho San Pedro companies began to lease lands to Mexican farmers. Mexican farmers grew crops that could be harvested within a short time period, from forty-five to sixty days. In Carson's recollection, some Mexican farmers grew flowers such as geraniums because many of them had worked as farmworkers under a European immigrant geranium farmer. They recovered the productivity of the farms in six months and "did pretty well" in growing geraniums.[27]

While Carson's recollection is a significant testimony about what happened after Japanese removal in relation to ethnic Mexicans, the business records of the Rancho San Pedro companies reveal even more about the transition from Japanese to Mexican farmers. In fact, the transition was not always smooth. In 1940, a Japanese family farmer leased a seventeen-acre parcel of land named "lease #2" for the period from July 1, 1940, to June 30, 1943, under the name of Ichirō Haijima, who was born in 1916 in Los Angeles. Their lease contract was canceled on May 1, 1942 due to their removal. About a month later, new tenants Vaughn Guzelain and William Beisel replaced the Haijima family with the lease contract, which would expire on June 30, 1945. Guzelain and Beisel began to grow flowers but did not stay long. In January 1943, Guzelain and Beisel transferred the lease to the Jones family, who had moved into the former Japanese farm, as mentioned earlier. The Jones family, however, also did not stay in the farm for too long. After these white tenants left the former Haijima farm, a tenant farmer, Angelo Ornelas, leased it on November 1, 1943. Although his lease contract does not say the nationality or ethnicity, Ornelas was most likely, given his name and the small size of the land he leased, an ethnic Mexican; also it was Carson's recollection that Japanese farms were taken over mostly by Mexicans. The 1942 Los Angeles City Directory lists a man named Angelo Ornelas who was a grocer in Boyle Heights; it is possible that this was the same Ornelas who, having enough capital and knowledge, took over the former Haijima family land. As described in a handwritten map (see Map 3) owned by the Carson Estate Company, the piece of land where the complicated transition from Japanese Haijima to Mexican Ornelas occurred is now part of the northwestern area of the California State University at Dominguez Hills.[28] Another example of the Japanese-Mexican transition of farmland was the fourteen-acre land formerly leased by a Japanese family under the name of Haruo Imaizumi. The Imaizumi family's farm was first taken over by a tenant named Hanko Franco, whose ethnicity is not clear, in May 1942. Franco was expected to lease the land until April 1945 but, for unknown reasons, left there by the end of 1942. Then, in January 1943, a Mexican farmer, Manuel Torres, took over six acres of the land formerly leased by the Imaizumi family (Torres continued to lease his six-acre land at least until 1950). This series of transitions from the Japanese to whites, and then to Mexicans, as recorded in these land lease contracts, illustrates the rapid demographic changes in the rural areas of Los Angeles County during the 1940s.[29]

TABLE 1. List of Japanese tenants in Rancho San Pedro along the rural routes from the post office in Compton, February 10, 1942

Name	Address		Acreage
Henry Aoto	Route 2, Box 833	Compton	7
Yutako Endow	Route 2, Box 827	Compton	10
H. Hamamoto	Route 2, Box 847	Compton	5
T. Ik[e]moto	Route 2, Box 849	Compton	8
George Kimura	P.O. Box 208	Compton	24
T. Matsumura	Route 2, Box 828	Compton	5
S. Matsunaga	Route 2, Box 822	Compton	10
M. Nak[a]shima	Route 2, Box 830	Compton	35
S. Nambu	Route 1, Box 859	Compton	12.86
T. Oka	Route 2, Box 840	Compton	5
T. Sugano	Route 2, Box 865-A	Compton	10.5
Sei Sujishi	Route 2, Box 805	Compton	6
F. Takeuchi	Route 2	Compton	17.3
I. Watanabe	Route 2, Box 848	Compton	5

SOURCE: Box 194, Rancho San Pedro Collection, Gerth Archives and Special Collections, University Library, California State University, Dominguez Hills.

There is further evidence of the transition from Japanese to Mexican tenancy in Rancho San Pedro. A list of new tenants made by the Dominguez Estate Company in 1943 recorded eighteen non-Japanese tenants, all of whom had Spanish-surnames except one. The tenants' names were R. Lopez, P. Hurtado, P. Cruz, F. Garcia, M. De Luna, Angel Acosta, Sebastian Venegas, and so forth. These new tenants were most likely ethnic Mexicans based on Carson's recollection that Japanese farms were taken over mostly by Mexicans and the fact that most foreign-born residents with Spanish surnames were Mexicans in Los Angeles County at the time. The list also recorded their rural route addresses telling us the exact places where these Mexican tenants lived during their tenancy and, more importantly, that many of their addresses were similar with those of former Japanese tenants. If we compare the list of forty-two Japanese tenants in 1942 and the list of seventeen Mexican tenants in 1943, we can observe that twelve Mexican tenants lived in the area where fourteen Japanese family farmers had lived before mass evacuation, along the rural routes from the post office in Compton (see Tables 1 and 2). These Japanese tenants grew vegetables in farms in the northeastern part of Rancho San Pedro. In one case, an ethnic Mexican tenant Joe Uribe and a former Japanese tenant M. Nakashima had the identical address of "Route 2, Box 830, Compton." This strongly suggests that Uribe moved into the former Nakashima's home after Japanese Internment began.[30]

It is likely that Uribe acquired only a small part of the former Nakashima land, as Uribe farmed only 3.6 of the 35 acres Nakashima once farmed. On November 24,

TABLE 2. List of Mexican tenants in Rancho San Pedro along the rural routes from the post office in Compton, 1943

Name	Address		Acreage
R. Lopez	P.O. Box 254	Compton	12.4
P. Cruz	Route 1, Box 842	Compton	2.3
F. Garcia	P.O. Box 24	Compton	4.0
M. De Luna	P.O. Box 523	Compton	12.4
D. De Luna	Route 2, Box 837	Compton	7.6
B. Lara	Route 2, Box 844	Compton	8.1
Jess. Medina	1212 North Acacia St.	Compton	6.7
Angel Acosta	Route 1, Box 834	Compton	2.9
Sebastian Venegas	Route 1, Box 837	Compton	9.5
Joe Uribe	Route 2, Box 830	Compton	3.6
P. Granado	Route 2, Box 824-C	Compton	4.3
Jose Verela	Route 2, Box 825	Compton	14.5

SOURCE: Box 194, Rancho San Pedro Collection, Gerth Archives and Special Collections, University Library, California State University, Dominguez Hills.

1943, the Dominguez Estate Company wrote a letter to Uribe saying, "According to our recent measurement of your land, we find you are farming 3.6 acres. Therefore, we are charging you for the current year beginning May 1, 1943 on the adjusted acreage." Including this letter, the company sent at least sixteen letters to new tenants, mostly ethnic Mexicans recorded on the above list, informing about the exact size of their farms. Their farm sizes in the list ranged from 3.6 to 14.5 acres, slightly smaller than the former Japanese farms in the same area. Usually, tenants made lease contracts after the size of land was determined. However, in the hurried and chaotic situation caused by the sudden disappearance of Japanese farmers, the company seems to have allowed new tenants to work the lands even before the sizes of their farms were precisely measured.[31]

CONTINUING TRIRACIAL RELATIONS DURING THE WAR

Land lease contracts tell us not only about the transition from Japanese to Mexican farmers but also about the cordial support provided by the Rancho San Pedro companies to former Japanese tenants. They kept their Japanese tenants until the very moment when the US government removed them. Not all white landowners were supportive to Japanese tenant farmers after the Pearl Harbor attack. For example, some landowners in Stockton in Northern California canceled the lease contracts with Japanese farmers right after the Pearl Harbor attack.[32] However, it is important for us to recognize that ethnic Japanese farmers in Southern

California's Rancho San Pedro lost their lands because of Japanese Internment, not because of the Pearl Harbor attack. As demonstrated by the red-ink handwritten memos on the Rancho San Pedro companies' lease contracts, for example, "Cancelled 4-6-42. Tenant Evacuated by U.S. Gov't" or "Tenant evacuated by U.S. Gov't May, 1942," Internment triggered a major management challenge for the Rancho San Pedro real estate companies.[33] John Victor Carson was so supportive of his Japanese tenants that many were very grateful to Carson during this difficult period. In May 1942, the Miyakawa family, a former Japanese tenant, sent a postcard to Carson from the Tulare Assembly Center showing their gratitude:

> We reached here about 6:30 in the evening on Thursday. The trip was long and its weather was so hot that practically all the passengers have gone to sleep but the beautiful scenery of the mountains and the desert were the only thing that kept us awake. We are now staying in the barrack no E-3 which is very cool and a nice place. So far everything is better than what we had expected. We thank you ever so much for everything you've done to us and we'll write to you again. Truly yours.[34]

Carson's support continued even after Japanese tenants were evacuated to the camps. Carson never hesitated to provide affidavits for those Japanese who were under investigation or others who wanted to gain permission to leave camps to work outside. On September 19, 1942, Misao Miyakawa, a Nisei daughter of Japanese immigrants Makoto and Tomiji Miyakawa and probably the same person who sent the above postcard, sent a letter to Carson from the Gila River Relocation Center and asked him to write an affidavit for her father, who was under investigation at the time. She wrote:

> How are you? We are now in the Gila Relocation Center and all of us are just fine. The desert heat is very severe and the sand storm is the only thing that causes us trouble.... Mr. Carson, I may cause you great deal of trouble but would you kindly make me out an affidavit of my father? This affidavit may forward him for another hearing. I'll appreciate very much if you can do so by proving his honesty, his residence of nearly sixteen years in Dominguez Hill, tilling the soil and has done anything wrong during these years. If you can, would you please send it as early as possible[?][35]

Within a week, Carson sent Misao his affidavit, which said, "Makoto Miyakawa has been a tenant of Dominguez Estate Company for several years, during which time, to the best of my knowledge, he has been an honest, industrious and law abiding member of his community and has reared and educated a family in this country. I have no knowledge that he has been associated with or has contributed to any foreign society or organization."[36] Right after receiving it, on September 27, Misao wrote back to Carson and appreciated his prompt support for the Miyakawa family, saying, "We'll never forget your kindness."[37] Since the Miyakawa family leased the land from the Del Amo Estate Company in Rancho San Pedro as well,

Misao sent the same request to the company. Eugenio Cabrero, the company's secretary, quickly responded to Misao's request and sent his affidavit back. It is most likely that these two Rancho San Pedro companies cooperated in supporting former Japanese tenants since their affidavits were very similar.[38]

A former Nisei farmer Henry Chiyozō Takeuchi also benefited from his trusting relationship with Carson, when he needed an affidavit for himself to get permission to leave the relocation center for outside employment or education. On May 7, 1943, Dillon Myer, director of the War Relocation Center, sent a letter to Carson requesting his affidavit about Takeuchi. A week later, Carson sent his affidavit emphasizing Takeuchi's good character, writing "he and his family were agricultural tenants of this company for many years prior to the evacuation of the Japanese from the Pacific Coast in May, 1942. It is my belief that Mr. Takeuchi was born here and educated in the public schools of this community. His reputation in the community is very good and as a vegetable farmer he is considerably above average."[39] These exchanges of letters and affidavits demonstrate the depth of the mutual trust between landowners and Japanese farmers in Rancho San Pedro, which should be remembered as one of important facts in the history of Japanese Internment.

Back in the 1930s, the trusting relationship between landowners and Japanese farmers in Rancho San Pedro was behind their collaboration in fighting against Mexican strikers. Nonetheless, Carson and Japanese tenants were not anti-Mexican. They were anti-union. Carson's grandmother Victoria Domínguez was one of the six daughters of Manuel Domínguez who successfully kept the family's land ownership during the turbulent period of the transition from the Mexican to American rule. Victoria married an Anglo-American George Henry Carson in 1857 but continued to speak almost only Spanish at home because she wanted her children to be able to speak Spanish. Although her grandson John Victor Carson did not learn to speak Spanish, his American wife, Alice, was fluent in Spanish since she was born and raised in Mexico. Carson had stayed in Mexico with Alice for "many, many months down in Mexico." Although Carson was a rich person whose life was very different from working-class Mexicans, he was familiar with Mexican culture and people.[40]

More important is the fact that Japanese farmers in Rancho San Pedro had close relationships with some Mexican workers as well. After being transferred to a "relocation center" in Arkansas, Henry Chiyozō Takeuchi received a letter from Carson inquiring about the properties of Takeuchi left in Rancho San Pedro. Takeuchi wrote back, "Thanks ever so much for your kind letter and also to bring our attention concerning our buildings." He explained that his family had sold their wooden flumes and pipe but kept the buildings to store their personal properties or rent as living quarters. Since his properties were removed, he wanted to rent his buildings during his absence. In addition, Takeuchi wrote, "Since our personal property has been moved away, I would like to rent the buildings. If you can[,] avoid rent from the one building which Julian Rodriguez is occupying if he is still living there." And "If this can't be done[,] tell Julian that I'll refund it when I return to California." Takeuchi seemed to be concerned that Rodriguez had to spend extra money for housing due to the changing situation. Takeuchi added, "The rent for the building, I will leave it up to you and your staff to work out the best plan." Rodriguez was almost certainly an ethnic Mexican considering his Spanish name, his relationship to Takeuchi, and his residence on farmland. It seems that Takeuchi was willing to pay Rodriguez for leaving his house to lease a more expensive building or lease the same building whose rent was newly set by Carson's company, while entrusting Carson in handling how to rent his buildings. As Takeuchi cared about the financial situation of Rodriguez, we can infer that the Takeuchi family and Rodriguez had a good relationship. In his letter, Takeuchi also sketched the size and location of his family's buildings (see Map 4) such as "living quarters, "boy room," "tractor garage," "small garage," and "Julian's Rodri[g]ue[z] House." Most Mexican farmworkers came to Japanese farms only when they found jobs, but Rodriguez lived together with the Takeuchi family as his house was very close to the Takeuchi family's house as demonstrated in the map.[41]

The basic socioeconomic structure that ruled Japanese agriculture in Los Angeles County was the triracial hierarchy in which Japanese farmers leased lands from whites and hired ethnic Mexicans. Because of this hierarchy, Los Angeles agriculture maintained a multiethnic environment and created a site of interethnic labor conflicts between Japanese and Mexicans. Letters exchanged between Carson and Japanese evacuees during the war, however, demonstrate another side of the triracial relations in which Japanese, Mexicans, and white landowners developed mutual trust and cooperated to keep Los Angeles farmland profitable. Japanese Internment eliminated the presence of Japanese farmers from Los Angeles County but could not completely obliterate the mutual trust developed in their triracial relationship. In the history of immigrants, the workplace is oftentimes a site of economic inequality. Yet, the workplace can also be the site of close contact enabling mutual understanding and making fluid and unstable the racial and class boundaries.

Los Angeles farmland was the *transpacific workplace* where Japanese and Mexicans who crossed the Pacific Ocean and the US-Mexico border interacted with each other weaving their respective experiences into a history of immigrant Los Angeles that developed both interethnic conflicts and mutual understanding. For a better understanding of interethnic relations, we should focus not only on what wartime hysteria created but also on what it did not easily change, and the context behind this resilience. By looking at this context, we can understand the nature of

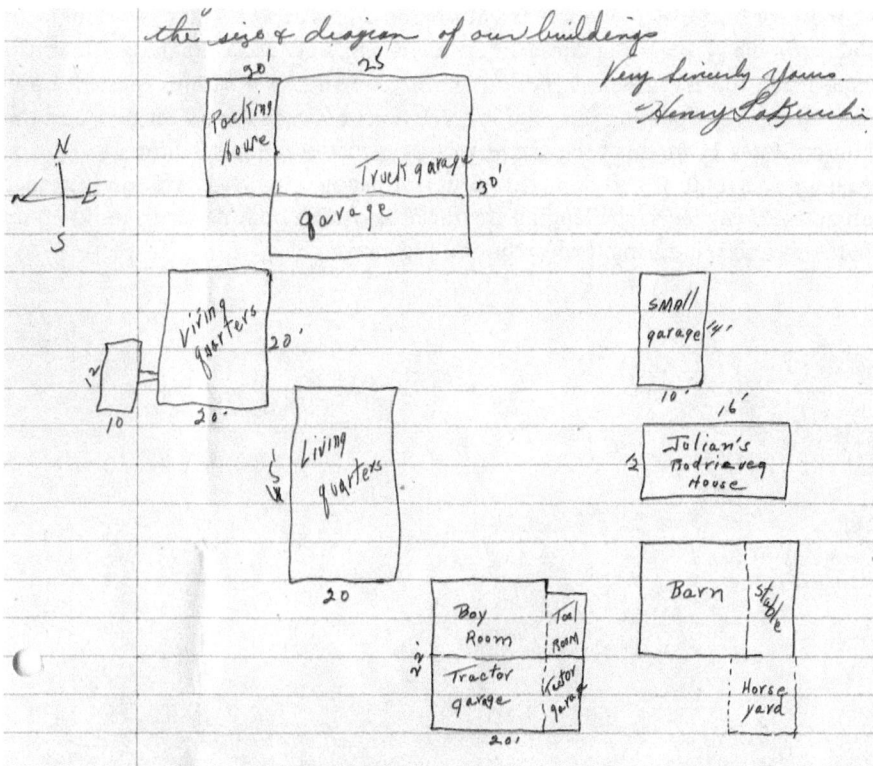

MAP 4. Buildings owned by former Japanese tenant Henry Chiyozō Takeuchi in Rancho San Pedro. It shows that Takeuchi lived with a Mexican farmworker Julian Rodriguez before Japanese removal. Courtesy of Rancho San Pedro Collection, Gerth Archives and Special Collections, CSU Dominguez Hills.

race and class relations in an immigrant society as more fluid and situational even in the time of economic and military crises.

Japanese Internment marked the end of this history of Japanese-Mexican relations in Los Angeles agriculture. It brought the end to the triracial hierarchy in Los Angeles agriculture as well as the transborder ethnic Japanese community in the US-Mexico borderlands. Then, the local real estate companies in Rancho San Pedro, under the management of John Victor Carson, had serious trouble finding new tenants who would replace the Japanese, and the government aid for the replacement did not help them enough. Again, like the Bracero Program, it was mainly ethnic Mexicans who acquired and revitalized the former Japanese lands in Rancho San Pedro. Even after Japanese removal, Carson provided genuine support for his former Japanese tenants based on his experiences of working with them for many years. Japanese Internment was not just a Japanese American experience. It was rather a larger multiethnic Los Angeles wartime experience created by rapidly changing international relations between Japan, Mexico, and the United States. From this perspective, we can see better the social dimension of Los Angeles society in which different groups of people interacted with one another on an everyday level, challenging the racial and class boundaries in multiethnic Los Angeles even during the wartime emergency.[42]

Conclusion

The eighteen-year period between the Immigration Act of 1924 and the mass removal of the ethnic Japanese population in 1942 was a traumatic and consequential chapter in the local history of multiethnic Los Angeles and a significant part of the history of the triangular relationship between Japan, Mexico, and the United States. This period witnessed the development and sudden demise of two distinct ethnoracial relationships centered around Japanese and Mexicans of Los Angeles County. One of these relationships was within the transborder ethnic Japanese community of the US-Mexico borderlands and the other was the triracial hierarchy in Los Angeles agriculture in which Japanese farmers leased land from white landowners and hired Mexican workers. These local and transnational relationships together formed the socioeconomic and geopolitical dynamics of the Pacific Coast of the US-Mexico borderlands, intersecting with each other through the concerns held by the peoples and governments of Japan, Mexico, and the United States. Particularly regarding Japanese-Mexican relations in Los Angeles, *La Opinión* wrote in spring 1942 that there was "enough material for a long paragraph." In fact, there were enough documents for a book. By using primary sources written in Japanese, Spanish, and English, this book has explored Japanese-Mexican relations from a transpacific perspective.

A simple but important fact is that Los Angeles farmland made Japanese, Mexicans, and white Americans interact with one another on an everyday or regular basis. Their interactions generated serious interethnic conflict but also prompted efforts toward mutual understanding that helped them accommodate each other beyond the dominant racial and class boundaries of this period. In the 1930s, agricultural strikes launched by Mexican workers played a significant role in bringing the Japanese side to the negotiating table and making farmers better understand the poor working conditions of Mexican workers. Although these groups were different in terms of race and class, they shared the same immigrant workplace. Based on interplay in their everyday life, there were moments when Mexicans could be treated not simply as strikers but as people who had legitimate reasons to demand better working conditions, and Japanese not as inhumane employers or enemy aliens but as negotiable or reliable resident farmers even in times of intense Japanese-Mexican labor conflict and wartime emergency in Los Angeles County in the 1930s and 1940s.

By looking at both local and international factors, this book has highlighted how the unique social dimensions of this triracial interaction challenged existing racial and class boundaries in the region, revealing the level of fluidity and contingency in racial and class relations that shaped the negotiations and accommodations reached by these different Pacific borderlands groups. The El Monte Berry Strike of 1933 intensified the racial, class, and national boundaries between Japanese and Mexicans in the local context of Los Angeles agriculture. These boundaries, however, proved to be fluid and unstable in the transnational context of the US-Mexico borderlands as demonstrated by the Mexicali Japanese who supported Los Angeles Mexicans despite their ethnic ties with Los Angeles Japanese farmers. Three years later, the Venice Celery Strike created two sets of Japanese-Mexican alliances: anti-labor (against union recognition) and pro-labor (for union recognition). The creation of these alliances between Japanese and Mexicans whose race and class were different proves the situational nature of Japanese-Mexican relations in Los Angeles farmland that were influenced but not determined by their racial and class differences. In such a situation, Japanese immigrant nationalism was rather compatible with a multiethnic understanding that Japanese immigrants should make efforts to build better relations with both white Americans and ethnic Mexicans. By the time of the Pacific War, this long-standing interethnic interplay in Los Angeles farmland had created a strong basis for Mexicans and white Americans to be able to regard their Japanese neighbors as farmers and residents without completely succumbing to the prevailing anti-Japanese hysteria of Los Angeles County. In such interactions, I believe, we can trace the history of transborder Los Angeles.

After World War II, many ethnic Japanese internees returned to Los Angeles County. Their population reached 36,761 in 1950, which was almost the same number recorded in 1940.[1] However, they could not rebuild their ethnic agricultural community to the prewar level. World War II brought a dramatic change in the demography and industry of California by multiplying the manufacturing economy during war years and by attracting about 1.6 million Americans from other states. People continued to migrate to California even after the war. Between July 1945 and July 1947, more than one million people moved to California, which caused rapid urbanization and created a housing shortage. Los Angeles County, one of the primary industrial regions of the US West, experienced this remarkable change like few other places.[2] When former ethnic Japanese farmers returned to Los Angeles County, many were not able to lease or buy lands because of rapid industrialization and urbanization, even in the places that used to be major Japanese agricultural areas such as the coastal regions or the Gardena, San Gabriel, or San Fernando Valleys. These areas included the places analyzed in this book such as El Monte, Venice, Gardena, and Dominguez Hills. For example, before the war, the Gardena Valley had from eight hundred to one thousand Japanese farming families. But after the war, only seventy to eighty Japanese families resumed their agricultural work. Those Japanese who had an ambition to resume agriculture on a large-scale moved from Los Angeles County to other places in neighboring Ventura and Orange Counties. By 1959, only 2,500 acres of land were cultivated by 150–200 Japanese families in Los Angeles County, an almost 90 percent decrease from the prewar level. On the other hand, the gardening and nursery industries replaced perishable crop agriculture as the major ethnic Japanese industry in postwar Los Angeles. Japanese immigrants had been known to be good at these businesses since before the war and these businesses could make larger profits from urbanization.[3] After all, in Los Angeles County, the postwar socioeconomic situation did not see the return of the highly institutionalized triracial hierarchy that had existed in prewar Japanese agriculture.

In the postwar period, remaining Japanese farms in California have been cultivated first by the Nisei and later by the Sansei (the third generation). Mexican immigrant and Mexican American farmworkers became increasingly important in California agriculture largely because of the Bracero Program implemented from 1942 to 1964. In the 1970s, Japanese Nisei farmers came into conflict with Mexican American workers organized by the United Farm Workers (UFW) under the leadership of César Chávez. In 1976, the UFW campaigned for Proposition 14 that would secure enough funding for the newly established Agricultural Labor Relations Board and guarantee the right of UFW organizers to enter the fields. At that time, the Nisei Farmers League led by Harry Kubo, a Japanese American farmer in Fresno County, responded fiercely to challenge Proposition 14. Kubo emphasized the importance of Japanese farmers' property rights that were once violated by Japanese Internment in the past, emotionally affirming, "It will never be repeated."[4] Thus, the ethnic Japanese wartime experience affected Japanese-Mexican relations even in the 1970s. Even today, no matter whether they conflict with Mexicans or not, Japanese American farmers still depend on Mexican immigrant farmworkers. However, postwar Japanese-Mexican relations are different from what existed in prewar Los Angeles County in terms of the proportion of the immigrant-generation tenant farmers, the involvement of the Japanese and Mexican governments, and in the transnational connection between the Japanese-Mexican relations in Los Angeles and those in Baja California, Mexico.

The demise of Japanese-Mexican relations in Los Angeles agriculture, however, does not suggest that Los Angeles ceased being a meeting place between Americans and Asian and Latin American immigrants. Today's Koreatown is a good example that demonstrates the different social layers of close Asian-Latin American interactions. Even outside Los Angeles, an increasing number of communities have come to develop immigrant workplaces where Asians and Latin Americans interact with one another. This book can thus serve as a historical lesson to understand today's Asian-Latin American relations in the United States. Across the chapters, it has analyzed interethnic conflicts and accommodations in prewar Los Angeles farmland, what can be called a *transpacific workplace*, from the local and international perspectives, shedding light on the less visible social dimension in which Japanese tenant farmers, Mexican farmworkers, and white Americans regularly interacted with each other. They engaged in interethnic negotiations, nurturing a certain level of mutual understanding beyond differences in their racial and class status, and making the racial and class boundaries fluid and situational, even amid the serious economic and military conflicts that defined the Pacific borderlands of the 1930s and 1940s.

Although the immigrant workplace often operates along racial and class lines, it should not be regarded only as a site that produces racial and class boundaries and inequalities. As shown in this book, the immigrant workplace should be conceptualized as a social space that can nurture mutual understanding between different groups of people, often thanks to the negotiations prompted by those who face more difficulties such as agricultural strikers, to destabilize the existing dominant racial and class boundaries of a particular place and time. This conclusion—formed as it is by using a transnational, transpacific lens—helps us understand the immigrant experience within the inevitable and continuing processes of interethnic interplay and negotiations in their everyday life, not within the fixed racial and class categories of our thought and analysis. What is more important is to observe, understand, and direct such historical processes of interethnic negotiations toward a better understanding of how to generate more trusting interethnic relations in immigrant workplaces not only in the United States but also in any country whose society and economy depend largely on immigrants and their descendants of diverse backgrounds.

NOTES

INTRODUCTION

1. Lon Kurashige, Madeline Y. Hsu, and Yujin Yaguchi argue that the emerging field of transpacific history sees people's struggles within and around the Pacific Ocean "as not simply national problems, but as articulations of transpacific processes and circumstances that have produced new relationships and modes of explanation." Lon Kurashige, Madeline Y. Hsu, and Yujin Yaguchi, "Introduction: Conversations on Transpacific History," *Pacific Historical Review* 83, no. 2 (May 2014): 187–188.

2. This book uses *ethnic Japanese* to mean people of Japanese origin and likewise *ethnic Mexicans* people of Mexican origin, including both immigrants and their US-born descendants, based on David Gutiérrez's definition of *ethnic Mexicans*, which means "the total Mexican-origin population of the United States, citizen and alien alike." See David G. Gutiérrez, *Walls and Mirrors: Mexican Americans, Mexican Immigrants, and the Politics of Ethnicity* (Berkeley: University of California Press, 1995), 218. This book also considers Japanese and Mexican immigrants basically as *ethnoracial* minorities since the ethnic and racial categories cannot completely be separated in theory and reality. Nevertheless, it mainly uses the terms *ethnic* and *interethnic* to describe Japanese and Mexicans as a group of immigrants and their mutual relations, putting importance on the agency of immigrants and their cultural and national ties with their home countries. On the other hand, when situating these immigrant groups in relation to the white majority, it mainly uses the terms *racial* and *triracial* to emphasize the aspect that they were minorities racialized within a white-dominant American society.

3. In 1930, the total population of Los Angeles County was 2,208,492 and its nonwhite population was 258,610. US Census Office, *Twelfth Census of the United States: 1900*,

Population (Washington, DC, 1901), Table 34, "Foreign Born Population, Distributed According to Country of Birth, by Counties," 738–739; US Census Bureau, *Fifteenth Census of the United States: 1930, Population* (Washington, DC, 1932), Table 13, "The Composition of the Population, by Counties: 1930" and Table 17, "Indians, Chinese, and Japanese, 1910 to 1930, and Mexicans, 1930, for Counties and for Cities of 25,000 or More," 252, 260, 266. In the city of Los Angeles in 1930, the ethnic Japanese population was 21,081 and the ethnic Mexican population was 97,116, covering 71 percent of the whole nonwhite population in the city. For a more detailed explanation of Japanese and Mexican immigration histories before 1924, see chapter 1.

4. For the history of American nativism and racial nationalism behind the 1924 Act, see John Higham, *Strangers in the Land: Patterns of American Nativism, 1860–1925* (New Brunswick, NJ: Rutgers University Press, 1955; 1988); Gary Gerstle, *American Crucible: Race and Nation in the Twentieth Century* (Princeton, NJ: Princeton University Press, 2001). For the anti-Japanese movement in California, see Roger Daniels, *The Politics of Prejudice: The Anti-Japanese Movement in California* (New York: Atheneum, 1968). For the impact of the 1924 Act on US-Japan relations, Toshihiro Minohara, *Hainichi imin hō to nichi-bei kankei* [The Japanese Exclusion Act and Japan-US relations] (Tokyo: Iwanami Shoten, 2002); Masako Iino, *Mō hitotsu no nichi-bei kankeishi: Hunsō to kyōchō no naka no nikkei amerikajin* [Another history of Japan-US relations: Japanese Americans in conflicts and cooperation] (Tokyo: Yūhikaku, 2000). For the role of pro-Japanese egalitarians who opposed the implementation of Japanese exclusion, see Lon Kurashige, *Two Faces of Exclusion: The Untold History of Anti-Asian Racism in the United States* (Chapel Hill: University of North Carolina Press, 2016).

5. Mae M. Ngai, *Impossible Subjects: Illegal Aliens and the Making of Modern America* (Princeton, NJ: Princeton University Press, 2004), 1–9. For the racialization of ethnic Mexicans, see also Kelly L. Hernández, *Migra!: A History of the U.S. Border Patrol* (Berkeley: University of California Press, 2010); John Mckiernan-González, *Fevered Measures: Public Health and Race at the Texas-Mexico Border, 1848–1942* (Durham, NC: Duke University Press, 2012).

6. The 1920s is generally remembered as the time of international cooperation and relatively stable relations between the United States and Japan. See Ryuji Hattori and Toshihiro Minohara, "Washinton taisei 1920 nendai" [The Washington regime in the 1920s], in *Nichi-bei kankeishi* [The history of Japan-US history], ed. Makoto Iokibe (Tokyo: Yūhikaku, 2008), 83–109.

7. Regarding Japanese nationalism after World War I, Prasenjit Duara contends that Japanese nationalism became radical and developed with "the ideology of pan-Asianism, which claimed to protect an authentic Asia and thus justified the expansion [in Asia] as a holy war against the West." See Prasenjit Duara, *Sovereignty and Authenticity: Manchukuo and the East Asian Modern* (Lanham, MD: Rowman & Littlefield Publishers, 2003), 34. According to Eiji Oguma, in the mid-1920s, the Japanese discourse on the *kokutai* polity, which placed the emperor at the center of Japanese sovereignty, came to embrace the idea that the Japanese nation had historically been successful in assimilating other ethnic groups, which ideologically justified Japanese colonization in East Asia. See Eiji Oguma, *Tan'itsu minzoku shinwa no kigen: "Nihonjin" no jigazō no keifu* [The origin of the myth

of ethnic homogeneity: The genealogy of "Japanese" self-images] (Tokyo: Shinyōsha, 1995), 148–150, 167–169.

8. As for Japanese immigrant nationalism, Yuji Ichioka wrote, "Victims of racial oppression can repudiate their oppressors in different ways. Patriotic identification with Japan was a way by which the Issei psychologically turned away from the America that had rejected them." See Yuji Ichioka, *Before Internment: Essays in Prewar Japanese American History*, ed. Gordon H. Chang and Eiichiro Azuma (Stanford, CA: Stanford University Press, 2006), 199.

9. For the historical development of *mestizaje* and the Mexican cultural nationalist movement, see Kelly R. Swarthout, *"Assimilating the Primitive": Parallel Dialogues on Racial Miscegenation in Revolutionary Mexico* (New York: Peter Lang, 2004).

10. Neil Foley explains, "Regardless of how the census classified them, Anglo Americans rarely regarded Mexicans as belonging to the white race. Neither did most Mexicans—they identified themselves simply as *mexicanos*." Neil Foley, *Mexicans in the Making of America* (Cambridge, MA: Harvard University Press, 2014), 50.

11. Natalia Molina, *How Race Is Made in America: Immigration, Citizenship, and the Historical Power of Racial Scripts* (Berkeley: University of California Press, 2014), 3–5. For previous studies related to interethnic interactions in California, for example, see Carey McWilliams, *Factories in the Field: The Story of Migratory Farm Labor in California* (Berkeley: University of California Press, 1939; 2000); Tomás Almaguer, *Racial Fault Lines: The Historical Origins of White Supremacy in California* (Berkeley: University of California Press, 1994; 2009); Karen Isaksen Leonard, *Making Ethnic Choices: California's Punjabi Mexican Americans* (Philadelphia: Temple University Press, 1992); Grace Peña Delgado, *Making the Chinese Mexican: Global Migration, Localism, and Exclusion in the U.S.-Mexico Borderlands* (Stanford, CA: Stanford University Press, 2012); Rudy P. Guevarra Jr., *Becoming Mexipino: Multiethnic Identities and Communities in San Diego* (New Brunswick, NJ: Rutgers University Press, 2012); George J. Sánchez, "'What's Good for Boyle Heights Is Good for the Jews': Creating Multiculturalism on the Eastside during the 1950s." *American Quarterly* 56, no. 3 (September 2004): 633–661; Scott Kurashige, *The Shifting Grounds of Race: Black and Japanese Americans in the Making of Multiethnic Los Angeles* (Princeton, NJ: Princeton University Press, 2008); Allison Varzally, *Making a Non-White America: Californians Coloring Outside Ethic Lines, 1925–1955* (Berkeley: University of California Press, 2008); Mark Wild, *Street Meeting: Multiethnic Neighborhoods in Early Twentieth-Century Los Angeles* (Berkeley: University of California Press, 2005); Eiichiro Azuma, *Between Two Empires: Race, History, and Transnationalism in Japanese America* (New York: Oxford University Press, 2005).

12. Camilla Fojas and Rudy P. Guevarra Jr. emphasize the importance of creating a new field of study that compares Asian Pacific American and Latin American studies. See Camilla Fojas and Rudy P. Guevarra Jr., eds., *Transnational Crossroads: Remapping the Americas and the Pacific* (Lincoln: University of Nebraska Press, 2012). For the studies that link Asian American studies with Native American studies, see Karen J. Leong and Myla Vicenti Carpio, eds., "Carceral States," *Amerasia Journal* 42, no. 1 (2016). This relative shortage of studies on Asian-Mexican relations seems to be the result of historiographical gap between Asian American studies and Mexican American studies. First, this gap

seems to come from different historical experiences between Asian and Mexican immigrants. Asian immigrants who came from the Eastern Hemisphere were treated as a racial threat, legally excluded from immigration and naturalization. Mexican immigrants were originally from the Western Hemisphere and were largely marginalized and exploited, or internally colonized, under US imperialism. Second, this gap exists because the civil rights movement of the 1960s encouraged and supported the development of ethnic studies by Asian American and Mexican American scholars rather separately except for a few scholars such as Ronald Takaki and Tomás Almaguer. See Ronald Takaki, *A Different Mirror: A History of Multicultural America* (New York: Little, Brown and Company, 1993); Almaguer, *Racial Fault Lines*.

13. Mae Ngai takes a comparative approach to the experiences of Mexicans and Asians and shows the nature of US immigration policy by narrating the experiences of different ethnoracial groups, respectively. Her study demonstrates the similarity of ethnic Mexican and Asian experiences, both of whom were racialized by immigration policy as illegal, criminal, and ineligible for naturalization. Natalia Molina examines the process in which public health policy constructed racial categories in multiracial Los Angeles that influenced Mexicans and Asians. See Ngai, *Impossible Subjects*; Natalia Molina, *Fit to Be Citizens?: Public Health and Race in Los Angles, 1879–1939* (Berkeley: University of California Press, 2006).

14. Natalia Molina has explored how the racialization of Asians influenced the racialization of Mexicans under what she calls the "immigration regime" of 1924. Molina contends that her works take a relational treatment that "recognizes that race is a mutually constitutive process and thus attends to how, when, where, and to what extent groups intersect" by focusing particularly on how "the racialization of one group affected the other." While I respect her definition of "relational" and her great contribution in linking the Mexican experience with the Asian experience, I still regard her works as part of comparative studies because they do not focus on actual interactions of different racialized groups and different nation-states. Natalia Molina, "Examining Chicana/o History through a Relational Lens," *Pacific Historical Review* 82, no. 4 (November 2013): 521–522; *How Race Is Made in America*, 1–6. As another example of comparative studies, see Erika Lee and Judy Yung, *Angel Island: Immigrant Gateway to America* (New York: Oxford University Press, 2010).

15. Leonard, *Making Ethnic Choices*; Sánchez, "'What's Good for Boyle Heights Is Good for the Jews.'" For a detailed history of Boyle Heights, see George J. Sánchez, *Boyle Heights: How a Los Angeles Neighborhood Became the Future of American Democracy* (Oakland: University of California Press, 2021).

16. We should remember that some comparative studies have done relational analyses, as we see in the important works of Carey McWilliams and Tomás Almaguer on Japanese-Mexican relations in agriculture. See McWilliams, *Factories in the Field*, 246–248; *Southern California: An Island on the Land* (Salt Lake City: Peregrine Smith Books, 1946; 1973), 374; Almaguer, *Racial Fault Lines*, ix, 7, 183–213.

17. For scholarly works and discussions on transnationalism, see Luis Eduardo Guarnizo and Michael Peter Smith, "The Locations of Transnationalism," in *Transnationalism from Below*, ed. Guarnizo and Smith (Piscataway, NJ: Transaction Publishers, 1998); Madeline Y. Hsu, *Dreaming of Gold, Dreaming of Home: Transnationalism and Migration*

between the United States and South China, 1882–1943 (Stanford, CA: Stanford University Press, 2000); Alicia Schmidt Camacho, *Migrant Imaginaries: Latino Cultural Politics in the U.S.-Mexico Borderlands* (New York: New York University Press, 2008); Shelley Fisher Fishkin, "Crossroads of Cultures: The Transnational Turn in American Studies: Presidential Address to the American Studies Association, November 12, 2004," *American Quarterly* 57, no. 1 (March 2005): 17–57; C. A. Bayly, Sven Beckert, Matthew Connelly, Isabel Hofmeyr, Wendy Kozol and Patricia Seed, "AHR Conversation: On Transnational History," *American Historical Review* 111, no. 5 (December 2006): 1441–1464.

18. Peña Delgado, *Making the Chinese Mexican*. Robert Chao Romero also argues that from the late nineteenth century, "the Chinese created a transnational commercial orbit in resistance, and adaptation" to the Chinese Exclusion Act and that their activities involved "a multinational socioeconomic network spanning China, Latin America, and the United States." See Robert Chao Romero, *The Chinese in Mexico, 1882–1940* (Tucson: University of Arizona Press, 2010), 1–5. For more studies on the Chinese in the US-Mexico borderlands, see Jason Oliver Chang, *Chino: Anti-Chinese Racism in Mexico, 1880–1940* (Urbana: University of Illinois Press, 2017); Verónica Castillo-Muñoz, *The Other California: Land, Identity, and Politics on the Mexican Borderlands* (Oakland: University of California Press, 2017). For the US-Canada borderlands, see Kornel S. Chang, *Pacific Connections: The Making of the U.S.-Canadian Borderlands* (Berkeley: University of California Press, 2012).

19. Azuma, *Between Two Empires*, 187–207. According to Azuma, Japanese farmers in 1930s Stockton regarded Mexicans as docile and attempted to hire them to reduce their reliance on Filipino farmworkers. For Japanese-Filipino relations, see also, Chris Friday, *Organizing Asian American Labor: The Pacific Coast Canned-Salmon Industry, 1870–1942* (Philadelphia: Temple University Press, 1994).

20. Eiichiro Azuma, "Japanese Immigrant Settler Colonialism in the U.S.-Mexican Borderlands and the U.S. Racial-Imperialist Politics of the Hemispheric 'Yellow Peril,'" *Pacific Historical Review* 83, no. 2 (May 2014): 255–276.

21. Although the Chinese were the precursor of Asian immigrants in this region, the ethnic Chinese population in Los Angeles County was quite small (5,330 in 1940) compared to the ethnic Japanese (36,866 in 1940) before the Pacific War largely as a consequence of the Chinese Exclusion Act of 1882. They did not make up the highly populated and institutionalized triracial hierarchy like the one developed by Japanese, Mexicans, and whites in Los Angeles farmland. US Census Bureau, *Sixteenth Census of the United States: 1940, Population* (Washington, DC, 1943), Table 25, "Indians, Chinese, and Japanese by Sex, for Counties, and for Cities of 10,000 to 100,000," 567.

22. "Map Reveals Jap Menace," "Network of Japanese Farms Covers Vital Southland Defense Areas," *Los Angeles Times*, March 4, 1942. The *Times* identified the source of the map: "Information compiled by County Agricultural Commissioner Harold J. Ryan and County Assessor John R. Quinn was consolidated into the master map. Working with these two men were County Surveyor Alfred Jones and Dist. Atty. John F. Dockweiler." And the newspaper explained the additions to the map: "Times Staff Artist Charles H. Owens shows, in black, the approximate location of the many plots of land, either owned by or leased by Japs." It is worth noting that the map gives an exaggerated impression that Japanese were densely populated in the Palos Verdes Peninsula, the militarily important southwestern

coastal area of Los Angeles County, although in reality only about fifty Japanese families lived there at the time. In 1929, about forty-five Japanese farming families lived in the Palos Verdes area. Their population in 1940 was likely to be very similar to that of 1929 because the ethnic Japanese population did not significantly increase from 1930 to 1940, largely due to the Immigration Act of 1924. See Minamikashū Nihonjin Shichijūnenshi Kankō Iinkai [Publishing committee of Japanese in Southern California], ed., *Minamikashū nihonjin shichijūnenshi* [Japanese in Southern California: A history of 70 years] (Los Angeles: Nanka Nikkeijin Shōgyō Kaigisho, 1960), 59; US Census Bureau, *Sixteenth Census of the United States: 1940, Population* (Washington, DC, 1943), Table 4, "Race by Nativity and Sex for the State: 1850 to 1940," 516.

CHAPTER 1. THE 1924 IMMIGRATION ACT AND ITS UNINTENDED CONSEQUENCE IN THE US-MEXICO BORDERLANDS

1. Kōji Higashi, *Beiboku jūō* [Traveling down and across the United States and Mexico] (Tokyo: Seikyōsha, 1920), preface by Hisayoshi Shimazu, preface by the author, 274–302. For the reaction of Mexican officials and immigrants against Henry Ashurst, see F. Arturo Rosales, *¡Pobre Raza!: Violence, Justice, and Mobilization among México Lindo Immigrants, 1900–1936* (Austin: University of Texas Press, 1999), 23.

2. Higashi, *Beiboku jūō*, preface by the author, 301.

3. "Imin wo Mekishiko e okure" [Send emigrants to Mexico], *Yomiuri Shimbun*, June 1, 1924; "Yūbō na Bokukoku ijū" [Migration to Mexico is hopeful], *Rafu Shimpo*, September 9, 1924.

4. Louise Pubols, "Born Global: From Pueblo to Statehood," in *A Companion to Los Angeles*, ed. William Deverell and Greg Hise (Malden, MA: Wiley-Blackwell, 2010), 21–25. Kevin Starr, *California: A History* (New York: Modern Library, 2007), 24, 32.

5. Pubols, "Born Global," 21–25. For the involvement of the Gabrieliño-Tongva people in pre-Hispanic interactions between California and other places in the American Southwest, see Erin M. Smith and Mikael Fauvelle, "Regional Interactions between California and the Southwest: The Western Edge of the North American Continental System," *American Anthropologist* 117, no. 4 (December 2015): 710–721.

6. Pubols, "Born Global," 31; Albert Camarillo, *Chicanos in California: A History of Mexican Americans in California* (Sparks, NV: Materials for Today's Learning, 1984: 1990), 5–7.

7. Pubols, "Born Global," 30–33; David Hombeck, "Land Tenure and Rancho Expansion in Alta California, 1784–1846," *Journal of Historical Geography* 4, no. 4 (1978): 376–379; Starr, *California*, 58; Dominguez Rancho Adobe Museum, "History," online at https://dominguezrancho.org/domingo-rancho-history/, accessed February 18, 2021.

8. Andrew C. Isenberg and Thomas Richards Jr. argue that "it was not until the end of the nineteenth century... [that] manifest destiny—particularly Polk's acquisitions of Oregon, Texas, and much of northern Mexico—assumed its aura of inevitability." See Andrew C. Isenberg and Thomas Richards Jr., "Alternative Wests: Rethinking Manifest Destiny," *Pacific Historical Review* 86, no. 1 (2017): 4–17.

9. Starr, *California*, 64, 73; Pubols, "Born Global," 35.

10. Sucheng Chan, *Asian Americans: An Interpretive History* (Boston: Twayne Publishers, 1991), 30–31; Walter Licht, *Industrializing America: The Nineteenth Century* (Baltimore: Johns Hopkins University Press, 1995), 82, 97–98, 126–128. For the congressional debates over the transcontinental railroad bill, see John Lauritz Larson, *Internal Improvement: National Public Works and the Promise of Popular Government in the Early United States* (Chapel Hill: University of North Carolina Press, 2001), 240–255. For the ideological driving force of the Civil War, see Eric Foner, *Free Soil, Free Labor, Free Men: The Ideology of the Republican Party before the Civil War* (New York: Oxford University Press, 1970; 1995); Michael A. Morrison, *Slavery and the American West: The Eclipse of Manifest Destiny and the Coming of the Civil War* (Chapel Hill: University of North Carolina Press, 1999).

11. Starr, *California*, 146; Carey McWilliams, *Southern California: An Island on the Land* (Salt Lake City: Peregrine Smith Books, 1946; 1973), 118–125. For the rapid expansion of the railroad network and public antagonism against it in late nineteenth-century California, see William Deverell, *Railroad Crossing: Californians and the Railroad, 1850–1910* (Berkeley: University of California Press, 1996).

12. Robert M. Fogelson, *The Fragmented Metropolis: Los Angeles, 1850–1930* (Cambridge, MA: Harvard University Press, 1967), 21, 63, 72, 75, 78–82, 95; US Census Bureau, *Fourteenth Census of the United States: 1920, Population* (Washington, DC, 1922), Table 9, "Composition and Characteristics of the Population, for Counties," and Table 12, "Country of Birth of the Foreign-Born White, for Counties and for Cities of 10,000 or More," 114, 124; Stephanie Lewthwaite, "Race, Place, Ethnicity in the Progressive Era," in *A Companion to Los Angeles*, ed. William Deverell and Greg Hise (Malden, MA: Wiley-Blackwell, 2010), 48–51.

13. Mark Wild, *Street Meeting: Multiethnic Neighborhoods in Early Twentieth-Century Los Angeles* (Berkeley: University of California Press, 2005), 18; Fogelson, *The Fragmented Metropolis*, 75–76; US Census Bureau, *Fourteenth Census of the United States*, Table 9, Table 12, 114, 124. Douglass Flamming explains that middle-class African Americans were "*bound and determined* to keep Jim Crow out of their new home [in Los Angeles, and] believed in the transformative power of the West." See Douglass Flamming, *Bound for Freedom: Black Los Angeles in Jim Crow America* (Berkeley: University of California Press, 2005), 14.

14. Lawrence J. Jelinek, *Harvest Empire: A History of California Agriculture* (San Francisco: Boyd & Fraser, 1979; 1982), 4–5, 40, 57–59, 62; Cletus E. Daniel, *Bitter Harvest: A History of California Farmworkers, 1870–1941* (Berkeley: University of California Press, 1981), 15–19, 33–35, 69; David Vaught, *Cultivating California: Growers, Specialty Crops, and Labor 1875–1920* (Baltimore: Johns Hopkins University Press, 1999), 9; Richard Steven Street, *Beasts of the Field: A Narrative History of California Farmworkers, 1769–1913* (Stanford, CA: Stanford University Press, 2004), xix.

15. Jelinek, *Harvest Empire*, 55, 68–72; Daniel, *Bitter Harvest*, 27–29, 50, 64; Street, *Beasts of the Field*, xviii; Tomás Almaguer, *Racial Fault Lines: The Historical Origins of White Supremacy in California* (Berkeley: University of California Press, 1994; 2009), 153–154, 183–204; Paul Kramer, "Empire against Exclusion in Early 20th Century Trans-Pacific History," *Nanzan Review of American Studies* 33 (2011): 16, 28. In the late 1880s, some farmers attempted to hire black farmworkers due to the exclusion of Chinese workers but failed because black workers soon found better paying jobs. See Delores Nason McBroome, "Harvests of Gold: African American Boosterism, Agriculture, and Investment in Allensworth

and Little Liberia," in *Seeking El Dorado: African Americans in California*, ed. Lawrence B. de Graaf, Kevin Mulroy, and Quintard Taylor (Seattle: University of Washington Press, 2001), 152.

16. The nature of California's industrialized agriculture that had fully taken hold in the early twentieth century is an important theme for historians. As early as the 1930s, Carey McWilliams demonstrated that the system of large land ownership helped create a highly exploitative economic structure of California agriculture. Cletus E. Daniel sees "the powerlessness of farmworkers" rather than the national or ethnic origin as a defining factor in labor-management relations in California agriculture. On the other hand, Tomás Almaguer contends that "race and the racialization process in California became the central organizing principle of group life," which meant white supremacy in the Southwest. Richard Steven Street states, "Class provides unifying meaning to the disparate experiences of the many races and nationalities" since the Spanish colonial period, while recognizing white supremacy as one of the foundational factors of California Agriculture. See Carey McWilliams, *Factories in the Field: The Story of Migratory Farm Labor in California* (Berkeley: University of California Press, 1939; 2000), 7; Daniel, *Bitter Harvest*, 11, 67, 71; Almaguer, *Racial Fault Lines*, 7; Street, *Beasts of the Field*, xix, xxi.

17. George J. Sánchez, *Becoming Mexican American: Ethnicity, Culture, and Identity in Chicano Los Angeles, 1900-1945* (New York: Oxford University Press, 1993), 17-37; Aito Shinohara, "Kyōwakoku no ayumi: Mekishiko," in *Ratenamerika sekai*, ed. Yoshio Masuda, Yoshiro Yamada, and Hidefuji Someda (Kyoto: Sekaishisōsha, 1984), 104-105; Camarillo, *Chicanos in California*, 33; David G. Gutiérrez, *Walls and Mirrors: Mexican Americans, Mexican Immigrants, and the Politics of Ethnicity* (Berkeley: University of California Press, 1995), 40-45.

18. US Census Office, *Twelfth Census of the United States: 1900, Population* (Washington DC, 1901), Table 33, "Foreign Born Population, Distributed According to Country of Birth, by States and Territories," 734; US Census Bureau, *Fourteenth Census of the United States*, Table 12, 124; Sánchez, *Becoming Mexican American*, 19, 72-73.

19. Francisco E. Balderrama, *In Defense of La Raza: The Los Angeles Mexican Consulate and the Mexican Community, 1929 to 1936* (Tucson: University of Arizona Press, 1982), 3-4.

20. In 1900 in Los Angeles County, the Japanese population was only 209 while the Chinese population was 2,951. See US Census Office, *Twelfth Census of the United States*, Table 34, "Foreign Born Population, Distributed According to Country of Birth, by Counties," 739.

21. Yuji Ichioka, *The Issei: The World of the First Generation Japanese Immigrants, 1885-1924* (New York: Free Press, 1988), 42-43; Masaaki Kodama, *Nihon iminshi kenkyū josetsu* [Introduction to Japanese migration history] (Hiroshima: Keisuisha, 1992), 11-18, 26, 518-521; Marius B. Jansen, *The Making of Modern Japan* (Cambridge, MA: Harvard University Press, 2000), 372-377; Teruko Kumei, *Gaikokujin wo meguru shakaishi: Kindai Amerika to nihonjin imin* [A social history of foreigners: Modern America and Japanese immigrants] (Tokyo: Yūzankaku, 1995), 80-82.

22. For the periodization of the history of Japanese overseas migration before World War II, see Kodama, *Nihon iminshi kenkyū josetsu*, i-ii, 518-521; Ichioka, *The Issei*, 52; Minamikashū Nihonjin Shichijūnenshi Kankō Iinkai [Publishing committee of Japanese in Southern California], ed., *Minamikashū nihonjin shichijūnenshi* [Japanese in Southern

California: A history of 70 years] (Los Angeles: Nanka Nikkeijin Shōgyō Kaigisho, 1960), 7–8, 13 (hereafter cited as *Minamikashū nihonjin shichijūnenshi*). For the lives of early Japanese immigrants in Hawai'i and California at the turn of the twentieth century, see Ichioka, *The Issei*; Ronald Takaki, *Strangers from a Different Shore: A History of Asian Americans* (New York: Little, Brown, and Company, 1989; 1998).

23. In 1873, the Japanese government set up a new consulate in San Francisco. In the same year, the Japanese consulate in San Francisco did a survey on Japanese residents and reported that there were sixty-eight Japanese men, eight women, and four kids in California. Many immigrants resided in San Francisco as a "school boy" who lived with a white American family as a domestic worker while attending school. In 1884, twenty-four Japanese immigrants lived in Los Angeles as domestic workers, restaurant employees, and so forth. *Minamikashū nihonjin shichijūnenshi*, 5–6, 661; Ichioka, *The Issei*, 24–27; US Census Office, *Twelfth Census of the United States*, Table 34, 739; US Census Bureau, *Fourteenth Census of the United States*, Table 9, 114, and "Supplemental Tables for Indian, Chinese, and Japanese Population," 132.

24. Masakazu Iwata, *Planted in Good Soil: A History of the Issei in United States Agriculture*, 2 vols. (New York: Peter Lang Publishers, 1992), 1:111, 153–154, 298.

25. Ibid., 292, 400.

26. Noritaka Yagasaki, *Imin nōgyō: Kariforunia no nihonjin imin shakai* [Immigrant agriculture: The Japanese immigrant society in California] (Tokyo: Kokonshoin, 1993), 51–53; Leonard Broom and Ruth Riemer, *Removal and Return: The Socio-Economic Effects of the War on Japanese Americans* (Berkeley: University of California, Press, 1949), 74, 85.

27. *Minamikashū nihonjin shichijūnenshi*, 53.

28. Dōjun Ochi, ed., *Minamikashū nihonjinshi kō-hen* [History of Japanese in Southern California, second volume] (Los Angeles: Nanka Nikkeijin Shōgyō Kaigisho, 1957), 61; Iwata, *Planted in Good Soil*, 1:397–400; *Minamikashū nihonjin shichijūnenshi*, 80–84, 88.

29. The ethnic Japanese population of Los Angeles County increased from 19,911 in 1920 to 36,866 in 1940 and that of Los Angeles City increased from 11,618 in 1920 to 23,321 in 1940. Broom and Riemer, *Removal and Return*, 8.

30. While the Ninth and Seventh Markets dealt with vegetables and fruits, there was a Japanese flower market on Los Angeles Street established in 1913 and later moved to Wall Street in 1941. *Minamikashū nihonjin shichijūnenshi*, 66–68, 115–117, 377–378, 662.

31. US Census Bureau, *Fourteenth Census of the United States*, Table 9, 114; US Census Bureau, *Fifteenth Census of the United States:1930, Population* (Washington, DC 1932), Table 2, "Color, Nativity, and Sex, for the State, Urban and Rural," and Table 13, "Composition of the Population, by Counties," 233, 252; Starr, *California*, 178–180; McWilliams, *Southern California*, 183–194; Ricardo Romo, *East Los Angeles: History of a Barrio* (Austin: University of Texas Press, 1983), 6; Yoshiaki Katada, "1930 nendai ni itaru nichi-bei kankei no gaiyō: Beikoku taiheiyō gan shuyōkō toriatsukai kamotsu to bōeki kōro no kōsatsu wo tōshite" [An exploration of the United States-Japanese trade relationships during the period approaching the 1930s: An examination of the changes of exports and imports in major ports along the US Pacific Coast and shipping routes between the US and Japan], *NUCB Journal of Economics and Information Science* 58, no. 2 (March 2014): 101; Sánchez, *Becoming Mexican American*, 69. For the Owens Valley, see Morrow Mayo,

"The Rape of Owens Valley," and Remi Nadeau, "There It Is—Take It," in *Los Angeles: Biography of a City*, ed. John Caughey and LaRee Caughey (Berkeley: University of California Press, 1977), 222–235.

32. US Census Bureau, *Fourteenth Census of the United States*, Table 12, 124; US Census Bureau, *Fifteenth Census of the United States*, Table 17, "Indians, Chinese, and Japanese, 1910 to 1930, and Mexicans, 1930, for Counties and for Cities of 25,000 or More," 266.

33. Eiichiro Azuma describes that "before the Pacific War, the Japanese of southern California and the northern Baja peninsula constituted what can be termed a 'transborder' community," although he does not discuss the impact of the 1924 Act on the transborder ethnic Japanese community. See Eiichiro Azuma, "Community Formation across the National Border: The Japanese of the U.S.-Mexican Californias," *Review: Literature and Arts of the Americas* 39, no. 1 (2006): 30–44.

34. Seiichi Akana, *Tsūzoku Beikoku imin hō kōwa* [Lecture on US immigration laws] (Tokyo: Hakubundō, 1929), 2–28, Rare Books, Huntington Library, San Marino, California. For the nativism behind the 1924 Act, see John Higham, *Strangers in the Land: Patterns of American Nativism, 1860–1925* (New Brunswick, NJ: Rutgers University Press, 1955; 1988). For Matson's article, see William Deverell, *Whitewashed Adobe: The Rise of Los Angeles and the Remaking of Its Mexican Past* (Berkeley: University of California Press, 2004), 172, 199.

35. Lon Kurashige, *Two Faces of Exclusion: The Untold History of Anti-Asian Racism in the United States* (Chapel Hill: University of North Carolina Press, 2016), introduction, ch. 4, and ch. 5.

36. Aristide R. Zolberg, *A Nation by Design: Immigration Policy in the Fashioning of America* (Cambridge, MA: Harvard University, 2006), 245; Mae M. Ngai, *Impossible Subjects: Illegal Aliens and the Making of Modern America* (Princeton, NJ: Princeton University Press, 2004), 1–9, 254.

37. The Japanese in Los Angeles knew that another major purpose of the 1924 Act was to restrict Southern and Eastern European immigrants. See Akana, *Tsūzoku Beikoku imin hō kōwa*, 3.

38. "Beikoku wa berabō daga Nihon mo taishi taido wo hansei seyo" [The United States is outrageous, but Japan should reflect on its attitude toward China], *Rafu Shimpo*, June 4, 1924; Zhaocheng Wang, "Ichi shinajin kara" [From a Chinese], *Tokyo Asahi Shimbun*, September 28, 1922; Ochi, ed., *Minamikashū nihonjinshi kō-hen*, 92. As for the situation of Chinese immigrant workers in 1920s Japan, see Yasuhisa Abe, "1920 nendai no Tōkyō fu ni okeru chūgokujin rōdōsha no shūgyō kōzō to kyojū bunka" [The occupational structure and residential differentiation of Chinese workers in Tokyo Prefecture during the 1920s], *Jinbun chiri* 51, no. 1 (1999): 40–41.

39. "Kokujokubi" [Day of national disgrace], *Rafu Shimpo*, May 28, 1924; "Beitaishikan no yakeato de nihonjin fungai seppuku" [An infuriated Japanese cut his abdomen in front of the U.S. Embassy], *Rafu Shimpo*, June 1, 1924; "Kanashimubeki giseisha" [A victim we should lament over], *Rafu Shimpo*, June 4, 1924.

40. Yuji Ichioka, *Before Internment: Essays in Prewar Japanese American History*, ed. Gordon H. Chang and Eiichiro Azuma (Stanford, CA: Stanford University Press, 2006), 53. See also Mitsuhiro Sakaguchi, *Nihonjin Amerika iminshi* [History of Japanese immigrants in the United States] (Tokyo: Fuji Shuppan, 2001), 23–31, 321.

41. Sakaguchi, *Nihonjin Amerika iminshi*, 273–300; "Kokuseki ridatsusha no gekizō" [A dramatic increase of those who renounce citizenship], *Osaka Mainichi Shimbun*, July 11, 1924; "Kokuseki hō chū kaisei" [Amendment of the Nationality Act], *Rafu Shimpo*, July 18, 1924.

42. Tomoko Makabe, "Ethnic Hegemony: The Japanese Brazilians in Agriculture, 1908–1968," *Ethnic and Racial Studies* 22, no. 4 (January 1999): 704.

43. The Japanese government encouraged Japanese emigration to South America by providing travel subsidy in hopes of reducing the number of unemployed in Japan. See Kodama, *Nihon iminshi josetsu*, i–ii; Makabe, "Ethnic Hegemony," 718; Mitsuhiro Sakaguchi, "Shutsu imin no kioku" [Memory of emigration], in *Imin kenkyū to tabunka kyōsei* [Immigration studies and multicultural coexistence], ed. Japanese Association for Migration Studies (Tokyo: Ochanomizu Shobō, 2011), 86–87.

44. Nichi-Boku Kōryūshi Henshū Iinkai [Editorial committee of history of Japan-Mexico interaction], ed., *Nichi-boku kōryūshi* [History of Japan-Mexico interaction] (Tokyo: PMC Shuppan, 1990), 422–423 (hereafter cited as *Nichi-boku kōryūshi*).

45. Tsuneji Chino to Chiyoko Fujioka, February 2, 1958, Folder 2, Box 59, Japanese American Research Project Collection, Special Collections, University of California, Los Angeles, Los Angeles, California (hereafter cited as JARP); *Minamikashū nihonjin shichijūnenshi*, 381.

46. Central Japanese Association of Southern California, meeting minutes, February 7, 1924, Box 229, Japanese American Research Project Collection, National Diet Library, Tokyo, Japan (hereafter cited as JARP-NDL). From 2002 to 2004, the National Diet Library of Japan purchased microfilms of some materials from the Japanese American Research Project Collection preserved in the Special Collections, Charles E. Young Library of the University of California, Los Angeles.

47. Central Japanese Association of Southern California, meeting minutes, April 3, 1924, Box 229, JARP-NDL.

48. "Chūō Nihonjin Kai de, chikaku Bokukoku chōsa ka" [Central Japanese Association will conduct research of Mexico soon], *Rafu Shimpo*, May 3, 1924; Central Japanese Association of Southern California, meeting minutes, April 29 1924, Box 229, JARP-NDL.

49. Dudley O. McGovney, "The Anti-Japanese Land Laws of California and the Other States," *California Law Review* 35, no. 1 (March 1947): 7–60. In 1924, Japanese immigrants in San Francisco conducted research about Japanese migration to Georgia and Florida and concluded that the Japanese would need more than two thousand dollars to begin agriculture in those states. Japanese Association of the United States, report on states outside California, November 1924, Box 263, JARP-NDL.

50. "Bokukoku nōen shihaisha wa Kashū ni okeru nihonjin" [Japanese in California to control farms in Mexico], *Rafu Shimpo*, July 10, 1924.

51. "Bokukoku wa shokun wo matsu" [Mexico is waiting for you], *Rafu Shimpo*, May 17, 1924.

52. Andrey Kobayashi and Midge Ayukawa, "A Brief History of Japanese Canadians," in *Encyclopedia of Japanese History of the Descendants in the Americas: An Illustrated History of the Nikkei*, ed. Akemi Kikumura-Yano (Walnut Creek, CA: AltaMira Press, 2002), 155–156; Masumi Izumi, "Tetsujōmō naki kyōsei shūyōjo: Dai niji taisen ka no nikkei

kanadajin" [Concentration camps without barbed wire: Japanese Canadians during World War II], *Ritsumeikan gengo bunka kenkyū* 25, no. 1 (2013): 122–123.

53. Roger Daniels, *The Politics of Prejudice: The Anti-Japanese Movement in California* (New York: Atheneum, 1968), 32, 73.

54. Torimatsu Ozono, "Bokukoku jijō (4)" [The situation of Mexico], *Rafu Shimpo*, July 20, 1924.

55. Torimatsu Ozono, "Bokukoku jijō (1)," *Rafu Shimpo*, July 17, 1924; "Bokukoku jijō (2)," *Rafu Shimpo*, July 18, 1924.

56. Ozno, "Bokukoku jijō (1)," *Rafu Shimpo*, July 17, 1924. *La Opinión* had the same understanding that Mexicans lacked the ambition for savings. See Raul D. Tovares, "*La Opinión* and Its Contribution to the Mexican Community's Adaptation to Life in the US," *Latino Studies* 7, no. 4 (December 2009): 490.

57. "Futatabi Bokukoku ijūsha e chūi wo ataetai" [I want to send a reminder to those who move to Mexico], *Rafu Shimpo*, May 4, 1924.

58. Kumaichi Horiguchi, acting deputy minister of the Japanese Legation in Mexico, to Jutarō Komura, minister of foreign affairs of Japan, May 26, 1911, 5-3-2-0-154, Bokukoku nairan kankei teikoku shinmin no songai baishō ikken [Demand for compensation for damage of Japanese subjects related to Mexican civil war], vol. 1, Diplomatic Archives of the Ministry of Foreign Affairs of Japan (DAMFAJ), Minato-ku, Tokyo, Japan (hereafter cited as 5-3-2-0-154, vol. 1, DAMFAJ). The Japan Center for Asian Historical Records (JACAR), a Japanese government's online digital archives, makes publicly available a large number of historical documents of the Japanese government including those preserved in the DAMFAJ and the National Archives of Japan (NAJ). See https://www.jacar.go.jp, accessed August 6, 2019.

59. Grace Peña Delgado, *Making the Chinese Mexican: Global Migration, Localism, and Exclusion in the U.S.-Mexico Borderlands* (Stanford, CA: Stanford University Press, 2012), 104–105, 106–110, 113.

60. "Shinajin haiseki" [Anti-Chinese exclusion], *Rafu Shimpo*, June 4, 1924.

61. "Bokukoku seibu shoshū nite shinajin mondai okoru" [Chinese problem discussed in western states of Mexico], *Rafu Shimpo*, September 7, 1924.

62. A *Rafu Shimpo* article reported on the disappearance of a Chinatown in Orange County and wrote, "Discriminated against again and again, the Japanese could face the similar destiny [like the Chinese did]." See "Kemuri no you ni kiesatta Orenji no shinamachi" [Orange County Chinatown vanished like a puff of smoke], *Rafu Shimpo*, June 18, 1924. For the history of anti-Chinese racism in Mexico, see Jason Oliver Chang, *Chino: Anti-Chinese Racism in Mexico, 1880–1940* (Urbana: University of Illinois Press, 2017).

63. Keiichi Itō, acting deputy minister of the Japanese Legation in Mexico, to Yasuya Uchida, minister of foreign affairs, June 1, 1922, 5-3-2-0-154, vol. 1, DAMFAJ.

64. "Bokukoku shisatsu hōkokukai" [A debrief session about the research in Mexico], *Rafu Shimpo*, September 5, 1924; "Shisatsu go no tai bokusaku" [A plan regarding Mexico after the research], *Rafu Shimpo*, September 6, 1924. Dobashi and Matsuoka gave another talk to Japanese farmers in Orange County, see "Anahaimu: Bokukoku shisatsu dan" [Anaheim: A talk on the research in Mexico], *Rafu Shimpo*, September 12, 1924.

65. "Yūbō na Bokukoku ijū," *Rafu Shimpo*, September 9, 1924; "Bokukoku shisatsu dan shōhō (3)" [Detailed reports of the research in Mexico], *Rafu Shimpo*, September 12, 1924; "Bokukoku shisatsu dan shōhō (4)," *Rafu Shimpo*, September 13, 1924; "Bokukoku shisatsu dan shōhō (5)," *Rafu Shimpo*, September 14, 1924.

66. "Bokukoku shisatsu dan shōhō (1)," *Rafu Shimpo*, September 10, 1924.

67. Jansen, *The Making of Modern Japan*, 578; Hyun Ok Park, *Two Dreams in One Bed: Empire, Social Life, and the Origins of the North Korean Revolution in Manchuria* (Durham, NC: Duke University Press, 2005), 49, 51.

68. Ryoichi Imai, "Manshū nōgyō imin ni okeru jinushika to sono ronri" [Becoming landowners and its logics in the agricultural immigration to Manchuria], in *Nihon teikoku wo meguru jinkō idō no kokusai shakai gaku* [Migration and repatriation: The rise and fall of the Japanese Empire], ed. Sinzo Araragi (Tokyo: Fuji Shuppan, 2008), 219; Sakio Tsurumi, "Imin to bōeki" [Immigration and trade], in *Kaigai ijū* [Overseas migration], ed. Nihon Imin Kyōkai [Migration Association of Japan] (Tokyo: Nihon Imin Kyōkai, 1923), 72–73.

69. "Dobashi Wataru kun ga meki hime ni" [Mr. Wataru Dobashi and a Mexican princess], *Rafu Shimpo*, September 7, 1924.

70. "Bokukoku shisatsu dan shōhō (6)," *Rafu Shimpo*, September 16, 1924.

71. "Tasū nōka Bokukoku shisatsu" [Many farmers visiting Mexico], *Rafu Shimpo*, July 4, 1924; "Nakamura Mankichi kun ikkō, Bokukoku shisatsu" [A group led by Mr. Mankichi Nakamura, research in Mexico], *Rafu Shimpo*, August 10, 1924; "Bokukoku tochi shisatsu no tochū, jidōsha tempuku shite Nakamura Genpei shi zanshi shi" [On the way to visit Mexico for land research, Mr. Genpei Nakamura died due to a car accident], *Rafu Shimpo*, September 16, 1924. Regarding Japanese farmers in Lancaster, the *Rafu nenkan* [Rafu yearbook and directory] 1910 recorded seventeen Japanese landowners in Lancaster in 1910. See also Iwata, *Planted in Good Soil*, 1:440.

72. "Bokukoku kinensai, Wakasugi ryōji enzetsu" [Consul Wakasugi will give a speech at the Mexican festival], *Rafu Shimpo*, September 16, 1924.

73. Kaname Wakasugi, Japanese consul in Los Angeles, to Keishirō Matsui, minister of foreign affairs of Japan, June 4, 1924, 6-1-2-72, Zaigai teikoku kōkan setchi zakken [Miscellaneous reports on the establishment of overseas imperial diplomatic offices], vol. 1, DAMFAJ, Minato-ku, Tokyo, Japan (hereafter cited as 6-1-2-72, vol. 1, DAMFAJ); "Shakai-teki ni haiseki saretsutsu dōshite dōka shieruka" [How could the Japanese assimilate when they are socially excluded?], *Rafu Shimpo*, June 3, 1924.

74. Kaori Hayashi, *A History of the Rafu Shimpo: Japanese and Their Newspaper in Los Angeles* (Osaka: Union Press, 1997), 65.

75. Kaori Hayashi, *Nikkei jānaristo monogatari* [Nikkei journalist stories] (Tokyo: Shinzansha Shuppan, 1997), 135–141.

76. Shirō Fujioka, "Hainichi jōkō wo fukumu Beikoku shin imin hō (4)" [The new US immigration act that has the Japanese exclusion clause], *Rafu Shimpo*, June 1, 1924.

77. Hayashi, *Nikkei jānarisuto monogatari*, 145.

78. "Kanashimubeki giseisha," *Rafu Shimpo*, June 4, 1924; "Shisatsu go no tai bokusaku," *Rafu Shimpo*, September 6, 1924.

79. Shirō Fujioka, *Ayumi no ato: Hokubei tairiku nihonjin kaitaku monogatari* [Traces of a journey: A story of Japanese pioneers in the North American continent] (Los Angeles: Ayumi no Ato Kankō Kōenkai, 1957), 74.

80. Satarō Yamada, *Gojin no kaitaku subeki kaigai yūbō no fugen* [My thoughts regarding promising overseas sources of wealth for our development] (Tokyo: Keibunsha, 1925), 1–9, 233.

81. "Imin seisaku shishin toshite Bokukoku Kenkyū Kai setsuritsu" [Foundation of the Mexico Study Society for emigration policy], *Rafu Shimpo*, September 26, 1924.

82. "Bokukoku Jijō Kenkyū Kai" [The Mexico Study Society], *Rafu Shimpo*, October 3, 1924.

83. "Katsuro kaihatsu subeku Bokukoku Hatten Kyōkai umaru" [The Mexico Development Society established to find new opportunities], *Rafu Shimpo*, October 10, 1924. While the group was generally called the Mexico Study Society, it was occasionally called the Bokukoku Hatten Kyōkai (Mexico Development Society).

84. Naotarō Kobayashi and Yoshimasa Itō, *Mekishiko shokumin no shiori* [Leaflet for settlement in Mexico] (Los Angeles: Rafu Bokukoku Kenkyū Kai, 1925), preface by authors, 3, 29, Folder 4, Box 1, Arthur Ito Papers, Huntington Library, San Marino, California.

85. "Bokukoku nenkan" [The Mexican almanac], *Rafu Shimpo*, July 11, 1924; "Ichigo kōsakusha no kyūjō" [Plight of berry growers], *Rafu Shimpo*, June 29, 1924. Another advertisement of the Mexican almanac said, "In the time when we hear a lot of voices on the development of Mexico, this is a treasury for the Japanese in the United States." "Bokukoku nenkan," *Rafu Shimpo*, September 27, 1924. Throughout this book, I have used MeasuringWorth.com to convert the monetary value of the first half of the twentieth century into its relative value of 2020. See MeasuringWorth.com, online at http://www.measuringworth.com, accessed December 29, 2021.

86. "Seito boshū" [Recruiting new students], *Rafu Shimpo*, August 10, 1924.

87. Nichi-Boku Kyōkai [The Japan-Mexico Society], *Nichi-Boku Kyōkai hō* [Japan-Mexico Society bulletin], vol. 1, April 30, 1926, Folder 10, Box 271, JARP, 190–192. This organization is different from another Nichi-Boku Kyōkai established in 1956 in Mexico. See *Nichi-boku kōryūshi*, 651–653.

88. Nichi-Boku Kyōkai, *Nichi-Boku Kyōkai hō*, vol. 1, April 30, 1926, Folder 10, Box 271, JARP, 190–192.

89. "Bokukoku Kenkyū Kai no umareta toki" [When the Mexico Study Society was created], *Rafu Shimpo*, October 22, 1924.

90. Nichi-Boku Kyōkai, *Nichi-Boku Kyōkai hō*, vol. 1, April 30, 1926, Folder 10, Box 271, JARP, 195–196.

91. Mexican Legation in Japan to the Mexican Ministry of Foreign Affairs, December 22, 1922, Folder 77, Box 3, Collection Gaveta 45, Archivo Histórico Genaro Estrada [Genaro Estrada Historical Archive], Secretaría de Relaciones Exteriores [Ministry of Foreign Affairs], Mexico City, Mexico (hereafter cited as AHGE).

92. Eduardo F. Hay, minister of the Mexican Legation in Japan, to the Ministry of Foreign Affairs of Mexico, June 2, 1924, Folder 210, Box 5, Collection Gaveta 21, AHGE.

93. "Mekishiko daitōryō Nihon imin kangei wo seimei" [The Mexican president welcomes Japanese immigrants], *Tokyo Asahi Shimbun*, April 18, 1924; "Hōjin shokumin to

Bokukoku shoshimbun no ronchō" [Japanese settlements and opinions of Mexican newspapers], *Rafu Shimpo*, April 25, 1924.

94. "Mekishiko mo kotowaru" [Mexico rejects, too], *Yomiuri Shimbun*, April 25, 1924.

95. Fujioka, *Ayumi no Ato*, 75–76.

96. Ryuji Hattori and Toshihiro Minohara, "Washinton taisei 1920 nendai" [The Washington regime in the 1920s] in *Nichi-bei kankeishi* [The history of Japan-US history], ed. Makoto Iokibe (Tokyo: Yūhikaku, 2008), 83–109; Toshihiro Minohara, *Hainichi imin hō to nichi-bei kankei* [The Japanese Exclusion Act and Japan-US relations] (Tokyo: Iwanami Shoten, 2002), 218.

97. Nichi-Boku Kyōkai, *Nichi-Boku Kyōkai hō*, vol. 1, April 30, 1926, Folder 10, Box 271, JARP, 4–15. In August 1924, the *Tokyo Asahi Shimbun* reported the rumor that Kimura had departed to Mexico to explore the possibility of sending Japanese immigrants to the Pacific Coast area of Mexico. To the press, the Ministry of Foreign Affairs of Japan denied the rumor probably because the ministry did not want to arouse attention from the US government. See "Nihon ga shihon wo ire, Bokukoku de menka saibai setsu, Kimura jimukan no nyūboku ni tomonau uwasa" [Cotton production in Mexico with Japanese capital, a rumor about Secretary Kimura's visit to Mexico], *Tokyo Asahi Shimbun*, August 22, 1924.

98. Nichi-Boku Kyōkai, *Nichi-Boku Kyōkai hō*, vol. 1, April 30, 1926, Folder 10, Box 271, JARP, 197–201.

99. "Imin wo Mekishiko e okure," *Yomiuri Shimbun*, June 1, 1924. The *Rafu Shimpo* reported about the *Yomiuri*'s editorial. See "Bokukoku e tasū imin wo okure" [Send many emigrants to Mexico], *Rafu Shimpo*, June 3, 1924.

100. "Iminka setchi ni kansuru gaimu daijin no iken" [An opinion of the minister of foreign affairs regarding setting up the immigration division], *Choya Shimbun*, August 5, 1891; *Nichi-boku kōryūshi*, 140–169; Koichiro Yaginuma, "Kindai Mekishiko no sangyō kaihatsu ni okeru nihonjin imin: 'Imin gaisha' no hensen to nihonjin Mekishiko 'keiyaku imin' wo chūshin ni" [Japanese immigrants and the development of modern Mexican industries—the history of "emigration companies" and Japanese "contract immigrants" in Mexico], *Kanda gaigo daigaku kiyō* 12 (March 2000): 212–215.

101. Iyo Kunimoto, "Kindai nichi-boku kankei no keisei to Beikoku 1888–1910" [The formation of modern Japan-Mexico relations and the United States, 1888–1910], *Ratenamerika ronshū* 11–12 (1978): 90–94; *Nichi-boku kōryūshi*, 338; María Elena Ota Mishima, "Características Sociales y Económicas de Los Migrantes Japoneses en México," in *Destino México: Un estudio de las migraciones asiáticas a México, siglo XIX y XX*, ed. María Elena Ota Mishima (Mexico City: Colegio de México, Centro de Estudios de Asia y Africa, 1997), 56; Daniels, *The Politics of Prejudice*, 41, 44; Greg Robinson, *A Tragedy of Democracy: Japanese Confinement in North America* (New York: Columbia University Press, 2009), 14. In 1924, a Japanese government report about the Gentlemen's Agreement explained, "The Japanese government has been taking stricter control of Japanese laborers who intend to go to the neighboring foreign territories of the United States in order to prevent them from illegally entering the United States." See Ministry of Foreign Affairs of Japan, "Shinshi kyōyaku" [Gentlemen's Agreement], 1924, GiTS-6, Dai 50 gikai setsumei sankō shiryō [Report prepared for the 50th Diet], DAMFAJ.

102. Ministry of Foreign Affairs of Japan, "Issues related to Mexico," 1926, GiTS-11, Dai 52 gikai setsumei sankō shiryō [Report prepared for the 52nd Diet], DAMFAJ; Fujioka, *Ayumi no ato*, 72–74.

103. María Elena Ota Mishima, *Siete Migraciones Japonesas en México, 1890–1978* (Mexico City: Colegio de México, Centro de Estudios de Asia y Africa, 1985), 67; Jerry García, *Looking Like the Enemy: Japanese Mexicans, the Mexican State, and US Hegemony, 1897–1945* (Tucson: University of Arizona Press, 2014), 79.

104. Ministry of Foreign Affairs of Japan, "Chūnanbei zairyū hōjin gaikyō" [The situation of overseas Japanese in Central and South America], 1934, GiAM-3, Dai 67 kai teikoku gikai setsumei sankō shiryō jō-kan [Explanatory report prepared for the 67th Imperial Diet, vol. 1], DAMFAJ. Jerry García writes that the total Japanese population in Mexico was estimated to be 5,967 in 1930. See García, *Looking Like the Enemy*, 79.

105. "Bokukoku imin gekizō ka" [A dramatic increase of immigrants in Mexico?], *Rafu Shimpo*, May 22, 1924.

106. Dirección General de Estadística, Secretaría de la Economía Nacional de México, *Quinto Censo de Población, Baja California Distrito Norte* (Mexico D. F., 1935), 11, Folder 1, Box 72, Collection Gobierno del Estado, Archivo Histórico del Estado de Baja California [Historical Archive of the State of Baja California], Mexicali, Mexico (hereafter cited as AHEBC); Yolanda Sánchez Ogás, *Asalto a Las Tierras 75 Aniversario, 1937–2012* (Mexicali: AM Impresiones, 2012), 30.

107. Catalina Velázquez Morales, *Los inmigrantes chinos en Baja California 1920–1937* (Mexicali: Universidad Autónoma de Baja California, 2001), 49–50, 59.

108. Nihon Mekishiko Ijūshi Hensan Iinkai [Editorial committee of history of Japanese migration to Mexico], ed., *Nihon Mekishiko ijūshi* (1971), 200–205 (hereafter cited as *Nihon Mekishiko ijūshi*); *Nichi-boku kōryūshi*, 422–424.

109. Ota Mishima, *Siete Migraciones Japonesas en México, 1890–1978*, 63–64.

110. *Nichi-boku kōryūshi*, 423–424, 438–439, 516; *Nihon Mekishiko ijūshi*, 200–206.

111. Dirección General de Estadística, *Quinto Censo de Población, Baja California Distrito Norte*, 32; Japanese Association of Mexicali to Ken Yanagisawa, acting deputy minister of the Japanese Legation in Mexico, June 13, 1931, M-1-3-0-1_1, Zaigai teikoku kōkan kankei zakken/Setchi kankei [Miscellaneous documents relating to overseas imperial diplomatic offices/relating to establishment], vol. 1, DAMFAJ. The Ministry of Foreign Affairs of Japan recorded nearly eight hundred Japanese residents in Mexicali and less than one hundred Japanese in Tijuana in 1931. See Ken Yanagisawa to Kijūrō Shidehara, minister of foreign affairs of Japan, April 29, 1931, M-2-2-0-1_3_2, Honshō narabini zaigai kōkan'in shutchō kankei zakken/Honshōin oyobi zaigai kōkan'in kaigai shutchō no bu (Soshakuchi, inin tōchi chiiki wo fukumu)/Zaibei kakukan [Miscellaneous documents relating to overseas diplomatic offices/overseas assignments of ministry officials and diplomatic office staff members (including leased and mandated territories)/Offices in the United States], vol. 2, DAMFAJ, Minato-ku, Tokyo, Japan (hereafter cited as M-2-2-0-1_3_2, vol. 2, DAMFAJ).

112. Yasutarō Taki, *Mekishiko kokujō taikan: Shokumin shichijūnenshi* [Mexico, great friend of Japan: A seventy-year history of Japanese settlement] (Mexico City: Mehiko Shimpōsha, 1968), 255–258.

113. *Nichi-boku kōryūshi*, 440.

114. Nichi Boku Kyōkai, *Nichi-Boku Kyōkai hō*, vol. 2, March 30, 1927, Folder 10, Box 271, JARP, 316–324.

115. Catalina Velázquez Morales, ed., *Baja California: Un presente con historia* (Mexicali: Universidad Autónoma de Baja California, 2002), 104.

116. Gobierno del Distrito Norte de la Baja California, information of Japanese Kiyoya Hayasaka, November 1929, Folder 90, Box 40, Collection Dirección General de Gobierno, Archivo General de la Nación [National Archives of Mexico], Secretaría General de Gobernación, Mexico City, Mexico (hereafter cited as AGN); Taki, *Mekishiko kokujō taikan*, 274.

117. *Ozawa v. United States*. 260 US 178 (1922).

118. Dirección General de Estadística, *Quinto Censo de Población, Baja California Distrito Norte*, 32, 35.

119. Secretaría de Gobernacion, "Pide se le informe si los extranjeros naturalizados pueden adquirir dominio en tierras y aguas," December 1929, Folder 32, Box 3, Collection Dirección General de Gobierno, AGN.

120. Taki, *Mekishiko kokujō taikan*, 244.

121. Ibid., 298. Ayumi Takenaka, "The Japanese in Peru: History of Immigration, Settlement, and Racialization," *Latin American Perspectives* 31, no. 3 (May 2004): 85.

122. Except for Baja California, the majority of Japanese immigrant men in Mexico married Mexican women in the 1930s. See García, *Looking Like the Enemy*, 85.

123. *Nichi-boku kōryūshi*, 516–518.

124. Ota Mishima regards the period from 1921 to 1940 as one of the three periods when the Japanese increased in Mexico. In this period, fishermen were one of the major groups of Japanese immigrants. See Ota Mishima, *Siete Migraciones Japonesas en México, 1890–1978*, 88–93. As for the Japanese fishery in the Baja California region, see Shigeru Sugiyama, "1930 nendai Mekishiko ni okeru nihon ebi torōru gyogyō to nichi-boku-bei sangoku kankei ni kansuru kenkyū" [The Japanese prawn trawl fishery and the trinational relationship between Japan, Mexico, and the United States in 1930s Mexico], Research report of project funded by Grant-in-Aid for Scientific Research (C) of the Japan Society for the Promotion of Science (April 2008); Yuko Konno, "Senzen no Kariforunia shū ni okeru hannichi gyogyō hōan wo meguru tatakai" [The struggle over anti-Japanese fishing bills in pre-World War II], *Imin kenkyū nempō* 22 (March 2016): 63–77.

125. *Nichi-boku kōryūshi*, 429–433.

126. Gobierno del Distrito Norte de la Baja California, *Periódico Oficial*, July 10, 1924, Biblioteca Central Mexicali [Mexicali Central Library], Universidad Autónoma de Baja California, Mexicali.

127. Nichi Boku Kyōkai, *Nichi-Boku Kyōkai hō*, vol. 2, March 30, 1927, Folder 10, Box 271, JARP, 321.

128. *Nichi-boku kōryūshi*, 433–435

129. Kunimoto, "Kindai nichi-boku kankei no keisei to Beikoku 1888–1910," 83–84, 87.

130. Council meeting minutes, "Nihon koku Mekishiko koku kan tsūshō kōkai jōyaku on hijun no ken" [Regarding the ratification of the treaty of commerce and navigation between Japan and Mexico], March 18, 1925, Sūmitsuin kaigi hikki [Council meeting minutes], Sū-D00562100, NAJ. Ota Mishima also touches upon the treaty to explain the

immigration of Japanese fishermen. See Ota Mishima, *Siete Migraciones Japonesas en México, 1890–1978*, 88–92.

131. Eiichiro Azuma, "Japanese Immigrant Settler Colonialism in the U.S.-Mexican Borderlands and the U.S. Racial-Imperialist Politics of the Hemispheric 'Yellow Peril,'" *Pacific Historical Review* 83, no. 2 (May 2014): 274.

132. Furuya reported that the United States had twenty-six consulates in Mexico. Shigetsuna Furuya, minister of the Japanese Legation in Mexico, to Keishirō Matsui, minister of foreign affairs of Japan, May 31, 1924, 6-1-2-72, vol. 1, DAMFAJ.

133. Kaname Wakasugi, Japanese consul in Los Angeles, to Keishirō Matsui, June 4, 1924, 6-1-2-72, vol. 1, DAMFAJ.

134. Kijūrō Shidehara, minister of foreign affairs of Japan, to Wakasugi, Masanao Hanihara, Japanese ambassador in the United States, and Ujirō Ōyama, Japanese consul general in San Francisco, July 23, 1924, 6-1-2-72, vol. 1, DAMFAJ; Ministry of Foreign Affairs of Japan, November 1, 1927, M-2-1-0-10_33, Kakkoku chūzai teikoku ryōji ninmen kankei zakken [Miscellaneous reports on appointment and dismissal of imperial consulate officials in foreign countries], DAMFAJ.

135. "Mekishiko Kenkyū Kai to shushi senden, Yodogawa fuku ryōji kangei kai no seikai" [The Mexico Study Society, welcoming party for vice consul Yodogawa], *Rafu Shimpo*, October 22, 1924.

136. Hayashi, *Nikkei jānarisuto monogatari*, 147; "Kyūchi ni tateru nōgyōka" [Farmers in peril], *Rafu Shimpo*, December 17, 1924.

137. Nichi Boku Kyōkai, *Nichi-Boku Kyōkai hō*, vol. 2, March 30, 1927, Folder 10, Box 271, JARP, 319–321.

138. "Hatten no kibō sukunaki Bokukoku teikashū hantō" [Little hope in Mexico's Baja California Peninsula], *Rafu Shimpo*, September 9, 1926.

139. Ota Mishima, "Características Sociales y Económicas," 55–57, 60–63, 104–110.

140. Eiichiro Azuma writes that "the latter half of the 1920s saw a rise in the number of Issei resettlers to northwestern Mexico. Between 1924 and 1931, 275 and 274 Issei households went through Tijuana and Mexicali, respectively, resettling elsewhere in Baja California." Azuma asserts this drawing on statistics compiled by historian María Elena Ota Mishima and assuming that those Japanese crossing Mexican border cities such as Tijuana and Mexicali were former Japanese residents in the United States who wanted to "resettle" in Mexico. However, Ota Mishima's statistics are neither about "Issei resettlers" from the United States nor about their households but simply about from where Japanese immigrants entered Mexico and where they lived. In fact, many Japanese immigrants first landed at San Francisco, moved through US territory, and finally entered Mexico via Mexicali and Tijuana. For example, a Japanese *yobiyose* immigrant Kieya Hayasaka landed at San Francisco on October 16, 1924 and a week later entered Mexicali by train via Los Angeles. The US government allowed Japanese migrants to move through the US territory to enter Mexico. See Azuma, "Japanese Immigrant Settler Colonialism," 270–271; Ota Mishima, *Destino México*, 60–63, 104–110; Taki, *Mekishiko kokujō taikan*, 274–275; Mexican Legation in Japan to the Mexican Ministry of Foreign Affairs, December 22, 1922, Folder 77, Box 3, Collection Gaveta 45, AHGE; Akana, *Tsūzoku beikoku imin hō*, 20–22.

141. Nichi Boku Kyōkai, *Nichi-Boku Kyōkai hō*, vol. 2, March 30, 1927, Folder 10, Box 271, JARP, 52–84.

142. Ministry of Foreign Affairs of Japan, May 1932, Tsū3_97, Bokukoku "Ensenada" hōmen ni okeru honpōjin no hatten jōkyō/1932 nen" [Development circumstances of Japanese in the Ensenada area, Mexico/1932], DAMFAJ; *Nihonjin Mekishiko ijūshi*, 205–206; Azuma, "Community Formation across the National Border," 40–41.

143. The consulate in Mazatlán was closed in 1935. Since then, the Japanese Legation in Mexico oversaw Baja Japanese through a consular office in Tijuana. See Ministry of Foreign Affairs of Japan, "The reasons for the decision to set up a new consular office in Tijuana," 1931, M-2-2-0-1_3_2, vol. 2, DAMFAJ; Ministry of Foreign Affairs of Japan, regarding the new allocation of consular work in Mexico, July 11, 1935, M-1-3-0-1_3, Zaigai teikoku kōkan kankei zakken (Miscellaneous reports on overseas imperial diplomatic offices), vol. 2, DAMFAJ.

144. McBroome, "Harvests of Gold," 149–180.

145. *Nichi-boku kōryūshi*, 472–477, 516.

146. Ibid.; *Nihonjin Mekishiko ijūshi*, 182.

147. For example, an editorial of the *Rafu Shimpo* criticized the murderer who killed Mashiko as "the enemy of the whole Japanese community." See "Mashiko kun (Mr. Mashiko)," *Rafu Shimpo*, December 23, 1926; "Mekishikari nikkai ni hōka shi" [Japanese Association of Mexicali set on fire], *Rafu Shimpo*, December 18, 1926; "Chūnichikai yori ryō kanji, Mekishikari shutchō" [Two secretaries of the Central Japanese Association visit Mexicali], *Rafu Shimpo*, December 23, 1926; "Shōda Taiheiyō no ue nimo giwaku no ten koshi" [Very suspicious Taiheiyo Shōda], *Rafu Shimpo*, December 25, 1926.

148. Interview by the author, Iwao Ichikawa, January 28, 2016, in Mexicali.

CHAPTER 2. THE DEEPENING OF JAPANESE-MEXICAN
RELATIONS IN TRIRACIAL LOS ANGELES

1. Minamikashū Nihonjin Shichijūnenshi Kankō Iinkai [Publishing committee of Japanese in Southern California], ed., *Minamikashū nihonjin shichijūnenshi* [Japanese in Southern California] (Los Angeles: Nanka Nikkeijin Shōgyō Kaigisho, 1960), 53, 57 (hereafter cited as *Minamikashū nihonjin shichijūnenshi*); Carey McWilliams, *Factories in the Field: The Story of Migratory Farm Labor in California* (Berkeley: University of California Press, 1939; 2000), 243–249.

2. The triracial hierarchy in Southern California was unique in the sense that it consisted of Japanese, Mexicans, and white Americans. Different types of triracial hierarchy also developed in other areas. For example, before World War II, in Northern California, Japanese farmers leased lands from white landowners and hired Filipino workers. By the early decades of the twentieth century in Hawai'i, some Portuguese had begun to work as field supervisors on sugar plantations and found themselves in an intermediate position between Anglo-Saxon plantation owners and Asian laborers such as Japanese and Filipinos. See Eiichiro Azuma, *Between Two Empires: Race, History, and Transnationalism in Japanese America* (New York: Oxford University Press, 2005); Moon-kie Jung, *Reworking*

Race: The Making of Hawaii's Interracial Labor Movement (New York: Columbia University Press, 2006), ch. 3.

3. David Vaught argues that from the late nineteenth century to the early twentieth century, agricultural labor relations particularly in California orchards and vineyards were shaped mainly by the "everyday interplay" between growers and other actors, such as their workers, communities, marketing cooperatives, other growers, and the state and federal governments. During this period, California growers identified themselves as the guardians of their harvest and saw their work as a way of life rather than just a business. When the state and federal governments came to ensure a sufficient labor supply from Mexico after World War I, however, California growers became part of so-called "industrialized agriculture," as characterized by Paul S. Taylor in the 1930s. See David Vaught, *Cultivating California: Growers, Specialty Crops, and Labor 1875–1920* (Baltimore: Johns Hopkins University Press, 1999).

4. Middleman minorities are immigrant groups who occupy an intermediate position between the elite and masses, face societal hostility, and succeed in occupations that can be easily liquidated. Their social status as sojourners or strangers strengthens their ethnic solidarity and economy and thus aggravates the hostility in the host society. See Edna Bonacich and John Modell, *Economic Basis for Ethnic Solidarity: Small Business in the Japanese American Community* (Berkeley: University of California Press, 1980); Bonacich, "A Theory of Middleman Minorities," *American Sociological Review* 38, no. 5 (October 1973): 583–594.

5. Chamber of Commerce of the United States, *Mexican Immigration: A Factual Report Reviewing Mexican Immigration to the United States from the Viewpoint of Its Economic, Social, Political and International Implications, with Less Extended Treatment of Immigration from Other Western Hemisphere Countries*, July 1930, 59, Box 80, George Pigeon Clements Papers, Special Collections, University of California, Los Angeles (hereafter cited as Clements Papers).

6. Sucheng Chan, *Asian Americans: An Interpretive History* (Boston: Twayne Publishers, 1991), 39. According to Nobuya Tsuchida, Japanese immigrants who arrived at the United States after the 1910s tended to become farmworkers or sharecroppers for established Japanese farmers. In hope of having more stable jobs, many of these latecomers became gardeners in the urban area. See Nobuya Tsuchida, "Japanese Gardeners in Southern California, 1900–1941," in *Labor Immigration under Capitalism: Asian Workers in the United States before World War II*, ed. Lucie Cheng and Edna Bonacich (Berkeley: University of California Press, 1984), 444.

7. Matt Garcia, *A World of Its Own: Race, Labor, and Citrus in the Making of Greater Los Angeles, 1900–1970* (Chapel Hill: University of North Carolina Press, 2001), 95.

8. *Minamikashū nihonjin shichijūnenshi*, 58; Lon Kurashige, *Japanese American Celebration and Conflict: A History of Ethnic Identity and Festival in Los Angeles, 1934–1990* (Berkeley: University of California Press, 2002), 23–24; Masakazu Iwata, *Planted in Good Soil: A History of the Issei in United States Agriculture*, 2 vols. (New York: Peter Lang Publishers, 1992), 1:290–291; Bonacich and Modell, *Economic Basis for Ethnic Solidarity*, 253.

9. Mae M. Ngai, *Impossible Subjects: Illegal Aliens and the Making of Modern America* (Princeton, NJ: Princeton University Press, 2004), 64–75. George J. Sánchez, *Becoming*

Mexican American: Ethnicity, Culture, and Identity in Chicano Los Angeles, 1900–1945 (New York: Oxford University Press, 1993), 57; Ricardo Romo, *East Los Angeles: History of a Barrio* (Austin: University of Texas Press, 1983), ch. 6.

10. Sánchez, *Becoming Mexican American*, 61–62.

11. Kelly L. Hernández, *Migra!: A History of the U.S. Border Patrol* (Berkeley: University of California Press, 2010), 36–37.

12. The intensification of border control was not exclusively operated by the US government. The Mexican government also wanted to prevent unsanctioned border crossing and played an important role in the development of the binational border enforcement. Ibid., 85, 89–90.

13. Abraham Hoffman, *Unwanted Mexican Americans in the Great Depression: Repatriation Pressures 1929–1929* (Tucson: University of Arizona Press, 1974), 26–30; David G. Gutiérrez, *Walls and Mirrors: Mexican Americans, Mexican Immigrants, and the Politics of Ethnicity* (Berkeley: University of California Press, 1995), 53–54.

14. Governor C. C. Young's Mexican Fact-Finding Committee, *Mexicans in California*, October 1930, Box 62, Clements Papers (hereafter cited as *Mexicans in California*), 159.

15. Lawrence J. Jelinek, *Harvest Empire: A History of California Agriculture* (San Francisco: Boyd & Fraser, 1979; 1982), 62–63.

16. California Development Association, *Survey of the Mexican Labor Problem in California*, 1928, Box 63, Clements Papers (hereafter cited as *Survey of the Mexican Labor Problem in California*), 1.

17. Sánchez, *Becoming Mexican American*, 69–70; Kevin Starr, *California: A History* (New York: Modern Library, 2007), 178, 182.

18. *Survey of the Mexican Labor Problem in California*, 2, 8, 10, 15. The California Development Association was founded in 1921. See Stephanie S. Pincetl, *Transforming California: A Political History of Land Use and Development* (Baltimore: Johns Hopkins University, 1999), 76–77.

19. *Survey of the Mexican Labor Problem in California*, 11; University of California, Los Angeles, Special Collections, "Finding Aid for the George Pigeon Clements Papers, 1825–1945," 1997, Online Archive of California, online at https://oac.cdlib.org/findaid/ark:/13030/tf2q2nb1h7/, accessed December 25, 2021.

20. Other historians have also discussed Clements's categorization of Mexicans. See Romo, *East Los Angeles*, 86–87; Gutiérrez, *Walls and Mirrors*, 48–49; Garcia, *A World of Its Own*, 101–103.

21. *Survey of the Mexican Labor Problem in California*, 11–12.

22. Regarding the history of racial mixing and the Mexican cultural nationalist movement in the 1920s, see Kelley R. Swarthout, *"Assimilating the Primitive": Parallel Dialogues on Racial Miscegenation in Revolutionary Mexico* (New York: Peter Lang, 2004).

23. Neil Foley, *Mexicans in the Making of America* (Cambridge, MA: Harvard University Press, 2014), 50; Devra Weber, "Introducción," in *El inmigrante mexicano: La historia de su vida, entrevistas completas, 1926–1927*, by Manuel Gamio, compiled by Devra Weber, Roberto Melville, and Juan Vicente Palerm (Mexico: Miguel Ángel Porrúa, 2002), 66–67.

24. *Survey of the Mexican Labor Problem in California*, 11, 17.

25. White agribusiness leaders incorporated the anti-Japanese discourse once used to implement Japanese exclusion into their pro-Mexican and still very racist argument, which shows a transpacific process in which a new form of *redirecting racism* emerged from the convergence of racialization experiences of Japanese and Mexicans in California. See Yu Tokunaga, "From Anti-Japanese to Anti-Mexican: Linkages of Racialization Experiences in 1920s California," in *Race and Migration in the Transpacific*, ed. Yasuko Takezawa and Akio Tanabe (London: Routledge, forthcoming). In Japanese, see Yu Tokunaga, "Hainichi kara haiboku e: 1920 nendai kariforunia shū ni okeru jinshuka keiken no rensa" [From anti-Japanese to anti-Mexican: Linkages of racialization experiences in 1920s California], in *Kantaiheiyō chiiki no idō to jinshu: Tōchi kara kanri e, sōgū kara rentai e* [Migration and race in the transpacific: From rule to control, from encounter to solidarity], ed. Akio Tanabe, Yasuko Takezawa, and Ryuichi Narita (Kyoto: Kyoto University Press, 2020).

26. William Deverell, *Whitewashed Adobe: The Rise of Los Angeles and the Remaking of Its Mexican Past* (Berkeley: University of California Press, 2004), ch. 5.

27. Casiano Pagdilao Coloma, "A Study of the Filipino Repatriation Movement," master's thesis, University of Southern California, 1939; Rudy P. Guevarra Jr., *Becoming Mexipino: Multiethnic Identities and Communities in San Diego* (New Brunswick, NJ: Rutgers University Press, 2012), 35–36.

28. *Survey of the Mexican Labor Problem in California*, 12; Albert Camarillo, *Chicanos in California: A History of Mexican Americans in California* (Sparks, NV: Materials for Today's Learning, 1984; 1990), 43; Romo, *East Los Angeles*, ch. 4; Sánchez, *Becoming Mexican American*, ch. 9.

29. *Survey of the Mexican Labor Problem in California*, 17.

30. Romo, *East Los Angeles*, 8.

31. Santa Monika no nōka 11 ken tachinoki" [11 farmers evicted from Santa Monica], *Rafu Shimpo*, February 24, 1924.

32. Jelinek, *Harvest Empire*, 63.

33. *Survey of the Mexican Labor Problem in California*, 8.

34. *Minamikashū nihonjin shichijūnenshi*, 18–19, 53, 56.

35. Ken'ichi Kodama was born in Hawai'i in 1893. Like Kodama, many Hawaiian-born Nisei moved to California and worked as farmers. Territory of Hawaii, Office of the Secretary, birth certificate of Ken'ichi Kodama, June 1910; The Del Amo Estate Company to Kodama, March 22, 1924; Kodama to the Del Amo Estate Company, 1924, Folder 6, Box 87, Del Amo Estate Company Collection, Gerth Archives and Special Collections, University Library, California State University, Dominguez Hills, Carson, California (hereafter cited as Del Amo Estate Company Collection). For the California Alien Land Law ballot of 1920, Lon Kurashige points out that "it was not insignificant that more than 200,000 Californians opposed the measure," which shows us the complicated dimension of anti-Asian politics in the 1920s. See Lon Kurashige, *Two Faces of Exclusion: The Untold History of Anti-Asian Racism in the United States* (Chapel Hill: University of North Carolina Press, 2016), 124.

36. Kōichi Ono to Gregorio del Amo, February 7, 1925, Folder 2, Box 96, Del Amo Estate Company Collection.

37. For the term *meki*, see Fuminori Minamikawa, "Vernacular Representations of Race and the Making of a Japanese Ethnoracial Community in Los Angeles," in *Trans-Pacific*

Japanese American Studies: Conversations on Race and Racializations, ed. Yasuko Takezawa and Gary Y. Okihiro (Honolulu: University of Hawai'i Press, 2016), 115–116.

38. "Hakuchū Yamamoto Hōsekiten e mekidoro ga shin'nyū" [Infiltration of a Mexican robber into Yamamoto Jewelry in daylight], *Rafu Shimpo*, June 25, 1924.

39. "Chihō nōka wo arasu sagikan to mekidoro" [Bandits and Mexican robbers looting rural farmers], *Rafu Shimpo*, June 26, 1924.

40. For other *Rafu Shimpo* articles that used the term *meki* in 1924, see "Meki dorobō nimei wo hodaku" [Two Mexican robbers arrested], July 22; "Asamadaki mekidoro ga oitsumerarete taiho" [Early morning, a Mexican robber was chased and arrested], August 27; "Daisen na meki" [A bold move of Mexicans], September 5; "Jukusuichū ni mekidoro ga ichimai kanban wo shikkei" [A Mexican robber stole a sign while the owner was sleeping], September 27; "Meki no jidōsha dorobō taiho su" [Mexican who stole a car was arrested], September 28; "Hoteru no iriguchi de machifuseta meki" [A Mexican ambush near the hotel entrance], October 17. The *Shin Sekai*, an ethnic Japanese paper based in San Francisco, also reported at least five incidents related to Mexicans using the term *mekidoro* from 1917 to 1931. All the incidents reported by the *Shin Sekai* happened in the Fresno or Los Angeles areas according to the search result of the Hoji Shinbun Digital Collection administered by the Hoover Institution at Stanford University. See the Hoji Shinbun Digital Collection, online at https://hojishinbun.hoover.org, accessed December 20, 2017.

41. Alonso's pseudonym is Carlos Almazán, and Velázquez's Anastacio Torres in the English edition of the book. See Miguel Alonso, interview by Luis Felipe Recinos, Los Angeles, California, April 18, 1927; Zeferino Velázquez, interview by Luis Felipe Recinos, Los Angeles, California, April 20, 1927; list of pseudonyms, Gamio, *El inmigrante mexicano*, 357–362, 402–404, 568–570. For the interviews translated in English, see Manuel Gamio, *The Mexican Immigrant: His Life-Story* (New York: Arno Press, 1969), 55–58, 87–91.

42. "Konketsu furyō shōnen Kishi Tonī" [Mixed-blood delinquent child Tony Kishi], *Rafu Shimpo*, September 5, 1924. For the history of the Whittier School in relation to minority youths, see Miroslava Chaves-Garcia, *States of Delinquency: Race and Science in the Making of California's Juvenile Justice System* (Berkeley: University of California Press, 2012).

43. Hyoue Okamura, "'Hāfu' wo meguru gensetsu: Kenkyūsha ya shiensha no chojutsu wo chūshin ni" [Discourses of hafu: In writings of scholars and supporters], in *Jinshu shinwa wo kaitai suru, vol. 3, Hybridity: "Chi" no seijigaku wo koete* [Dismantling the race myth, vol. 3, Hybridity: Beyond the politics of "blood"], ed. Kohei Kawashima and Yasuko Takezawa (Tokyo: University of Tokyo Press, 2016), 42.

44. Leti Volpp, "American Mestizo: Filipinos and Antimiscegenation Laws in California," *UC Davis Law Review* 33, no. 4 (1999): 802–803; Paul Spickard, *Japanese Americans: The Formation and Transformations of an Ethnic Group* (New Brunswick, NJ: Rutgers University Press, 1996; 2009), 35, 66. Although most Japanese immigrants opposed intermarriage, some thought intermarriage was necessary for the future ethnic Japanese community. See Paul Spickard, *Mixed Blood: Intermarriage and Ethnic Identity in Twentieth-Century America* (Madison: University of Wisconsin Press, 1989), 61–62.

45. Constantine Panunzio, "Intermarriage in Los Angeles, 1924–33," *American Journal of Sociology* 47, no. 5 (March 1942): 691–694; Greg Robinson, "The Early History of

Mixed-Race Japanese Americans," in *Hapa Japan: History*, vol. 1, ed. Duncan Ryuken Williams (New York: Kaya Press, 2017), 226.

46. For example, a *Rafu Shimpo* article about the decline of Chinatowns in California wrote, "Mexicans and Southern European immigrants prosper in [former] Chinatowns." See "Kemuri no you ni kiesatta Orenji no shinamachi" [Orange County Chinatown vanished like a puff of smoke], *Rafu Shimpo*, June 18, 1924.

47. For example, see "Hitō dojin seifu wo ikaku" [Native Filipinos threaten the government], *Rafu Shimpo*, August 29, 1924. The Hoji Shinbun Digital Collection created by the Hoover Institution of Stanford University hits 182 *Rafu Shimpo* Japanese articles with the search word "dojin."

48. Yukichi Fukuzawa, *Sekai kuni zukushi* [All the countries of the world], vol. 6 (Tokyo: Keiō Gijuku Zōhan, 1869). A large number of Fukuzawa's works can be read digitally in Digital Collections of Keio University Libraries. See Dejitaru de Yomu Fukuzawa Yukichi, online at http://dcollections.lib.keio.ac.jp/en/fukuzawa, accessed January 25, 2018.

49. Masato Kuwabara and Masao Gabe, eds., *Ezochi to Ryūkyū* [Ezochi and Ryukyu] (Tokyo: Yoshikawa Kōbunkan, 2001), 126–128. The Japanese government promoted the assimilation of the Ainu modeling the US assimilation policy toward Native Americans. See Eiji Oguma, *Tan'itsu minzoku shinwa no kigen: "Nihonjin" no jigazō no keifu* [The origin of the myth of ethnic homogeneity: The genealogy of "Japanese" self-images] (Tokyo: Shinyōsha, 1995), 81.

50. Tomohide Banzai, "Kindai Nihon no jinshu sutereo taipu no keisei katei to mainoritii ni taisuru gendaiteki henken no kenkyū" [Studies on the formation processes of ethnic stereotypes and the prejudice toward minorities in modern age of Japan], a research report of project funded by Grant-in-Aid for Scientific Research (C) (2) of Japan Society for the Promotion of Science (March 2002), 58–59.

51. According to the *Daigenkai* dictionary, the third meaning of *dojin* was "a doll made from clay." See Fumihiko Ōtsuki, "Dojin," *Daigenkai* (Tokyo, 1934), 552.

52. "Bokukoku jijō (2)" [The situation of Mexico], *Rafu Shimpo*, July 18, 1924.

53. Saichirō Koshida, acting deputy minister of the Japanese Legation in Mexico, to Kijūro Shidehara, minister of foreign affairs of Japan, March 4, 1926, B-3-5-2-224, Kakkoku ni okeru nōgyō kankei zakken [Miscellaneous reports on agriculture in other countries], vol. 2, Diplomatic Archives of the Ministry of Foreign Affairs of Japan, Minato-ku, Tokyo, Japan.

54. Naotarō Kobayashi and Yoshimasa Itō, *Mekishiko shokumin no shiori* [Leaflet for settlement in Mexico] (Los Angeles, 1925), preface by Keiichi Itō, Arthur Ito Papers, Huntington Library, San Marino, California.

55. Shirō Fujioka, "Hainichi jōkō wo fukumu Beikoku shin imin hō (4)" [The new US immigration act that has the Japanese exclusion clause], *Rafu Shimpo*, June 1, 1924. The victory of Japan over Russia was a factor that strengthened anti-Japanese racism. See Jung, *Reworking Race*, 79, 81; Roger Daniels, *The Politics of Prejudice: The Anti-Japanese Movement in California* (New York: Atheneum, 1968), 27.

56. Tenorio's pseudonym is Miguel Chávez in the English edition of the book. See Fortino V. Tenorio, interview by M. Robles, Los Angeles, California, April 15, 1927; list of

pseudonyms, Gamio, *El inmigrante mexicano*, 329–330, 568–570. For the interviews translated in English, see Gamio, *The Mexican Immigrant*, 168–170.

57. Japanese Chamber of Commerce of Southern California, meeting minutes, 1918, Box 272, Japanese American Research Project Collection, National Diet Library, Tokyo, Japan (hereafter cited as JARP-NDL).

58. One example is Ralph Lazo, a Mexican-Irish American who was born in 1924 and grew up in Los Angeles. Lazo is well known for registering as Japanese and going to Manzanar along with his Japanese American friends during World War II. See Brian Niiya, ed., *Encyclopedia of Japanese American History: An A-to-Z Reference from 1868 to the Present*, updated edition (New York: Checkmark Books, 2021), 257–258. For the multiracial neighborhood of Boyle Heights, see George J. Sánchez, *Boyle Heights: How a Los Angeles Neighborhood Became the Future of American Democracy* (Oakland: University of California Press, 2021).

59. Romo, *East Los Angeles*, 3–6.

60. Ibid., 80–88; Camarillo, *Chicanos in California*, ch. 3 and 4; Sánchez, *Becoming Mexican American*, ch. 8 and 9. For the history of class and race segregation in Los Angeles, see Laura Redford, "The Intertwined History of Class and Race Segregation in Los Angeles," *Journal of Planning History* 16, no. 4 (November 2017): 305–322.

61. Camarillo, *Chicanos in California*, 38.

62. The naturalization rates of Mexican immigrants in Los Angeles were as low as 10.7 percent in 1910, 3.3 percent in 1920, and 13.8 percent in 1940. See Francisco E. Balderrama, *In Defense of La Raza: The Los Angeles Mexican Consulate and the Mexican Community, 1929 to 1936* (Tucson: University of Arizona Press, 1982), 8.

63. Gutiérrez, *Walls and Mirrors*, 89.

64. Sánchez, *Becoming Mexican American*, 109.

65. Weber, "Introducción," 66.

66. Emory S. Bogardus, "The Mexican Immigrant and Segregation," *American Journal of Sociology* 36, no. 1 (July 1930): 78.

67. For the relationship between the Japanese government and local Japanese associations in California, see Yuji Ichioka, "Japanese Associations and the Japanese Government: A Special Relationship, 1909–1926," *Pacific Historical Review* 46, no. 3 (August 1977): 409–437.

68. "Sato shin ryōji niwa hajimete taiken no sonchō" [The first experience for the new consul Sato to be a village mayor], *Rafu Shimpo*, November 7, 1929.

69. Monica Lozano, interview by Shirley Biagi, Washington Press Club Foundation, December 13, 1993, http://beta.wpcf.org/oralhistory/loz.html, accessed November 27, 2017. In 1920s Los Angeles, there were several Spanish-language newspapers. See Nicolás Kanellos and Helvetia Martell, *Hispanic Periodicals in the United States, Origins to 1960: A Brief History and Comprehensive Bibliography* (Houston, TX: Arte Público Press, 2000). San Antonio had been the largest Mexican concentration until Los Angeles overtook the lead in the 1920s. See Romo, *East Los Angeles*, 80.

70. Raul D. Tovares, "*La Opinión* and Its Contribution to the Mexican Community's Adaptation to Life in the US." *Latino Studies* 7, no. 4 (December 2009): 481.

71. "Precios de suscripción," *La Opinión*, September 16, 1926; "Subscription Rate," *Rafu Shimpo*, September 21, 1926. *La Opinión* as a historical newspaper is available online at Google News Archive, at https://news.google.com/newspapers, accessed July 27, 2021.

72. "Dos palabras"; Teodoro Torres Jr., "El secreto profesional en el periodismo"; José Vasconcelos, "El soplo," *La Opinión*, September 16, 1926.

73. Tovares, "*La Opinión* and Its Contribution," 487–488.

74. Ibid., 487–493.

75. "Inglés en pocas semanas," *La Opinión*, September 16, 1926; "El Inglés sin Maestro," *La Opinión*, November 2, 1926.

76. As for the advertisement of a Spanish-language school on the *Rafu Shimpo*, see chapter 1.

77. "The Hara Co.," *La Opinión*, October 3 and 17, 1926.

78. "The Hara Co.," *La Opinión*, January 2, 1927. The Hara Company continued to place its advertisement on the New Year's Day of 1928. See "The Hara Co.," *La Opinión*, January 1, 1928. In the Plaza area where Mexicans enjoyed recreational and cultural activities, they patronized Japanese pool halls, too. Romo, *East Los Angeles*, 83.

79. George L. Cady, *Report of Commission on International and Interracial Factors in the Problems of Mexicans in the United States*, ca. 1928, Box 62, Clements Papers, 27.

80. "Dr. T. Ichioka"; "Doctor M. Shinohara," *La Opinión*, December 1, 1928; Dr. T. Ichioka"; "Doctor M. Shinohara," *La Opinión*, January 1, 1931. There were other Japanese doctors as well as Chinese doctors who provided medical care to Mexican residents in Los Angeles. Chinese doctors specialized in Chinese herbal remedies. For example, see "Está Ud. Enfermo? D. K. Tuey," *La Opinión*, January 1, 1929.

81. *Mexicans in California*, 123.

82. "El Cónsul Sr. Pesqueira es sindicalista," *La Opinión*, November 6, 1927.

83. *Mexicans in California*, 123–124. Devra Weber, "The Organizing of Mexicano Agricultural Workers in Imperial Valley and Los Angeles, 1928–34, An Oral History Approach," *Aztlán* 3, no. 2 (1972): 329. As for the foundation of the CUOM, see also Sánchez, *Becoming Mexican American*, 231–232.

84. *Mexicans in California*, 125.

85. Camarillo, *Chicanos in California*, 42. According to Rudy P. Guevarra Jr., contemporary sociologist Emory S. Bogardus did not think Mexicans were able to organize, either. See Guevarra, *Becoming Mexipino*, 101

86. *Mexicans in California*, 125–126.

87. Gutiérrez, *Walls and Mirrors*, 34; Camarillo, *Chicanos in California*, 37.

88. *Minamikashū nihonjin shichijūnenshi*, 380–384.

89. *Mexicans in California*, 14, 129.

90. Nativist efforts to set a quota on Mexican immigrants in Congress finally ended in 1932. According to Benjamin Montoya, the Mexican government had sought to stop the flow of emigrants since the 1920s but opposed the Box Bill because it presumed that Mexicans were racially inferior. See Benjamin C. Montoya, "A Grave Offense of Significant Consequences: Mexican Perspectives on U.S. Immigration Restriction during the Late 1920s," *Pacific Historical Review* 87, no. 1 (Spring 2018): 333–355.

91. As for Mexican Repatriation, see Balderrama, *In Defense of La Raza*, 20–25.

92. Monica Lozano, interview by Shirley Biagi.

93. Sánchez, *Becoming Mexican American*, 210, 225. William Deverell has explored how the pavement construction of the Los Angeles River in the 1930s created the dividing line between Anglo American and Mexican American residents in Los Angeles. See Deverell, *Whitewashed Adobe*, ch. 3.

94. Balderrama, *In Defense of La Raza*, 22-23.

95. J. A. H. Kerr, "To Our Mexican Friends," *Los Angeles Chamber of Commerce Bulletin*, May 1931, Box 80, Clements Papers; Bruce A. Findlay, manager of the Chamber's Exploitation and Public Relations Department, to A. G. Arnoll, the Chamber's secretary and general manager, May 15, 1931, Box 80, Clements Papers; "Un mensaje de amistad a la colonia," *La Opinión*, May 13, 1931.

96. Balderrama, *In Defense of La Raza*, 16, 23-24.

97. George P. Clements to A. G. Arnoll, June 11, 1931, Box 80, Clements Papers.

98. The list of founding members of the CUOM including Flores appeared in the report *Mexicans in California*. See *Mexicans in California*, 126.

CHAPTER 3. TRANSPACIFIC BORDERLANDS

1. Lawrence J. Jelinek, *Harvest Empire: A History of California Agriculture* (San Francisco: Boyd & Fraser, 1979; 1982), 70-71; Devra Weber, *Dark Sweat, White Gold: California Farm Workers, Cotton, and the New Deal* (Berkeley: University of California Press, 1994), ch. 3; Cletus E. Daniel, *Bitter Harvest: A History of California Farmworkers, 1870-1941* (Berkeley: University of California Press, 1981), ch. 4.

2. Ronald W. López, "The El Monte Berry Strike of 1933," *Aztlán* 1, no. 1 (April 1970): 101-102, 105-106.

3. "Los Japoneses de Baja California apoyan a los huelguistas," *La Opinión*, June 30, 1933. The original Spanish messages are "La Asociación Japonesa de la Baja California . . . ha averiguado que el proceder de estos súbditos japoneses en California es inhumano y atentatorio a las relaciones de amistad y cooperación que deben existir entre el patrón y el trabajador."

4. Abraham Hoffman, "The El Monte Berry Pickers' Strike, 1933: International Involvement in a Local Labor Dispute," *Journal of the West* 12, no. 1 (1973): 71-84; Francisco E. Balderrama, *In Defense of La Raza: The Los Angeles Mexican Consulate and the Mexican Community, 1929 to 1936* (Tucson: University of Arizona Press, 1982); Gilbert G. González, *Mexican Consuls and Labor Organizing: Imperial Politics in the American Southwest* (Austin: University of Texas Press, 1999); "The 1933 Los Angeles County Farm Workers Strike," *New Political Science* 20, no. 4 (December 1998): 441-458. A contemporary scholar Charles B. Spaulding, who made the first observation of the strike, explained that the strike increased the social distance between Japanese and Mexicans while strengthening ties between Japanese and whites. See Charles B. Spaulding, "The Mexican Strike at El Monte, California," *Sociology and Social Research* 18 (July-August 1934): 571-580.

5. López, "The El Monte Berry Strike of 1933"; Devra Weber, "The Organizing of Mexicano Agricultural Workers: Imperial Valley, and Los Angeles 1928-34, An Oral History Approach," *Aztlán* 3, no. 2 (1972): 307-350; Charles Wollenberg, "Race and Class in Rural California: The El Monte Berry Strike of 1933," *California Historical Quarterly* 51,

no. 2 (July 1972): 155–164. For the viewpoint of Communist organizers in the strike, see Daniel, *Bitter Harvest*. Vicki Ruiz recorded the memories of a Mexican American resident in El Monte who witnessed the strike. See Vicki Ruiz, *From Out of the Shadows: Mexican Women in Twentieth-Century America* (New York: Oxford University Press, 1998; 2008), 75–77. George J. Sánchez refers to the Mexican government's involvement in the strike. See George J. Sánchez, *Becoming Mexican American: Ethnicity, Culture, and Identity in Chicano Los Angeles, 1900–1945* (New York: Oxford University Press, 1993), 235–238.

6. For brief mentions, see David J. O'Brien and Stephen S. Fugita, *The Japanese American Experience* (Bloomington: Indiana University Press, 1991), 30–31; Noritaka Yagasaki, *Imin nōgyō: Karifornia no nihonjin imin shakai* [Immigrant Agriculture: The Japanese immigrant society in California] (Tokyo: Kokonshoin, 1993), 79–80; Eiichiro Azuma, *Between Two Empires: Race, History, and Transnationalism in Japanese America* (New York: Oxford University Press, 2005), 270.

7. For "trans-Pacific-borderlands," see Grace Peña Delgado, *Making the Chinese Mexican: Global Migration, Localism, and Exclusion in the U.S.-Mexico Borderlands* (Stanford, CA: Stanford University Press, 2012).

8. US Census Bureau, *Fifteenth Census of the United States: 1930, Population* (Washington, DC, 1932), Table 13, "The Composition of the Population, by Counties: 1930," and Table 17, "Indians, Chinese, and Japanese, 1910 to 1930, and Mexicans, 1930, for Counties and for Cities of 25,000 or More," 252, 266.

9. López, "The El Monte Berry Strike of 1933," 103; Spaulding, "The Mexican Strike at El Monte, California," 571–572; Ruiz, *From Out of the Shadows*, 75–76.

10. "Sweet, Sad Latino Life of Yesterday," *Los Angeles Times*, September 27, 1992.

11. Mokichi Fukushima, secretary official in Tijuana, to Yasuya Uchida, minister of foreign affairs of Japan, July 11, 1933, I-4-4-0-2, Gaikoku ni okeru rōdō sōgi kankei zakken [Miscellaneous documents relating to labor disputes in foreign countries], vol. 1, Diplomatic Archives of the Ministry of Foreign Affairs of Japan (DAMFAJ), Minato-ku, Tokyo, Japan (hereafter cited as I-4-4-0-2, vol.1, DAMFAJ); Toshito Satō, consul in Los Angeles, to Uchida, June 17, 1933, I-4-4-0-2, vol.1, DAMFAJ. The Japan Center for Asian Historical Records (JACAR), a Japanese government's online database, makes publicly available a large number of historical documents preserved in the DAMFAJ. See https://www.jacar.go.jp, accessed February 4, 2019. Although berries were picked on a crate basis like other crops, the payment for berry pickers was arranged on an hourly basis since they picked various types of berries with different crate values. See Ross H. Gast to George Pigeon Clements, manager of the Agricultural Department of the Los Angeles Chamber of Commerce, June 27, 1933, Box 64, George Pigeon Clements Papers, Special Collections, University of California, Los Angeles, Los Angeles, California (hereafter cited as Clements Papers).

12. Carey McWilliams, *Factories in the Field: The Story of Migratory Farm Labor in California* (Berkeley: University of California Press, 1939; 2000), 247–249.

13. "800 pizcadores más van a la huelga," *La Opinión*, June 6, 1933; López, "The El Monte Berry Strike of 1933," 102–104; Spaulding, "The Mexican Strike at El Monte, California," 573. For the successful involvement of the CAWIU and the contribution of the ethnic Mexican community in the 1933 cotton strike, see Daniel, *Bitter Harvest*, ch. 6; Weber, *Dark Sweat, White Gold*, ch. 3.

14. "Kai! Shirane Shizuko jō" [Good job! Miss. Shizuko Shirane], *Nichibei Shimbun*, June 9, 1933; López, "The El Monte Berry Strike of 1933," 104; Daniel, *Bitter Harvest*, 143–146.

15. "800 pizcadores más van a la huelga," *La Opinión*, June 6, 1933.

16. Ibid.; "Arrestos al cundir la huelga de los pizcadores mexicanos!," *La Opinión*, June 7, 1933; Weber, "The Organizing of Mexicano Agricultural Workers," 326–329. González, "The 1933 Los Angeles County Farm Workers Strike," 446. The UCOM and la Confederación de Uniones de Campesinos y Obreros Mexicanos (CUCOM) were not the same organization, since the latter was formally established on July 15, 1933, after the end of the El Monte strike. See Spaulding, "The Mexican Strike at El Monte, California," 575; González, *Mexican Consuls and Labor Organizing*, 111. Moreover, in primary sources produced during the strike, the union led by Flores appears as the UCOM. See "Concluye la huelga al rendirse los Japoneses," *La Opinión*, July 7, 1933; Copy of the contract between the Central Japanese Association of Southern California and la Unión de Campesinos y Obreros Mexicanos (hereafter cited as contract), July 6, 1933, I-4-4-0-2, vol. 1, DAMFAJ. For the founding of the CUOM, see chapter 2.

17. "Arrestos al cundir la huelga de los pizcadores mexicanos!," *La Opinión*, June 7, 1933; Weber, *Dark Sweat, White Gold*, 85.

18. "Sweet, Sad Latino Life of Yesterday," *Los Angeles Times*, September 27, 1992.

19. Katsuma Mukaeda and Masatoshi Nakamura, *Zaibei no higojin* [Kumamoto people in the United States] (Los Angeles, 1931), 637–638, Katsuma Mukaeda Papers, Japanese American National Museum, Los Angeles, California; Alexandra Giffen, Finding aid for the Katsuma Mukaeda Papers, online at Online Archives of California, http://www.oac.cdlib.org/findaid/ark:/13030/c8fx7fx0/entire_text/, accessed October 27, 2017.

20. "Fukami kanji, shi wo toshite" [Secretary Fukami, risking his life], *Rafu Shimpo*, June 10, 1933; "Boshū ni ōjite, beikokujin ga sattō" [Americans flooded into the office upon recruitment], *Rafu Shimpo*, June 10, 1933; "Bokukokujin higyō taisaku de" [A measure against the Mexican strike], *Rafu Shimpo*, June 10, 1933; "Ichigo no debana wo orare, tetteiteki no dageki desu" [They spoiled the harvest of berries, devastating damage], *Rafu Shimpo*, June 11, 1933. Fukami's last name appeared as "Fukamizu" in Japanese newspaper articles, while Spanish and English sources spelled it as "Fukami." It is likely that he introduced himself as "Fukami" to Mexicans and Americans as it was easier for non-Japanese speakers to pronounce.

21. "Kai! Shirane Shizuko jō," *Nichibei Shimbun*, June 9, 1933. For the experiences of Nisei, see David K. Yoo, *Growing Up Nisei: Race, Generation, and Culture among Japanese Americans of California, 1924–1949* (Urbana: University of Illinois Press, 2000); Lon Kurashige, *Japanese American Celebration and Conflict: A History of Ethnic Identity and Festival in Los Angeles, 1934–1990* (Berkeley: University of California Press, 2002); Yuji Ichioka, *Before Internment: Essays in Prewar Japanese American History*, ed. Gordon H. Chang and Eiichiro Azuma (Stanford, CA: Stanford University Press, 2006); John Modell, "Class or Ethnic Solidarity: The Japanese American Company Union," *Pacific Historical Review* 38, no. 2 (1969): 193–206.

22. "Editorials by G. H. N.," *Rafu Shimpo* (English section), June 8, 1933. George Hideo Nakamoto was born in Fresno in around 1906 and joined the *Rafu Shimpo* as a coeditor of its English section in 1933 after studying journalism at the University of California–Berkeley

and Columbia University. In 1938, seeing little hope in the future of himself in racist US society, he left the *Rafu Shimpo* to work for the Domei News, a Japanese news agency. He gained Japanese citizenship in 1942 and died in Japan in 1988. See Kaori Hayashi, *A History of the Rafu Shimpo: Japanese and Their Newspaper in Los Angeles* (Osaka: Union Press, 1997), 79–81.

23. Minamikashū Nihonjin Shichijūnenshi Kankō Iinkai [Publishing committee of Japanese in Southern California], ed., *Minamikashū nihonjin shichijūnenshi* [Japanese in Southern California: A history of 70 Years] (Los Angeles: Nanka Nikkeijin Shōgyō Kaigisho, 1960), 58, 667 (hereafter cited as *Minamikashū nihonjin shichijūnenshi*).

24. Gast to Clements, June 28, 1933; Clements to W. G. Arnoll, July 26, 1933, Box 64, Clements Papers; Wollenberg, "Race and Class in Rural California," 161–163.

25. "Huelga de 125 Mexicanos aquí," *La Opinión*, June 4, 1933; "Bokukokujin sutoraiki de benisu nōka no taikai" [Farmers in Venice hold a convention as to the strike of Mexicans], *Rafu Shimpo*, June 3, 1933; "Bōryoku sae mochiite higyō sanka wo kyōyō suru, Gādena heigen ni bokujin nashi" [Even with violence, they force people to join the strike, Mexicans are now absent in the Gardena Valley], *Rafu Shimpo*, June 19, 1933; "Domingusu wo osotta ittai" [A group that attacked the Dominguez area], *Rafu Shimpo*, June 11, 1933.

26. According to the Mexican consulate in Los Angeles, the number of Mexican families was 8,750 in Orange County, 3,750 in Ventura County, and 1,250 in San Luis Obispo County in 1933. See Luis Lupián G, "Informe de la visita practicada al Cosulado de México en Los Angeles, California, durante los días del 27 de abril al 31 de mayo de 1933," June 6, 1933, Folder 266, Box 29, Collection Gaveta 30, Archivo Histórico Genaro Estrada [Genaro Estrada Historical Archive], Secretaría de Relaciones Exteriores [Ministry of Foreign Affairs], Mexico City, Mexico (hereafter cited as Collection Gaveta 30, AHGE).

27. "Huelga de 125 Mexicanos aquí," *La Opinión*, June 4, 1933; "Bokukokujin sutoraiki de Benisu nōka no taikai" [Farmers in Venice hold a convention as to the strike of Mexicans], *Rafu Shimpo*, June 3, 1933; "Bōryoku wo sae mochiite higyō sanka wo kyōyō suru, Gādena heigen ni bokujin nashi," *Rafu Shimpo*, June 19, 1933. "Domingusu wo osotta ittai," *Rafu Shimpo*, June 11; "Nōen higyō mo tetsudatte" [Thanks to the agricultural strike], *Rafu Shimpo*, June 19, 1933; "Sankō yamanote hōmen no hitode no hojū" [Workers supplied in the San Pedro mountain area], *Rafu Shimpo*, June 26, 1933.

28. "Huelga de 125 Mexicanos aquí; "Actua El Vice-Consul Ricardo Hill," *La Opinión*, June 6, 1933.

29. Luis Lupián G, "Informe de la visita practicada al Cosulado de México en Los Angeles, California; Balderrama, *In Defense of La Raza*, 9–10.

30. Mexican Consulate in Los Angeles, "Informe de protección. Junio de 1933," June 1933, Folder 2, Box 626, Collection Departamento Consular (IV), Archivo Histórico Genaro Estrada, Secretaría de Relaciones Exteriores, Mexico City, Mexico (hereafter cited as Collection Departamento Consular [IV], AHGE).

31. "El Consulado unifica a los huelgistas," *La Opinión*, June 13, 1933.

32. Ibid.; "Benisu higyō ni kanshite, Hiru ryōji wa kataru" [Consul Hill talks about the Venice strike], *Rafu Shimpo*, May 7, 1936.

33. "Nōen sutoraiki de nichi-boku ryōjikan no sesshō" [Negotiation between the Japanese and Mexican consulates regarding the agricultural strike], *Rafu Shimpo*, June 8, 1933;

"Higyō bokukokujin no shii wa dōkoku jinshu ni taisuru" [Mexican strikers' demonstration is against their own country's race], *Kashu Mainichi*, July 9, 1933. Historical newspaper articles of the *Kashu Mainichi* are available online at the Hoji Shinbun Digital Collection administered by the Hoover Institution at Stanford University, https://hojishinbun.hoover.org/, accessed December 21, 2020.

34. Satō to Uchida, July 18, 1933, I-4-4-0-2, vol. 1, DAMFAJ.

35. "Satō ryōji no raichaku" [The arrival of Consul Satō], *Rafu Shimpo*, November 5, 1929; *Minamikashū nihonjin shichijūnenshi*, 378–379; Yoshiaki Katada, "1930 nendai ni itaru nichi-bei kankei no gaiyō: Beikoku taiheiyō gan shuyōkō toritsukai kamotsu to bōeki kōro no kōsatsu wo tōshite" [An exploration of the United States-Japanese trade relationships during the period approaching the 1930s: An examination of the changes of exports and imports in major ports along the US Pacific Coast and shipping routes between the US and Japan], *NUCB Journal of Economics and Information Science* 58, no. 2 (March 2014): 107–108.

36. *Minamikashū nihonjin shichijūnenshi*, 668. For the impact of the Manchuria Incident on the ethnic Japanese community, see Ichioka, *Before Internment*.

37. "Nichi-Bei Kyōkai shusai no Satō ryōji kangeikai" [The welcome party for Consul Satō held by the Japan-American Society], *Rafu Shimpo*, November 27, 1929; "Seikatsu kaizen to hōritsu sonchō wo" [Improvement of life and respect for laws], *Rafu Shimpo*, January 1, 1931.

38. López, "The El Monte Berry Strike of 1933," 105. In August 1933, Lawrence Ross, the Communist Party spokesman, wrote, "The El Monte strike was a costly lesson, but highly valuable." See Daniel, *Bitter Harvest*, 153.

39. Daniel, *Bitter Harvest*, 147.

40. "Kai! Shirane Shizuko jō," *Nichibei Shimbun*, June 9, 1933.

41. For Karl Yoneda, see Mark Wild, *Street Meeting: Multiethnic Neighborhoods in Early Twentieth-Century Los Angeles* (Berkeley: University of California Press, 2005), 191. On the other hand, the *Rafu Shimpo* consistently shows us that Japanese tenant farmers, who were mostly immigrants and not US born, had antipathy against Communists.

42. "Shitsugyōsha to sakeibunshi, higyō kakudai no gen'in" [The unemployed and leftists, the reason behind the expansion of the strike], *Rafu Shimpo*, June 11, 1933.

43. "Kanken to teikei shi sakeibunshi wa issō suru hōshin" [In cooperation with authorities, leftists should be removed], *Rafu Shimpo*, June 10, 1933.

44. Satō to Uchida, June 23, 1933, I-4-4-0-2, vol. 1, DAMFAJ; "Calles envía dinero a los huelguistas," *La Opinión*, June 21, 1933; "Calles envía $600 más a los huelguistas," *La Opinión*, June 22, 1933; López, "The El Monte Berry Strike of 1933," 106; Ricardo Pozas, "El Maximato: El partido del hombre fuerte, 1929–1934," *Estudios de historia moderna y contemporánea de México* 9 (1983): 251–279; Mexican Consulate in Los Angeles, "Informe de protección. Junio de 1933," June 1933, Folder 2, Box 626, Collection Departamento Consular (IV), AHGE.

45. López, "The El Monte Berry Strike of 1933," 106; González, *Mexican Consuls and Labor Organizing*, 113.

46. "Calles envía dinero a los huelguistas," *La Opinión*, June 21, 1933. Bustamante was the former general organizer of the CUOM in the late 1920s when anti-Mexican nativism

became strong in the US Southwest. At that time, Bustamante lived in Los Angeles and provided the ethnic Mexican community with a critical view on debates about the so-called "Mexican Problem" through his articles in *La Opinión*, while asking the Mexican government to restrict further Mexican emigration to the United States. See Yu Tokunaga, "'Mekishikojin mondai' to imin media: 1920 nendai Rosanzerusu ni okeru haigaishugi to mekishikojin imin no teikō" [The 'Mexican problem' and immigrant media: Mexican immigrants' resistance against nativism in 1920s Los Angeles], *Amerikashi kenkyū* 42 (August 2019): 3–18.

47. "Boicot anti-Nipón en Ciudad Juárez," *La Opinión*, June 22, 1933.

48. For the CROM, see José Manuel Lastra Lastra, "El sindicalismo en México," *Anuario mexicano de historia del derecho* 14 (2002): 37–85.

49. Satō to Uchida, June 23, 1933, I-4-4-0-2, vol. 1, DAMFAJ. Hoffman reveals that the US Ambassador to Mexico Josephus Daniels had a cordial relationship with the Mexican secretary of foreign affairs José M. Puig Casaraunc, showing a supportive stance toward Mexican farmworkers during the strike as part of the Good Neighbor Policy. See Hoffman, "The El Monte Berry Pickers' Strike, 1933," 75.

50. Satō to Uchida, July 1 and 18, 1933, I-4-4-0-2, vol. 1, DAMFAJ; "To Our Mexican Friends," *Los Angeles Chamber of Commerce Bulletin*, May 1931, Box 80, Clements Papers. While López and González explain that Japanese tenant farmers agreed to pay twenty cents an hour on June 26, a Japanese diplomatic document says that they agreed to pay eighteen cents an hour. The Japanese side most likely took into consideration both skilled and less-skilled workers and calculated average hourly wages of piecework and overtime work. See López, "The El Monte Berry Strike of 1933," 107–108; González, "The 1933 Los Angeles County Farm Workers Strike," 452; Gast to Clements, June 27, 1933, Box 64, Clements Papers. For Mexican Repatriation, see Balderrama, *In Defense of La Raza*, 22–23.

51. Gast to Clements, June 27, 1933, Box 64, Clements Papers.

52. López, "The El Monte Berry Strike of 1933," 107–108.

53. Satō to Uchida, June 23, 1933, I-4-4-0-2, vol. 1, DAMFAJ; Yoshiatsu Hori, minister of the Japanese Legation in Mexico, to Satō, June 24, 1933, I-4-4-0-2, vol. 1, DAMFAJ.

54. Satō to Uchida, July 1 and 18, 1933, I-4-4-0-2, vol. 1, DAMFAJ.

55. Ibid.; "Kore ijō no chingin neage wa nihonjin nōka no jimetsu" [Raising wages will lead to the self-destruction of Japanese farmers], *Rafu Shimpo*, June 28, 1933.

56. "Japanese Growers Spurn Mexican Strikers' demand for Special Privileges," *Rafu Shimpo* (English section), June 28, 1933. An editorial in the English section contended that Japanese farmers should be better organized to confront "an organized minority" of strikers. See "The Unorganized Majority," *Rafu Shimpo* (English section), July 2, 1933.

57. Yagasaki, *Imin nōgyō*, 51–58. In 1941, the per capita income for all Japanese Americans was $671, while the per capita income for all California civilians was $982. See Leonard Broom and Ruth Riemer, *Removal and Return: The Socio-economic Effects of the War on Japanese Americans* (Berkeley: University of California, Press, 1949), 13, 20–22.

58. Satō to Uchida, July 1, 1933, I-4-4-0-2, vol. 1, DAMFAJ

59. "Jitai wo akka seru higyō to bokujin gawa shunōbu no iken" [The strike that exacerbates the situation and the opinions of Mexican leaders], *Rafu Shimpo*, June 29, 1933;

"Local Mexican Leaders Voice Opinions to the Rafu Shimpo; Consul Martínez Issues Statement Pleading for Amity," *Rafu Shimpo* (English section), June 29, 1933. While Japanese reporters interviewed Mexican representatives from the standpoint of Japanese farmers, they also showed sympathy toward Mexican strikers by acknowledging their difficult living conditions.

60. "Mueren de hambre 2 niños en la huelga de pizcadores," *La Opinión*, June 30, 1933. According to Natalia Molina, among Mexicans living in rural areas of Los Angeles County, their infant mortality rates were as many as 100 deaths per 1,000 live births in 1927, which was more than twice as high as among whites and Japanese residents. Natalia Molina, *Fit to Be Citizens?: Public Health and Race in Los Angles, 1879–1939* (Berkeley: University of California Press, 2006), 93–94.

61. "La cámara del trabajo decreta el boicot anti-japonés," *La Opinión*, July 1, 1933. For the Cámara Nacional del Trabajo, see Víctor López Villafañe, *La formación del sistema político mexicano*, third edition (Mexico City: Siglo Veintiuno Editores, 1986; 1993), 121–122.

62. "Los niponés abren al público sus plantaciones," *La Opinión*, June 30, 1933; "Officers Watch Picketing Army," *Los Angeles Times*, June 30, 1933.

63. "Officers Watch Picketing Army," *Los Angeles Times*, June 30, 1933; "Higyōdan demo" [Strikers' demonstration], *Rafu Shimpo*, June 30, 1933; Lisa McGirr, *Suburban Warriors: The Origins of the New American Right* (Princeton, NJ: Princeton University Press, 2001), 37. The Japanese consulate did not mention any injury to Japanese subjects regarding the incident. See Sato to Uchida, July 1, I-4-4-0-2, vol. 1 DAMFAJ.

64. Satō to Uchida, July 18, I-4-4-0-2, vol. 1 DAMFAJ.

65. "Action to End Strike Begun," *Los Angeles Times*, July 1, 1933; "El gobernador de California intervino ya en la huelga," *La Opinión*, July 1, 1933.

66. Mexican Consulate in Los Angeles, "Informe de protección. Junio de 1933," June 1933, Folder 2, Box 626, Collection Departamento Consular (IV), AHGE

67. "Dan nuevo impulso al movimiento," *La Opinión*, June 28, 1933; "El movimiento está tomando proporciones serias, dijo el Cónsul Martínez," *La Opinión*, June 30, 1933. Flores and Vice Consul Hill blamed the Japanese as an inferior ethnic group who caused the strike, instead of blaming the social structure where growers in general and white landowners had control over farmworkers. See González, *Mexican Consuls and Labor Organizing*, 106–107.

68. Satō to Uchida, June 23, July 1 and 18, 1933, I-4-4-0-2, vol. 1, DAMFAJ.

69. Gast to Clements, June 27, 1933, Box 64, Clements Papers; McWilliams, *Factories in the Field*, 246–247; The State of California, Department of Industrial Relations, "History of California Minimum Wage," online at http://www.dir.ca.gov/iwc/minimumwagehistory.htm, accessed December 29, 2018.

70. Hori to Uchida, June 15, 1933; Fukushima to Uchida, July 11, 1933, I-4-4-0-2, vol. 1, DAMFAJ.

71. Hori to Uchida, June 29, 1933, I-4-4-0-2, vol. 1, DAMFAJ; "Así lo anunció anoche el Consulado, y el comité abrió una investigación," *La Opinión*, June 30, 1933.

72. "Bokukoku kakumei tō sōsai ga issendoru wo sōkin" [The chairman of the Partido Nacional Revolucionario sent $1,000)], *Kashu Mainichi*, June 30, 1933; Mexican Consulate

in Los Angeles, "Informe de protección. Junio de 1933," June 1933, Folder 2, Box 626, Collection Departamento Consular (IV), AHGE

73. Hori to Uchida, June 30, 1933, I-4-4-0-2, vol. 1, DAMFAJ; "Un grave peligro para la Baja California," *El Excélsior*, May 9, 1933; Jerry García, *Looking Like the Enemy: Japanese Mexicans, the Mexican State, and US Hegemony, 1897–1945* (Tucson: University of Arizona Press, 2014), 93.

74. Nichi-Boku Kōryūshi Henshū Iinkai [Editorial committee of history of Japan-Mexico interaction], ed., *Nichi-boku kōryūshi* [History of Japan-Mexico interaction] (Tokyo: PMC Shuppan, 1990), 478–481 (hereafter cited as *Nichi-boku kōryūshi*).

75. See chapter 1.

76. Even before the El Monte strike, anti-Japanese sentiment was increasing in the northern regions of Mexico, such as Baja California, due to Japanese expansion in Asia. See García, *Looking Like the Enemy*, 93.

77. Ministry of Foreign Affairs of Japan, "Bokukoku teikashū ni haken suru ryōjikan'in ni kansuru ken" [Regarding the consular staff member to be sent to Baja California], 1931, M-2-2-0-1_3_2, Honshō narabini zaigai kōkan'in shutchō kankei zakken/honshōin oyobi zaigai kōkan'in kaigai shutchō no bu (Soshakuchi, inin tōchi chiiki wo fukumu)/ Zaibei kakukan [Miscellaneous documents relating to overseas diplomatic offices/overseas assignments of ministry officials and diplomatic office staff members (including leased and mandated territories)/offices in the United States], vol. 2, DAMFAJ.

78. Fukushima to Uchida, July 11, 1933, I-4-4-0-2, vol. 1, DAMFAJ. In mid-June of 1933, Fukushima visited Los Angeles for consular meetings and told the *Kashu Mainichi*, "Mexican workers' strike in Southern California has no influence in the Baja California region." See "Boku seifu ni nakitsuku sutoraiki gumi" [The strikers' group begs the Mexican government], *Kashu Mainichi*, June 19, 1933.

79. "Mensajes de los Japoneses de Baja California, apoyando la huelga de los pizcadores," *La Opinión*, June 30, 1933. Although *La Opinión* called the Japanese organization the Asociación Japonesa de la Baja California, it was actually the Japanese Association of Mexicali. See Fukushima to Uchida, July 11, 1933, I-4-4-0-2, vol. 1, DAMFAJ.

80. Fukushima to Uchida, June 28 and 29, and July 11, 1933, I-4-4-0-2, vol. 1, DAMFAJ. In late July of 1933, Guajardo acknowledged the fact that the Mexicali Japanese made the donation when he was interviewed by a local Mexicali newspaper *Mercurio*. See "Mandaron dinero los Japoneses?," *Mercurio*, July 29, 1933, Miscellaneous Newspaper Collection, 1704–1970, Special Collections and Archives, University of California, Irvine (hereafter cited as Miscellaneous Newspaper Collection).

81. García, *Looking Like the Enemy*, 89.

82. Jason Oliver Chang, *Chino: Anti-Chinese Racism in Mexico, 1880–1940* (Urbana: University of Illinois Press, 2017), 1–30, 184–186, 194–197.

83. "El boycot contra los niponés," *El Hispano-Americano*, June 25, 1933, I-4-4-0-2, vol. 1, DAMFAJ.

84. "Mekishikari hōmen ni hainichi no kisei ugoku" [Growing anti-Japanese sentiment in the Mexicali area], *Rafu Shimpo*, June 28, 1933.

85. "Mexicali in Boycott of Japanese Merchants," *Kashu Mainichi* (English section), June 29, 1933; "Crisis . . .," *Kashu Mainichi* (English section), June 30, 1933; "Appare hōjin

nōka" [Great job, Japanese farmers], *Kashu Mainichi*, July 2, 1933; "Crisis Reached in Farm Labor Problems," *Kashu Mainichi* (English section), July 2, 1933.

86. Erika Lee, "Orientalisms in the Americas: A Hemispheric Approach to Asian American History," *Journal of Asian American Studies* 8, no. 3 (October 2005): 235–256.

87. Hori to Uchida, July 2, 1933, I-4-4-0-2, vol. 1, DAMFAJ.

88. Sucheng Chan, *Asian Americans: An Interpretive History* (Boston: Twayne Publishers, 1991), 111; Ronald Takaki, *Strangers from a Different Shore*, updated and revised edition (1989; repr., New York: Little, Brown, and Company, 1998), 268–269.

89. Satō to Uchida, July 5, 1933, I-4-4-0-2, vol. 1, DAMFAJ.

90. Satō to Uchida, July 6, 1933, I-4-4-0-2, vol. 1, DAMFAJ; "Daihyōsha namida wo nonde shūgawa chōteian wo shōnin" [Japanese representatives accept the proposal, holding back tears], *Rafu Shimpo*, July 6, 1933.

91. Contract, July 6, 1933, I-4-4-0-2, vol. 1, DAMFAJ. The full text of the contract appeared on the *Rafu Shimpo*'s English section. See "Full Text of Agreement," *Rafu Shimpo* (English section), July 8, 1933.

92. "Strikers Make Pay Pact," *Los Angeles Times*, July 7, 1933.

93. "Concluye la huelga al rendirse los Japoneses," *La Opinión*, July 7, 1933; Contract, July 6, 1933, I-4-4-0-2, vol. 1, DAMFAJ. The Mexican government praised themselves for their role in the strike, as we can see in their words that "the favorable circumstances ... together with that of General Calles, probably saved the Mexican workmen of California from the most serious situation that has ever confronted them." See Hoffman, "The El Monte Berry Pickers' Strike, 1933," 80. Meanwhile, a number of strike organizers, who had a close relationship with the Communist Party, strongly criticized the deal arguing that Mexican representatives sold out to the Japanese side. After the negotiation, Guillermo (William) Velarde, the undersecretary of the Mexican union who attended the final meetings alongside Flores, accused the Mexican consulate and Flores of making too many concessions to Japanese tenant farmers. See Weber, "The Organizing of Mexicano Agricultural Workers," 331.

94. "Chōin wa nattaga bokukokujin no kisan sukunashi" [Despite the agreement, few Mexicans returned], *Rafu Shimpo*, July 7, 1933; "Nihonjin ga yatowanu to bokukokujin rōdōsha himei" [Mexican workers cry that Japanese are not employing them], *Rafu Shimpo*, July 12, 1933. Charles B. Spaulding observed that some Mexican farmworkers had a strong impression that the Japanese discriminated against the former strikers after the agreement was signed. See Spaulding, "The Mexican Strike at El Monte, California," 577.

95. Mexican Consulate in Los Angeles, "Informe de protección. Junio de 1933," June 1933, Folder 2, Box 626, Collection Departamento Consular (IV), AHGE

96. Satō to Uchida, July 18, 1933, I-4-4-0-2, vol. 1, DAMFAJ.

97. Yagasaki, *Imin nōgyō*, 58–59, 79–80.

98. "Jisshitsuteki niwa 16 sen 6 rin" [Actually it is 16.6 cents], *Rafu Shimpo*, July 6, 1933; "Chōin wa natta ga bokukokujin no kisan sukunashi," *Rafu Shimpo*, July 7, 1933.

99. Sei Fujii, "Attitude of Los Angeles Leaders in Strike Settlement Wins Praise, Sei Fujii Stresses Amity with Mexicans," *Kashu Mainichi* (English section), July 7, 1933. On July 2, Fujii wrote in the English section, "This newspaper further expresses deep sympathy for the families of our Mexican friends who are out of work because of this unfortunate

controversy." Fujii, "Amity Still Exists, Says Fujii as Present Farm Situation Outlined," *Kashu Mainichi* (English section), July 2, 1933.

100. "Yoshida, Yoshizaki ryōshi ga kukyō wo shakumei" [Mr. Yoshida and Mr. Yoshizaki explained their difficult situation], *Rafu Shimpo*, July 14, 1933. *Kashu Mainichi* did not report Yoshida and Yoshizaki's visit to Los Angeles, as far as the author knows.

101. Ibid.

102. Satō to Uchida, July 18, 1933, I-4-4-0-2, vol. 1, DAMFAJ.

103. "La Sociedad Japonesa de Ensenada, lamenta el conflicto existente entre trabajadores mexicanos y japoneses en Los Angeles, Cal," *El Faro*, July 8, 1933, Miscellaneous Newspaper Collection.

104. Fukushima to Uchida, July 11, 1933, I-4-4-0-2, vol. 1, DAMFAJ. Although Fukushima did not report the Ensenada Japanese' statement to Tokyo, it is most likely that he knew it given the close relationship between him and Japanese residents in Baja California.

105. *Nichi-boku kōryūshi*, 440–445; María Elena Ota Mishima, *Siete Migraciones Japonesas en México, 1890–1978* (Mexico City: Colegio de México, Centro de Estudios de Asia y Africa, 1985), 87. For the pragmatic aspect of the *ejido* program under the Cárdenas administration, see Nicole Mottier, "Calculating Pragmatism: The High Politics of the Banco Ejidal in Twentieth-century Mexico," *The Americas* 74, no. 3 (July 2017): 331–363.

106. See *Minamikashū nihonjin shichijūnenshi*, 58–59, 667; Edna Bonacich and John Modell, *Economic Basis for Ethnic Solidarity: Small Business in the Japanese American Community* (Berkeley: University of California Press, 1980), 253.

107. Clements to W. G. Arnoll, November 23, 1937, Box 64, Clements Papers.

108. F. L. S. Harman to Clements, August 23, 1933, Box 62, Clements Papers.

109. Jelinek, *Harvest Empire*, 71.

CHAPTER 4. ETHNIC SOLIDARITY OR INTERETHNIC ACCOMMODATION

1. Yuko Matsumoto, "1936 nen Rosanjerusu serori sutoraiki to nikkei nōgyō komyunitī" [The Los Angeles Celery Strike of 1936 and the Japanese agricultural community], *Shirin* 75, no. 4 (July, 1992): 484–513.

2. Francisco E. Balderrama briefly mentions that the Venice strike ended up without union recognition for Mexican workers. See Francisco E. Balderrama, *In Defense of La Raza: The Los Angeles Mexican Consulate and the Mexican Community, 1929 to 1936* (Tucson: University of Arizona Press, 1982), 102. Stuart Jamieson touches upon the important fact that 385 Japanese farmers had signed an agreement with Mexican strikers by July 1936. Although he writes that the strike was settled "on the basis of 60-percent union preference in employment and a minimum wage of 30 cents per hour for field labor," this was not the case, since the Venice strike did not end with a formal settlement in 1936 as described in this chapter. See US Department of Labor, Bureau of Labor Statistics, *Labor Unionism in American Agriculture*, by Stuart Jamieson (Washington: GPO, 1945), 124–125. David J. O'Brien and Stephen S. Fugita touch upon the El Monte and Venice strikes but overlook the internal divides within the ethnic Japanese community in Los Angeles and in the larger

US-Mexico borderlands. See David J. O'Brien and Stephen S. Fugita, *The Japanese American Experience* (Bloomington: Indiana University Press, 1991), 30–32.

3. Noritaka Yagasaki, *Imin nōgyō: Kariforunia no nihonjin imin shakai* [Immigrant agriculture: The Japanese immigrant society in California] (Tokyo: Kokonshoin, 1993), 43–46, 57, 69; Minamikashū Nihonjin Shichijūnenshi Kankō Iinkai [Publishing committee of Japanese in Southern California], ed., *Minamikashū nihonjin shichijūnenshi* [Japanese in Southern California: A history of 70 years] (Los Angeles: Nanka Nikkeijin Shōgyō Kaigisho, 1960), 59, 88 (hereafter cited as *Minamikashū nihonjin shichijūnenshi*).

4. Mexican Consulate in Los Angeles, "Informe de protección correspondiente al mes de julio de 1935," July 31, 1935, Folder 101(I), Box 5, Collection Gaveta 8, Archivo Histórico Genaro Estrada [Genaro Estrada Historical Archive], Mexico City, Mexico (hereafter cited as AHGE). The Los Angeles Regional Labor Board first functioned under the National Labor Board, an agency authorized by the National Industrial Recovery Act of 1933, which was later replaced by the National Labor Relations Board organized under the Wagner Act. See Louis B. Perry and Richard S. Perry, *A History of the Los Angeles Labor Movement, 1911–1941* (Berkeley: University of California Press, 1963), 311–315.

5. Devra Weber, *Dark Sweat, White Gold: California Farm Workers, Cotton, and the New Deal* (Berkeley: University of California Press, 1994), 82, 105.

6. "Estalló la huelga de pizcadores," *La Opinión*, April 19, 1936; The Federated Farmers Association of Southern California [*Nanka Nōkai Renmei*, hereafter *Nōkai Renmei*], antistrike measure report, July 1936, I-4-4-0-2_2, Gaikoku ni okeru rōdō sōgi kankei zakken (Higyō taigyō wo fukumu)/Beikoku no bu [Miscellaneous documents relating to labor disputes in foreign countries (including strikes and sabotages)/The United States of America], vol. 1, Diplomatic Archives of the Ministry of Foreign Affairs of Japan, Minato-ku, Tokyo, Japan (hereafter cited as I-4-4-0-2_2, vol. 1, DAMFAJ).

7. "Ichi jikan no saitei sanjussen" [At least 30 cents per hour], *Rafu Shimpo*, May 6, 1936; "3 mil pizcadores en huelga!," *La Opinión*, April 20, 1936; Devra Weber, "The Organizing of Mexicano Agricultural Workers: Imperial Valley, and Los Angeles 1928–34, An Oral History Approach," *Aztlán* 3, no. 2 (1972): 331. For Mexican labor activists and their relations with Lilliam Monroe, see Gilbert G. González, *Labor and Community: Mexican Citrus Worker Villages in a Southern California County, 1900–1950* (Urbana: University of Illinois Press, 1994), ch. 6. Although the Venice strike did not play out directly with the labor movement in Mexico, there were historical relationships between the strike and the labor movement in Mexico and the United States. First, the CUCOM, like la Confederación de Uniones Obreras Mexicanas (CUOM), was modeled after the structure and ideology of la Confederación Regional Obrera Mexicana (CROM), the Mexican union that was founded in 1918 and influential until 1928 and had listed the CUCOM as an affiliate by 1933. Second, Velarde was the son of a founding member of the Industrial Workers of the World (IWW) that had supported Mexican workers in California. The IWW worked closely with el Partido Liberal Mexicano (PLM). Devra Weber observes, "The PLM-IWW alliance taught a lesson in internationalism that made Mexican leftists more open to working with their Anglo counterparts and laid a basis for alliances between Mexicans and Anglos of the U.S. Communist party in the 1920s and 1930s." Weber, *Dark Sweat, White Gold*, 85–86.

8. "3 mil pizcadores en huelga," *La Opinión*, April 20, 1936; "Kaiketsu wa sōhō no tame to, rōdōsha gawa no iibun, sutoraiki iinkai no ichiin, Ishida Kōken shi raisha dan" [Solving for both sides, workers' explanation, a strike committee member, Mr. Kōken Ishida visits the *Rafu Shimpo*], *Rafu Shimpo*, May 2, 1936.

9. Nōkai Renmei, anti-strike measure report, July 1936, I-4-4-0-2_2, vol. 1, DAMFAJ; George Clements, manager of the Agricultural Department of the Los Angeles Chamber of Commerce, to A. E. Hanson, March 18, 1936, Box 64, George Pigeon Clements Papers, Special Collections, University of California, Los Angeles, (hereafter cited as Clements Papers); "1500 pizcadores rompen la huelga; abandonan la CUCOM," *La Opinión*, June 8, 1936; "Fujii Kamai shachō no shōdō de, Gādena no ichibu nōka mekishikan yunion to keiyaku musubi" [Encouraged by the Kashu Mainichi's President, a group of Gardena farmers signed a contract with the Mexican union], *Rafu Shimpo*, June 18, 1936.

10. Los Angeles Chamber of Commerce, "Offices and Directors Associated Farmers of Los Angeles County," ca. 1936, Box 64, Clements Papers.

11. Nōkai Renmei, anti-strike measure report, July 1936, I-4-4-0-2_2, vol. 1, DAMFAJ.

12. Clements to A. G. Arnoll, secretary of Los Angeles Chamber of Commerce, May 18, 1936, Box 64, Clements Papers. In Clements' letter, the FFWU was written as the Filipino Labor Union. In a letter from Velarde to Katō, it appeared as the FFWU, and the CUOM was included as one of the unions supported by the CUCOM in the Venice strike. See Guillermo Velarde to Shin'ichi Katō, April 6, 1936, Box 64, Clements Papers.

13. "Pikettā no bōkō ni kanken ga sairuidan" [The authority threw tear gas bombs against violent picketers], *Rafu Shimpo*, April 25, 1936.

14. "8 mexicanos huelguistas de Venice, heridos en un motín," *La Opinión*, April 25, 1936.

15. "Ryōsha gankyō ni aitaiji shi" [Both parties face off], "Romita nōka mo jieisaku" [Farmers in Lomita take a self-defense measure], *Rafu Shimpo*, April 25, 1936.

16. Nōkai Renmei, anti-strike measure report, July 1936, I-4-4-0-2_2, vol. 1, DAMFAJ.

17. Ibid.

18. Matsumoto, "1936 nen Rosanjerusu serori sutoraiki to nikkei nōgyō komyunitī," 69.

19. "Nōen no higyō" [Strike in farms], "Sōgo fujo no seishin kara giyūdan tatsu" [The spirit of mutual aid in the giyūdan], *Rafu Shimpo*, April 28, 1936.

20. Arthur E. Clark, executive secretary of the Associated Farmers of Los Angeles County, to Eugene Biscailuz, Los Angeles Sheriff, May 1, 1936, Box 64, Clements Papers.

21. Nōkai Renmei, anti-strike measure report, July 1936, I-4-4-0-2_2, vol. 1, DAMFAJ; "Reconocimiento de la unión," *La Opinión*, April 29, 1936; The Venice Industrial Association [Benisu Sangyō Kumiai], statement, *Rafu Shimpo*, June 2, 1936; Central strike committee, an open letter on the Venice strike, May 2, 1936, Folder 3, Box 1, Karl G. Yoneda Papers, Modern Japanese Political History Materials Room, National Diet Library of Japan, Tokyo (hereafter cited as Yoneda Papers). The original documents of the Yoneda Papers are preserved in the Special Collections, Charles E. Young Library of the University of California, Los Angeles.

22. "Shūdōsha jūbun de, giyūdan raien wo jitai, Benisu de rōdōsha kādo saiyō" [With enough workers, giyūdan's visit declined, introduction of the worker's card in Venice],

Rafu Shimpo, May 9, 1936; "Ragun nōen sutoraiki, dai yon shūme ni hairu" [The Los Angeles County strike now in the fourth week], *Rafu Shimpo*, May 11, 1936.

23. Clarke A. Chambers, *California Farm Organizations: A Historical Study of the Grange, the Farm Bureau, and the Associated Farmers, 1929–1941* (Berkeley: University of California Press, 1952), 70–71.

24. "8 mexicanos huelguistas de Venice, heridos en un motín," *La Opinión*, April 25, 1936; "Fujii Kamai shachō no shōdō de, Gādena no ichibu nōka mekishikan yunion to keiyaku musubi," *Rafu Shimpo*, June 18, 1936.

25. "Nōen sōgi no kaiketsu no michi" [A solution for the agricultural strike], *Rafu Shimpo*, May 1, 1936; "Sutoraiki taisaku toshite Seinen Seigidan soshiki" [The establishment of the Youth League for Justice], *Rafu Shimpo*, May 4, 1936; "San Gēburu heigen rōdōsha fukki shi" [The return of workers in the San Gabriel Valley], *Rafu Shimpo*, May 5, 1936; "San Gēburu mo higyō boppatsu ni sonau" [The San Gabriel farmers prepare for the outbreak of strikes], *Rafu Shimpo*, May 8, 1936.

26. "Yunion mitomenu to ganbari" [Working hard not to recognize unions], *Rafu Shimpo*, May 2, 1936; "Benisu higyō ni kanshi, Hiru ryōji wa kataru" [Consul Hill talks about the Venice strike], *Rafu Shimpo*, May 7, 1936.

27. "8 mexicanos huelguistas de Venice, heridos en un motín," *La Opinión*, April 25, 1936; "Los niponés no aceptan un arreglo," *La Opinión*, May 2, 1936. For the transition from Calles to Cárdenas, see Víctor López Villafañe, *La Formación del Sistema Político Mexicano*, third edition (Mexico City: Siglo Veintiuno Editores, 1986; 1993), 45–55.

28. The 21st district office of the National Labor Relations Board, "Strike of Mexican Field Workers," April 17, 1936, Folder 4, Box 1, RG25, Records of the National Labor Relations Board, National Archives at Riverside, Riverside, California (hereafter cited as RG25, NAR).

29. The 15th district office of the National Labor Relations Board, "Agreement San Diego Field Workers," August 22, 1935, Folder 2, Box 1, RG25, NAR.

30. Mexican Consulate in Los Angeles, "Informe de protección correspondiente al mes de julio de 1935," July 31, 1935, Folder 101(I), Box 5, Collection Gaveta 8, AHGE.

31. Central strike committee, an open letter on the Venice strike, May 2, 1936, Folder 3, Box 1, Yoneda Papers.

32. "Kaiketsu wa sōhō no tame to, rōdōsha gawa no iibun, sutoraiki iinkai no ichiin, Ishida Kōken shi raisha dan," *Rafu Shimpo*, May 2, 1936. The *Rafu Shimpo* called Ishida's organization the Kashū Nihonjin Nōen Rōdōsha Kumiai Nanka Rengō [Southern California Federation of the Japanese Farm Workers Union of California].

33. Ibid.

34. Shin'ichi Katō, "Nōka gawa no tachiba (2)" [The position of farmers], *Rafu Shimpo*, May 5, 1936.

35. See chapter 3.

36. "Huelguistas y cosecheros en un arreglo," *La Opinión*, May 13, 1936.

37. "Nōen sutoraiki, zenji ta chiiki ni kakudai ka" [The strike gradually seems to be spreading to other areas], *Rafu Shimpo*, May 13, 1936.

38. "Kaiketsu wa sōhō no tame to, rōdōsha gawa no iibun, sutoraiki iinkai no ichiin, Ishida Kōken shi raisha dan," *Rafu Shimpo*, May 2, 1936; Katō, "Nōka gawa no tachiba (3)," *Rafu Shimpo*, May 6, 1936.

39. "Nōen sutoraiki, zenji ta chiiki ni kakudai ka," *Rafu Shimpo*, May 13, 1936; "Tairitsu sen'eika shinagaramo kyokumen tenkai no kizashi miraru" [While conflict aggravated, a sign of moving on to the next stage], *Rafu Shimpo*, May 14, 1936. In mid-May, Clements sent letters to the sheriff and police chiefs of Los Angeles to thank their support for Japanese farmers. See Clements to James E. Davis, chief of the Los Angeles Police Department, May 15, 1936, Box 64, Clements Papers; Clements to Eugene Biscailuz, Sheriff of Los Angeles County, May 15, 1936, Box 64, Clements Papers.

40. "Nōen sutoraiki, zenji ta chiiki ni kakudai ka," *Rafu Shimpo*, May 13, 1936; "Romita de shii" [Demonstration in Lomita], *Rafu Shimpo*, May 13, 1936; "Tairitsu sen'eika shinagaramo kyokumen tenkai no kizashi miraru," *Rafu Shimpo*, May 14, 1936; "Higyōdan shii ni nōka fungai" [Farmers infuriated about the strikers' demonstration], *Rafu Shimpo*, May 16, 1936; "San Pīdoro yamate e, higyōdan taikyo sattō" [Strikers arrive at the mountain side of San Pedro in large number], *Rafu Shimpo*, May 18, 1936; Noboru Murakami, diary, May 15, 1936, Box 130, Noboru Murakami Papers, Japanese American Research Project Collection, Special Collections, University of California, Los Angeles.

41. Nōkai Renmei, anti-strike measure report, July 1936, I-4-4-0-2_2, vol. 1, DAMFAJ.

42. "Katō shihainin, higyō kanbu to kaiken" [Manager Katō met with strike leaders], *Rafu Shimpo*, May 8, 1936.

43. Nōkai Renmei, anti-strike measure report, July 1936, I-4-4-0-2_2, vol. 1, DAMFAJ; "Nōen sutoraiki jiken, tsuini chōteikan no te e" [The agricultural strike problem will be handled by the mediator], *Rafu Shimpo*, May 20, 1936; "Nōren iin to higyōdan kanbu, dai yoji kaiken mo mata monowakare" [Nōkai Renmei members and strike leaders, fourth meeting ended in disagreement], *Rafu Shimpo*, May 23, 1936.

44. "Nōren iin to higyōdan kanbu, dai yoji kaiken mo mata monowakare," *Rafu Shimpo*, May 23, 1936.

45. Nōkai Renmei, anti-strike measure report, July 1936, I-4-4-0-2_2, vol. 1, DAMFAJ.

46. Ibid.; "Nōen sutoraiki jiken, tsuini chōteikan no te e," *Rafu Shimpo*, May 20, 1936.

47. "Zenkai no Mukaeda kyōtei wa kōsei datō da, Bākā chōteikan kisha ni kataru" [The previous Mukaeda agreement was fair and appropriate, mediator Barker talks to us], *Rafu Shimpo*, May 22, 1936; "Nōren iin to higyōdan kanbu, dai yoji kaiken mo mata monowakare," *Rafu Shimpo*, May 23, 1936.

48. Shōji Nagumo, "Kisho sutoraiki sokumenkan (1)" [Letter about the strike from a different perspective], *Rafu Shimpo*, May 23, 1936. Nagumo created a beautiful Japanese garden in the "relocation center" at Manzanar during World War II. As for the history of the Southern California Gardener Unions' Federation, see "Nanka Teien Gyōsha Renmei sōritsu 60 shūnen" [60th anniversary of the Southern California Gardener Unions' Federation], *Rafu Shimpo*, February 19, 2015, online at https://www.rafu.com/, accessed January 25, 2021.

49. As Tsuchida explains, most Japanese gardeners were latecomers who migrated to the United States after the implementation of the Alien Land Laws and could not establish a strong base in agriculture. This prevented them from becoming established farmers

but forced them to work as farmworkers. In this situation, they came to see gardening as a more stable and rewarding job. See Nobuya Tsuchida, "Japanese Gardeners in Southern California, 1900–1941," in *Labor Immigration under Capitalism: Asian Workers in the United States before World War II*, ed. Lucie Cheng and Edna Bonacich (Berkeley: University of California Press, 1984), 443–446, 459–460.

50. Nōkai Renmei, anti-strike measure report, July 1936, I-4-4-0-2_2, vol. 1, DAMFAJ.

51. "Nōka no sōi wo hyōji shi kaiketsu wo iin ni ichinin" [Leaving the solution to the committee's discretion as a collective will of farmers], *Rafu Shimpo*, May 21, 1936.

52. Matsumoto, "1936 nen Rosanjerusu serori sutoraiki to nikkei nōgyō komyunitī," 69–70.

53. "Shōnō no tachiba ni kansuru tōsho" [A letter regarding the position of small-scale farmers], *Kashu Mainichi*, May 30, 1936.

54. In 1931, the *Rafu Shimpo* installed a new rotary press that could print about twenty-five thousand copies per hour, helping them keep a prominent position as a Japanese language newspaper in Southern California. See Dōjun Ochi, ed., *Minamikashū nihonjinshi kō-hen* [History of Japanese in Southern California, second volume] (Los Angeles: Nanka Nikkeijin Shōgyō Kaigisho, 1957), 97.

55. "Grist for the Mill," *Kashu Mainichi* (English section), May 20, 1936; "Sōgo fujo no seishin kara giyūdan tatsu" [The spirit of mutual aid in the giyūdan], *Rafu Shimpo*, April 28, 1936; "Nōen higyō ni tsuki seinendan tatsu" [A youth group launched due to the agricultural strike], *Kashu Mainichi*, May 13, 1936; "Nisei Workers Aid Farms in Strike Area," *Rafu Shimpo* (English section), May 1, 1936; "San Gabriel to Hold Nisei Mass Meeting Saturday," *Kashu Mainichi* (English section), May 20, 1936; "Nōen sōgi ni kanshi nōkai renmei kanbu ni kugen wo teisu" [Regarding the agricultural strike, I make a critical comment to the Nokai Renmei leaders], *Kashu Mainichi*, May 29, 1936. An editorial of the *Rafu Shimpo*'s English section praised the cooperation of Nisei but criticized Nisei living in the city area, writing that "the several score Nisei who contributed their time and labor in cutting the Venice celery crop this past week were chiefly from the neighboring farm areas. But few were from the city." See "A Question Mark," *Rafu Shimpo* (English section), May 3, 1936.

56. Nōkai Renmei, anti-strike measure report, July 1936, I-4-4-0-2_2, vol. 1, DAMFAJ. Lucio was the representative of the Comisión Honorífica de Santa Ana, an ethnic Mexican organization affiliated to the Mexican consulate. See "El Cónsul Hill se defiende," *La Opinión*, June 13, 1936.

57. González, *Labor and Community*, 146–148.

58. "Zenson ikka no daikentō" [The whole village united as one family to fight], *Rafu Shimpo*, May 20, 1936; Kō Murai, *Zaibei nihonjin sangyō sōran* (Los Angeles: Beikoku Sangyō Nippōsha, 1940), 651, Murai Family Papers, Japanese American National Museum, Los Angeles, California.

59. "24 heridos y 40 arrestados en la huelga de pizcadores," *La Opinión*, May 26, 1936.

60. "Nōen higyō wo kage de ayatsuru, aka no joō, Monrō joshi" [Monroe, the queen of reds, who masterminds the strike], *Rafu Shimpo*, May 26, 1936; "Strike Violence Increases," *Rafu Shimpo* (English section), May 26, 1936.

61. "Domingusu nōkumi, kinkyū ketsugi" [Farmers' association in Dominguez Hills adopted an emergency resolution], *Rafu Shimpo*, May 26, 1936.

62. "Domingusu oka nōen higyō bōryokuka zakkan" [Thoughts on the eruption of violence in Dominguez Hills], *Kashu Mainichi*, May 29, 1936.
63. "24 heridos y 40 arrestados en la huelga de pizcadores," *La Opinión*, May 26, 1936.
64. Ibid.
65. "El comité pro-huelga lanza una excitativa," *La Opinión*, May 31, 1936.
66. "Pikettā sattō, shūdōsha wo ikaku" [Picketers flood into the area, threatening workers], *Rafu Shimpo*, May 20, 1936; "Nōen shinnyū no higyōdan" [Strikers encroaching in the farms], *Rafu Shimpo*, May 28, 1936; "Heigen nai seinendan no kessoku" [Solidarity of the youth league in the Valley], *Rafu Shimpo*, May 29, 1936.
67. "Bōkō pikettā, yūzai no senkoku" [Guilty verdict on violent picketers], *Rafu Shimpo*, June 4, 1936; "Bōkō pikettā ni rokkagetsuno taikei" [Prison sentence for six months to violent picketers], June 5, 1936; "San Gēburu keikai" [Vigilance needed in San Gabriel], *Rafu Shimpo*, June 5, 1936.
68. "Victoria de los pizcadores," *La Opinión*, May 29, 1936; "Shinkō chū datta kaiketsu kōshō" [Negotiation for solution was in progress], *Rafu Shimpo*, May 29, 1936.
69. "Shinkō chū datta kaiketsu kōshō," *Rafu Shimpo*, May 29, 1936.
70. "Nihonjin nōka shichijū mei yunion to keiyaku" [70 Japanese farmers signed a contract with the union], *Kashu Mainichi*, May 29, 1936; "50 Growers Sign," *Kashu Mainichi* (English section), May 29, 1936.
71. "Gādena hōmen no yunion shōnin wa tonda dema" [A bad false rumor about Gardena farmers recognizing unions], *Rafu Shimpo*, June 1, 1936. Another article said that Ueda was the only person who signed the contract with the union. See "Yunion to shōmei wa nisei rīsu meiginin" [Who signed the contract with the union was a *Nisei* lessee], *Rafu Shimpo*, June 8, 1936.
72. "Farms Hold United Front in L. A. Strike," *Rafu Shimpo* (English section), June 1, 1936.
73. Nōkai Renmei, anti-strike measure report, July 1936, I-4-4-0-2_2, vol. 1, DAMFAJ; Matsumoto, "1936 nen rosanjerusu serori sutoraiki to nikkei nōgyō komyunitī," 69.
74. Nōkai Renmei, anti-strike measure report, July 1936, I-4-4-0-2_2, vol. 1, DAMFAJ; "Yunion wo hanareta bokukokujin 1,500 chingin kyōtei wo musubu" [1,500 Mexicans who had left the union signed the wage agreement], "Kaiketsu ni honsō shita ryō iin kinzen" [Both committee members who worked hard for solution are delighted], *Rafu Shimpo*, June 8, 1936; "Sutoraiki kaishō sezu to" [The strike not solved], *Rafu Shimpo*, June 9, 1936; "1500 pizcadores rompen la huelga; abandonan la CUCOM," *La Opinión*, June 8, 1936.
75. "1500 pizcadores rompen la huelga; abandonan la CUCOM," *La Opinión*, June 8, 1936; "Bokukokujin rōdōsha yunion wo hōki" [Mexican workers abandoned the union], *Rafu Shimpo*, June 8, 1936; "Kaiketsu ni honsō shita ryō iin kinzen," *Rafu Shimpo*, June 8, 1936; "Jikyoku taisaku zikkō iinkai, kari keiyaku kyōtei wo shōnin su" [Anti-strike measure committee acknowledged a provisional agreement], *Rafu Shimpo*, June 9, 1936.
76. "Sutoraiki kaishō sezu to," *Rafu Shimpo*, June 9, 1936.
77. "Kaiketsu ni honsō shita ryō iin," *Rafu Shimpo*, June 8, 1936.
78. "Japanese Ranks Split on Unions," *Los Angeles Times*, June 18, 1936; "Fujii Kamai shachō no shōdō de, Gādena no ichibu nōka mekishikan yunion to keiyaku musubi," *Rafu Shimpo*, June 18, 1936.

79. Nōkai Renmei, anti-strike measure report, July 1936, I-4-4-0-2_2, vol. 1, DAMFAJ.
80. "Bobu Ueda kun no yunionmen shiyō keiken dan" [Bob Ueda's experience of using union men], *Kashu Mainichi*, July 1, 1936.
81. Arthur Clark, executive secretary of the Associated Farmers of Los Angeles County, to the Board of Direction of the Associated Farmers of Los Angeles County, June 11, 1936, Box 64, Clements Papers. It seems that Clark thought that a group of labor activists in the San Joaquin Valley was involved in the Venice strike, although other Spanish and Japanese primary sources analyzed in this book do not indicate their direct involvement.
82. Ibid.
83. Arnoll to Clements, June 20, 1936, Box 64, Clements Papers.
84. Clark to the Board of Direction of the Associated Farmers of Los Angeles County, June 11, 1936, Box 64, Clements Papers.
85. Ibid.
86. Nōkai Renmei, anti-strike measure report, July 1936, I-4-4-0-2_2, vol. 1, DAMFAJ; Katsuma Mukaeda, "Sen-man no tabi kara" [From my trip in Korea and Manchuria], *Rafu Shimpo*, June 4 to 6, 1936.
87. Katsuma Mukaeda, "Sen-man no tabi kara," *Rafu Shimpo*, June 4 to 6, 1936.
88. Nōkai Renmei, anti-strike measure report, July 1936, I-4-4-0-2_2, vol. 1, DAMFAJ; "Nōen sutoraiki sankagetsu" [The agricultural strike has continued for three months], *Rafu Shimpo*, July 9, 1936.
89. "Nōen sutoraiki sankagetsu," *Rafu Shimpo*, July 9, 1936. *La Opinión* did not detail the provisional agreement but mentioned only hourly wages, the applied period, and no recognition of closed shop. See "Bases para terminar el movimiento," *La Opinión*, July 11, 1936.
90. "Sōgi kaiketsu no kōrōsha, Mukaeda shi kataru" [Contributor to the solution for the strike, Mr. Mukaeda talks], *Rafu Shimpo*, July 9, 1936.
91. Nōkai Renmei, anti-strike measure report, July 1936, I-4-4-0-2_2, vol. 1, DAMFAJ. Regarding the Dominguez Hills white landowners' statement, Matsumoto mentioned it as part of "an attempt of pressure and control over ethnic Japanese farmers." Her argument seems to be based on the assumption that the decision of white landowners one-sidedly controlled or influenced the situation of Japanese farmers. By taking a closer look at the local context, however, I argue that most Japanese farmers and landowners in the Dominguez Hills area were determined to fight together against strikers largely because of their genuine mutual trust, which will be explained in chapter 6. See Matsumoto, "1936 nen Rosanjerusu serori sutoraiki to nikkei nōgyō Komyunitī," 65–66.
92. "Fracasaron los arreglos en la huelga," *La Opinión*, July 14, 1936.
93. Clark to the Board of Direction of the Associated Farmers of Los Angeles, June 11, 1936, Box 64, Clements Papers; "Mekishikan sutoraiki Orenji gun e tobihi" [The Mexican strike has spread to Orange County], *Rafu Shimpo*, June 10, 1936.
94. "Enshu gawa to Bokukoku ryōji, tairitsu mondai wo jakki" [Farmers' side and the Mexican consul invoke a conflict], *Rafu Shimpo*, June 13, 1936; "El Cónsul Hill se defiende," *La Opinión*, June 13, 1936.
95. "El líder de la CUCOM, preso!," *La Opinión*, July 15, 1936.
96. "Está ya en libertad el Sr. Velarde," *La Opinión*, July 17, 1936.

97. "Terminaron ayer 2 huelgas: La de México y La de Orange," *La Opinión*, July 26, 1936; "Hundreds Jailed as Citrus Rioters Attack Workers," *Los Angeles Times*, July 7, 1936; "Citrus War End Nears," *Los Angeles Times*, July 17, 1936; "Eight Hurt in Battle," *Los Angeles Times*, July 26, 1936.

98. Kōichi Hori, consul in Los Angeles, to Hachiro Arita, minister of foreign affairs of Japan, August 18, 1936, I-4-4-0-2_2, vol. 1, DAMFAJ; Nōkai Renmei, anti-strike measure report, July 1936, I-4-4-0-2_2, vol. 1, DAMFAJ.

99. "Hori ryōji tōbu shisatsu" [Consul Hori travels on the East Coast], *Rafu Shimpo*, June 13, 1936.

100. The 21st district office of the National Labor Relations Board, weekly report, July 10, 1936, Folder 1, Box 1, RG25, NAR.

101. Towne Nylander, director of the Los Angeles Regional Labor Board, to Ralph T. Seward, regional attorney, March 12, 1937, Folder 3, Box 1, RG25, NAR. On Nylander, see Perry and Perry, *A History of the Los Angeles Labor Movement, 1911–1941*, 313, 496.

102. Clements to Arnoll, August 13, October 12, and November 27, 1936, Box 64, Clements Papers; Arthur E. Clark, executive secretary of the Associated Farmers of Los Angeles County, ca. October, 1936, Box 64, Clements Papers. For the relationship between Hill and radical labor organizers, see Gilbert G. González, *Mexican Consuls and Labor Organizing: Imperial Politics in the American Southwest* (Austin: University of Texas Press, 1999), 118–121.

103. "Nōsangyō wo tōshite no nichibei shinzen wo kōchō" [Deepening Japan-US relations through agriculture], *Rafu Shimpo*, February 24, 1936.

104. "Fue firmado un ventajoso contrato entre las empresas agrícolas y los pizcadores," *La Opinion*, April 29, 1937; *Minamikashū Nihonjin Shichijūnenshi*, 388; Jamieson, *Labor Unionism in American Agriculture*, 127–128. In 1937, the CUCOM merged with other leftist organizations into the United Cannery, Agricultural, Packing, and Allied Workers of America, the agricultural branch of the Congress of Industrial Organizations. See Weber, *Dark Sweat, White Gold*, 159–160, 164–165.

105. Katsuma Mukaeda, interview by Dave Biniasz, November 28, 1973, Japanese American Project, Oral History Program at California State University, Fullerton, Special Collections, University of California, Los Angeles, Los Angeles, California.

106. Cletus E. Daniel, *Bitter Harvest: A History of California Farmworkers, 1870–1941* (Berkeley: University of California Press, 1981), 176.

CHAPTER 5. JAPANESE INTERNMENT
AS AN AGRICULTURAL LABOR CRISIS

1. Kumezō Hachimonji, diary, December 7 and 9, 1941, Folder 2, Box 61, Kumezo Hachimonji Papers, Japanese American Research Project Collection, Special Collections, University of California, Los Angeles, Los Angeles, California.

2. Commission on Wartime Relocation and Internment of Civilians, *Personal Justice Denied* (1982, repr., Washington, DC: Civil Liberties Public Education Fund and University of Washington Press, 1997) (hereafter cited as *Personal Justice Denied*), Summary, 18. As for the decision-making process of Japanese Internment, see Morton Grodzins, *Americans Betrayed: Politics and the Japanese Evacuation* (Chicago: University of Chicago Press,

1949; 1974); Jacobus tenBroek, Edward N. Barnhart, and Floyd W. Matson, *Prejudice, War and the Constitution: Causes and Consequences of the Evacuation of the Japanese Americans in World War II* (Berkeley: University of California Press, 1954; 1970); Roger Daniels, *The Decision to Relocate the Japanese Americans* (Philadelphia: Lippincott, 1975); Greg Robinson, *By Order of the President: FDR and the Internment of Japanese Americans* (Cambridge, MA: Harvard University Press, 2001); Brian Masaru Hayashi, *Democratizing the Enemy: The Japanese American Internment* (Princeton, NJ: Princeton University Press, 2004); Alice Yang Murray, *Historical Memories of the Japanese American Internment and the Struggle for Redress* (Stanford, CA: Stanford University Press, 2008); Lon Kurashige, *Two Faces of Exclusion: The Untold History of Anti-Asian Racism in the United States* (Chapel Hill: University of North Carolina Press, 2016).

3. For the impact of Japanese Internment on non-Japanese minorities, see Scott Kurashige, *The Shifting Grounds of Race: Black and Japanese Americans in the Making of Multiethnic Los Angeles* (Princeton, NJ: Princeton University Press, 2008), 161–169; R. J. Smith, *The Great Black Way: L.A. in the 1940s and the Lost African-American Renaissance* (New York: Public Affairs, 2006), 139–153; Greg Robinson, *After Camp: Portraits in Midcentury Japanese American Life and Politics* (Berkeley: University of California Press, 2012), 105–122; Allison Varzally, *Making a Non-White America: Californians Coloring Outside Ethnic Lines, 1925–1955* (Berkeley: University of California Press, 2008), 122–123. See also George J. Sánchez, "Disposable People, Expendable Neighborhoods," in *A Companion to Los Angeles*, eds. William Deverell and Greg Hise (Malden, MA: Blackwell Publishing, 2010), 129–146.

4. It is generally explained that the ethnic Japanese in Hawai'i were not interned because of their economic importance in the islands. For example, see Sucheng Chan, *Asian Americans: An Interpretive History* (Boston: Twayne Publishers, 1991), 127. While acknowledging the importance of ethnic Japanese workers in wartime Hawai'i, Akihiro Yamakura argues that Japanese Internment on the mainland and the military rule of Hawai'i during World War II were "essentially the same in terms of the vigilance against the ethnic Japanese and the intention to contain them." Akihiro Yamakura, *Shiminteki jiyū: Amerika nikkeijin senji kyōsei shūyō no rīgaru hisutorī* [Civil liberties: A legal history of the wartime incarceration of the people of Japanese ancestry in America] (Tokyo: Sairyūsha, 2011), 120.

5. "Accounts 'Frozen,'" *Rafu Shimpo* (English section), December 9, 1942.

6. Laurence I. Hewes Jr., regional director of the Farm Security Administration, to district officers and field agents of the Wartime Farm Adjustment Program of the Farm Security Administration, March 15, 1942, Carton 2, W. R. Ralston Papers, Bancroft Library, University of California, Berkeley (hereafter cited as Ralston Papers); US Congress, House of Representatives, Hearings before the Select Committee Investigating National Defense Migration, 77th Cong., 2nd session, March 6, 7, and 12, 1942 (hereafter cited as Tolan Committee), 11658; Minamikashū Nihonjin Shichijūnenshi Kankō Iinkai [Publishing committee of Japanese in Southern California], ed., *Minamikashū nihonjin shichijūnenshi* [Japanese in Southern California: A history of 70 years] (Los Angeles: Nanka Nikkeijin Shōgyō Kaigisho, 1960, 58 (hereafter cited as *Minamikashū nihonjin shichijūnenshi*).

7. Masakazu Iwata, *Planted in Good Soil: A History of the Issei in United States Agriculture*, 2 vols. (New York: Peter Lang Publishers, 1992), 1:294; Leonard Broom and Ruth

Riemer, *Removal and Return: The Socio-Economic Effects of the War on Japanese Americans* (Berkeley: University of California Press, 1949), 74.

8. US Census Bureau, *Sixteenth Census of the United States: 1940, Population* (Washington, D.C., 1943), Table 4, "Race, by Nativity and Sex, for the United States: 1850 to 1940," and Table 25, "Indians, Chinese, and Japanese by Sex, for Counties, and for Cities of 10,000 to 100,000," 19, 516, 567; Broom and Riemer, *Removal and Return*, 13, 74, 85.

9. "San nōsan shijō no nichi-bei-shi jin ga taisaku kyōgi" [Japanese, Americans, Chinese of the three produce markets hold a meeting to discuss measures], *Rafu Shimpo*, December 10, 1941.

10. "Senjika no Shō Tōkyō, hotondo zenbu heiten, issei no ginkō yokin hikidashi kinshi" [Little Tokyo in the wartime, almost all closed, banking transactions by Issei are prohibited], *Rafu Shimpo*, December 10, 1941.

11. US Department of Agriculture, *Food for Freedom: Informational Handbook 1943*, November 1942, 3, online at https://archive.org/details/foodforfreedomin14unit, accessed October 9, 2018.

12. Dave Davidson, chairman of the California USDA Defense Board, to chairmen of USDA County Defense Boards, December 10, 1941, Carton 2, Ralston Papers; US Department of Agriculture, *Food for Freedom*, 36.

13. "Nihonjin wa yokin wo hyaku doru made hikidaseru" [Japanese allowed to withdraw up to $100], *Rafu Shimpo*, December 12, 1941.

14. "Nihonjin wa shukka seyo" [The Japanese need to ship], *Rafu Shimpo*, December 12, 1941; *Minamikashū nihonjin shichijūnenshi*, 59.

15. As for prewar Japanese immigrant nationalism, see Yuji Ichioka, *Before Internment: Essays in Prewar Japanese American History*, eds. Gordon H. Chang and Eiichiro Azuma (Stanford, CA: Stanford University Press, 2006), ch. 8.

16. "Nōsan shijō narabini haikyū wa heijō no kinō ni fukusu" [Produce markets and distribution recovered to normal], *Rafu Shimpo*, December 12, 1941; "Nihonjin wa shukka seyo," *Rafu Shimpo*, December 12, 1941; "Sā yasai ga kita" [Vegetables have come], *Rafu Shimpo*, December 13, 1941; "Mise mo hiraite Shō Tōkyō kakkizuku" [Shops open, Little Tokyo revitalized], *Rafu Shimpo*, December 13, 1941.

17. P. A. Minges, "Report on the Effects of the Japanese War on the Japanese Alien and Native-Born Vegetable Growers of California," December 29, 1941, Carton 2, Ralston Papers.

18. Ibid. For Japanese-Filipino relations in Stockton, see Eiichiro Azuma, *Between Two Empires: Race, History, and Transnationalism in Japanese America* (New York: Oxford University Press, 2005), 187–207.

19. Minges, "Report on the Effects of the Japanese War." Minges also critically argued that the freezing and "the speedy work in unblocking Japanese assets may have created the impression in the east that most of California vegetables are produced by Japanese," which could result in a boycott of Japanese vegetables that would help the competitors in other states "seize this opportunity to cut in on California produce."

20. "We Are 100 Percent for the United States," *Rafu Shimpo* (English section), December 9, 1941; "Zaibei dōhō shoshi e keikoku" [Warning for fellow Japanese in the United States], *Rafu Shimpo*, December 10, 1941; "Minasama eno gochūi" [Warning to all], *Rafu*

Shimpo, December 11, 1941; "Minasama eno onegai" [Request to all], *Rafu Shimpo*, December 13, 1941.

21. "Anti-Axis Committee formed by J.A.C.L," *Rafu Shimpo* (English section), December 9, 1942; "Sūjiku datō sen ni nisei katsuyaku" [Nisei are active in fighting against Axis Powers], *Kashu Mainichi*, December 10, 1941; "Minasama eno onegai," *Rafu Shimpo*, December 13, 1941.

22. "Nihon kankei denpō" [Telegrams related to Japan], *Rafu Shimpo*, June 25, 1924; "Minasama eno onegai," *Rafu Shimpo*, December 13, 1941.

23. *Personal Justice Denied*, 54–55, 70; tenBroek, et al, *Prejudice, War, and the Constitution*, 76–77.

24. Regarding the anti-Japanese politics and the Democratic Party in California in the early twentieth century, see Toshihiro Minohara, *Kariforunia shū hainichi undō to nichi-bei kankei: Imin mondai wo meguru nichi-bei masatsu* (Tokyo: Yūhikaku, 2006). Olson won the gubernatorial election in 1938 with a policy plan that intended to support farmworkers and even strikers with sufficient relief payments when necessary. His administration also attempted to mediate labor disputes and inspect farm labor camps. By the end of 1939, however, California farm employers succeed in forcing Olson to drop his initial ideas. See Lawrence J. Jelinek, *Harvest Empire: A History of California Agriculture* (San Francisco: Boyd & Fraser, 1979; 1982), 72.

25. "Oruson shū chiji nikkei shimin ni yōbō" [Governor Olson's demand for Japanese American citizens], *Rafu Shimpo*, December 13, 1941.

26. Broom and Riemer, *Removal and Return*, 13.

27. Culbert Olson, "Defense," January 28, 1942, Carton 5, Culbert L. Olson Papers, Bancroft Library, University of California, Berkeley (hereafter cited as Olson Papers). For the presidential proclamation issued on January 14, 1942, see "Western Alien Register First," *Los Angeles Times*, January 16, 1942.

28. For the California plan, see Daniels, *The Decision to Relocate the Japanese Americans*, 36–39.

29. Culbert Olson, "National Defense," speech before the 17th District American Legion, Los Angeles, February 20, 1942, Carton 5, Olson Papers.

30. "Kashū nihonjin no torishimari ni" [Regarding the control of the Japanese in California], *Rafu Shimpo*, February 5, 1942; "Ōruson Kashū chiji ga hōsō" [Governor Olson broadcast], *Kashu Mainichi*, February 5, 1942; "Okuchi eno nihonjin tachinoki, Oruson chiji hantai" [Governor Olson opposes the evacuation of the Japanese to inland areas], *Rafu Shimpo*, February 6, 1942.

31. "Olson Kashū chiji issei nisei no kyōryoku wo yōbō" [California Governor Olson demands cooperation of Issei and Nisei], *Rafu Shimpo*, February 7, 1942; "State Attitude Outlined by Olson at Confab," *Rafu Shimpo* (English section), February 7, 1942. For Akira Komai, see Chris Komai, "Revival: Rafu Shimpo," Discover Nikkei, March 7, 2014, online at http://www.discovernikkei.org/en/journal/2014/3/7/revival-rafu-shimpo, accessed October 10, 2018. The militarily important areas to which Olson was referring were not the Military Areas No. 1 and No. 2 designated after Executive Order 9066. As of February 5, for instance, in Los Angeles County, these military areas were far smaller than the so-called Military Areas. The map of Military Areas delineated after Executive Order 9066 appeared

in the *Los Angeles Times* in March 1942. See "Army Lists Areas Barred to Aliens," *Los Angeles Times*, March 4, 1942.

32. "State Attitude Outlined by Olson at Confab," *Rafu Shimpo* (English section), February 7, 1942.

33. Daniels, *The Decision to Relocate the Japanese Americans*, 37. The Associated Farmers, a farmers' organization with which Japanese farmers cooperated in order to break the Venice Celery strike in 1936, was also a proponent of the use of Japanese labor within California under the supervision of the government authorities. See Grodzins, *Americans Betrayed*, 32–34.

34. Roscoe E. Bell, secretary of the California Agricultural (Land Use) Planning Committee of the USDA Bureau of Agricultural Economics, to chairmen of County Farm Labor Subcommittees, February 2, 1942, Carton 2, Ralston Papers.

35. Ibid.; Roscoe E. Bell to the California USDA War Board, February 11, 1942, Carton 2, Ralston Papers. Governor Olson was aware that anti-Japanese sentiment was strong, particularly in Imperial County. In February 1942, R. W. Ware and Elmer W. Heald, sheriff and district attorney of Imperial County, sent a telegram to Olson to tell him that sending the evacuated Japanese to Imperial Valley would complicate defense and could cause a conflict with the local Filipino population, and that Mexican officials of Baja California were also concerned about the relocation of the Japanese to the neighboring Imperial Valley. See "Protest against Sending Jap Evacuees to Valley Answered," *Los Angeles Times*, February 14, 1942.

36. Daniels, *The Decision to Relocate the Japanese Americans*, 36–39; tenBroek, et al, *Prejudice, War, and the Constitution*, 86, 205.

37. Grodzins, *Americans Betrayed*, 67–76.

38. Tolan Committee, 11679, 11685, 11691. At the Tolan Committee, W. S. Rosecrans, agricultural coordinator of the Los Angeles County Defense Council and former president of the Los Angeles Chamber of Commerce, testified that the lands of Los Angeles County "are not purely agricultural lands" and "are, in themselves, in a transition period" for industrial purposes or settlement.

39. Walter Lippmann, "The Fifth Column on the Coast," *Washington Post*, February 12, 1942; *Personal Justice Denied*, 80; Robinson, *By Order of the President*, 123; Daniels, *The Decision to Relocate the Japanese Americans*, 49; "Kanken ni furachi na soburi wo suru minohodo wo shiranu chikan ari" [There are some rogues who behave rudely to the authorities], *Rafu Shimpo*, February 24, 1942.

40. For the American Legion, see tenBroek, et al, *Prejudice, War, and the Constitution*, 43–46; Grodzins, *Americans Betrayed*, 38–43.

41. Olson, "National Defense."

42. Tolan Committee, 11629–11642; Olson, "National Defense"; "Tsurare gun demo nihonjin okotowari" [Japanese rejected in Tulare County, too], *Rafu Shimpo*, February 22, 1942. The aggression of the Japanese military in Asia in the initial period of the war strengthened war hysteria in the United States. See, for example, *Personal Justice Denied*, 28. As for the Tolan Committee and debates on Japanese farms during the war, see also Connie Y. Chiang, *Nature Behind Barbed Wire: An Environmental History of the Japanese American Incarceration* (New York: Oxford University Press, 2018), 12–39. On March 10,

1942, in San Francisco, representatives of JACL chapters held a meeting to discuss their position regarding mass evacuation; they adopted a resolution that they would willingly cooperate with mass evacuation to prove their loyalty to the United States. See "Ikanaru gisei mo amanjite shinoban" [We will endure any sacrifice], *Rafu Shimpo*, March 11, 1942.

43. Tolan Committee, 11629–11642.

44. "Oruson Kashū chiji, ontō naru shoken" [Moderate opinion of Governor Olson], *Kashu Mainichi*, March 7, 1942. Olson said, "It is our baby, all of us—the United States of America. It seems to me when the Federal Government decides as to the most feasible places to go, and the Federal Government pays for that, that that is the program we all ought to follow and those who stand in the way ought to get out of it." See Tolan Committee, 11642. The *Rafu Shimpo* translated the "baby" part as "ethnic Japanese are children of the United States." See "Kain iinkai ni okeru chiji, shichō no shōgen" [Testimonies of the governor and the mayor at the Lower House Committee], *Rafu Shimpo*, March 7, 1942.

45. Grodzins, *Americans Betrayed*, 100–102; Page Smith, *Democracy on Trial: The Japanese American Evacuation and Relocation in World War II* (New York: Simon & Schuster, 1995), 119–120; "Rinkorun yo ni araba kanarazuya yokuryū sen, Bōron shichō" [If Lincoln were alive, he would have interned them, says Mayor Bowron], *Rafu Shimpo*, February 13, 1942; "Tāminaru tō kyojūsha, sanjūnichi inai tachinoki meirei ka" [Residents of Terminal Island, evacuation to be ordered within thirty days?], *Rafu Shimpo*, February 13, 1942.

46. Tolan Committee, 11642–11652. Bowron had come to consider that the civil and human rights of the ethnic Japanese population should be sacrificed for the greater good of the non-Japanese majority in Los Angeles. In February 1942, Bowron wrote in his letter to Congressman John Costello, "I would hate to see the three million people in the Los Angeles metropolitan area greatly inconvenienced, business activity slowed up, traffic congested, and the people given unnecessary cause for fear, merely because of the presence here of 40,000 Japanese, only a limited portion of whom might be expected to do something dangerous." See Grodzins, *Americans Betrayed*, 104–105.

47. "Kain iinkai ni okeru chiji, shichō no shōgen," *Rafu Shimpo*, March 7, 1942; Togo Tanaka, "An Open Letter," *Rafu Shimpo* (English section), March 8, 1942.

48. Tolan Committee, 11629–11642.

49. "Army Will Move 5000 Japs by End of Week," *Los Angeles Times*, April 1, 1942; *Personal Justice Denied*, 112; "Tomato Harvest Action Pledged; Palos Verdes, Facing Loss of Crop, Will Place Matter before Council," *Los Angeles Times*, September 22, 1942.

50. Deborah Cohen, *Braceros: Migrant Citizens and Transnational Subjects in the Postwar United States and Mexico* (Chapel Hill: University of North Carolina Press, 2011), 21–28.

51. Culbert Olson, "Mexican Labor," July 2, 1942, Carton 5, Olson Papers. At the time of my research in 2016, some parts of Olson's radio speech script were illegible because of the way in which the documents were bound.

52. Ibid. Interestingly, Olson's radio speech was reported by the *Los Angeles Times* but not broadcast in Los Angeles, possibly because it clearly conflicted with the uncompromising policy of Mayor Bowron against the ethnic Japanese population. See "Olson Threatens to Ask Jap Use," *Los Angeles Times*, July 3, 1942.

53. "DeWitt Vetoes Using Japs in Harvest Crisis," *Los Angeles Times*, July 9, 1942; Ed Ainsworth, "As You Might Say—," *Los Angeles Times*, July 10, 1942; "Project Agricultural Program Must Succeed," *Tulean Dispatch Daily*, June 12, 1943, online at https://ddr.densho.org/, accessed December 31, 2021.

54. Culbert Olson to President Franklin D. Roosevelt, August 19, 1942; Claude R. Wickard, secretary of agriculture, to Culbert Olson, August 27, 1942, Folder Migratory-120-A Thru-G, Box 7, RG96, Records of the Farmers Home Administration, 1918–1975, National Archives at College Park, College Park, Maryland.

55. Neil Foley, *Mexicans in the Making of America* (Cambridge, MA: Harvard University Press, 2014), 97, 101

56. Selfa A. Chew, *Uprooting Community: Japanese Mexicans, World War II, and the U.S.-Mexico Borderlands* (Tucson: University of Arizona Press, 2015), 53–55.

57. Ibid., 47: Greg Robinson, *A Tragedy of Democracy: Japanese Confinement in North America* (New York: Columbia University Press, 2009), 145–148.

58. In 1940, 4,942 Japanese lived in Mexico according to the Japanese government's survey. See Investigation Bureau, survey of Japanese overseas residents, 1940, Cho_17, Investigation Bureau, records of investigation, Diplomatic Archives of the Ministry of Foreign Affairs of Japan, Minato-ku, Tokyo, Japan.

59. Nichi-Boku Kōryūshi Henshū Iinkai [Editorial committee of history of Japan-Mexico interaction], ed., *Nichi-boku kōryūshi* [History of Japan-Mexico interaction] (Tokyo: PMC Shuppan, 1990) (hereafter cited as *Nichi-boku kōryūshi*), 575–576.

60. Robinson, *A Tragedy of Democracy*, 145–148.

61. *Nichi-boku kōryūshi*, 563–566.

62. "Medida contra los niponés en México," *La Opinión*, January 2, 1942.

63. "Declara El General Cárdenas, No hay bases de Japón en la Baja California"; "La Política Demográfica de México"; "Compre UD. bonos de la defensa," *La Opinión*, January 2, 1942.

CHAPTER 6. ENDURING INTERETHNIC TRUST IN RANCHO SAN PEDRO

1. Sucheng Chan, *Asian Americans: An Interpretive History* (Boston: Twayne Publishers, 1991), 126; Allison Varzally, *Making a Non-White America: Californians Coloring Outside Ethnic Lines, 1925–1955* (Berkeley: University of California Press, 2008), 122; Laurence I. Hewes Jr. to district officers and field agents of the Wartime Farm Adjustment Program of the Farm Security Administration, March 15, 1942, Carton 2, Ralston Papers, Bancroft Library, University of California, Berkeley (hereafter cited as Ralston Papers). For the FSA wartime operation regarding Japanese farms, see Connie Y. Chiang, *Nature Behind Barbed Wire: An Environmental History of the Japanese American Incarceration* (New York: Oxford University Press, 2018), 29–39.

2. Map of Rancho San Pedro, Map case 3, Folder 1, Drawer 2, Gerth Archives and Special Collections, University Library, California State University, Dominguez Hills, Carson, California; Masakazu Iwata, *Planted in Good Soil: A History of the Issei in United States Agriculture*, 2 vols. (New York: Peter Lang Publishers, 1992), 1:397–400; Minamikashū Nihonjin Shichijūnenshi Kankō Iinkai [Publishing committee of Japanese in Southern

California], ed., *Minamikashū nihonjin shichijūnenshi* [Japanese in Southern California: A history of 70 years] (Los Angeles: Nanka Nikkeijin Shōgyō Kaigisho, 1960), 79–88.

3. Eileen R. N. Sugiyama (Yoshimura), "Inventory and Analysis of Materials on the Arrival and Settlement of Japanese and Japanese Americans in the Dominguez Family Papers," revised draft #5, July 1, 1981, 14. Eileen Reiko Yoshimura has conducted a detailed research of the documents on ethnic Japanese residents, using the records of the real estate companies in Rancho San Pedro, as an undergraduate student at California State University, Dominguez Hills. Her research is significant in helping us to understand the daily lives and war experience of the Japanese population in Rancho San Pedro.

4. Judson Grenier, *Reminiscences of the Dominguez Rancho and the Carson Family: An Oral History by John Victor Carson*, second edition (Carson: California State University, Dominguez Hills, 1981), introduction.

5. Dominguez Estate Company, list of Japanese tenants, February 10, 1942, Box 194; Carson Estate Company, land lease contracts, Box 117 and 118, Rancho San Pedro Collection, Gerth Archives and Special Collections, University Library, California State University, Dominguez Hills, Carson, California (hereafter cited as Rancho San Pedro Collection); Del Amo Estate Company, list of Japanese tenants, February 10, 1942, Box 62, Del Amo Estate Company Collection, Gerth Archives and Special Collections, University Library, California State University, Dominguez Hills, Carson, California (hereafter cited as Del Amo Estate Company Collection).

6. Carson Estate Company, lease contract of Chieno Amate, February 25, 1941; To A. G. Hemming, memoranda, April 10 and 18, 1941; lease contract of Shigeru Amate, January 1, 1941; California State Board of Health, Bureau of Vital Statistics, birth certificate of Shigeru Amate, March 16, 1920, Box 117, Rancho San Pedro Collection. The issue dates of these documents indicate that the Carson Estate Company made some contracts retrospectively and let the Amate family use the land before they confirmed Shigeru's birth certificate.

7. Carson Estate Company, lease contract of Shigeru Amate, January 1, 1942; memorandum, February 13, 1942, Box 117, Rancho San Pedro Collection; Dominguez Estate Company, lease contract of Yoshio Amemiya, January 14, 1942, Box 192, Rancho San Pedro Collection.

8. Hewes, March 15, 1942, Carton 2, Ralston Papers. For his position, see US Congress, House of Representatives, Select Committee Investigating National Defense Migration, *National Defense Migration: Hearings before the Select Committee Investigating National Defense Migration*, 77th Cong., 2nd session, March 6, 7, and 12, 1942 (hereafter cited as Tolan Committee), 11653.

9. Tolan Committee, 11653–11660.

10. Grenier, *Reminiscences of the Dominguez Rancho and the Carson Family*, credits, introduction, 2, 43–44. Carson managed the land owned by the Dominguez Estate Company and Carson Estate Company, while the Del Amo family handled the farm operation of the Del Amo Estate Company.

11. Carson Estate Company, map of Horita's farm, ca. 1939; lease contract of Tōru Horita, July 1, 1941; lease contract of K. B. Jones and J. D. Jones, March 27, 1942; US Department of Agriculture, Farm Security Administration to the Carson Estate Company, June 25, 1942; US Department of Agriculture, Farm Security Administration, severance agreement, July 6, 1942, Box 117, Rancho San Pedro Collection.

12. Grenier, *Reminiscences of the Dominguez Rancho and the Carson Family*, 44–45.

13. Ibid., 45.

14. Farm Security Administration to Carson Estate Company, May 20, 1942; Carson Estate Company, memorandum, May 21, 1942; memorandum, June 24, 1942, Box 117, Rancho San Pedro Collection.

15. According to the Los Angeles City Directory of 1939, a person named William J. Commack was an engineer at the Los Angeles Fire Department and lived in Van Nuys. Los Angeles Directory Co., *Los Angeles City Directory* 1939 (Los Angeles, 1939), 383, online at http://rescarta.lapl.org/ResCarta-Web/jsp/RcWebBrowse.jsp, accessed July 20, 2017.

16. Chiang, *Nature Behind Barbed Wire*, 34.

17. Carson Estate Company, lease contract of Haruko Kurashige, May 21, 1941; lease contract of John J. Wong, May 19, 1942; memorandum, June 24, 1942, Box 118, Rancho San Pedro Collection; Varzally, *Making a Non-White America*, 122.

18. Grenier, *Reminiscences of the Dominguez Rancho and the Carson Family*, 34, 45.

19. US Census Bureau, *Sixteenth Census of the United States: 1940, Population* (Washington, DC, 1943), Table 24, "Foreign-Born White, by Country of Birth, by Counties, and for Cities of 10,000 to 100,000," 564; Zaragoza Vargas, *Labor Rights Are Civil Rights: Mexican American Workers in Twentieth-Century America* (Princeton, NJ: Princeton University Press, 2005), 224.

20. Vargas, *Labor Rights Are Civil Rights*, 224, 233–234. For the wartime experiences of Mexican American female workers, see Elizabeth R. Escobedo, *From Coveralls to Zoot Suits: The Lives of Mexican American Women on the World War II Home Front* (Chapel Hill: University of North Carolina Press, 2013), 99–100.

21. For the Mexican American experience in the Sleepy Lagoon murder case during World War II, see Mauricio Mazon, *The Zoot-Suit Riots: The Psychology of Symbolic Annihilation* (Austin: University of Texas Press, 1984;1995), 6, 22–24.

22. Ralph Lazo, a Mexican-Irish teen, registered as a Japanese and went to internment along with his Japanese American friends. Guy Gabaldon, another Mexican American who was raised by a Japanese family in Boyle Heights, later saved more than one thousand Japanese soldiers and civilians by persuading them to surrender in Saipan during the war. See Varzally, *Making a Non-White America*, 139; "Guy Gabaldon, 80; WWII Hero Captured 1,000 Japanese on Saipan," *Los Angeles Times*, September 6, 2006.

23. "Ichioka Tsutayo dokutoru shin iin kaigyō" [Dr. Tsutayo Ichioka opens her new clinic], *Rafu Shimpo*, January 30, 1942; "Nueva oficina de la Dra. Ichioka," *La Opinión*, February 3, 1942.

24. José Ruiz Velis, "El 'Pequeño Tokio' ha muerto," *La Opinión*, April 19, 1942. This article is cited and translated by Greg Robinson. See Greg Robinson, *After Camp: Portraits in Midcentury Japanese American Life and Politics* (Berkeley: University of California Press, 2012), 122.

25. Greg Robinson conducted a careful analysis of *La Opinión*'s coverage on Japanese Internment. See Robinson, *After Camp*, ch. 6.

26. "Una gran oportunidad," *La Opinión*, April 27, 1942.

27. Grenier, *Reminiscences of the Dominguez Rancho and the Carson Family*, 45.

28. Carson Estate Company, lease contract of Ichirō Haijima, July 1, 1940; lease contract of Vaughn Guzelain and William Beisel, June 12, 1942; lease contract of Angelo Ornelas (His last name was misspelled as Ornelos on the contract), November 1, 1943; Carson Estate Company, map, n.d.; State of California, Department of Public Health, Vital Statistics, birth certificate of Ichirō Haijima, August 5, 1916; Southern California Floral Industry, transfer of lease, January 8, 1943, Box 117, Rancho San Pedro Collection; Los Angeles Directory Co., *Los Angeles City Directory 1942* (Los Angeles, 1942), 2765.

29. Carson Estate Company, lease contract of Haruo Imaizumi, July 1, 1940, Box 118, Rancho San Pedro Collection; Carson Estate Company, lease contract of Manuel Torres, December 15, 1942; lease contract of Hanko Franco, May 1, 1942, Box 118, Rancho San Pedro Collection.

30. Dominguez Estate Company, list of Japanese tenants, February 10, 1942; list of non-Japanese tenants, 1943, Box 194, Rancho San Pedro Collection; Map of Rancho San Pedro, Map Case 3, Folder 1, Drawer 2, Special Collections, Gerth Archives and Special Collections, University Library, California State University, Dominguez Hills, Carson, California. According to the US Census of 1940, non-Mexican Latin Americans and Spaniards in Los Angeles County numbered only 4,498, while Mexicans numbered 59,260 as foreign-born whites. See US Census Bureau, *Sixteenth Census of the United States: 1940, Population* (Washington, DC, 1943), Table 24, "Foreign-Born White, by Country of Birth, by Counties, and for Cities of 10,000 to 100,000," 564.

31. Dominguez Real Estate Company to Joe Uribe, November 24, 1943, Box 194, Rancho San Pedro Collection. Similar letters from the company to new tenants are preserved in the Rancho San Pedro Collection.

32. Eiichiro Azuma, *Between Two Empires: Race, History, and Transnationalism in Japanese America* (New York: Oxford University Press, 2005), 207. On the other hand, in March 1942, many growers in Stockton sent letters to the California Agricultural War Board and expressed their willingness to keep ethnic Japanese farmworkers on their lands until the middle of July. See Chiang, *Nature Behind Barbed Wire*, 21.

33. For example, see Carson Estate Company, lease contract of Momoo Mochizuki, July 1, 1940 (canceled on April 6, 1942), and of Ichirō Hayima (Haijima), July 1, 1940 (canceled in May 1942), Box 117, Rancho San Pedro Collection.

34. M. Miyakawa to J. V. Carson, May 11, 1942, Box 194, Rancho San Pedro Collection.

35. Misao Miyakawa to J. V. Carson, September 19, 1942, Box 194, Rancho San Pedro Collection; California State Board of Health, Bureau of Vital Statistics, birth certificate of Misao Miyakawa, March 31, 1924, Box 93, Del Amo Estate Company Collection.

36. J. V. Carson, affidavit about Makoto Miyakawa, September 24, 1942, Box 194, Rancho San Pedro Collection.

37. Misao Miyakawa to J. V. Carson, September 27, 1942, Box 194, Rancho San Pedro Collection.

38. Misao Miyakawa to the Del Amo Estate Company, September 19, 1942; Eugenio Cabrero, affidavit about Makoto Miyakawa, September 30, 1942; Misao Miyakawa to Eugenio Cabrero, October 2, 1942, Box 93, Del Amo Estate Company Collection.

39. D. S. Myer, director of the War Relocation Authority, to J. V. Carson, May 7, 1943; Carson to the War Relocation Authority, May 14, 1943, Box 194, Rancho San Pedro Collection.

40. Grenier, *Reminiscences of the Dominguez Rancho and the Carson Family*, introduction, 36.

41. Henry Chiyozō Takeuchi to J. V. Carson, February 16, 1943; Henry Chiyozō Takeuchi, Bill of Sale, February 16, 1943, Box 194, Rancho San Pedro Collection. On the map, Rodriguez's name appears to be misspelled as "Rodrizueg."

42. Further research should be done to explore whether what happened in Rancho San Pedro during the war happened in other rural areas of Los Angeles County.

CONCLUSION

1. U.S. Census Bureau, *Seventeenth Census of the United States: 1950, Population* (Washington DC, 1952), Table 47, "Indians, Japanese, and Chinese, by Sex, for Selected Counties and Cities," 5-179.

2. Kevin Starr, *California: A History* (New York: Modern Library, 2007), 235-239.

3. Japanese agriculture in the Imperial Valley, which was one of prominent sites of Japanese agriculture before the Pacific War, declined after the war, since white and other nonwhite tenants replaced the Japanese during the war and continued to farm lands after the war. Minamikashū Nihonjin Shichijūnenshi Kankō Iinkai [Publishing committee of Japanese in Southern California], ed., *Minamikashū nihonjin shichijūnenshi* [Japanese in Southern California: A history of 70 years] (Los Angeles: Nanka Nikkeijin Shōgyō Kaigisho, 1960), 78-79, 100-101, 133-134; Leonard Broom and Ruth Riemer, *Removal and Return: The Socio-Economic Effects of the War on Japanese Americans* (Berkeley: University of California, Press, 1949), 74. Japanese nonfiction writer Yoshimi Ishikawa has written about his experience of working as a farmhand with Mexican workers in 1960s Southern California. See Yoshimi Ishikawa, *Sutoroberī rōdo*, vol. 1 and 2 (Tokyo: Hayakawa Shobō, 1988).

4. Matt Garcia, *From the Jaws of Victory: The Triumph and Tragedy of Cesar Chavez and the Farm Worker Movement* (Berkeley: University of California Press, 2012), 163-174; "Harry Kubo 84; Farm Leader Was Defender of Private Property Rights," *Los Angeles Times*, December 16, 2006.

BIBLIOGRAPHY

PRIMARY SOURCES

Manuscript Materials

The United States

Bancroft Library, University of California, Berkeley

    Culbert L. Olson Papers
    W. R. Ralston Papers

Gerth Archives and Special Collections, University Library, California State University, Dominguez Hills, Carson

    Del Amo Estate Company Collection
    Ishibashi Collection
    Rancho San Pedro Collection

Huntington Library, San Marino

    Arthur Ito Papers
    Rare Books

Japanese American National Museum, Los Angeles

    Katsuma Mukaeda Papers
    Murai Family Papers

La Historia Society Museum, El Monte

Special Collections and Archives, University of California, Irvine

Miscellaneous Newspaper Collection, 1704–1970

Special Collections, University of California, Los Angeles

California State University, Fullerton Oral History Program, Japanese American Project Oral History Collection
George Pigeon Clements Papers
Japanese American Research Project (JARP), University of California, Los Angeles
Kumezo Hachimonji Papers
Noboru Murakami Papers
Pre-war Japanese Socio-cultural Organizations
Shiro Fujioka Papers

USC Digital Libraries, University of Southern California, Los Angeles

California Historical Society Collection, 1860–1960

US National Archives at College Park, College Park, MD

RG96, Records of the Farmers Home Administration, 1918–1975

US National Archives at Riverside, Riverside, CA

RG25, Records of the National Labor Relations Board

Japan

Diplomatic Archives of the Ministry of Foreign Affairs of Japan, Tokyo (DAMFAJ)

Bokukoku "Ensenada" hōmen ni okeru honpōjin no hatten jōkyō (Tsū3_97)
Bokukoku nairan kankei teikoku shinmin no songai baishō ikken (5-3-2-0-154)
Dai 50 gikai setsumei sankō shiryō (GiTS-6)
Dai 52 gikai setsumei sankō shiryō (GiTS-11)
Dai 67 kai teikoku gikai setsumei sankō shiryō jō-kan (GiAM-3)
Gaikoku ni okeru rōdō sōgi kankei zakken (higyō taigyō wo fukumu)/Beikoku no bu (I-4-4-0-2_2)
Honshō narabini zaigai kōkan'in shutchō kankei zakken (M-2-2-0-1_3_2)
Investigation Bureau, records of investigation (Cho_17)
Kakkoku chūzai teikoku ryōji ninmen kankei zakken (M-2-1-0-10_33)
Kakkoku ni okeru nōgyō kankei zakken (B-3-5-2-224)
Zaigai teikoku kōkan kankei zakken/Setchi kankei (M-1-3-0-1_1)
Zaigai teikoku kōkan kankei zakken (M-1-3-0-1_3)
Zaigai teikoku kōkan setchi zakken (6-1-2-72)

Modern Japanese Political History Materials Room, National Diet Library, Tokyo

Central Japanese Association of Southern California, meeting minutes (Original documents are preserved in the JARP, UCLA)

Karl Yoneda Papers (Original documents are preserved in the JARP, UCLA)

National Archives of Japan, Tokyo (NAJ)

Sūmitsuin kaigi hikki (Sū-D00562100)

Reference Room, Japanese Overseas Migration Museum, Yokohama

Shūgakukan Research Library, Ritsumeikan University, Kyoto

Mexico

Genaro Estrada Historical Archive (Archivo Histórico Genaro Estrada), Mexico City (AHGE)

Collection Departamento Consular IV
Collection Gaveta 8
Collection Gaveta 21
Collection Gaveta 30

Historical Archive of the State of Baja California (Archivo Histórico del Estado de Baja California), Mexicali (AHEBC)

Collection Gobierno del Estado

Mexicali Central Library (Biblioteca Central Mexicali), Universidad Autónoma de Baja California, Mexicali

Periódico Oficial (1924)

Mexico-Japan Association (Asociación México-Japonesa), Mexico City

National Archives of Mexico (Archivo General de la Nación), Mexico City (AGN)

Collection Dirección General de Gobierno

Newspapers and Periodicals

Choya Shimbun. 1891 (Tokyo)
El Excélsior. 1933 (Mexico City)
El Faro. 1933 (Ensenada)
El Hispano-Americano. 1933 (Tijuana)
Kashu Mainichi. 1933, 1936, 1941, 1942 (Los Angeles)
La Opinión. 1924, 1926, 1927, 1928, 1929, 1931, 1933, 1936, 1937, 1942 (Los Angeles)

Los Angeles Times. 1933, 1936, 1942, 1992, 2006 (Los Angeles)
Mercurio. 1933 (Mexicali)
Osaka Mainichi Shimbun. 1924 (Osaka)
Rafu Shimpo. 1924, 1926, 1929, 1931, 1933, 1936, 1941, 1942, 2015 (Los Angeles)
Tokyo Asahi Shimbun. 1922, 1924 (Tokyo)
Tulean Dispatch Daily. 1943 (Tule Lake)
Yomiuri Shimbun. 1924 (Tokyo)

Government Publications

Governor C. C. Young's Mexican Fact-Finding Committee. *Mexicans in California.* Sacramento: California State Printing Office, 1930.
US Census Office. *Twelfth Census of the United States: 1900. Population.* Washington, DC: GPO, 1901.
US Census Bureau. *Thirteenth Census of the United States: 1910, Population.* Washington, DC: GPO, 1913.
———. *Fourteenth Census of the United States: 1920, Population.* Washington, DC: GPO, 1923.
———. *Fifteenth Census of the United States: 1930, Population.* Washington, DC: GPO, 1933.
———. *Sixteenth Census of the United States: 1940, Population.* Washington, DC: GPO, 1943.
———. *Seventeenth Census of the United States: 1950, Population.* Washington, DC: GPO, 1952.
US Congress. House of Representatives. Select Committee Investigating National Defense Migration. *Hearings on National Defense Migration.* 77th Cong., 2nd sess., Washington, DC: GPO, 1942.
US Department of Agriculture. *Food for Freedom: Information Handbook 1943.* Washington, DC: GPO, 1942.
US Department of Labor, Bureau of Labor Statistics. *Labor Unionism in American Agriculture.* By Stuart Jamieson. Bulletin No. 836. Washington, DC: GPO, 1945.

Theses and Unpublished Papers

Pagdilao Coloma, Casiano. "A Study of the Filipino Repatriation Movement." Master's thesis, University of Southern California, 1939.
Sugiyama, Eileen R. N. "Inventory and Analysis of Materials on the Arrival and Settlement of Japanese and Japanese Americans in the Dominguez Family Papers," revised draft #5. Research paper, History Department, California State University, Dominguez Hills, 1981.

Published Books and Articles

Akana, Seiichi. *Tsūzoku Beikoku imin hō kōwa.* Tokyo: Hakubundō, 1929.
Bogardus, Emory S. "The Mexican Immigrant and Segregation." *American Journal of Sociology* 36, no. 1 (1930): 74–80.
Fujioka, Shirō. *Ayumi no ato: Hokubei tairiku nihonjin kaitaku monogatari.* Los Angeles: Ayumi no Ato Kankō Kōenkai, 1957.

Fukuzawa, Yukichi. *Sekai kuni zukushi*. Vol. 6. Tokyo: Keiō Gijuku Zōhan, 1869.
Gamio, Manuel. *El inmigrante mexicano: La historia de su vida, entrevistas completas, 1926–1927*. Compiled by Devra Weber, Roberto Melville, and Juan Vicente Palerm. Mexico City: Miguel Ángel Porrúa, 2002.
———. *The Mexican Immigrant: His Life-Story*. New York: Arno Press, 1969.
Higashi, Kōji. *Beiboku jūō*. Tokyo: Seikyōsha, 1920.
Kobayashi, Naotarō, and Yoshimasa Itō. *Mekishiko shokumin no shiori*. Los Angeles: Rafu Bokukoku Kenkyū Kai, 1925.
Los Angeles Directory Co. *Los Angeles City Directory* 1939. Los Angeles: Los Angeles Directory Co. Publishers, 1939.
Minamikashū Nihonjin Shichijūnenshi Kankō Iinkai, ed. *Minamikashū nihonjin shichijūnenshi*. Los Angeles: Nanka Nikkeijin Shōgyō Kaigisho, 1960.
Mukaeda, Katsuma, and Masatoshi Nakamura. *Zaibei no higojin*. Los Angeles: Nanka Kumamoto Kaigai Kyōkai, 1931.
Murai, Kō. *Zaibei nihonjin sangyō sōran*. Los Angeles: Beikoku Sangyō Nippōsha, 1940.
Nichi-Boku Kōryūshi Henshū Iinkai, ed. *Nichi-boku kōryūshi*. Tokyo: PMC Shuppan, 1990.
Nihon Mekishiko Ijūshi Hensan Iinkai, ed. *Nihon Mekishiko ijūshi*. N.p: Nihon Mekishiko Ijūshi Hensan Iinkai, 1971.
Ochi, Dōjun, ed. *Minamikashū nihonjinshi kō-hen*. Los Angeles: Nanka Nikkeijin Shōgyō Kaigisho, 1957.
Ōtsuki, Fumihiko. *Daigenkai*. Tokyo: Fuzanbō, 1934.
Spaulding, Charles B. "The Mexican Strike at El Monte, California." *Sociology and Social Research* 18 (1934): 571–580.
Taki, Yasutarō. *Mekishiko kokujō taikan: Shokumin shichijūnenshi*. Mexico City: Mehiko Shimpōsha, 1968.
Tsurumi, Sakio. "Imin to bōeki." In *Kaigai ijū*, edited by Nihon Imin Kyōkai, 65–75. Tokyo: Nihon Imin Kyōkai, 1923.
Yamada, Satarō. *Gojin no kaitaku subeki kaigai yūbō no fugen*. Tokyo: Keibunsha, 1925.

SECONDARY SOURCES

Abe, Yasuhisa. "1920 nendai no Tōkyō fu ni okeru chūgokujin rōdōsha no shūgyō kōzō to kyojū bunka." *Jinbun chiri* 51, no. 1 (1999): 40–41.
Almaguer, Tomás. *Racial Fault Lines: The Historical Origins of White Supremacy in California*. 1994. Reprint, Berkeley: University of California Press, 2009.
Azuma, Eiichiro. *Between Two Empires: Race, History, and Transnationalism in Japanese America*. New York: Oxford University Press, 2005.
———. "Community Formation across the National Border: The Japanese of the U.S.-Mexican Californias." *Review: Literature and Arts of the Americas* 39, no.1 (2006): 30–44.
———. "Japanese Immigrant Settler Colonialism in the U.S.-Mexican Borderlands and the U.S. Racial-Imperialist Politics of the Hemispheric 'Yellow Peril.'" *Pacific Historical Review* 83, no. 2 (May 2014): 255–276.

Balderrama, Francisco E. *In Defense of La Raza: The Los Angeles Mexican Consulate and the Mexican Community, 1929 to 1936.* Tucson: University of Arizona Press, 1982.

Banzai, Tomohide. "Kindai Nihon no jinshu sutereo taipu no keisei katei to mainoriti ni taisuru gendaiteki henken no kenkyū." Research report of project funded by Grant-in-Aid for Scientific Research (C) (2) of Japan Society for the Promotion of Science (March 2002).

Bayly, C. A., Sven Beckert, Matthew Connelly, Isabel Hofmeyr, Wendy Kozol, and Patricia Seed. "AHR Conversation: On Transnational History." *American Historical Review* 111, no. 5 (December 2006): 1441–1464.

Bonacich, Edna. "A Theory of Middleman Minorities." *American Sociological Review* 38, no. 5 (October 1973): 583–594.

Bonacich, Edna, and John Modell. *Economic Basis for Ethnic Solidarity: Small Business in the Japanese American Community.* Berkeley: University of California Press, 1980.

Broom, Leonard, and Ruth Riemer. *Removal and Return: The Socio-Economic Effects of the War on Japanese Americans.* Berkeley: University of California, Press, 1949.

Camarillo, Albert. *Chicanos in California: A History of Mexican Americans in California.* 1984. Reprint, Sparks, NV: Materials for Today's Learning, 1990.

Castillo-Muñoz, Verónica. *The Other California: Land, Identity, and Politics on the Mexican Borderlands.* Oakland: University of California Press, 2017.

Chambers, Clarke A. *California Farm Organizations: A Historical Study of the Grange, the Farm Bureau, and the Associated Farmers, 1929–1941.* Berkeley: University of California Press, 1952.

Chan, Sucheng. *Asian Americans: An Interpretive History.* Boston: Twayne Publishers, 1991.

Chang, Jason Oliver. *Chino: Anti-Chinese Racism in Mexico, 1880–1940.* Urbana: University of Illinois Press, 2017.

Chang, Kornel S. *Pacific Connections: The Making of the U.S.-Canadian Borderlands.* Berkeley: University of California Press, 2012.

Chao Romero, Robert. *The Chinese in Mexico, 1882–1940.* Tucson: University of Arizona Press, 2010.

Chaves-Garcia, Miroslava. *States of Delinquency: Race and Science in the Making of California's Juvenile Justice System.* Berkeley: University of California Press, 2012.

Chew, Selfa A. *Uprooting Community: Japanese Mexicans, World War II, and the U.S.-Mexico Borderlands.* Tucson: University of Arizona Press, 2015.

Chiang, Connie Y. *Nature Behind Barbed Wire: An Environmental History of the Japanese American Incarceration.* New York: Oxford University Press, 2018.

Cohen, Deborah. *Braceros: Migrant Citizens and Transnational Subjects in the Postwar United States and Mexico.* Chapel Hill: University of North Carolina Press, 2011.

Commission on Wartime Relocation and Internment of Civilians. *Personal Justice Denied.* 1982. Reprint, Washington, DC: Civil Liberties Education Fund, 1997.

Daniel, Cletus E. *Bitter Harvest: A History of California Farmworkers, 1870–1941.* Berkeley: University of California Press, 1981.

Daniels, Roger. *The Decision to Relocate the Japanese Americans.* Philadelphia: Lippincott, 1975.

———. *The Politics of Prejudice: The Anti-Japanese Movement in California*. New York: Atheneum, 1968.

Deverell, William. *Railroad Crossing: Californians and the Railroad, 1850–1910*. Berkeley: University of California Press, 1996.

———. *Whitewashed Adobe: The Rise of Los Angeles and the Remaking of Its Mexican Past*. Berkeley: University of California Press, 2004.

Duara, Prasenjit. *Sovereignty and Authenticity: Manchukuo and the East Asian Modern*. Lanham, MD: Rowman & Littlefield Publishers, 2003.

Escobedo, Elizabeth R. *From Coveralls to Zoot Suits: The Lives of Mexican American Women on the World War II Home Front*. Chapel Hill: University of North Carolina Press, 2013.

Fishkin, Shelley Fisher. "Crossroads of Cultures: The Transnational Turn in American Studies: Presidential Address to the American Studies Association, November 12, 2004." *American Quarterly* 57, no. 1 (March 2005): 17–57.

Flamming, Douglass. *Bound for Freedom: Black Los Angeles in Jim Crow America*. Berkeley: University of California Press, 2005.

Fogelson, Robert M. *The Fragmented Metropolis: Los Angeles, 1850–1930*. Cambridge, MA: Harvard University Press, 1967.

Fojas, Camilla, and Rudy P. Guevarra Jr., eds. *Transnational Crossroads: Remapping the Americas and the Pacific*. Lincoln: University of Nebraska Press, 2012.

Foley, Neil. *Mexicans in the Making of America*. Cambridge, MA: Harvard University Press, 2014.

Foner, Eric. *Free Soil, Free Labor, Free Men: The Ideology of the Republican Party before the Civil War*. 1970. Reprint, New York: Oxford University Press, 1995.

Friday, Chris. *Organizing Asian American Labor: The Pacific Coast Canned-Salmon Industry, 1870–1942*. Philadelphia: Temple University Press, 1994.

García, Jerry. *Looking Like the Enemy: Japanese Mexicans, the Mexican State, and US Hegemony, 1897–1945*. Tucson: University of Arizona Press, 2014.

Garcia, Matt. *From the Jaws of Victory: The Triumph and Tragedy of Cesar Chavez and the Farm Worker Movement*. Berkeley: University of California Press, 2012.

———. *A World of Its Own: Race, Labor, and Citrus in the Making of Greater Los Angeles, 1900–1970*. Chapel Hill: University of North Carolina Pres, 2001.

Gerstle, Gary. *American Crucible: Race and Nation in the Twentieth Century*. Princeton, NJ: Princeton University Press, 2001.

González, Gilbert G. *Labor and Community: Mexican Citrus Worker Villages in a Southern California County, 1900–1950*. Urbana: University of Illinois Press, 1994.

———. *Mexican Consuls and Labor Organizing: Imperial Politics in the American Southwest*. Austin: University of Texas Press, 1999.

———. "The 1933 Los Angeles County Farm Workers Strike." *New Political Science* 20, no. 4 (December 1998): 441–458.

Grenier, Judson. *Reminiscences of the Dominguez Rancho and the Carson Family: An Oral History by John Victor Carson*, second edition. Carson: California State University, Dominguez Hills, 1981.

Grodzins, Morton. *Americans Betrayed: Politics and the Japanese Evacuation*. 1949. Reprint, Chicago: University of Chicago Press, 1974.

Guarnizo, Luis Eduardo, and Michael Peter Smith, eds. *Transnationalism from Below*. Piscataway, NJ: Transaction Publishers, 1998.
Guevarra Jr., Rudy P. *Becoming Mexipino: Multiethnic Identities and Communities in San Diego*. New Brunswick, NJ: Rutgers University Press, 2012.
Gutiérrez, David G. *Walls and Mirrors: Mexican Americans, Mexican Immigrants, and the Politics of Ethnicity*. Berkeley: University of California Press, 1995.
Hattori, Ryuji, and Toshihiro Minohara. "Washington taisei 1920 nendai." In *Nichi-bei kankeishi*, edited by Makoto Iokibe, 83-109. Tokyo: Yūhikaku, 2008.
Hayashi, Brian Masaru. *Democratizing the Enemy: The Japanese American Internment*. Princeton: Princeton University Press, 2004.
Hayashi, Kaori. *A History of the Rafu Shimpo: Japanese and Their Newspaper in Los Angeles*. Osaka: Union Press, 1997.
———. *Nikkei Jānarisuto Monogatari*. Tokyo: Shinzansha Shuppan, 1997.
Hernández, Kelly L. *Migra!: A History of the U.S. Border Patrol*. Berkeley: University of California Press, 2010.
Higham, John. *Strangers in the Land: Patterns of American Nativism, 1860-1925*. 1955. Reprint, New Brunswick, NJ: Rutgers University Press, 1988.
Hoffman, Abraham. "The El Monte Berry Pickers' Strike, 1933: International Involvement in a Local Labor Dispute." *Journal of the West* 12, no. 1 (1973): 71-84.
———. *Unwanted Mexican Americans in the Great Depression: Repatriation Pressures 1929-1929*. Tucson: University of Arizona Press, 1974.
Hombeck, David. "Land Tenure and Rancho Expansion in Alta California, 1784-1846." *Journal of Historical Geography* 4, no. 4 (1978): 371-390.
Hsu, Madeline Y. *Dreaming of Gold, Dreaming of Home: Transnationalism and Migration between the United States and South China, 1882-1943*. Stanford, CA: Stanford University Press, 2000.
Ichioka, Yuji. *Before Internment: Essays in Prewar Japanese American History*. Edited by Gordon H. Chang and Eiichiro Azuma. Stanford, CA: Stanford University Press, 2006.
———. *The Issei: The World of the First Generation Japanese Immigrants, 1885-1924*. New York: Free Press, 1988.
———. "Japanese Associations and the Japanese Government: A Special Relationship, 1909-1926." *Pacific Historical Review* 46, no. 3 (August 1977): 409-437.
Iino, Masako. *Mō hitotsu no nichi-bei kankeishi: Hunsō to kyōchō no naka no nikkei Amerikajin*. Tokyo: Yūhikaku, 2000.
Imai, Ryoichi. "Manshu nōgyō imin ni okeru jinushika to sono ronri." In *Nihon teikoku wo meguru jinkō idō no kokusai shakai gaku*, edited by Sinzo Araragi, 217-254. Tokyo: Fuji Shuppan, 2008.
Isenberg, Andrew C., and Thomas Richards Jr. "Alternative Wests: Rethinking Manifest Destiny." *Pacific Historical Review* 86, no. 1 (2017): 4-17.
Ishikawa, Yoshimi. *Sutoroberī rōdo*, 2 vols. Tokyo: Hayakawa Shobō, 1988.
Iwata, Masakazu. *Planted in Good Soil: A History of the Issei in United States Agriculture*, 2 vols. New York: Peter Lang Publishers, 1992.
Izumi, Masumi. "Tetsujōmō naki kyōsei shūyōjo: Dai niji taisen ka no nikkei kanadajin." *Ritsumeikan gengo bunka kenkyū* 25, no. 1 (2013): 119-135.

Jansen, Marius B. *The Making of Modern Japan*. Cambridge, MA: Harvard University Press, 2000.
Jelinek, Lawrence J. *Harvest Empire: A History of California Agriculture*. 1979. Reprint, San Francisco: Boyd & Fraser, 1982.
Jung, Moon-kie. *Reworking Race: The Making of Hawaii's Interracial Labor Movement*. New York: Columbia University Press, 2006.
Kanellos, Nicolás, and Helvetia Martell. *Hispanic Periodicals in the United States, Origins to 1960: A Brief History and Comprehensive Bibliography*. Houston, TX: Arte Público Press, 2000.
Katada, Yoshiaki. "1930 Nendai ni itaru nichi-bei kankei no gaiyō: Beikoku taiheiyō gan shuyōkō toriatsukai kamotsu to bōeki kōro no kōsatsu wo tōshite." *NUCB Journal of Economics and Information Science* 58, no. 2 (March 2014): 87–111.
Kobayashi, Andrey, and Midge Ayukawa, "A Brief History of Japanese Canadians." In *Encyclopedia of Japanese History of the Descendants in the Americas: An Illustrated History of the Nikkei*, edited by Akemi Kikumura-Yano, 150–161. Walnut Creek: AltaMira Press, 2002.
Kodama, Masaaki. *Nihon iminshi kenkyū josetsu*. Hiroshima: Keisuisha, 1992.
Komai, Chris. "Revival: Rafu Shimpo," *Discover Nikkei*, March 7, 2014. Accessed July 3, 2017. http://www.discovernikkei.org/en/journal/2014/3/7/revival-rafu-shimpo.
Konno, Yuko. "Senzen no Kariforunia shū ni okeru hannichi gyogyō hōan wo meguru tatakai." *Imin kenkyū nempō* 22 (March 2016): 63–77.
Kramer, Paul. "Empire against Exclusion in Early 20th Century Trans-Pacific History." *Nanzan Review of American Studies* 33 (2011): 13–32.
Kumei, Teruko. *Gaikokujin wo meguru shakaishi: Kindai Amerika to nihonjin imin*. Tokyo: Yūzankaku, 1995.
Kunimoto, Iyo. "Kindai nichi-boku kankei no keisei to Beikoku 1888–1910." *Ratenamerika ronshū* 11–12 (1978): 83–102.
Kurashige, Lon. *Japanese American Celebration and Conflict: A History of Ethnic Identity and Festival in Los Angeles, 1934–1990*. Berkeley: University of California Press, 2002.
———. *Two Faces of Exclusion: The Untold History of Anti-Asian Racism in the United States*. Chapel Hill: University of North Carolina Press, 2016.
Kurashige, Lon, Madeline Y. Hsu, and Yujin Yaguchi. "Introduction: Conversations on Transpacific History." *Pacific Historical Review* 83, no.2 (May 2014): 183–188.
Kurashige, Scott. *The Shifting Grounds of Race: Black and Japanese Americans in the Making of Multiethnic Los Angeles*. Princeton, NJ: Princeton University Press, 2008.
Kuwabara, Masato, and Masao Gabe, eds. *Ezochi to Ryūkyū*. Tokyo: Yoshikawa Kōbunkan, 2001.
Larson, John Lauritz. *Internal Improvement: National Public Works and the Promise of Popular Government in the Early United States*. Chapel Hill: University of North Carolina Press, 2001.
Lastra, José Manuel Lastra. "El sindicalismo en México." *Anuario Mexicano de Historia del Derecho* 14 (2002): 37–85.
Lee, Erika. "Orientalisms in the Americas: A Hemispheric Approach to Asian American History." *Journal of Asian American Studies* 8, no.3 (October 2005): 235–256.

Lee, Erika, and Judy Yung, *Angel Island: Immigrant Gateway to America*. New York: Oxford University Press, 2010.
Leonard, Karen Isaksen. *Making Ethnic Choices: California's Punjabi Mexican Americans*. Philadelphia: Temple University Press, 1992.
Lewthwaite, Stephanie. "Race, Place, Ethnicity in the Progressive Era." In *A Companion to Los Angeles*, edited by William Deverell and Greg Hise, 40–55. Malden, MA: Wiley-Blackwell, 2010.
Licht, Walter. *Industrializing America: The Nineteenth Century*. Baltimore: Johns Hopkins University Press, 1995.
López, Ronald W. "The El Monte Berry Strike of 1933." *Aztlán* 1, no. 1 (April 1970): 101–114.
López Villafañe, Víctor. *La formación del sistema político mexicano*. Third edition. 1986. Reprint, Mexico City: Siglo Veintiuno Editores, 1993.
Lozano, Monica. Interview by Shirley Biagi. Washington Press Club Foundation. December 13, 1993. Accessed January 25, 2018. http://beta.wpcf.org/oralhistory/loz.html.
Makabe, Tomoko. "Ethnic Hegemony: The Japanese Brazilians in Agriculture, 1908–1968." *Ethnic and Racial Studies* 22, no. 4 (January 1999): 702–723.
Matsumoto, Yuko. "1936 nen Rosanjerusu serori sutoraiki to nikkei nōgyō komyunitī." *Shirin* 75, no. 4 (July 1992): 484–513.
Mayo, Morrow. "The Rape of Owens Valley." In *Los Angeles: Biography of A City*, edited by John Caughey and LaRee Caughey, 222–231. Berkeley: University of California Press, 1977.
Mazon, Mauricio. *The Zoot-Suit Riots: The Psychology of Symbolic Annihilation*. 1984. Reprint, Austin: University of Texas Press, 1995.
McBroome, Delores Nason. "Harvests of Gold: African American Boosterism, Agriculture, and Investment in Allensworth and Little Liberia." In *Seeking El Dorado: African Americans in California*, edited by Lawrence B. de Graaf, Kevin Mulroy, and Quintard Taylor, 149–180. Seattle: University of Washington Press, 2001.
McGirr, Lisa. *Suburban Warriors: The Origins of the New American Right*. Princeton, NJ: Princeton University Press, 2001.
McGovney, Dudley O. "The Anti-Japanese Land Laws of California and the Other States." *California Law Review* 35, no. 1 (March 1947): 7–60.
Mckiernan-González, John. *Fevered Measures: Public Health and Race at the Texas-Mexico Border, 1848–1942*. Durham: Duke University Press, 2012.
McWilliams, Carey. *Factories in the Field: The Story of Migratory Farm Labor in California*. 1939. Reprint, Berkeley: University of California Press, 2000.
——— . *Southern California: An Island on the Land*. 1946. Reprint, Salt Lake City: Peregrine Smith Books, 1973.
Minamikawa, Fuminori. "Vernacular Representations of Race and the Making of a Japanese Ethnoracial Community in Los Angeles." In *Trans-Pacific Japanese American Studies: Conversations on Race and Racializations*, edited by Yasuko Takezawa and Gary Y. Okihiro, 107–132. Honolulu: University of Hawai'i Press, 2016.
Minohara, Toshihiro. *Hainichi imin hō to nichi-bei kankei*. Tokyo: Iwanami Shoten, 2002.
——— . *Kariforunia shū hainichi undō to nichi-bei kankei: Imin mondai wo meguru nichi-bei masatsu*. Tokyo: Yūhikaku, 2006.

Modell, John. "Class or Ethnic Solidarity: The Japanese American Company Union." *Pacific Historical Review* 38, no. 2 (May 1969): 193–206.

Molina, Natalia. "Examining Chicana/o History through a Relational Lens." *Pacific Historical Review* 82, no. 4 (November 2013): 520–541.

———. *Fit to Be Citizens?: Public Health and Race in Los Angles, 1879–1939*. Berkeley: University of California Press, 2006.

———. *How Race Is Made in America: Immigration, Citizenship, and the Historical Power of Racial Scripts*. Berkeley: University of California Press, 2014.

Montoya, Benjamin C. "A Grave Offense of Significant Consequences: Mexican Perspectives on U.S. Immigration Restriction during the Late 1920s." *Pacific Historical Review* 87, no. 1 (Spring 2018): 333–355.

Mottier, Nicole. "Calculating Pragmatism: The High Politics of the Banco Ejidal in Twentieth-century Mexico." *The Americas* 74, no. 3 (July 2017): 331–363.

Morrison, Michael A. *Slavery and the American West: The Eclipse of Manifest Destiny and the Coming of the Civil War*. Chapel Hill: University of North Carolina Press, 1999.

Nadeau, Remi. "There It Is—Take It." In *Los Angeles: Biography of A City*, edited by John Caughey and LaRee Caughey, 231–235. Berkeley: University of California Press, 1977.

Ngai, Mae M. *Impossible Subjects: Illegal Aliens and the Making of Modern America*. Princeton, NJ: Princeton University Press, 2004.

Niiya, Brian, ed. *Encyclopedia of Japanese American History: An A-to-Z Reference from 1868 to the Present*, updated edition. New York: Checkmark Books, 2021.

O'Brien, David J., and Stephen S. Fugita. *The Japanese American Experience*. Bloomington: Indiana University Press, 1991.

Oguma, Eiji. *Tan'itsu minzoku shinwa no kigen: "Nihonjin" no jigazō no keifu*. Tokyo: Shinyōsha, 1995.

Okamura, Hyoue. "'Hāfu' wo meguru gensetsu: Kenkyūsha ya shiensha no chojutsu wo chūshin ni." In *Jinshu shinwa wo kaitai suru, vol.3, Hybridity: "Chi" no seijigaku wo koete*, edited by Kohei Kawashima and Yasuko Takezawa, 37–67. Tokyo: University of Tokyo Press, 2016.

Ota Mishima, María Elena. "Características sociales y económicas de los migrantes japoneses en México." In *Destino México: Un estudio de las migraciones asiáticas a México, siglo XIX y XX*, edited by María Elena Ota Mishima, 55–121. Mexico City: Colegio de México, Centro de Estudios de Asia y Africa, 1997.

———. *Siete migraciones japonesas en México, 1890–1978*. Mexico City: Colegio de México, Centro de Estudios de Asia y Africa, 1985.

Panunzio, Constantine. "Intermarriage in Los Angeles, 1924–1933." *American Journal of Sociology* 47, no. 5 (March 1942): 690–701.

Park, Hyun Ok. *Two Dreams in One Bed: Empire, Social Life, and the Origins of the North Korean Revolution in Manchuria*. Durham, NC: Duke University Press, 2005.

Peña Delgado, Grace. *Making the Chinese Mexican: Global Migration, Localism, and Exclusion in the U.S.-Mexico Borderlands*. Stanford, CA: Stanford University Press, 2012.

Perry, Louis B., and Richard S. Perry. *A History of the Los Angeles Labor Movement, 1911–1941*. Berkeley: University of California Press, 1963.

Pincetl, Stephanie S. *Transforming California: A Political History of Land Use and Development*. Baltimore: Johns Hopkins University, 1999.

Pozas, Ricardo. "El Maximato: El partido del hombre fuerte, 1929–1934." *Estudios de Historia Moderna y Contemporánea de México* 9 (1983): 251–279.

Pubols, Louise. "Born Global: From Pueblo to Statehood." In *A Companion to Los Angeles*, edited by William Deverell and Greg Hise, 20–39. Malden, MA: Wiley-Blackwell, 2010.

Redford, Laura. "The Intertwined History of Class and Race Segregation in Los Angeles." *Journal of Planning History* 16, no. 4 (November 2017): 305–322.

Robinson, Greg. *After Camp: Portraits in Midcentury Japanese American Life and Politics*. Berkeley: University of California Press, 2012.

———. *By Order of the President: FDR and the Internment of Japanese Americans*. Cambridge, MA: Harvard University Press, 2001.

———. "The Early History of Mixed-Race Japanese Americans." In *Hapa Japan: History*. Vol. 1. Edited by Duncan Ryuken Williams, 225–250. New York: Kaya Press, 2017.

———. *A Tragedy of Democracy: Japanese Confinement in North America*. New York: Columbia University Press, 2009.

Romo, Ricardo. *East Los Angeles: History of a Barrio*. Austin: University of Texas Press, 1983.

Rosales, F. Arturo. *¡Pobre Raza!: Violence, Justice, and Mobilization among México Lindo Immigrants, 1900–1936*. Austin: University of Texas Press, 1999.

Ruiz, Vicki. *From Out of the Shadows: Mexican Women in Twentieth-Century America*. 1998. Reprint, New York: Oxford University Press, 2008.

Sakaguchi, Mitsuhiro. *Nihonjin Amerika iminshi*. Tokyo: Fuji Shuppan, 2001.

———. "Shutsu imin no kioku." In *Imin kenkyū to tabunka kyōsei*, edited by Japanese Association for Migration Studies, 80–103. Tokyo: Ochanomizu Shobō, 2011.

Sánchez, George J. *Becoming Mexican American: Ethnicity, Culture, and Identity in Chicano Los Angeles, 1900–1945*. New York: Oxford University Press, 1993.

———. *Boyle Heights: How a Los Angeles Neighborhood Became the Future of American Democracy*. Oakland: University of California Press, 2021.

———. "Disposable People, Expendable Neighborhoods." In *A Companion to Los Angeles*, edited by William Deverell and Greg Hise, 129–146. Malden, MA: Wiley-Blackwell, 2010.

———. "'What's Good for Boyle Heights Is Good for the Jews': Creating Multiculturalism on the Eastside during the 1950s." *American Quarterly* 56, no. 3 (September 2004): 633–661.

Sánchez Ogás, Yolanda. *Asalto a las tierras 75 aniversario, 1937–2012*. Mexicali: AM Impresiones, 2012.

Schmidt Camacho, Alicia. *Migrant Imaginaries: Latino Cultural Politics in the U.S.-Mexico Borderlands*. New York: New York University Press, 2008.

Shinohara, Aito. "Kyowakoku no ayumi: Mekishiko." In *Ratenamerika sekai*, edited by Yoshio Masuda, Yoshiro Yamada, and Hidefuji Someda, 100–109. Kyoto: Sekaishisōsha, 1984.

Smith, Erin M., and Mikael Fauvelle. "Regional Interactions between California and the Southwest: The Western Edge of the North American Continental System." *American Anthropologist* 117, no. 4 (December 2015): 710–721.

Smith, Page. *Democracy on Trial: The Japanese American Evacuation and Relocation in World War II*. New York: Simon & Schuster, 1995.
Smith, R. J. *The Great Black Way: L.A. in the 1940s and the Lost African-American Renaissance*. New York: Public Affairs, 2006.
Spickard, Paul. *Japanese Americans: The Formation and Transformations of an Ethnic Group*. 1996. Reprint, New Brunswick, NJ: Rutgers University Press, 2009.
———. *Mixed Blood: Intermarriage and Ethnic Identity in Twentieth-Century America*. Madison: University of Wisconsin Press, 1989.
Starr, Kevin. *California: A History*. New York: Modern Library, 2007.
Street, Richard Steven. *Beasts of the Field: A Narrative History of California Farmworkers, 1769–1913*. Stanford, CA: Stanford University Press, 2004.
Sugiyama, Shigeru. "1930 nendai Mekishiko ni okeru Nihon ebi torōru gyogyō to nichiboku-bei sangoku kankei ni kansuru kenkyū," Research report of project funded by Grant-in-Aid for Scientific Research (C) of the Japan Society for the Promotion of Science (April 2008).
Swarthout, Kelley R. *"Assimilating the Primitive": Parallel Dialogues on Racial Miscegenation in Revolutionary Mexico*. New York: Peter Lang, 2004.
Takaki, Ronald. *A Different Mirror: A History of Multicultural America*. New York: Little, Brown and Company, 1993.
———. *Strangers from a Different Shore: A History of Asian Americans*. 1989. Reprint, New York: Little, Brown, and Company, 1998.
Takenaka, Ayumi. "The Japanese in Peru: History of Immigration, Settlement, and Racialization." *Latin American Perspectives* 31, no. 3 (May 2004): 77–98.
tenBroek, Jacobus, Edward N. Barnhart, and Floyd W. Matson. *Prejudice, War and the Constitution: Causes and Consequences of the Evacuation of the Japanese Americans in World War II*. 1954. Reprint, Berkeley: University of California Press, 1970.
Tokunaga, Yu. "From Anti-Japanese to Anti-Mexican: Linkages of Racialization Experiences in 1920s California." In *Race and Migration in the Transpacific*, edited by Yasuko Takezawa and Akio Tanabe. London: Routledge, forthcoming.
———. "'Mekishikojin mondai' to imin media: 1920 nendai Rosanzerusu ni okeru haigaishugi to mekishikojin imin no teikō." *Amerikashi kenkyū* 42 (August 2019): 3–18.
Tovares, Raul D. "*La Opinión* and Its Contribution to the Mexican Community's Adaptation to Life in the US." *Latino Studies* 7, no. 4 (December 2009): 480–498.
Tsuchida, Nobuya. "Japanese Gardeners in Southern California, 1900–1941." In *Labor Immigration under Capitalism: Asian Workers in the United States before World War II*, edited by Lucie Cheng and Edna Bonacich, 435–467. Berkeley: University of California Press, 1984.
Vargas, Zaragoza. *Labor Rights Are Civil Rights: Mexican American Workers in Twentieth-Century America*. Princeton, NJ: Princeton University Press, 2005.
Varzally, Allison. *Making a Non-White America: Californians Coloring Outside Ethic Lines, 1925–1955*. Berkeley: University of California Press, 2008.
Vaught, David. *Cultivating California: Growers, Specialty Crops, and Labor 1875–1920*. Baltimore: Johns Hopkins University Press, 1999.

Velázquez Morales, Catalina, ed. *Baja California: Un presente con historia*. Mexicali: Universidad Autónoma de Baja California, 2002.

———. *Los inmigrantes chinos en Baja California 1920–1937*. Mexicali: Universidad Autónoma de Baja California, 2001.

Volpp, Leti. "American Mestizo: Filipinos and Antimiscegenation Laws in California." *UC Davis Law Review* 33, no. 4 (1999): 795–835.

Weber, Devra. *Dark Sweat, White Gold: California Farm Workers, Cotton, and the New Deal*. Berkeley: University of California Press, 1994.

———. "Introducción." In *El inmigrante mexicano: La historia de su vida, entrevistas completas, 1926–1927*, by Manuel Gamio, compiled by Devra Weber, Roberto Melville, and Juan Vicente Palerm, 21–91. Mexico: Miguel Ángel Porrúa, librero-editor, 2002.

———. "The Organizing of Mexicano Agricultural Workers, Imperial Valley and Los Angeles, 1928–34, An Oral History Approach." *Aztlán* 3, no. 2 (1972): 307–350.

Wild, Mark. *Street Meeting: Multiethnic Neighborhoods in Early Twentieth-Century Los Angeles*. Berkeley: University of California Press, 2005.

Wollenberg, Charles. "Race and Class in Rural California: The El Monte Berry Strike of 1933." *California Historical Quarterly* 51, no. 2 (July 1972): 155–164.

Yagasaki, Noritaka. *Imin nōgyō: Kariforunia no nihonjin imin shakai*. Tokyo: Kokonshoin, 1993.

Yaginuma, Koichiro. "Kindai Mekishiko no sangyō kaihatsu ni okeru nihonjin imin: 'Imin gaisha' no hensen to nihonjin Mekishiko 'keiyaku imin' wo chūshin ni." *Kanda gaigo daigaku kiyō* 12 (March 2000): 203–228.

Yamakura, Akihiro. *Shiminteki jiyū: Amerika nikkeijin senji kyōsei shūyō no rīgaru hisutorī*. Tokyo: Sairyūsha, 2011.

Yang Murray, Alice. *Historical Memories of the Japanese American Internment and the Struggle for Redress*. Stanford, CA: Stanford University Press, 2008.

Yoo, David K. *Growing Up Nisei: Race, Generation, and Culture among Japanese Americans of California, 1924–1949*. Urbana: University of Illinois Press, 2000.

Zolberg, Aristide R. *A Nation by Design: Immigration Policy in the Fashioning of America*. Cambridge, MA: Harvard University, 2006.

INDEX

Acosta, Angel, 170
African Americans, 16, 49–50, 187–88n15
Agricultural Industrial Workers Union of America (AIWUA), 109
Agricultural Workers Industrial League (AWIL), 76
Ainu people, 63
Alien Land Laws, 27, 42, 81, 88
Alonso, Miguel, 61–62
Amate, Chieno, 162–63
Amate, Shigeru, 162–63
American Civil War, 15
American Eugenics Society, 55
American Federation of Labor (AF of L), 17, 72, 117, 129, 133
anti-Japanese sentiment, 2, 28–30, 88, 91–97, 104, 143, 147, 149, 152, 155, 202n25, 228n35
Arizona, 27, 96, 125
Arnoll, A. G., 74, 130
Ashurst, Henry, 12
Asia, 2, 14, 32
Asian-Mexican relations, 183–84n12
Asians, racialization of, 184n14
Associated Farmers of Contra Costa County, 112
Associated Farmers of Los Angeles County, 108–9, 111, 129, 134

Atchison, Topeka and Santa Fe Railroad, 15–16, 103
Azuma, Eiichiro, 5–6, 46, 190n33, 198n140

Baja California, 7–8, 12–13, 24, 42, 49, 77, 90, 92, 96, 101, 158; African Americans in seeking a haven from racial discrimination, 49–50; Japanese community in, 46, 157–58; Japanese fishing activities in, 45–46; large Japanese population of, 40; as a symbolic site, 46
Balderrama, Francisco E., 77
Barker, Thomas, 97–99, 119–20, 132
Beisel, William, 169
Bell, Roscoe E., 147–48
Bendetsen, Karl R., 148
Benítez, David, 125–26, 126*fig.*, 127, 130–31
Biscailuz, Eugene, 111
Blackwood, William, 17
Bogardus, Emory S., 66
Bonacich, Edna, 54
border control, 44, 54, 201n12
Bowron, Fletcher, 152–53, 229n46
Box Bill, 55, 206n90
Boyle Heights, Los Angeles, 4–5, 19, 65
Bracero Program, 1, 10, 138, 154, 156, 160, 179

Brazil, 26
Bustamante, Luis F., 86, 211–12n46

Cabrero, Eugenio, 173
California, 13–14, 178; Mexican California, 14–15; number of Mexican-born residents in (1900–1920), 19; prohibition on intermarriage in, 62–63. *See also* California, agriculture in
California, agriculture in, 188n16; defining aspects of Japanese agriculture in Southern California, 20–21; Filipino labor and California agriculture, 55; industrialized agriculture in, 17, 55–56
California Alien Land Laws (1913, 1920), 2, 21, 26, 60, 81, 88, 144
California Board of Health, 58
California Development Association, 56, 58, 60
California Packing Corporation, 103
California USDA Defense Board, 140
California USDA War Board, 147
Calles, Plutarco Elías, 30, 85, 89–94, 114, 130
Calles, Rodolfo Elías, 95
Camacho, Ávila, 156–57
Cámara Nacional del Trabajo (National Chamber of Labor), 89
Cammack, William J., 166
Cannery and Agricultural Workers' Industrial Union (CAWIU), 76–77, 79, 84–85
capitalism, 77; racial, 18
Cárdenas, Lázaro, 102, 114, 130, 156–58
Carson, Alice, 173
Carson, George Henry, 173
Carson, John Victor, 164, 166–67, 169, 172–73, 175–76
Carson Estate Company, 161–64, 166–67, 169
Casaraunc, José M. Puig, 86
Central Industrial Association of Southern California (Nanka Chūō Sangyō Kumiai), 112, 141
Central Japanese Association of Southern California (Nanka Chūō Nihonjin Kai), 26–27, 31, 48, 72, 80, 98, 100, 110, 112, 119
Chang, Jason Oliver, 95
Chávez, César, 179
China, 5, 12–14, 97; Chinese laborers in California, 17
Chinese Exclusion Act (1882), 17, 20, 54
"Chinese Problem," the, 30
citizenship, 25–26, 28, 54, 151; Mexican, 44, 66, 168

Ciudad Juárez, 86
Clark, Arthur, 129, 134–35, 223n81
Clark, Thomas B., 145
Clements, George Pigeon, 56–58, 73–74, 103, 109, 130, 134–35, 220n39; racial categorizations of Mexicans, 57–58
Coachella Valley, 55
Colima, 31, 36, 48
Colina, Rafael de la, 74
colonialism, settler, 36
Colorado River Land Company, 41–42, 102
Colusa County, California, 147–48
Commission on International and Interracial Factors in the Problems of Mexicans in the United States, 69
Communists, 76–77, 79, 82, 85, 110; anti-Communists, 57, 84, 108; Japanese, 115
Confederación de Uniones de Campesinos y Obreros Mexicanos (CUCOM), 108–14, 122, 125–27, 129, 131–35, 217n7; contract with signed by Ueda, 124, 128; criticism of Japanese farmers during the Venice Celery Strike, 123; CUCOM version of what happened in Dominguez Hills during the Venice Celery Strike, 123; Mexicans who did not follow the order of the CUCOM, 123; shift in focus from Los Angeles to Orange County, 133; and the strengthening of solidarity of Mexican workers, 123
Confederación de Uniones Obreras Mexicanas (CUOM), 53, 67, 71–73, 80, 218n12
Confederación Regional Obrera Mexicana (CROM), 71–72, 86, 217n7

Daniel, Cletus E., 85
Daniels, Roger, 145
Davidson, Dave, 140–41
Deguchi, Masato, 109, 115, 118–19, 122, 130
Del Amo Estate Company, 60, 162, 172
Delgado, Grace Peña, 5
De Moran, A. E., 36
Department of Protection of the Mexican Consulate, 83
Deverell, William, 58
DeWitt, John, 145–48, 155
Díaz, Porfirio, 18, 30
Dobashi, Wataru, 31–34, 48
dojin, 53, 63–65
Domínguez, Christóbal, 162
Domínguez, Manuel, 14–15, 162, 164, 173

Domínguez, Victoria, 173
Dominguez Estate Company, 161–62, 170–72
Dominguez Hills, 60–61, 82, 108, 110, 118, 122–23, 132, 179, 223n91
Donovan, J. O., 145

Egashira, Teizō, 48
ejidos, 102
El Dorado County, California, 147
El Excélsior, 92
El Hispano-Americano, 95
El Monte, Los Angeles, 66, 113, 168, 179; white landowners association in, 81
El Monte Berry Strike, 8, 77, 105–6, 110–11, 114–16, 123, 130, 178, 215n93; arrest of Communists during, 85; expansion of, 86; as an international problem, 78–89; rapid spread of, 81–83; role of the Mexican consulate in, 84–85, 90–91; settlement of, 97–104; strong support of from labor organizations, 86; transnational dimension of, 77, 91–92
El Nuevo Mundo, 122
el Partido Nacional Revolucionario (National Revolutionary Party [PNR]), 89, 92
Enomoto, Takeaki, 40
Ensenada, 44–45, 49, 157–58; statement of Japanese immigrants in, 101, 101*fig*.
Espinosa, J., 133
Essay on the Inequality of the Human Races, An (Comte de Gobineau), 62
ethnic Japanese/ethnic Mexicans, definition of, 181n2
Europe, 13, 32, 39

Farm Security Administration (FSA), 160, 163–66, 168
Federation of Japanese Associations in Southern California (Minamikashū Rengō Nihonjin Kai), 72
Filipino Federated Workers Union (FFWU), 109
Filipino Repatriation Act (1935), 58
Filipinos, 6, 17, 21, 55, 58, 60, 63, 142, 153
Fitzgerald Edward H., 113, 133
Flores, Armando, 74, 80–81, 85, 89–91, 98–100, 213n67
Flores Magón, Ricardo, 80
Foley, Neil, 57
Food-for-Freedom Program, 140, 163
food security, 138–39, 150, 152–53
Ford, Leland, 144, 149

Franco, Hanko, 169
Fresno County, California, 20, 142, 147, 179
Fugita, Stephen S., 216–17n2
Fujii, Sei, 99–100, 120, 127, 215–16n99
Fujioka, Shirō, 33–34, 38, 64
Fukami, Takashi, 80, 98
Fukushima, Mokichi, 43, 49, 93–95, 102, 214n78
Fukuzawa, Yukichi, 63

Gabrieliño-Tongva, 13–14
Gamio, Manuel, 57, 61, 66
Gardena, 21, 81–82, 110, 116–17, 124–26, 132, 179; Issei in, 121
Garza, Leandro, 65
Gast, Ross H., 87, 91
Gentlemen's Agreement (between Japan and the United States [1907 and 1908]), 21, 26, 40, 66–67, 195n101; nullification of, 41, 43, 45, 47, 158
giyūdan (volunteer corps), 110–11, 111*fig*., 112, 121
González, Gilbert G., 77, 86
González, Manuel, 98
Great Depression, the, 53, 73–75, 77, 103; and the development of the labor movement in the 1930s, 76
Grenier, Judson, 164
Guajardo, Edmundo, 94, 214n80
Gullion, Allen W., 148
Guzelain, Vaughn, 169

Hachimonji, Kumezō, 137
Haijima, Ichirō, 169
Hara Company, 69, 70*fig*.
Harbor City, California, 118, 122, 124
Harman, F. L. S., 103
Hasekura, Tsunenaga, 37
Hata, Naoki, 44
Hawai'i, ethnic Japanese in, 138, 148, 225n4
Hay, Eduardo F., 37–40
Hayasaka, Kieya, 43, 198n140
Hernández, Kelly L., 54
Hewes, Laurence I., Jr., testimony at the Tolan Committee, 163–64
Hicks Camp, 66, 79, 90, 123
Higashi, Kōji, 12–13
Hill, Ricardo, 83–84, 89, 113–14, 121–22, 125, 127, 129, 130–33, 213n67; resignation of, 134–35
Hoffman, Abraham, 77
Hokkaidō, 63
Holguin, Patty, 79
Hori, Kōichi, 118, 133–34

Hori, Yoshiatsu, 88, 92, 97
Horita, Tōru, 164

Ichikawa, Iwao, 51
Ichikawa, Mitsu, 50–51, 157–58
Ichikawa, Yonezō, 157
Ichioka, Toshio, 70, 167–68
Ichioka, Tsutayo, 167–68
Ichioka, Yuji, 183n8
illegal aliens, 3, 25, 54
Imaizumi, Haruo, 169
Immigration Act (1924), 1, 2, 21, 24–28, 40, 47, 52, 61, 76, 88, 177; and the nullification of the Gentlemen's Agreement, 41, 43, 45, 158
imperialism: Japanese, 141; US, 183–84n12
Imperial County, California, 41, 142, 228n35
Imperial Valley, 62, 143; Japanese agriculture in, 234n3
Imperial Valley Lettuce Strike, 76
Industrial Association of San Francisco, 103
Industrial Workers of the World (IWW), 17, 217n7
Inoue, Katsuichi, 124–25
Inoue, Masaji, 37
internment. *See* Japanese Internment
Ishida, Kōken, 108, 115, 117–19
Ishii, Itarō, 29–30, 32
Itani, Ichijirō, 37, 45
Iwata, Masakazu, 54

Jamieson, Stuart, 216–17n2
Japan, 39, 77, 86, 104, 177; effect of the Great Earthquake of 1906 on Japanese immigration, 20; imperial expansion of in East Asia, 3; Japan-Mexico relations, 13; Japanese enthusiasm for Mexico, 36–37; modernization of, 16, 18–22; southwestern prefectures of, 20
Japanese agriculture, in wartime California, 139–48; and skilled Japanese immigrants, 147–48
Japanese Agricultural Association of Mexicali, 44
Japanese American Citizens League (JACL), 144, 146, 150, 228–29n42; in San Gabriel Valley, 81
Japanese Association of Los Angeles (Rafu Nihojin Kai), 28, 112
Japanese Association of Mexicali, 42, 50
Japanese Chamber of Commerce of Southern California, 65
Japanese Exclusion Act, 25, 34, 37, 58

Japanese Farm Workers Union of California (JFWUC), 109, 115, 135
Japanese Internment, 9, 137–39, 157, 178; and the alleged military necessity of versus the actual economic necessity for, 148–53; and the Manzanar Camp, 154–55; Mexican workers as a solution to the removal of the Japanese, 153–59; and Roosevelt's Executive Order 9066, 149–50; and the Tule Lake Camp, 154–55
Japanese/Mexican immigrants/relations, 8; interethnic relations between, 1–4, 7–9, 167–68; labor conflicts of, 6; as racialized minorities in Los Angeles, 2; relational approach to, 4; role of in the agricultural development in Los Angeles County, 1
Japanese-Mexican relations, local and international, 97–99, 135–36, 177–80
Japanese Ministry of Foreign Affairs, 43, 47, 195n97, 196n111
"Japanese Problem," the, 8, 53
Japanese School of Mexicali, 44
Japan-Mexico Society (Nichi-Boku Kyōkai), 37–40, 43, 48
Japan-Mexico Treaty of Amity, Commerce, and Navigation (1924), 45–46
Jones, J. D., 164
Jones, Kenneth Bruce, 164
jus sanguinis (Japan) and *jus soli* (United States) principles, 26

Kai, Seijirō (Masajirō), 118, 126
Kasai, Fusao, 28
Kashu Mainichi, 78, 84, 92, 96, 99–100, 120, 128; as labor friendly, 121, 123; on Governor Olson, 146, 152; on the signing of a contract to raise wages between CUCOM and Bob Ueda, 124–25
Katō, Shin'ichi, 109, 113, 115–18, 120, 124–26, 126*fig.*, 129
Kern County, California, 17, 142, 147
Kerr, J. A. H., 73–74, 87
Kikuchi, Ryūsaku, 30
Kishi, Tony, 62
Kodama, Ken'ichi, 60–61, 202n35
Komai, Akira, 146
Komai, Toyosaku, 146
Kondō, Masaharu, 45
Kubo, Harry, 179
Kurashige, Haruko, 166
Kurashige, Lon, 24–25

INDEX

Kuwahara, Masakichi, 161
Kuwahara, Otokichi, 122

Lambert, Tom, 81
La Opinión, 8, 88, 96, 133, 158, 167–68, 177; approval of the government decision to relocate the Japanese as a military necessity, 168; reports on the El Monte strike in, 77, 79–80, 83, 89–90, 93, 99; editorial page of the first issue, 68; founding of, 67; influence on Japanese-Mexican conflicts, 53; interethnic history of, 65–75; practical advice provided to Mexicans in Los Angeles, 68–69; reports on the Venice Celery Strike, 108–10, 114, 116, 122–24, 126–27; statement of Japanese immigrants in Mexicali, 94*fig.*
La Prensa, 67
Latin America, 2
Lazo, Ralph, 205n58, 232n22
Leonard, Karen Isaksen, 4
Lippmann, Walter, 149
Little Liberia, 49–50
Little Tokyo, 11, 22, 108, 140, 142, 149; merchants of, 53–54
Lomita, California, 110, 118, 124
Long Beach, California, 16, 153
López, Ronald W., 77–78, 85
Los Angeles, 13–15, 59, 127–28, 135–136; development of farmland in, 16–17, 22*fig.*, 59–60; East Los Angeles, 66, 73; European immigrants to, 16; increase of Mexican immigrants to after Japanese exclusion, 52–53, 58–59; increase in population of due to immigration (1880–1900), 15–16; Japanese immigrants to, 19–20; medical care provided to Mexicans by Japanese doctors in, 69–70, 70*fig.*; Mexican immigrants to, 55–56, 65–67; migration of Japanese from to Mexico, 47; produce market in, 23*fig.*; relations between Los Angeles and Mexicali Japanese, 49–50; South Bay area of, 21, 60, 118
Los Angeles agriculture, 10*map*, 52, 180; and the *factories in the field* concept, 52; as the most important industry for Japanese immigrants, 128–29. *See also* triracial hierarchy, in Los Angeles agriculture
Los Angeles Chamber of Commerce, 17, 24, 73–74, 86–87, 91, 109, 129–130, 132, 148–49; Agricultural Department of, 56–58, 74, 87, 103, 109, 149; as a business partner of Japanese farmers, 149
Los Angeles County, 1, 11, 21, 83, 87–88, 91, 112, 129, 139, 145, 149, 178–79; Chinese population in, 185n21; Japanese population in, 2, 20, 24, 78–79, 178; Mexican population in, 2, 19, 24, 78–79, 167; socioeconomic impact of World War II on the ethnic Mexican community in, 167; total population of, 16, 181–82n3
Los Angeles Daily News, 124
Los Angeles Times, 36, 41, 90, 99, 127, 156; "Network of Japanese Farms Covers Vital Southland Defense Areas" article in, 10–11; report on the Japanese evacuation for harbor areas, 153–54
Lower California Mexican Land and Development Company, 49–50
Lozano, Ignacio, 67–68
Lozano, Monica, 67–68
Lucio, Lucas, 121–22, 127, 133

Macbeth, Hugh, 49
Manchuria, 31–32, 35, 84, 92, 131
Manifest Destiny, 14–15
Marcus, David, 89
Martínez, Alejandro, 84–85, 89–90, 92, 98–99, 101
Mashiko, Saburō, murder of, 50–51
Matson, Clarence, 24
Matsui, Keishirō, 46
Matsumoto, Yuko, 106, 223n91
Matsuoka, Ryōsaku, 31–34, 48
Mazatlán, establishment of a new Japanese consulate in, 46–47, 199n143
McWilliams, Carey, 52, 79, 184n16, 188n16
Meiji Restoration, 19
meki, 53, 59–65, 203n40
Merced County, California, 20, 147
mestizaje (racial mixing), 3, 57
mestizo, 57, 95
Mexicali, 8, 29, 49, 77, 157; Chinese immigrants in, 42; interethnic tension between Japanese and Mexican residents of, 93, 97; Japanese immigrants in, 41–44, 47–48, 50–51, 196n111, 198n140, 214n80; Mexicali Japanese, 93–96, 100, 102–3; as the primary cotton cultivation center in Mexico, 41–42
Mexican Agricultural Society, 168
Mexican Almanac, 36, 194n85

254   INDEX

Mexican-American War (1846–1848), 12, 15, 19
Mexican Fact-Finding Committee, 72–73
Mexican "greasers," 57–58
Mexican Ministry of Foreign Affairs, 38, 82, 90, 92, 107
Mexican Ministry of the Interior, 158
"Mexican peon," the, 55, 57
"Mexican Problem," the, 8, 53, 55, 72, 211–12n46
Mexican Revolution, 18, 30, 39–40, 46, 67, 80, 102
Mexicans, 24–25, 206n90; as "illegal aliens," 54; Japanese racial view of, 59–65
Mexico, 5, 32, 77, 86, 104, 177; anti-Japanese sentiment in, 29–30, 92–97; intermarriage between Japanese men and Mexican women in, 44; Japan-Mexico relations, 13, 45–46, 92, 113, 177; Japanese immigration to, 27, 40–41; Japanese population in, 41, 157, 230n58; modernization of, 16, 18; Spanish colonization of, 57
Mexico Study Society (Bokukoku Kenkyū Kai), 35–37, 40, 47, 194n83
Mibu, Naonori, 118
middleman minorities, 52, 54, 74, 78, 95–96, 200n4
Miller, Howard B., 149
Minami, Yemon, 126
Minges, P. A., 142–44, 163, 226n19
minzoku (race/ethnicity), 3
Miyakawa, Makoto, 172
Miyakawa, Misao, 172–73
Miyakawa, Tomiji, 172
MK Fisheries, 45
Modell, John, 54
Molina, Natalia, 4, 184nn13–14
Monroe, Lillian, 108–9, 122, 130, 134
Monterey County, California, 142
Morishita, Shin'ichi, 50
Moriyama, Keizaburō, 37
Mukaeda, Katsuma, 80, 98, 100, 119, 130–36
Murakami, Noboru, 118
Myer, Dillon, 173

Nagumo, Shōji, 120, 220n48
Nakamoto, George Hideo, 81, 88, 209–10n22
Nakamura, Genpei, 33
Nakamura, Kengorō, 118
Nakaoka, Gensaku, 42–43
Nakashima, M., 170–71
Nakazawa, Kiyoshi, 44
Nanka Nōkai Renmei (Federated Farmers Association of Southern California, or Southern California Farm Federation), 108–10, 112–13, 116–27, 129–35
National Labor Relations Board (NLRB), 114, 134
National Recovery Administration, 107
nationalism: American, 2–3, 24, 33; Japanese, 3, 182–83n7; Japanese immigrant, 9, 36, 64, 106, 117, 131, 178, 183n8; Mexican, 3, 8, 30, 77, 84, 95–96, 101–2, 104, 116
Native Americans, 13–14
Naturalization Act (1790), 43
Nayarit, 30–31, 48
Neve, Felipe de, 14
New Deal, the, 103, 105, 107, 136. *See also* Venice Celery Strike, Japanese immigrant nationalism and interethnic accommodation during
Ngai, Mae, 54, 184n13
Nisei Farmers League, 77, 179
Nishi, Kazuo, 109
Nylander, Towne, 134

O'Brien, David J., 216–17n2
Ōhashi, Chūichi, 43, 45, 47–48
Olson, Culbert, 9, 138, 144–51, 159–160, 227n24, 228n35, 229n44; radio speech of, 145–46, 154–56; testimony at the Tolan Committee, 151–53
Orange County, California, 87–88, 110, 115–16, 121–22, 125, 127, 129, 130, 133–34, 142, 192n62, 210n26
Ornelas, Angelo, 169
Ōta, Juzō (Toshizō), 121
Ota Mishima, María Elena, 41, 48, 197n124, 198n140
Otis, Harrison G., 41
Overseas Business Bulletin (Ministry of Foreign Affairs of Japan), 43
Ōyama, Ujirō, 65
Ozawa v. United States (1922), 2, 43–44
Ozono, Torimatsu, 28–29, 64

Pacheco, M., 83
Pacific Hotel (Taiheiyō Hotel), 65
Pacific Ocean, as a site of international trade, 39
Pacific War, the (during World War II), 2, 154, 156, 158, 167, 178, 190n33, 234n3
Palos Verdes, California, 82, 185–86n22
Panunzio, Constantine, 63
Partido Liberal Mexicano (PLM), 80, 217n7
Pearl Harbor, attack on, 6, 21, 128, 136, 139–40, 143–146, 148, 151, 157, 163, 168, 171–72

Periódico Oficial, 45
Perry, Matthew, 19
Peru, 26, 35, 42, 44, 48
Piñon, Blas, 110, 113
Placer County, California, 20, 147, 148
Puerto Ricans, 58
Pulido, Mike, 122

racialization, 3, 184n14, 188n16, 202n25
racism, of white agribusiness on Mexicans, 53–59; and anti-Mexican restrictionists, 54–55
Rafu Shimpo, 27, 31–37, 40, 47, 49–51, 61–62, 67–68, 78, 81–82, 89–90, 96, 99, 100, 104, 113, 115, 119, 123, 127, 140, 143–44, 146, 149, 168; articles of concerning Mexico, 28–30, 64; articles using the term *meki* in, 203n40; criticism of Fletcher Bowron's anti-Japanese sentiment, 152; editorial concerning the 1924 Immigration Act, 25; English section of, 88, 121, 125, 153; opinion on Communists, 85; on the reluctance to ship vegetables as an act of sabotage, 141–42; report on Olson's testimony before the Tolan Committee, 152; on the signing of a contract to raise wages between CUCOM and Bob Ueda, 124–25; support for Nōkai Renmei, 120
Rancho San Pedro, 10–11, 21, 60, 160, 161*map*, 231n3; continuing triracial relations in during the Pacific War, 171–76; Horita and Haijima farms in, 165*map*; Japanese tenants in, 170*tab*.; Mexican tenants in, 171*tab*.; triracial agriculture in old Spanish Rancho, 161–64; and wartime farms without new tenants but Mexicans, 164–71
raza (race or people), 3, 76–77, 123–24
Regional Labor Board, 107, 134, 217
Riverside County, California, 142, 147
Rodríguez, Abelardo, 85–86, 88, 91, 95, 157
Rodriguez, Julian, 173–74, 175*map*
Rolph, James, Jr., 90, 92, 98–99
Romero, Robert Chao, 185n18
Romo, Ricardo, 59
Roosevelt, Franklin D., 85, 92, 115, 145, 156; issuing of Executive order 9066 by, 139, 149–50
Roosevelt, Theodore, 41
Russia, 13, 64, 163
Russo-Japanese War (1904 and 1905), 32, 204n55

Sacramento County, California, 20, 147
Sacramento Valley, 55
Saigō, Jūtoku, 37
Sakaguchi, Kenjirō, 30
Sakai, Yoneo, 113
San Benito County, California, 147
San Bernardino County, California, 147
Sánchez, George J., 4, 54, 73, 207–8n5
San Diego, 27, 45; Japanese farmers in, 114–15
San Fernando Valley, 16, 108, 110, 179
San Francisco, 15–16, 20, 26, 191n49, 198n140; Japanese consulate in, 189n23
San Gabriel Mission, 13–14
San Gabriel Valley, 16, 21, 78–79, 81, 86, 90, 98, 110, 113, 122–24, 179
San Joaquin County, California, 147–48
San Joaquin Valley, 55, 129, 223n81
San José del Cabo, 45
San Pedro, 108, 118, 132, 153
Sansei, 179
Santa Barbara County, California, 142
Santa Monica, 16, 59
Satō, Toshito, 67, 83–91, 97–100; summary report concerning the El Monte strike, 100–101
Saylor, Anna L., 73
Seinen Seigidan (Youth League for Justice), 113
Shidehara, Kijūrō, 38–39
Shinohara, M., 70
Shirane, Shizuko, 81
Shōda, Kiyoji, 50–51
Sinaloa, Mexico, 14, 28, 38, 46, 48
Sleepy Lagoon murder case, 167
Solano County, California, 147–48
Solórzano, Jesús, 80
Sonora, Mexico, 14, 42, 48, 95; anti-Chinese campaign in, 30
Southern Pacific Railroad, 15–16, 103
Spanish Empire, 13; independence of the Republic of Mexico from, 14; missionaries of, 13–14
Spickard, Paul, 62
Stockton, California, 171, 185n19, 233n32
Survey of the Mexican Labor Problem in California (California Development Association report), 56, 58–60
Sutter County, California, 147–48

Takeuchi, Henry Chiyozō, 173–74; buildings owned by, 175*map*
Tanaka, Togo, 153
Tenorio, Fortino, 64
Thompson, J. M., 145
Tōi, Hiroshi, 85

Tokyo Asahi Shimbun, 25, 38
Tokyo Club, 50–51
Tolan Committee, 150–53, 163–64
Torrance, California, 21, 124, 153–54, 161
Torreón massacre, 30
Torres, Manuel, 169
Torres, Teodoro, Jr., 68
Tovares, Paul D., 68
Treaty of Guadalupe-Hidalgo (1848), 2–3, 15
transborder ethnic Japanese community, development of, 40–51. *See also* Ensenada; Mexicali; *yobiyose*
transpacific borderlands, 5, 78, 97, 104, 179
transpacific history, 1, 3–4, 181n1
transpacific workplace, 6–7, 78, 104, 106–7, 116, 127, 129, 135, 138, 174–75, 180
triracial hierarchy, 6, 185n21, 199–200n2; in Los Angeles agriculture, 1–2, 8–9, 52–53, 59–61, 75–76, 78, 81, 86–87, 106, 117, 128, 131, 136, 138, 168, 177, 179; triracial relations during World War II, 171–76; unsolved problems of, 97–104
Tsuchida, Nobuya, 120, 200n6, 220–21n49
Tsutsumi, Sankichi, 42
Tulare County, California, 142, 147–48, 151
Tydings-McDuffie Act (1934), 58

Uchida, Yasuya, 86, 92, 97
Ueda, Bob, 124–28, 132, 222n71
Umimoto, Tetsuo, 35
undocumented immigration, from Japan, 38, 41, 54, 195n101; from Mexico, 3, 52. *See also* illegal aliens
Unión de Campesinos y Obreros Mexicanos (UCOM), 80, 98, 108, 209n16
Union of Laborers and Field Workers, 114
United Farm Workers (UFW), 77, 179
United States, 1–2, 5, 32, 39, 77, 86, 104, 177; acquisition of California by, 12; annexation of Texas by, 12; anti-Japanese regulations of, 49; diplomatic concern in over the Japanese presence in Mexico, 46
United States-Mexico borderlands, 2, 4–8, 103–4; growing anti-Japanese sentiment in, 87–97; unintended consequence of the 1924 Immigration Act in, 12–51
Uribe, Joe, 170–71
US Border Patrol, 3, 54. *See also* border control
US Department of Agriculture (USDA), 138–40, 145–48, 150–51, 159–60, 163; on the unfreezing of Japanese assets, 142

US Department of Labor, 87, 91, 113, 133
US Department of Treasury, 139–40; recognition of the importance of Japanese agriculture by, 141
US-Japan relations, 12–13, 38–39, 84, 88, 130–31

Vasconcelos, José, 57, 68
Vaught, David, 52, 200n3
Velarde, Guillermo (William), 108–9, 116–19, 122, 124, 127–28, 131–34, 215n93, 217n7
Velázquez, Zeferino, 62
Venice, California, 81, 91, 179
Venice Celery Strike, 9, 104–6, 110–11, 127–28, 130–33, 178, 216–17n2; assistance of the California State government during, 119–20; beginning of, 107–8; consecutive negotiations between the Japanese and Mexican sides, 118–19; decline of, 130–31; expansion of the strike in Domínguez Hills, 122–23; and the *giyūdan* workforce, 110–11, 111*fig.*, 112, 121; the inter-Japanese divide and growing support for Mexicans during, 118–29; Japanese immigrant nationalism and interethnic accommodation during, 129–36; and the Los Angeles Chamber of Commerce, 109; provisional agreement between Nōkai Renmei and David Benítez, 125–27; role of union recognition during, 107–17; signing of a contract between CUCOM and Bob Ueda, 124–25

Wagner Act, 105–8, 114–15, 217n4
Wakasugi, Kaname, 33, 46–47
Wang, Zhaocheng, 25
War Manpower Commission, 154
Wartime Farm Adjustment Program, 163
Watson Land Company, 162
Weber, Devra, 57, 78, 217n7
West, Fred, 133
white Anglo-Saxon Americans, 24–25
white supremacy, 6, 52, 188n16
Wickard, Claude R., 140, 156
Wollenberg, Charles, 78
Wong, John J., 166–67
Works Progress Administration (WPA), 91
World War I, 3, 12, 19, 39, 42, 49, 150, 182n7, 200n3
World War II, 1, 22, 140, 164, 178; socioeconomic impact on the ethnic Mexican community in Los Angeles County, 167; triracial

relations during, 171–76. *See also* Japanese Internment

Yamada, Satarō, 34–35
yobiyose (relatives of Japanese residents in Mexico), 41, 43–46, 49–50, 157, 198n140

Yodogawa, Masaki, 47
Yolo County, California, 142, 147
Yomiuri Shimbun, 38, 40
Young, C. C., 72–73

Zoot Suit Riots, 167

Founded in 1893,
UNIVERSITY OF CALIFORNIA PRESS
publishes bold, progressive books and journals
on topics in the arts, humanities, social sciences,
and natural sciences—with a focus on social
justice issues—that inspire thought and action
among readers worldwide.

The UC PRESS FOUNDATION
raises funds to uphold the press's vital role
as an independent, nonprofit publisher, and
receives philanthropic support from a wide
range of individuals and institutions—and from
committed readers like you. To learn more, visit
ucpress.edu/supportus.

www.ingramcontent.com/pod-product-compliance
Lightning Source LLC
Chambersburg PA
CBHW021342230426
43666CB00006B/376